BUSINESS BRAHMINS

Business Brahmins

The Gauda Saraswat Brahmins of South Kanara

HARALD TAMBS-LYCHE

MANOHAR
2011

First published 2011

ISBN 978-81-7304-902-6

Published by
Ajay Kumar Jain *for*
Manohar Publishers & Distributors
4753/23 Ansari Road, Daryaganj
New Delhi 110002

Typeset by
FineCurve Computers,
Meerut City 250002

Printed at
Salasar Imaging Systems
New Delhi 110035

Contents

Acknowledgements

It was by chance that I came to work on South Kanara: I was still working on Gujarat, when my wife became attached to an Indo-French programme on the Ghat forest, and so I joined her in that region. From 1990 we did several short spells of fieldwork together there, exploring the *bhuta* cults and other aspects of Tulu society. I am deeply grateful to her for her collaboration, including her reading and commenting upon the present work.

By the late 1990s I gradually turned my attention to the study of the Gauda Saraswat Brahmin (GSB) community, which is the subject of this book. By 2003 the University of Picardie-Jules Verne granted me research leave for a semester, and so my wife, my daughter Suguna, and I were able to settle down in Udupi for six months, which became the main period of fieldwork for this research. My elder daughter Elisabeth, who was at college in France, also joined us during her Christmas holidays. Mohandas Borkar, estate agent, found us an apartment with his neighbours Mr. and Mrs. Acharya, and both families became our friends and helped us in a number of ways during our stay. Though the Borkars are not GSB, Mohandas' intimate knowledge of Udupi and its families was a great help, and his son Sunil also tried to help me learn Konkani. The lack of success is not his fault. Like others I mention here, they continued to help me when I returned later, several times, to Udupi to complete my data. My thanks to them all.

One of our first tasks was to find a school for Suguna, and this brought us into contact with K.K. Pai, head of 'the Pai empire' which figures greatly in this book – I thank him heartily for his friendly assistance. As I started to go from shop to shop to meet the GSB merchants, I was received courteously and there are too many people who helped me to mention them all individually. But I must give special thanks to Anant Airody and the elders of that family, as well as Shailesh Gundu Nanak and his elders. I spent a lot of time discussing with them both, and Shailesh also accompanied me to the lineage temples in Goa. Among others I should like to mention U.P. Kamath and his son.

A very special place in my research were the hours I spent with P.R. Kuduva, an amateur historian and an expert on the history of the GSB *maths*. The number of references to him in the text and the notes should speak for themselves. In Mangalore, M. Mukunda Prabhu, the historian, cheerfully shared his vast knowledge with me, as did K.C. Vasantha Madhava, whose work on the agrarian history of the region – which deserves to be far more widely known – has been a great inspiration. Michael Lobo, the author of several impressive works on the Catholic community, also offered his friendly assistance. Father Alexander D'Souza of the Konkani Academy, was also both friendly and helpful, as was the head and library staff at the Saint Aloysius College in Mangalore. The long interview I had with Mrs. Sadhana Kini, also helped my work greatly. Outside the GSB community, I must mention the time spent with my wife's assistant, Krishna Bhat, whose knowledge of the area is impressive, and not least, with my colleagues Dr. Krishnaia, Ashok Alva and Krishna Bhat, the director at the Regional Resource Centre for Folk Performing Arts. The use of their library and the assistance of its librarian were of great help to me. They all contributed greatly to my understanding of the area. Needless to say, any flaws in this work remain my own responsibility.

The reader will find reference to a number of others in the following pages, for unlike most anthropologists but like most local historians, I have used the real names of people I met and those I write about. Udupi is too special a place in South Kanara to mask successfully under another name, and the families and personalities I write about are mostly known to 'everybody' in Udupi. It would be obviously impossible to mask the realizations of the Tonse Pai family under a fictitious name, and since the other families, too, have made their own distinctive contribution to the town's history it would seem unfair to hide their accomplishments. But this also means that in trying to give an account of the place of these families in town life, I have had to include critical remarks as well as admiration, and so I sincerely hope that nobody will feel hurt. My point is that in a small town such as Udupi, the members of the town's bourgeoisie are, in effect, public personalities with all that implies. Nobody in K.K. Pai's position can hope to evade criticism: to me, his accomplishments constitute, in themselves, the proper answer to such critical remarks. Similarly, the portrait I have painted of various families – such as the Airodys – reflect, I hope, both their accomplishments and the kind of jealousy towards the successful that we should expect in any small-town milieu. My respect for the accomplishments of Udupi's GSB community is great, and I do hope this is evident to the reader.

Some readers may feel that this book deals with the growth of a small town in terms that give too much credit to the individuals and families of an emergent bourgeoisie. They will say, rightly, that great numbers of individuals from the lower castes were equally important in making the city. I do not contest this, but I wanted to paint a portrait not just of Udupi, but also of the GSB: naturally, as an anthropologist, I have privileged the role of my informants. But nobody can, I think, deny the crucial importance of the bourgeoisie in creating the kind of town Udupi has become, and nobody in Udupi would, in my view, deny the central place of the GSB in this context. Their role is important for Udupi, but equally for the way in which its GSB community constructs its own identity and culture. And since this role is paralleled, with all the different specifics of diverse urban histories, in other places where the GSB have been important, Udupi's history seems to me to offer a privileged access to understanding the GSB community.

This is, basically, a work from the field, and I apologize for the many points where further research on literature and sources might have brought us further. With many other claims on my time, I wanted to publish the present work without further delay, and so some loose ends had to be left for another occasion.

With all respect to friends and colleagues in South Kanara, I wish to dedicate the present work to my wife Marine Carrin, who brought me to the area, and to my daughters Suguna and Elisabeth, who helped make the stay memorable.

HARALD TAMBS-LYCHE

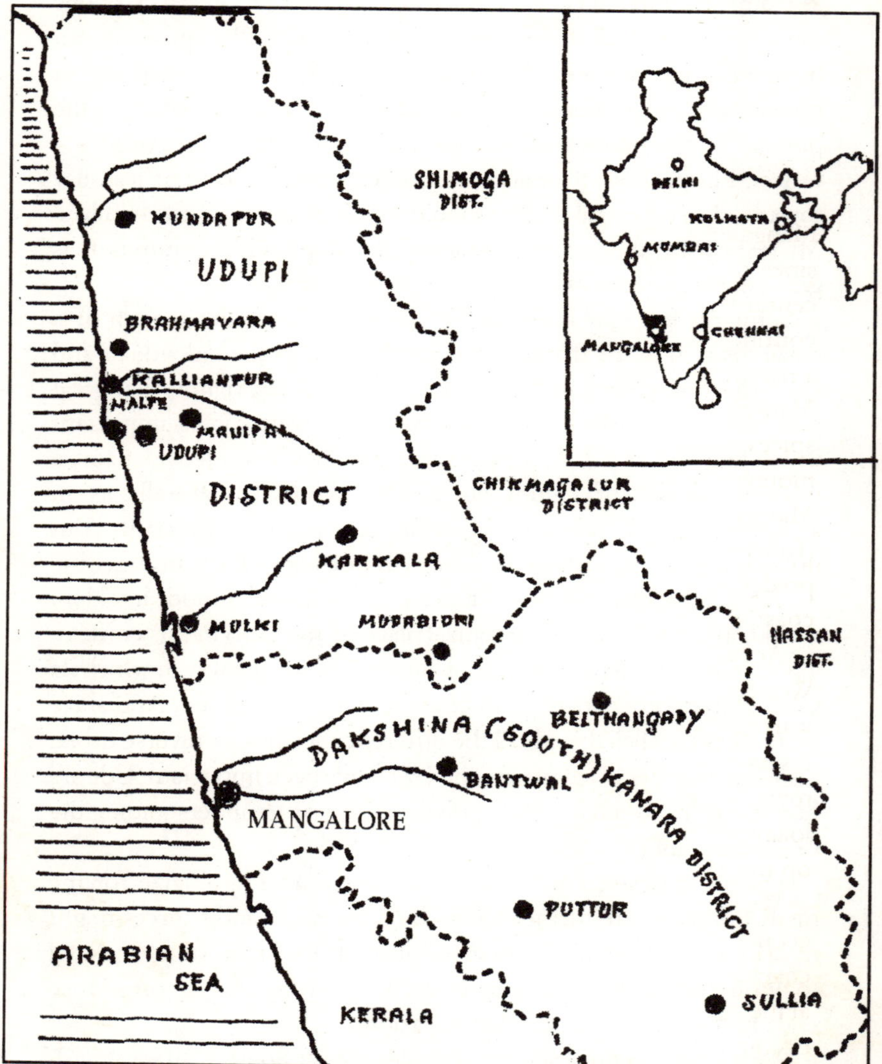

Fig. 1: Sketch map of South Kanara and its location in India

Introduction

Mangalore, some 700 km south of Mumbai, is a port known at least since the *Periplus of the Erythraean Sea,* written in the first or second century of our era. Its description of the roadstead, formed by the confluence of the Netravati and the Gurupura rivers and shielded by a narrow tongue of sand, is still valid today. Like the Malabar coast, Mangalore was known to early European traders for pepper and other spices, grown in the foothills of the Western Ghats. Though these mountains reach some 3,000 m, trade routes did cross them and Mangalore was an important port for the Vijayanagara empire (fourteenth to sixteenth century), as it must have been for its predecessors. Other ports, of varying importance, line the Kanara coast between Mangalore and Goa.

According to legend, the narrow stretch of land between the Western Ghats and the Arabian Sea was created when the Brahmin warrior Parashurama, seeking refuge after killing the Kshatriyas, threw his axe from the top of the Ghats. The sea receded. Whatever the myth, the coast has risen in recent geological periods, and sand and loam deposited by the rivers ensures that the land is still encroaching on the sea.

We may distinguish three zones of the country, differing in ecology, economy and social form (Kamath, 1982: 12-14). The coastal belt is characterized by fishing and coconut farming. Farther inland, we arrive at the rice fields, scattered between low hills, until we reach the foothills of the Ghats. Here, plantations of areca, pepper, and other spices take over. A number of rivers, overflowing during the heavy rains[1] but much reduced in the dry season, flow from the Ghats to the sea. Their inlets often divide into rivulets, where islands continuously form, so most harbours have changed constantly through the times. This complicates the history of the coast, as ports once important have lost their access to the sea, while others have come up. The merchant communities have moved in consequence.

South Kanara is not a poor area. It is densely populated[2] and has been exporting rice at least since the sixteenth century,[3] though it imports rice today. Most roads, where merchants and armies passed, ran east to west, along the dry ridges. The north-south route meandered between coast and inland, crossing the rivers inland on fords or, very rarely, bridges, with ferries across the wide estuaries. North-south communications, then, were largely by ship along the coast, as far as important commerce or military movements were concerned. Typically, Tipu built forts to the east along the valley from Mangalore towards the Ghats. He also fortified harbours where there may be no water now, since the coastline has changed.

The relative isolation of each village cluster[4] is less obvious today than it must have been before modern roads were built: whenever one leaves the route, the difficulty of the terrain is obvious. The forest is dense, the country hilly, and the rivers impassable during the rains. The forest constituted a real barrier to communication, so each traditional village was something of 'a world in itself'. Some villages were close to the roads, but most were away from them, in the forest. The area, then, represents a paradox: considerable commerce coexisted with an isolated countryside. We understand why no medieval empire bothered to take direct control of such villages: they could be left to themselves, provided the road was safe. The intermediary vassals known as the Tulu kings (Bhatt, 1975), may have provided the solution of nominal overlordship at minimal cost. It seems clear that the survival of the Tulu language – often seen as the most archaic of the present Dravidian languages – is related to this isolation.

Known as Tulunadu – the land of the Tulus – the countryside is linguistically and culturally distinct from neighbouring areas. It includes most of South Kanara and the adjoining Kasaragode district of Kerala. Tulu was seen as a minority language and was not taken into account when Indian state boundaries were adjusted to the language situation;[5] the official languages are Kannada, and Malayalam in Kasaragode. The northern border between Tulunadu and the Kannada-speaking areas runs along the various rivers which join the sea at Kallianpur, and coincides with the boundary of the dominant Bunt caste.[6]

The religion, too, is particular, and early British observers felt the *bhuta* cults (Brückner, 1995; Carrin and Tambs-Lyche, 2003) were reminiscences of Buddhism rather than a Hindu phenomenon. In fact, these cults for centuries coexisted, not with Buddhism, but with Jainism. *Bhutas* – or *daivas* – are clearly distinct from deities of the pan-Indian pantheon, though they are often said to be the *gana* (people, assistants) of Shiva. The *rajandaivas* or 'royal *bhutas*' are linked to traditional chiefdoms, usually headed by a Bunt family, though some were still ruled by Jains when the British arrived. The annual festivals (*nema*) of these deities are still important though the chiefdoms are gone. To their patrons, these rituals serve to confirm their continued importance, and maintain the unity of the local society of which they used to be the chiefs (Carrin and Tambs-Lyche, 2003). No Brahmins officiate ir the *bhuta* cults. The small-scale chiefdoms were separated by forests and represent, for India, a rather 'primitive', almost 'tribal', level of social and political integration. There was also a tradition of Tulu kings, but it does not imply a clear picture of political conditions at any specific time, though there existed a hierarchy of terms for political domains.[7] Today, these distinctions are of limited importance, but the myth of the Tulu kings are part of the common heritage of present-day Tulu speakers.

The latter see themselves as culturally distinct from people of surrounding areas, and today, there is a new stress on the specificity of being Tulu. This movement, concentrating on language, religion and literature, tends to treat Tulunadu as a kind of mini-nation, its frontiers defined in terms of cultural content.[8] A salient fact here is investment in the *bhuta* cults. New masks and jewellery are being made for them, and attendance at the *nemas*, the annual rituals of the 'royal' *bhutas*, is increasing.[9] This is a recent change, for at the beginning of the 1980s, these cults were in decline. It was difficult, then, to find mediums who still remembered and were capable of singing the *bhuta* epics, the *paddanas*; in effect, mediums were dying out. Tulu ethnicity, then, is manifesting itself as a cultural revival, where the language occupies a central place. The latter has no official status, and had – until recently – little written literature. This has changed radically since the 1970s, but the new writing is strongly turned towards folklore and folk culture. The *paddanas* sung at *bhuta* rituals, which have been collected and commented,[10] are important for the development of Tulu literature.[11] The traditional theatre, Yakshagana, also plays a role. Such theatre exists in both Kannada and Tulu language, but there has been a new wave of plays written in Tulu.[12]

The link with the *bhuta* cults imply that Tulu society tends to be seen in the image projected by the *nemas*: a paternalist structure where the old landlord families represent the traditional justice that the *bhuta* incarnates.

The Tulu movement is ethnic rather than regional, for Tulu speakers cannot be said truly to control their region. Konkani speakers dominate Mangalore city, the other towns, and the tertiary sector in general. So far, however, the movement has not developed a particular anti-Konkani stance.

The groups affected by this discourse on Tulu identity mainly have a rural base traditionally tied to agriculture. Central here are the Bunts, former chiefs, warriors and landowners. The most important Tulu-speaking caste among the peasantry are the Billavas (bowmen), whose traditional occupation was coconut farming and toddy production, but who became the predominant labour force in the rice-growing villages led by Bunt chiefs.[13] Several castes of specialists – from Brahmins to untouchables – may be added to this cluster of communities, all of them Tulu speakers.

At an even earlier date, the small Jain kingdoms[14] were themselves controllers of trade: but they flourished before the present rice zone had been drained and cleared. Thus they must mainly have controlled the roads along the ridges, leading to their plantations in the foothills of the Ghats. They tended to be vassals of larger states, such as Vijayanagara. Later, from the fifteenth or early sixteenth century, valley lands were cleared by the Billavas, moving inland from the coast. But the rights in the land were allotted to the Bunts, who thereby became vassals of the Jain kings. As rice production expanded, the Bunts effectively became chiefs of their villages, and the kings had little power to control them. It seems, indeed, that it was the land reclamation, led by the Bunts, which spelt the end of the Jain kingdoms. In the seventeenth century the Ikkeri Nayaks from the north, a dynasty that had been vassals of the Vijayanagara empire, extended their rule to the coastal regions. The Jain kingdoms lost whatever independence they had and the Bunts became, in effect, the local chiefs under Nayak rule in South Kanara.

No merchant caste is included in the Tulu group, except the Jains. Though they have indeed been active in the traditional export trades,[15] their relation to the Tulu ethnic movement is ambiguous. The predominant merchant community of the area today is the Konkanis, or the GSB. Their language is Konkani, an Indo-European and not a Dravidian language, their religion is a variant of Vaishnavite Hinduism – a minority are Shaivite – with few links to the *bhuta* cults; and they tend to be seen as 'immigrants' from Goa. They are patrilineal, while the Tulu speakers were – and to some degree still are – matrilineal.[16] Some Konkani families do in fact patronize *bhuta* cults, in their capacity as landowners. But it is more or less taken for granted that landowners in Tulunadu should propitiate the *bhutas*, since their cult is seen as metonymic of landownership. Here, indeed, the owner is seen, ideally, to 'belong to the land' and not vice versa.

Close to the GSB, culturally, are the Catholics, whose most important families were converted from that community. Nobody includes these 'Konkanis' among the Tulus, and in the popular view, common also among folklorists and historians, Tulu society represents the 'original' strata of the population, to which later newcomers, such as the GSB, have been added. It is the GSB community that is the subject of this book.

Before taking up this study, I had been working on Saurashtra, a peninsular region of Gujarat, north of Mumbai (1997, 2004). There, I concentrated on the opposition between mercantile and agrarian communities, between traders and chiefs. There are similarities between South Kanara and Saurashtra, for the latter's history, too, has been marked by its proximity to the trade routes. Like Mangalore, the city of Vallabhi, on the east coast of Saurashtra, was an important centre of trade in the early half of the first millennium AD. We know, largely from Jain sources, that this community dominated Vallabhi's commerce in the port's heyday from the fourth to the eighth century. Basing myself on Kosambi's analysis of early Indian empires, I concluded that the Vallabhi kingdom must have been based on revenue from trade. The kings controlled a network of towns and routes but their power over the countryside was limited to a narrow zone, where land was held partly by urban landowners, partly by free peasants loyal to the king.[17] Beyond this zone the countryside must have been 'tribal', bound to the kingdom by treaties but not controlled by it (1997). I interpret the relationship between the rural Tulu and the trading towns of South Kanara as pointing to a very similar pattern, which, however, persisted here to a much later date than in Saurashtra.

Vallabhi fell in or around AD 784, and I have analysed (1997) the changes in the following centuries. There is considerable evidence of immigration and it seems that the space beyond Vallabhi's control was gradually filled up with new, 'tribal', populations, changing the balance of power in the peninsula. After Vallabhi's fall, new states came into being, based on an alliance between a tribal population and a line of chiefs.[18] This analysis of the changes leading from 'classical' to 'medieval' India implies a development where cities and trade are older than the 'traditional' order of the countryside. Traders tend to look upon Saurashtra as peripheral to the towns they have lived in since 'times immemorial'. Yet in Saurashtra as in South Kanara, visions of 'traditional society' deal with a feudal system populated by heroic warriors and rustic simple folk, to the virtual exclusion of the trader.

This shows a problem central to the South Asian situation. We may delimit regions by social and cultural perceptions, but whose perceptions are we talking about? In South Kanara, as in Saurashtra, different perceptions of the region coexist (Tambs-Lyche, 1993). Just as the rural speakers of Saurashtra's local dialect Kathiawadi insist on the specificity of their region, so Tulu speakers insist on the particularity of theirs. In both cases, these regionally-minded groups are led by dominant castes, Rajputs in Saurashtra, Bunts in Tulunadu, and the region they perceive coincides with the area of their political dominance (Mayer, 1958), linked to the control of land and of agriculture. In both cases, the merchant castes, whose power base is largely independent of land tenure, transcend the perceived regional boundary.

Tulu historiography underlines the age of the cultural institutions central to Tulu identity, and in particular the age of the Tulu kingdom or kingdoms.[19] But when folklorists try to date the *bhuta* cults as we know them, they tend to converge on a date around the fifteenth or sixteenth century. My friends among Konkani historians put it even later.[20] Some elements of both cult and myths are, no doubt, older; the dating of the folklorists refers to the substantial parts of the *paddanas* as they are still sung at rituals.

Agricultural history, based mainly on inscriptions, indicates an intensive period of land reclamation around the sixteenth century. This was when Bunts led an expansion in rice cultivation, and agriculture and population moved down from the dry ridges. In the valleys, river banks and marshes were reclaimed by dams and canalization, and important here was the establishment of coconut plantations fencing off rice lands from streams and backwaters, using the Billavas' expertise in coconut culture (Vasantha Madhava, 1991: 117-26). Their role led to their taking to rice farming on tenancy contracts. Thus, the relationship between Bunt landowners and Billava tenants, and the 'traditional' Tulu village came into being.

This period of expansion may have been the the result of a fast growing market for rice, and we know that the Portuguese were important buyers: Goa's growing population could not be supplied from the colony's own fields. It seems, then, that the 'traditional' Bunt chiefdom is largely the creation of the 'rice boom' that followed from the Portuguese establishing themselves in Goa.[21]

There seem to have been three main categories of trade at Goa and South Kanara in the Portuguese period. First, there is the old export trade of the area, mainly pepper and spices. The exporters here were probably Jains: shipping to Europe was a Portuguese monopoly, while the Indian Ocean was served by the Gujaratis – and some Portuguese as well. In competition with them, the Muslim traders were seen as 'pirates' by the Portuguese. Second, there were imports from the Indian Ocean area to the kingdoms east of the mountains: best known is the supply of Persian and Arab horses to the Vijayanagara empire. These trade networks must have overlapped with those already mentioned, Gujaratis predominating, along with Portuguese and Arabs. The third type of commerce, however, was the import of rice from South Kanara to Goa. This trade, dominated by the GSB, became important very early in the sixteenth century and continued till modern times (Pearson, 1976, 1981; Subramaniam, 1993). Very probably, it was the GSB who financed the clearing of new lands for rice.

Subramaniam stresses the changes that characterize Asian societies in the sixteenth century. Criticizing the tendency to distinguish land-based, 'feudal' societies from trade-oriented states oriented towards the sea, he underlines the general increase in trade – whether in the Mughal empire, in Iran, or in Japan, as well as the emergence of many of the new seaborne domains (1993: 10-28). There was a rise of trade in the north-south direction, whereas earlier the main trend had been east-west. He also notes an important increase in the long-distance trade in food grains.[22] The restructuration of South Kanara as a rice-producing area dominated by the Bunts, and a trading sphere dominated by the GSB, seems to have been part of this wider process. Even before the coming of the Portuguese, the GSB may have been trading in rice, exporting to Oman and the Gulf. This would explain why some were established in South Kanara and Malabar well before the Portuguese period.

Rather than later immigrants to an established social and economic pattern, then, the GSB were among its founders. In other words, the 'traditional society' to which the Tulu ethnic revival refers, was dependent on and, in terms of social and economic organization, included the GSB merchants. To construct one as 'modern and external', the other as 'traditional and indigenous' – as is often done in South Kanara – seriously skews our understanding of the dynamics of the area.

The Konkanis themselves, however, tend to accept that they are 'immigrants'.[23] The term 'Gauda' is seen to refer to their origin from Bengal,[24] or alternatively to their northern origin, while 'Saraswati' refers to the lost river of Punjab, mentioned in the Vedas, reaching the sea through Rajasthan.[25] A very long line is constructed here going back to Punjab or Rajasthan – at the time of the Indus Valley Civilization, before the disappearance of the Saraswati River – by way of migration to Bengal or Gujarat, and then to Goa. Everybody agrees that Goa was their home before coming to the Tulu country. One explanation dominates with regard to this latter migration: due to Christian religious persecution, the GSB, as good Hindus, had to flee Portuguese territory. This is why the term 'refugee' is sometimes used by them, without any inference of stigma. Yet Konkani Catholics also migrated to the Tulu country at about the same time. As 'new

Christians' – along with the Jews – they were indeed suspected of continuing heathen practices and so may have felt as much threatened by the inquisition in Goa as the non-Christians. But for both groups there may also have been an economic motivation. We have seen that the rice trade was expanding, attracting the GSB: as for the Catholics, they were welcomed by the Nayak rulers as colonizers of waste land. Their specialty, then and later, was coconut cultivation. In both cases, there seems to have been substantial migration through the seventeenth and eighteenth centuries.

Religious persecution in Goa was particularly significant around 1570-80, though the inquisition lasted into the nineteenth century. Even at the best of times, however, there were restrictions on Hindu cults and temples in Portuguese territory. A very large number of temples were destroyed. Even so, two Hindu merchant communities continued to dominate the trade of Portuguese India: the Gujarati Banias[26] and the Konkani GSB (Pearson, 1976, 1981). This pattern was established before the inquisition came to Goa, but continued later. Clearly, though some GSB left Goa during these years, there were enough left to dominate local trade in and around Goa; long-distance trade (Africa, Red Sea, Gulf, South-East Asia) was dominated by the Gujaratis.[27] Evidently, then, the persecution in Goa has attained a disproportionate place in the collective memory of the Konkani GSB community.

According to Vasantha Madhava's fundamental work on the agrarian developments of South Kanara since medieval times, there was a sharp increase in the GSB community in the early decades of the eighteenth century (1991: 150). By this time, Goa was declining as a trade centre: the British and the French were gaining trade, territory and power. By the latter part of the century the Konkanis, both Hindu and Christian, were well established in North and South Kanara. When Hamilton arrived to survey the area after the British conquest in 1800, he described the GSB as merchants and shopkeepers, stressing that they tended to be well off (1807/1999: 12-13, 20-1, 58). The Konkani were seen by the British as much more literate, intelligent and progressive than any other group in the area,[28] and this is also the view the Konkanis have of themselves.

The 'village trader' in the Tulu country is often a GSB, while the community has a place in the old spice trade and its modern developments, such as areca and cashewnut. They have also bought plantations. Today, the GSB control, or are strongly present, in all kinds of trade in South Kanara, dealing in grains and fertilizers as well as consumer goods. They dominate banking and are strongly present in education.

In all towns and many large villages we find a temple to Venkatarama, an incarnation of Vishnu, seen as 'belonging to' the GSB. These temples are 'private', and administered by a committee of prominent members from the local GSB community.[29] The temple committee seems to function as the node of political and cultural leadership in the local GSB communities.[30] Venkatarama temples mainly cater to members of the caste. The GSB, then, while firmly entrenched in a strong socio-economic position, do not enter into a 'ritual hierarchy' like that enacted when the Bunt chief celebrates his 'royal' *bhuta.* Rather, they stay outside the local ritual order, underlining their separation from other castes.[31]

The GSB generally agree that they descend from the Brahmin population living in the valley of the Saraswati, the mythical river which disappeared more than 2,000 years ago. Fictive or not, this link to the Saraswati is central to GSB identity. In their view, it proves the ancient origin of their caste, linking it to other communities of Saraswat Brahmins present in different regions of India, many of which are prestigious. It shows the GSB not just as real Brahmins but as one of the most ancient Brahmin communities, with all that this implies for prestige and cultural self-assurance. This is particularly pertinent since the GSB, who eat fish and have unorthodox rituals, are not on the face of it the Brahmins towards which other communities would look for Sanskritization (Srinivas 1952, 1962, 1967). They are not priests – except for a separate community known as Bhats – but merchants, and proud of their commercial importance and status.

The prefix Gauda has caused much debate among the GSB and among scholars, for some hold that it implies a link to Bengal, while others stress that Gauda is an epithet applied to northern Brahmins.[32] I shall not enter the debate,[33] but the northern links are important to the GSB, since Hinduism and Brahmin culture came from the north, giving preeminence to northern as against Dravidian origins, just as northern Brahmins were traditionally seen as superior to those from the south. From the north, the ancestors of the GSB community arrived in Goa around the tenth century.[34] There, they adopted or developed the Konkani language. Goa is often seen in an idealized light, as a 'land of milk and honey,' from which the GSB were forced to flee or emigrate due to Portuguese persecution. As we have seen, this popular image needs to be qualified: there was emigration before the Portuguese came, the colonization brought opportunities for trade which led many GSB to settle in the south, and Goa was possibly getting overpopulated after the first centuries of Portuguese rule. But while these themes sometimes enter the discussion of the past among GSB, the idyllic image of Goa, and the idea of a forced diaspora remain pillars of caste identity.

Speakers of the Konkani language among Dravidian populations, the GSB are often known as Konkanis. Here, too, there are debates of importance to members of the community. Some deny that there is a Konkani community, since many different groups speak that language. Even so, Konkani language is an important identity marker, more so since there are several variants of the language, of which the GSB dialect is one. Some regret that the Catholics of South Kanara – most of whom were converted from GSB families – speak 'a purer Konkani than we do'. The language is highly esteemed, though there is a persistent claim that Konkani is not really a written language – which is far from the truth.[35] Yet the claim is significant: The assertion should be taken to mean that the language lacks a script of its own, often seen as emblematic of a language's identity and prestige in India. Unlike other regional languages, such as Kannada, Marathi or Gujarati, there has been no standardization of literary Konkani: efforts to produce a common standard invariably founder on the tendency, for each Konkani-speaking community, to use its own variant. There is a generally held idea that the language of the GSB reflects the history of the community: those that hold that the term Gauda refers to Bengal are eager to find links to Bengali in their vocabulary, while others claim that the forms in question may equally well stem from older Gujarati or Marathi. More defensible in linguistic terms is the assertion that Konkani is among the most archaic – and thus among the oldest and most prestigious[36] – of the Indo-European group of Indian languages; older than Marathi or Gujarati, its closest neighbours.

Goa occupies an important place in the image the GSB have of their history, not just in terms of nostalgia with regard to that beautiful region, but also since Goa is the origin of the present lineages of the caste, as well as the site of the temples of their lineage deities (*kuladevatas*). These temples are generally situated in the so-called 'new conquests' of Goan territory, which became Portuguese in the eighteenth century. The original temples and villages of the GSB lineages were situated inside the 'old conquests', and destroyed by the Portuguese in the sixteenth and early seventeenth century. The new temples were built outside Portuguese territory, and when the Portuguese gained authority over their 'new conquests', they had to accept the presence of these temples along with that of a Hindu majority.

Most GSB families still maintain a close link to these temples, where they go, or send representatives from the family, at least once a year. While some lineage temples have since been established in the south, most people still retain the link to their temple in Goa. The lineage deity and temple, along with the *gotra* and *pravara*,[37] are important markers of identity within the community. They, in addition to the family name and its place of origin locate each individual on a mental map – more or less complete, according to individual knowledge – of the community. Many GSB also speculate about their actual village of origin. Some actually do research – generally on an amateur basis – on this question. One source used is the priests of the present temples; another is the Portuguese archives in Goa. This mapping is at once structural and historical, and it is a main argument of this book that the synchronic and diachronic merge here, in what I shall call the historicity of the GSB community, so that 'social structure' effectively becomes, and is seen as, a product of historical events.[38]

Within these larger categories, the immediate identification of a member of the caste is twofold: there is the family name – transferred patrilineally though there may be several surnames to a lineage – and the name of the place where the current segment of the lineage established itself. Only occasionally is this the name of the village or town where the family currently resides: more commonly, it is the place from where the ancestor of the present local descent group came. Thus in the town of Udupi, where I did my main fieldwork, I know only one family using Udupi in their name: most names referred to villages in the vicinity, from where the grandfather or great-grandfather of my informants came and established himself at Udupi. The place-name is used as a first name but precedes it. Thus a well-known businessman in town in the last generation was Airody Radhakrishna Pai, where Airody is a village north of Udupi where the family stayed for some generations, Radhakrishna is the first name of the individual, and Pai is the family name. Very commonly, as in many middle-class castes in India, the person is referred to by his initials, thus A.R. Pai for this man.

The first initial thus commemorates part of the family's history, and sets it apart from other families using the same surname: the number of surnames in the caste is limited, so referring to 'Mr. Pai', for example, does not take us very far. The family is usually referred to by the combination of the first and the last name – 'He is an Airody Pai' or 'she is an Ammunje Nayak', for example. But these identifications take on a particular aspect when used in the local context, for this double designation also refers to what we may call the family firm. Thus the Ammunje Nayaks and the Airody Pais are two family dynasties in Udupi, identified historically with the first shop they opened in town, and in the present with the family firm or other well-known activity. The groups who identify with such a shop are *vaibhav* or *wagad*, 'families'. Structurally, a *vaibhav* or *wagad* is a local lineage segment, including all patrilineal descendants of the ancestor who first used the present place-name marker, or, alternatively, who moved to the present place and founded the present family firm.

The first shop has symbolic significance. Thus the Airodys, who now own perhaps a dozen shops in Udupi, have maintained their first shop in activity – where it all began – in the 1890s.[39] The Kalsanka Pai family meets for Diwali in their old family shop in the Udupi temple square.[40] Diwali has twin importance for the GSB merchant families: it is, as for many other Indian castes, the new year and an occasion for celebration: and as for most Indian merchants, an important part of the ritual is the renewal and the blessing of the account books. But since this ceremony is held, when possible, in the family's 'original' shop, it also celebrates the unity of the family as a community in the Durkheimian sense, and provides an occasion to remember the family history. The old shop marks the point where the lineage segmented into local kinship groups, and it is a sad situation if a split in the family makes it impossible to celebrate the commercial 'beginnings' together. These beginnings are also marked, in the old shops, by the portrait of its founder close to the family deities, on the wall behind the counter. Old shops often advertise their age on the signboard outside the shop; and the Airody Pais have produced a very interesting brochure to celebrate the centenary of the family enterprise, stressing their 'tradition of quality'.

For the individual, then, the first level with which he identifies is the *vaibhav*, known to himself and others as the combination of a place-name and a surname. This identification implies the history of the move to the present place and that of the family firm. People also know to which *gotra* (and sometimes *pravara*) each *vaibhav* belongs, as well as the identity of their *kuladevata* and at which temple (in Goa or in South Kanara) that deity is worshipped. Individuals of course know members of other *vaibhavs*: that of their wife and that of their mother, of other in-laws, and also – very often – those families who worship at the same *kuladevata* temple. The families who do so are seen as a kind of community at an intermediary level. Another kind of intermediary community is formed by the families belonging to the same *math* or monastery, and who share the same guru.[41] Then there are the families known from their own caste or village, and going to the same Venkatarama temple. Then again, there is the caste, seen as a community of language, culture, and origin from Goa. Finally, there is the longer link to the north, to the river Saraswati and to other Saraswat Brahmins spread over most of India. The link that the Saraswati provides with the beginnings of Indian history, and with the Indus Valley Civilization, tend to promote an identification with the roots of 'Indian culture' – which makes the GSB, in their own view, its prime representatives in their locality and region.

In many ways, this book differs from most anthropological monographs. Most striking, perhaps, is the fact that I have eschewed the anonymity usually accorded to informants.[42] Thus much of the book reads like local history, rather than structural analysis. One reason is simply that anonymity seems useless once Udupi is identified. The families we meet would be recognized by any Udupi reader, or anybody else familiar with the town. To speak of 'a well-known pilgrimage centre and district headquarters located in South Kanara, not far from Mangalore' would immediately identify the town and to say less would imply a distortion of key variables for understanding the setting. But there is another reason, of theoretical importance. As Dumont once put it; 'history is the process by which society reveals itself as what it is' (Dumont, 1957: 21). Societies do not exist in abstract, structural time, but only in concrete, historical circumstances. It is through the specifics of history that the generalities of social dynamics manifest themselves. Udupi, then, is not a 'typical' case of a small town in India, and the GSB are certainly not simply a 'case' of caste. Still, through the story of Udupi and its GSB community, we see a number of factors at work shaping the configuration we see today. Some of these factors are comparable to those found in the development of other small towns, in India or elsewhere. Others are peculiar to the particular constellation of factors we subsume under the term caste, related to the religious complex we call Hinduism, and so on. The approach followed here, then, is to relate specificities, and then, within the limits of the material, account for them in general anthropological or sociological terms.

This book deals with the particularities of the position occupied by the GSB, 'Business Brahmins', and their implications for our understanding of community belonging and cultural pluralism in India. To achieve this, I deal with different dimensions of social stratification, usually subsumed under class and ethnicity, as well as caste. The main point is to explain the position of the GSB as the outcome of factors belonging to all these dimensions. The GSB, in terms of class, constitute a major part of the bourgeoisie of South Kanara: they are a particular caste of Brahmins: and they are ethnically distinct from Tulu speakers. I argue that these dimensions merge into a whole not adequately caught by any single dimension: caste, class and ethnicity go together in constructing the regional social system of South Kanara.

NOTES

1. Some 3,000 mm (120 inches) annually.
2. In 1981 Dakshina Kannada District, which includes Mangalore and most of the Tulu country, had a population of 23,73,399 for an area of 8,441 sq km, or 281.2 per sq km. Even deducting the Mangalore agglomeration (3,05,513 inhabitants in 1981) this is a very high density for Karnataka: only Mandya and Bengaluru districts were more densely populated (Kamath, 1982; 390, 406-7).
3. See for example, Arasaratnam, 1987: 101, 108 and Bouchon, 1987: 166-7.
4. These units are described more specifically below (pp. 65-71).
5. Tulu has been a spoken dialect. It has a rich literature deposited in memory only through folklore. This language has rarely been employed as a documentary and literary medium. Barring a few epigraphs in this language making use of the Tulu script, which happens to be a variation of the Malayalam script, we have hardly any old literature written in Tulu (Bhatt, 1975: xiii).
6. The Bunts, like most Tulu speakers, are matrilineal by tradition, and ritual leadership, such as the right to receive the *bhuta*, belongs to the eldest male descendant of the elder sister. Since Independence, and particularly since the land reforms (the last of which were introduced in 1973), land is inherited patrilineally and is usually divided between siblings. Such division does not necessarily affect the ritual role of the family, and as elsewhere in India, juridical division of property is not always accompanied by fragmentation of the management unit.
7. Thus several villages (*uru*) might form a *magane*, again united under a common chief into a *seme*. A number of *seme* constituted a *nadu*.
8. I have discussed this movement elsewhere (2010; Carrin and Tambs-Lyche, 2003).
9. The ritual which recreates and revives traditional Tulu society is the *nema*, the annual festival of a royal *bhuta* (Brückner, 1995; Carrin and Tambs-Lyche, 2003). In the *nema*, the village is conceived as the property of a *bhuta*, and administered in 'trust' by a family of landholders. In the rice-growing middle zone, these are generally Bunts, the 'warriors' of the region and the typical patrons of *bhuta* cults. Most landowners still perform their traditional religious role. The old 'manor' (*gutu*) is still, ritually and in prestige terms, the centre of the village, though the landholders may now live in separate, newer buildings. It is in the 'manor' that the *bhuta's* regalia (*bandara*) are kept. These old houses have a spacious verandah, often decorated with beautiful wood carvings. Here, the chief received visitors and dependents; untouchables, however, are not allowed to enter the verandah.

10. Much work has been done by the Centre of Folklore Studies at Manipal near Udupi, started by the GSB Tonse Pai family and financed by the Ford Foundation. This work recalls the first stage of nationalism characterized by romanticism and a turn towards folk culture, which Hobsbawm (1975) sees as typical of small nations without a state. Indeed, the Finnish folklorist Lauri Honko, a main contributor, expressed the hope that the *paddanas* would do for Tulu identity what the Kalevala achieved for the Finns (1985). Still, no important Tulu politician has yet launched a demand for a Tulu national state. The parallel is apt in so far as we are dealing with people who, until these discoveries, were deemed to have languages but no literature. See also Chinnappa Gowda, 1983; Brückner, 1995; Honko, 1986; Carrin, 1998; 1999, Carrin and Tambs-Lyche, 2003; Vivek Rai, 1986 a and b, etc.
12. The complex of Pai institutions at Udupi and Manipal includes a Yakshagana centre, where the art is taught and practised. Several other cultural institutions, notably temples, have their own Yakshagana groups. These developments have been paving the way for a new Tulu literature, with a small but vigorous milieu of writers.
13. Billavas were also, traditionally, the 'soldiers' of the Bunts, and this role is ritually stressed. Like the Bunts, they are matrilineal. They have their own *bhutas*, quite distinct from the royal ones: the twin brothers Koti and Chennaya. Traditionally, their sanctuaries were seen by the Bunt landlord as their property, but today, they have often been taken over by the Billavas themselves. This is symptomatic of the Billava drive to emancipate themselves from their former position of servitude – and untouchability – while resistance to these changes from Bunts are indicative of the latter's efforts to keep the Tulu movement together.
14. According to S.U. Kamath, the early Jain chiefs were feudatories of the Chalukyas from above the Ghats who 'entered Tulunadu and carved out their own territory in the twelfth century. Others came under the Hoysalas (thirteenth century) and their power increased under the Vijayanagara rulers in the fourteenth century, when the local Alupa dynsty disappeared.
15. The Jains seem to have controlled plantations of areca nuts, pepper, and other export commodities for a long time. It is likely that their towns were based on this trade. The Jains also controlled some ports. It seems likely that it were the Muslims who drove the Jains from the coastal trade. Indeed, the Muslims of the present port of Bhatkal are said, by many inhabitants of the area including Jains, to be converts from Jainism.
16. For the matrilineal system of the Bunts, see Claus, 1978.

17. Njammasch has made an impressive analysis of this landownership pattern from inscriptions (1992a, b; 1993).
18. Thus the Chudasama kings of Junagadh were supported by the Ahirs, the line of the Jethwas of Porbandar by the Mers. See Tambs-Lyche, 1997. These political formations may have been similar to much later developments in Bundelkhand (Jain, 2002), highland Orissa (Schnepel, 2002), Bastar (Sundar, 1997), and elsewhere in central India at a much later date.
19. One based on or near Mangalore, another at Barakuru, north of the present-day Tulu-speaking area.
20. 'The *gutu* system (the Bunt manor dominating a village of tenants and labourers) came very late,' says M.M. Prabhu, a prominent GSB historian from Mangalore. 'The Bunts like to say it is very old. But in fact it only dates from around 1650.' By *gutu* system he means the traditional village of a Bunt chief and his Billava tenants.
21. This hypothesis does not exclude, of course, the presence of some rice-growing Bunt villages at an earlier date, for the coastal areas of the Persian Gulf were already importers of rice, and a trade link – largely run by Muslim merchants – to these lands had long been active. Nor do I deny the existence, prior to this date, of elements of the *bhuta* cults. Since Jainism, like Buddhism, was never a religion of the masses, it is probable that popular religion under Jain domination was the ancestor of the *bhuta* cults. Indeed, the *bhuta* cults of North Kanara, which lack the link through 'royal *bhutas*' to the chiefs, presents much simpler forms than in the south (Carrin, 2002) and may well be a surviving variant of the cults current when Jainism dominated South Kanara.
22. 'At the same time', he says, 'the rise of the port-centered states that we have described, such as Aden, Hurmuz and Melaka, led to the growth of a substantial trade in food grains and other items of bulk consumption. This trade, in relatively low-value and high-volume goods, may have existed earlier as well, but it would seem that the late fourteenth and fifteenth centuries witnessed a substantial expansion in its extent' (1993: 29).
23. An article in the Mumbai journal the *Kanara Saraswat* (principally a Chitrapur Saraswat journal) illustrates this sentiment perfectly: 'We become foreigners wherever we go . . . even in our own Kanara we are accustomed to this treatment, in spite of our long domicile there. There we became Kushasthalis, because Kanarese is not our mother tongue, and when we move out of it and settle, say, in Madras . . . we are treated as people of the west coast and have no *locus standi*; in the place of our

adaptation in Maharashtra we are Karwaris . . . (We have) a north Indian name and a south Indian existence' (*Kanara Saraswat*, 11, no. 1, April 1928: 16-20, cited by Conlon, 1977: 197).

24. Gowd or Gauda, a region of Bengal and eastern Bihar, is often equated with the historical region of Kosala.
25. Some years ago this tradition was still seen as 'mythical'. Recent research comfirms the former existence of a great river flowing from the foothills of the Himalaya with its estuary either north or south of Kacch (Valdiya, 2002).
26. Both Jain and Hindu.
27. There are a few examples of GSB families known to have taken part in this trade.
28. This point is stressed in the District Manual of South Kanara (Sturrock, 1894).
29. There is a parallel, here, to the way Jains and other merchant communities of Saurashtra run their temples.
30. This is clear from the history of banking in the area, where the GSB play a leading role. When their early banks recruited board members for new branches, they seem to have preferred temple committee members.
31. This again constitutes a parallel to the merchant castes of Gujarat.
32. Gauda used here as an epithet of northern Brahmins, the Panchagauda, as opposed to the southern Panchadravida.
33. My own opinion, however, is that the reference to the northern group of Brahmins is likely to be the correct interpretation of the term.
34. GSB historians concur on this date, among them P.R. Kuduva of Udupi and M.M. Prabhu of Mangalore. V.N. Kudva also gives this date in his book (1972).
35. This point will be discussed later.
36. 'It is really very close to Prakrit', says P.R. Kuduva.
37. See the chapter on kinship.
38. See also my similar argument, for Saurashtra, in Tambs-Lyche 2004: 163-4.
39. Some of the family asserted that their first shop in Udupi was opened in the 1860s; I go here by the date indicated in the brochure published on the centenary of their enterprise. Since the family were itinerant merchants before settling in Udupi, they may have had some permanent stall here earlier, but if so, this is not the one they now identify as their 'first shop'.
40. Though the shop in Kalsanka is now gone, people told me that one of the obstacles to widening the main street – an important thoroughfare –

through Kalsanka was the old house of the Kalsanka Pai family, which this influential family did not like to pull down.

41. These monasteries are particular to the caste and must not be confounded with the eight Madhava *maths* (the *Ashtamath*) at Udupi.
42. One price to pay for this lack of anonymity is, of course, the deletion of incidents and stories that could be considered as injurious or harmful to informants. I trust the reader will have an adequate understanding of small-town dynamics to infer the existence of such stories, of which there are many.

1

The Road Travelled

I was impressed with the historical consciousness of the GSB I met. Whenever we talked about the community, the discussion tended to turn towards its history: people talked of their origins in the north, of Goa, or of the itinerary of their family since their arrival in South Kanara. This does not mean that everybody is an amateur historian. But many know historians, amateurs or professionals, from the community, who are respected and have a ready audience. In this chapter I do not try to replace their views with mine, but rather to report, as an ethnographer, on the historical discourse I encountered in the field. Reference was made, here, to several works – notably in Kannada – that I have not been able to consult.[1]

Michael Lobo, doing historical and genealogical research among Konkani Christians, feels that most of them do not know much about their history. In his work he has had to look around for knowledgeable informants. I was more impressed than he has been with the general level of historical interest among informants. This may be due to conversion functioning as a watershed in the history of Catholics: few bother to go back farther than that. Since the Catholics came as agriculturalists, rather than businessmen, their history is punctuated by changing land tenures, which break the continuity as the families have moved. Still, several Catholic families are able to go back to the eighteenth century, a few even to the seventeenth, and many – in Mangalore – to the generation returning from captivity under Tipu to take up their old, or get new, lands in Mangalore.[2] Lobo, it must be said, was concerned with genealogies and precise historical facts, while I was more concerned with a general consciousness of the past. The two are not the same. It is not exact dates that concern my GSB informants, nor the details of genealogy. What interests them is closer to what anthropologists call myth, a historical narrative that will explain and legitimate the place they currently occupy in South Kanara society.[3] In terms of family history, there is not much difference between the GSB and the Christians. But the GSB are far more concerned with their 'mythical' past, before and during their stay in Goa.[4]

Thus I shall not myself enter the debate on how the Saraswat Brahmins migrated from the valley of the Saraswati to their settlements in Goa, where they became the ancestors of the GSB[5] (Fig. 1). Instead I shall cite people who are recognized by the community's members as their own historians, and so, whatever their disagreements, they form part of the field where identity is defined through historical debate and discourse. Their work, then, is part of the historical consciousness of the community, a theme which laymen as well as historians discuss freely.

Among the accomplished historians of the community, M. Mukunda Prabhu is highly regarded, inside as well as outside his caste. The 'M' stands for Manjeshwar, where his family was for a long time involved in the management of the temple, probably the first to be established by the community south of Goa. He has lived in Mangalore the last 28 years, and is often visited by people like myself, curious about the history of the caste and the region.

As to the links between Goa and the Saraswati valley, M.M. Prabhu stresses that there are a large number of Saraswats in Kacch, known as Kacchi Saraswats. He underlines that all the adjectival Brahmin names (Saraswat Brahmins, Shivalli Brahmins, Nagar Brahmins, and so on) are taken from place names, the name of a place of origin or the parents' place.[6]

According to S.S. Talmaki, says M.M. Prabhu, the Saraswats started to leave their original homeland toward the end of the third century BC. The Saraswats, he continues, originally came from the foothills of Himalaya,[7] then went to Kacch, to Afghanistan, and eastwards to Kosala.[8] His own work uses evidence from ritual texts – the *mantras*. According to that source, 'our Sankalpa starts from Kurukshetra[9] then to the Gaudakaranya,[10] then Godavari dakshina,[11] and then to Goa'. From there the ancestors came to Sankhyavati, near Sirsi in North Kanara. 'Malaya' refers to the woodland around there. In the formula found in the *Sankalpa* text, 'everything is in the locative case, you may add a word, but you cannot delete anything' – so the itinerary, he feels, is kept in the *Sankalpa mantra.* There is linguistic evidence too, he adds. Thus Puruka instead of Purusha is used by the GSB – as the Punjabis do. In Konkani, the word for medicine becomes *vokada*, from the original *okada.* There are some such linguistic distinctions which the GSB have retained even now.

One early branch descended from Kacch. A second branch brought the itinerary merchants.

> To distinguish us from the original settlement we were called Gauda Saraswats. To the Sahashti (in Goa) came, as the name indicates, sixty-six families: another thirty came to Tiswadi (in Goa), making a total of ninety-six families. When we came east to Kosala we arrived at the river Sowan or Swarnavati in Bihar, which we called Shanavati. It flows between Bihar and Orissa. Shanavati Sahasra thus means the thousand from Shanavati – not 96,000, as is often claimed. Shanavati refers to ninety-six villages of Kosala. . . . Another group from Dwarka settled at Kushusthali[12] – there is another one in Uttar Pradesh.

The place-names of origin were often attached to the new places – 'like New England' – feels M.M. Prabhu. The second branch of Saraswats arrived in Goa in the early tenth century, he says. But the Kacchi branch must have come earlier.[13] The Panchagauda category, he says, distinguishing northern Brahmins from those of the south, dates only from about the tenth century.[14] The implication, here, is that 'Gauda' in the GSB caste name predates this distinction and so must refer to the Gauda region of north-western Bengal and eastern Bihar.

Perhaps the most knowledgeable of the several local historians of the GSB community resident in Udupi is P.R. Kuduva, who has a watch shop near the Sanskrit College.[15] Kuduva, too, stresses the links of the GSB with the Saraswati River, which he associates with the Indus Valley Civilization, and with Dwarka: one term used by them is Dwarkesi – those who came from Dwarka.[16] Konkani, he stresses, is directly descended from Prakrit, 'which was the old form of Sanskrit'. The main cooking vessel is called *cherbi* in GSB dialect – a term directly related to the old term for the vessel used in the *yagna*,[17] called *choru* or *chervi.*

P.R. Kuduva on his part stresses that the term Gauda indicates the northern origin of the caste, as one of the Panchagauda groups. Saraswati is itself enough to indicate the community. The Saraswati

Brahmins are the only Brahmin community found all over India, he says. Everywhere, the Saraswats speak the language of their region. Konkani, he stresses, is directly linked to Prakrit, which he regards as older than Sanskrit. All this, of course, underlines the point that the GSB are among those Brahmin communities most closely related to the original Brahminical culture of ancient India.

M.V. Kamath, GSB journalist and writer, maintains that the Saraswats originally came from the doab between the Saraswati and Drishadvati rivers, described in the *Rigveda*, the *Brihat Samhita*, the *Markandeya Purana* and the *Bhagavata Purana*. 'There is also a special chapter, *Saraswatakhyana*, on the Saraswats in Shalya Parva of the *Mahabharata*. In it is depicted a twelve year famine during which the Vedic *shrotriyas* died and the Rishi Saraswata, "the foremost of the Rishis of unrivalled splendour and godlike mien", kept himself alive by eating fish' (Kamath, 1983: 1). This passage is often used by the GSB – usually without the scriptural reference – to explain their fish-eating habit. The *Buddhacharita* too has reference to the preservation of Vedic culture by the Saraswats, continues Kamath (ibid.).

Kamath cites from the evening *sandhya* of the Chitrapur Saraswats and 'some Vaishnava Saraswats' of Kanara:[18] *Namaste Sharadadevi Kasmirapuravasini* – 'we bow to Sharadadevi, resident of Kashmir' – and from that of the Shenvis (Shenoys): *Sarasvati Mahamaya Kasmiri-puravasini// Satadresamantat tam sarasvata mahammunim* 'we bow to Saraswati who is the great *maya* and the resident of Kashmir, and also to the great sage Saraswata residing in the neighbourhood of Satadri' (ibid.: 2-3).

This point clearly shows, in Kamath's view, the relationship to Kashmir, a land situated, it is felt, on the route the Vedic peoples must have taken into India,[19] and still the home of Brahmins generally viewed as among the most traditional and purest of all. These are of course the Pandits that Madan writes about (1987).

Of the introduction of Brahmins to the Parashuramashristi[20] – the Konkan, Kanara and Malabar coast – the *Skanda Purana* says:

> Thereafter, Parasurama brought ten munis (brahmans) who were residents of Triboira . . . [21] from among the Pancha Gaudas and established them on Pancha-Krosi and Kushasthali and Gomanchala (Goa). Their gotras were Bharadwaja, Kausika (Kamsa), Vatsa, Kaundinya, Kashyapa, Vasishta,

Jamadagni, Viswamitra, Gautama and Atri. They were brought for the purpose of *shraddha*, *yajna*, and *bhojana*. He settled them in Matagrama (Madgaon), Kushasthali (Kudathali or Kuttal) and Kardali (Keloshi).

(Kamath, 1983: 3)

The *gotras* mentioned here are all common among the present-day GSB, and they commonly suppose that they were the *gotras* of their ancestors in Goa. The *Skanda Purana*, then, seems to confirm the direct continuity of lineage from Parashurama's days till the present. The interpretation of place-names goes to show that the Purana effectively attests settlement in Goa, at the very localities were the GSB's ancestors were found in Portuguese times.

As in many historical constructions, the emphasis here is on continuity. For these historians of the community, there is a direct line leading from the Vedic immigration – or from the Indus Civilization – through the valley of the Saraswati, down to Goa, and then into South Kanara. Such continuity is, for all the historians cited, mainly attested by scriptural sources. There are minor differences in interpretation, but they are not central to the main theme of this book. What is clear is that these historians – and numerous others – are respected in the community for their knowledge of the past, and that such knowledge is in itself a commodity much sought after. As P.R. Kuduva says, 'people will come to me and ask me to contribute an article – the occasion is often an anniversary of a temple or some similar occasion – and so I feel I should oblige'. Typically, among laymen who lack historical knowledge themselves, the common answer to my questions was: 'you should talk to so-and-so, he is very knowledgeable about these matters'. The person in question was usually an acquaintance, and though its sources may be scriptural, the knowledge functions and is distributed as oral tradition. Occasionally somebody would show a book or refer to one, but mostly it is the authority of concrete, knowledgeable persons that is referred to. And when I went to see Prabhu or Kuduva, what I was given was effectively an oral lecture on GSB history.

In Goa, the community that became the Saraswat Brahmins came to occupy and own land in some of the central districts of the territory, notably in the island of Tiswadi, on which Panaji, the state capital, is situated. The Saraswats were certainly the dominant caste in Tiswadi, and possibly in other areas, and their mode of dividing the land and practising agriculture was to leave a lasting mark on the landscape.

There is evidence, says U.P. Kamath, a consulting engineer at Udupi, that the GSB came to Goa as a united group, an established community. 'You can see it from the physical features of the landscape of Tiswadi', he says. 'The bunds[22] between the rice fields there are rectilinear and absolutely equidistant: each field enclosed, then, represents a standard size.' The bunds here clearly serve to measure as well as to delimit each field. This, he underlines, is strikingly different from the fields and bunds of South Kanara, which follow the twists and turns of the landscape. The Goan pattern, he feels, must be evidence of communal agriculture, or at least a system of agriculture where land was distributed from a central agency, which would explain the importance of exact measurement. This pattern cannot stem from the Portuguese, for it is found only in former GSB territory, not in the rest of Goa. This, in fact, corresponds to what is stated on communal land use in Central Goa in the nineteenth century.[23] An important point here is that these are U.P. Kamath's own observations: they do not stem from a literary source, and so attest to the interest in their history common among the GSB.

The term communal agriculture, here, refers not so much to common ownership of land as to an integrated system, under some form of centralized community leadership, of dividing and demarcating the lands. Taken in this sense, the topographical evidence certainly does seem to attest to a concentrated and planned settlement, implying considerable autonomy and political organization on the part of the caste. This is corroborated by other evidence. 'Recognized as the founders of the villages (*gaonkar*)'[24] says Conlon of the Portuguese period, 'these brahman families collectively organized and enjoyed the produce of the best rice fields. Not all *gaonkars* were GSBs, but most GSB families held *gaonkar* rights' (1977: 18).

It might, of course, be argued that the planned aspect of agriculture in Goa may not have originated with the immigrant Brahmins, but with the authorities who allowed them to settle there. GSB historical constructions, however, are devoid of reference to this authority, and external evidence gives no obvious clue as to who they were. If the regular character of land allotments originated with an external authority, moreover, we still have to explain why it should have been applied only to the lands settled by the Saraswats. Thus Kamath's argument implies not only the existence of a strong internal organization of the Saraswats, but also relative autonomy: in other words, before the Portuguese came, the GSB ancestors were effectively the lords of the land. This point, as will be familiar to Indianists from the historical constructions of dominant castes elsewhere, in no way excludes allegiance to some superior level of authority: it shows only that within the limits of their own territory and jurisdiction, our Brahmins were able to organize themselves as they wanted. This leads to a further, important point: the asserted autonomy strengthens the image of Goa as the promised land, as 'our' land, as the cultural landscape created by the ancestors, which has become an important point for a community regretting its present dispersal and lack of territorial unity. If the GSB are not a dominant caste today, it is not because of a lack of the necessary qualities, but because they lost their land to a superior force (the Portuguese) and had to settle in the land of others.

The evidence from Portuguese records (Kamath refers here to Priolkar, 1961) makes it possible to identify a number of lines of descendance and their relationship to families among the GSB population today.

> On the one hand, you have there a complete listing of temples and villages, specifying which temple belonged to which village – these were the temples the Portuguese destroyed. So, for example, when a Shenoy lived in the village where the Ganesh temple was situated, he would belong to the *gotra* which has Ganapati as its lineage deity. And since surnames, *gotras* and lineage deities vary independently of each another, a Shenoy having Ganapati as lineage deity will belong to one particular *gotra*, which we will still find represented in the population of today.

There is scope for considerable future research here, for the Goa archives are said (Pearson, 1976) to contain data on the village level well beyond what was used by Priolkar.

U.P. Kamath also cites the term used for the wife's family – 'other people' in favour of the thesis that it was mainly GSB men who came to Goa, and that they married local women. The wives also call their husband *bamun*, i.e. 'Brahmin', which, he feels, goes to show that the women were not originally from a Brahmin caste. Others, as we shall see, point to intermarriage, but with Brahmin castes of the southern group. I would not, as an anthropologist, accept the interpretation of kinship terms of address in the way U.P. does, as I feel such usage must be explained within the framework of kinship structure rather than history.[25] But the long discussion I had with U.P. Kamath – who as an engineer surveys and evaluates property for sale – is one more piece of evidence as to the importance, among GSB intellectuals, of anything to do with the caste's history and origins: this sense of historicity was ever present in the discussions I had with them.

We have noted above how the first Saraswat settlers in Goa belonged to ten *gotras*, widely acknowledged as the original ones. Later, more Saraswats came, and M.V. Kamath, the journalist, cites an earlier historian:

> Within a short time, the whole of Goa was sprinkled with their colonies round their temples. It is possible that the colonists started life as agriculturists, traders and scribes and by dint of industry, good habits and character they soon came to be proprietors of large tracts of agricultural land within the island. They also won the esteem of the original inhabitants and assumed the role of their friends and advisers. (cited from V.M. Dubashi by Kamath, 1983: 3-4)

This is of course a reflection of how present-day GSB like to imagine their ancestors: in Dubashi's account, the lands in Goa were not the gift of some ruler or other, but acquired due to the 'industry, good habits and character' that, we may take as implicit, still characterize caste members. This, incidentally, fits straight into the image of a merchant caste, as we may ask why the alternatives – land gifted for ritual service, or won by military prowess – are not affirmed here. Merchants, in India as elsewhere, like to see themselves as 'self-made men'.

'They brought with them, of course, their own religious and social practices', says Kamath.

> It is possible that some of them married into the families of the Pancha-Dravida group of Brahmins already living south of the Vindhyas. But they were intent on retaining their foreignness which is probably the reason why they called themselves the Gauda Saraswat Brahmins, as Saraswat Brahmins who had come from Gauda desh. Of the various Saraswat communities

which are to be found in north India and the west coast, only the Saraswats of the west coast are known as Gauda Saraswat Brahmins. (1983: 4)

Let us note that 'foreignness' here carries an accent of rank and superior purity, since northern origin is a point of prestige among Brahmins. By keeping to 'their own religious and social practices' the GSB would have succeeded in keeping their very essence pure and unmixed. This point is particularly salient if it is admitted that inter-marriage with southern, and implicitly inferior, Brahmins have taken place, even if we assume, as U.P. Kamath, the engineer, does, that the GSB were accepting wives from other Brahmin castes but (implicitly) not giving them their daughters. Though marriage then would be in the proper, hypergamous mode, to admit female ancestors of lower rank may affect the purity of the line. To stress fidelity to tradition, however, shows that such inferior 'substance' [in Inden's sense of the term (1976)] has not in any way corrupted the essence of the caste.

Goa was taken by the Portuguese in 1510 (Subramaniam, 1993: 68), and soon became the centre of the Portuguese establishment in Asia, the Estado da India. For half a century this role seems to have provided considerable opportunity for the Brahmin population. But the situation changed with the introduction to Goa of the Inquisition in 1560. Signs of change were already evident in Portugal itself, where the liberal and humanist mood changed towards censorship in the early 1540s. The Inquisition had been officially set up in 1531, but was not very active until 1537-8 (ibid.: 83). In the beginning, the Inquisition mainly targeted the New Christians,[26] as it had done in Portugal, but it soon turned against Christian converts from Hinduism, suspected of pre-conversion practices. In 1540, all temples in Tiswadi were destroyed. Those in Bardes were razed in 1573 while Salcete's turn came in 1584-7. Temple lands were seized by the Church. Most Hindu rites and ceremonies were banned (Pearson, 1987: 117-18). By 1563, a royal mandate ordered the expulsion of all non-cultivating Brahmins from Portuguese territory (Machado Prabhu, 1999: 119). This did not mean that they all left, however. By 1623 there were still 150,000 Hindus in Goa (Pearson, 1987: 118). No doubt some GSB left, some remained. But for the latter, the cultural and social climate was hardly congenial, to say the least. While there are still some 250

Hindu temples in Goa, says one of the Alevoor Kinis, at least an equal number was destroyed by the Portuguese. Fonseca, in fact, says that 280 were 'razed to the ground' in the province of Salcete alone, in the year 1567 (1878/1986: 65). Certainly, a very large number were destroyed.

Portuguese Asia went through an economic crisis in 1545-52, with shipping on the Cape route continuing to decline into the 1560s. When trade to Portugal began to pick-up again in the 1570s, the Inquisition was active (Subramaniam, 1993: 84-6). It seems probable, therefore, that Goa gradually became less attractive to the GSB both in commercial and cultural terms, from the early sixteenth century, filled with new opportunities, towards and into the second half of the century. In this period, the influence of the *casados* – the Portuguese settled in India – over the viceroy's policy in Goa increased (ibid.: 93-4). They tended to use their influence against competing, indigenous traders.

Subramaniam stresses, however, that a large part of Portuguese trading activities in Asia – until the 1630s at least – was in fact done outside the effective authority of Portuguese rule. Thus the New Christians tended to dominate in East Asia and in the trans-Pacific trade, where they were safe for a long time from persecution (ibid.: 117-22). Thus we may well think that the GSB, too, retained many of their trading links to Goa even at a time when Hindu temples were destroyed in Goa itself.[27] To get away from Portuguese authority, it sufficed to go to the Kanara coast. After the fall of the Vijayanagara empire in 1565, three ports were, and for a limited time, controlled by the Portuguese. They were Honavara, Basrur and Mangalore (ibid.: 106). But as the kingdom of the Ikkeri Nayaks expanded in the void left by Vijaynagara's collapse, these ports fell to them in the mid-1650s (ibid.: 178). Well before that, the kingdom had offered safe refuge and rich trading opportunities to the immigrant GSB community.

But these immigrants found caste-fellows already settled in the south. There is information, from inscriptions and other sources, on the migration of the Konkanis to the Kanara coast before the Portuguese period. The earliest evidence we have of this is the Manjeshwar or Madananteshwara temple, south of Kasaragod in northern Kerala.[28] But I will let my insider historians speak, for the reasons given above. It is the oldest existing Konkani (GSB) temple, says P.R. Kuduva, dating from around AD 1200. It is very important in GSB history, adds M.M. Prabhu, whose family was, as we have seen, associated with it for a long time. According to him, the Manjeshwar temple was originally a Naga (snake) temple. 'But they found a *lingam* there, so it became an Ananteshwara[29] temple. Ranga Sharma, a GSB, discovered the *lingam*. Shesha (snake), Ishwara (Ananteshwara), and Narasimha are represented there.' M.M. Prabhu feels that the Narasimha image must have been donated by the Konkanis. The temple is first mentioned in the *Skanda Purana*,[30] says Prabhu. He stresses that his family was responsible for the Manjeshwar temple for a long time. In that context, he tells a story: One day he saw a cobra in his garden, but his father had always said that one must respect the snakes, so Mukunda told the cobra that he would make an offering to him the next time he went to Manjeshwar, that his father had taken care of the Manjeshwar temple – but that he wanted the *nag* to go away where he had come from. And, he says, the *nag* did exactly that: it turned around and disappeared. The story underlines, of course, the temple's link to the snake cult, as well as M.M. Prabhu's link to the temple. There was, in fact, an oracle of the god Shesha (snake) there until 1934. The medium was a GSB, and a descendant of the great Ranga Sharma.

M.M. Prabhu was among those who discovered a buried inscription at Heruru, near Mangalpadi. It mentions that the Alupa king Kulashekhara[31] had a palace in Manjeshwar. He was giving audience there – accompanied by his daughter – and she also gave a donation to the temple. Inscription 243 from Udupi, of AD 1321-2 mentions Virakula Shekhara as the ruler. His son Kumara Devarasa and leading citizens are mentioned as is the Manjeshwar temple. These inscriptions show that Manjeshwar was an important temple at the time of the Alupa kings, who ruled the Tulu-speaking country.[32] The dynasty disappeared in the fourteenth century.

Thus the age of the Manjeshwar temple, and its association with the GSB, is well attested, and there is no doubt that the community was indeed established at Manjeshwar well before the Portuguese came to India. Very likely, they were traders. The evidence suggests, then, as both M.M. Prabhu and P.R. Kuduva imply, that a GSB trading network along the coast was already active when Vasco da Gama reached Calicut, and that the Portuguese were using this network, as they used other existing trading links, while the Portuguese connection in its turn offered new opportunities, enabling the GSB traders to expand their operations.

By the eighteenth century the Manjeshwar temple used to pay tribute to the Domba Hegde of Vittala, says M.M. Prabhu, since it subsisted from cultivating lands which belonged to that prince. But after the fourth Anglo-Mysore war, which left the British in control of the area, the temple suspended payment since they were no longer sure who to pay. The Domba Hegde sent his army to collect the tribute and they plundered the temple. Then they returned to Tellicherry, where the Hegde was based at the time.[33] Some of the sacred objects were also taken to Vittala.

The Manjeshwar citizens petitioned Munro – who had become collector of Kanara – so by the end of the war, the British called for an explanation and ordered the Domba Hegde to hand back the temple's property as well as the land. He refused, and got a small army together to fight the British – but he was beaten and dethroned after one and a half years. After the looting of the Manjeshwar temple, continues M.M. Prabhu, GSB from Vittala were denied *prasad* there – the ban has now been lifted. The Vittala GSB, it may be noted, disposed of reserved seats on the Domba Hegde's audience verandah.[34] This, no doubt, attests to the Hegde's reconnaissance of their economic importance in his domain.

P.R. Kuduva's family, the Kochikar Kuduvas,[35] came to Mahé, the former French colony in Kerala, probably from Goa. His ancestor first came to Mahé as a representative of the Portuguese government in the seventeenth century. But he has found no records to trace the development of the family between that point and the end of the eighteenth century, in Tellicherry, where they moved from Mahé.[36] They then moved to Mangalore, to Padubidri between Mulki and Udupi, and finally to Udupi. He has tracked the family backwards for seven generations; at that time they were in Tellicherry. This must have been around 1800. Part of the family is still staying there. It was P.R. Kuduva's grandfather who moved to Udupi, some seventy years back, in the early 1930s. But his kinsman Kesho Kuduva had been established in Udupi since the 1850s, running a hardware shop in the temple square, on the corner of VT Street and the temple square. The Gundu Nayaks took over this property in the 1920s. This means that the Kochikar Kuduva hardware shop was there before Udupi developed from a pilgrimage centre into a town, and before the present GSB community really established itself there.

M.M. Prabhu uses rituals to demonstrate some of his historical points. To illustrate his view of the migrations of his community, he cites the *mantra* called Praksha Prasanna: 'the people are facing east, taking the vow, and electing a leader whom they then have to follow during the migration. The leader would be hitting with his *danda* the wood used to make axles for chariots – and wherever the wood fell, he would have to go, i.e. in that direction.'

The image is fascinating, and may have some relevance to the early period, when sizeable groups leaving the Saraswati Valley were looking for new lands. However that may be, it is likely that migration from Goa was different. We may imagine whole villages or large parts of them taking the decision to migrate rather suddenly, as when, for example, their temple had been razed to the ground. Still, there must have been many and different groups, and it is likely that sometimes just a single family took to the road. More to the point, perhaps, it is likely that these Saraswats already knew where to go: they were heading south, to lands outside the Portuguese domain. Some may indeed have chosen to go north or east, but if so, they must have been but a small minority of those who were to become the GSB.[37]

Concerning the migration to South Kanara about five hundred years ago, continues M.M. Prabhu, 'we have a vivid description by way of the Achurana Sutra: Women and children had to be seated in chariots, protected from sun and rain by parasols'. Clearly, says Prabhu, the Saraswats migrated with their families. The migration would have taken place, he feels, because of water problems: Achurana Sutra implies that they migrated with their cattle.

Again, there are some problems: water would not seem to have been a main problem in Goa, though over-population and diminishing holdings may have been a factor usually hidden behind a discourse dominated by the religious persecution. From what we know of the state of roads along the Kanara coast at the time, chariots would not have been a very practical proposition either. It certainly was not when Francis Buchanan (1807/1999: III) travelled through the country three hundred years later.[38] It is highly likely, however, that whole families migrated, and sometimes several together, as noted above. Taken as one, these descriptions of migration taken from ritual texts inform us, I think, mainly of an ideal of migration: a whole community together, with clear leadership, organized for travel in such a way as to protect women and children from hardship. The real migrations may have been rather different. But the elaboration of such an ideal tells us about the status of migratory moves in the GSB self-image. It tells us how this community, true to Brahmin ideals, would be able to uproot itself and move while still keeping to high standards of conduct and discipline. The image underlines that GSB migration – in spite of the pressures highlighted elsewhere in the discourse – was done in a way worthy of Brahmins.

Not all GSB left Goa, however. Among those that remained, Suba Kamat, who was connected with the customs in Goa, founded a trading house in 1750, in association with his four sons. Faced with declining trade in Goa, they established close links with the French, documented by some eight hundred letters in French at the Xavier's Centre of Historical Research, Goa, which have been studied by Ernestine Carreira (1990). Operating from Goa, with branches in Mumbai and Mahé, this trading firm was a main partner of the French. It acted as an intermediary between the Estado da India and the French, and as an intelligence agent for the French in British and Mahratta territory, using on occasion its own ships to link Mahé and Poona. It acted as a banker, commuting money between Poona, Mumbai, Surat, and the French possessions, and extended its service to a number of French mercenaries and adventurers serving with the Indian princes. It sold, bought and repaired ships for the French. With its French partners, in India and on Ile de France (Mauritius), it was heavily engaged in the slave trade. It traded with Europe, East Africa, Mauritius, Gujarat, Bengal, and China. Its links with France lasted till 1792, when the market for Oriental goods crashed in France as the revolution took its toll, while the British occupied the French possessions in India in 1793. Thus the GSB firm had to rebuild its networks to work with the British, and from 1810, like so many Mumbai traders, it entered the opium trade to China.

Konkanis were present in South Kanara before the Madhava *maths* were established in Udupi, says P.R. Kuduva. The Manjeshwar temple near Kochi was there even before Madhvacharya was born. In short, 'the Konkanis came here as traders long before the Portuguese came. . . . Our people', he continues, 'were here before the Shivalli Brahmins. The Saraswats were the first Brahmins to come to the Canara coast, known as the land of Parasurama. It was Parasurama who brought us to Goa,'[39] he continues, and 'later more (of us) came south under Portuguese pressure – but the Konkanis were there already.' P.R. Kuduva's point is clear: the GSB are not 'immigrants' in any ordinary sense of the term. If they differ from surrounding communities, it is because they are closer to the pan-Indian Brahminical culture.

Nowhere in the present organization of the community is this continuity across migration more clearly manifest than in the cult of the lineage deities, or *kuladevatas*. There are about fifty to sixty *kuladevata* temples in Goa. The one to Mahalasanarayani is the biggest and the most important, says a member of the Ammunje Nayak family. Mahalasa is called the Queen of Goa, or 'Saibini', while Damodar is called 'Saib'. Some, however, would claim that the temple to Shantadurga is as, or more important, than that to Mahalasa. It is striking how people seem to welcome questions about their *kuladevata*. Everybody among the GSB seems to have a real relationship to their deity in Goa. All are not equally fervent in their devotion, however, as indeed one might expect. There is considerable variation in the regularity with which people visit their lineage temple. Some, like the Airody Pais and the Parempali Nayaks go seldom or not at all, while others, like the Alevoor Kinis, the Ammunje Nayaks or the Gujjadi Shenoys, go regularly and maintain a close relation to the temple, contributing – as the Gujjadi Shenoys stress that they do – regularly to the temple funds. And, though they do not go very often, the Airody Pais have made some spectacular donations to their lineage temple.[40] The remark of a member of the Parempali Nayak family – 'everything was destroyed by the Portuguese at Goa' is in interesting contrast to the remarks of the others, who do not hesitate to bestow on the rebuilt temples the kind of devotion due to its predecessors.

Since the remark was made by a member of a family that seldom goes to Goa, we may perhaps suppose that the remark is meant to legitimize this abstention. May it be that the temple of the Parempali Nayaks, in contrast to the others, was not rebuilt?

According to M.M. Prabhu, the number of priests at Goa diminished a lot because of the GSB exodus, as many priests also migrated to the Kanara coast. Gauravas used to be the priests of the Goan temples and they still are: but now the GSB themselves become priests. The priestly role, however, is not really traditional among the GSB. Most priests I met stressed that though they were certainly Konkani, they were not GSB. According to them, they form a separate community, which does not marry the GSB. They use the term Bhat for themselves, which is also used as their surname. But other GSB stressed that Bhat is simply the term for a priest, and does not indicate a separate caste. And I certainly met younger recruits to the priesthood who came from ordinary GSB families.

Kuduva's *kuladevata* is Ganapati Mahamaya. The original temple to this pair of deities is at Candolim in Goa, called Ganapati Sansthan, but he prefers to go to the temple of the same deity at Shirali, some 5 km from Bhatkal.[41] His *ishtadevata* is Venkatarama. Like all Kuduva families he too belongs to the Kaushika *gotra*, so they all share the same *kuladevata* and no marriage can take place between Kuduvas.[42] One of Kuduva's sons is a computer specialist, working with the Ford agency in Mangalore. There are other Kuduvas in Udupi: thus there is a shop framing pictures at the southern end of V.T. Street. Kuduva is a surname only found in South Kanara and Goa.

P.R. Kuduva and U.A. Kamath have the same lineage god, though they do not belong to the same *gotra*. This means, of course, that they know each other from the temple. They underline the 'family atmosphere' of these temples. There the distance between devotee and priest is much reduced. For, says U.A. Kamath, 'when I go to my lineage temple, there will be no fence in front of the *garbaguddi*'.[43] Since only the GSB come, they are all allowed to go to the altar and perform the ritual themselves, except the women, of course. 'So it is in a very real sense my temple', he says. And since the same people come every year, they know each other, and they know, when they meet there, to which *gotra* each of them belongs.

M.M. Prabhu told me the story of the *murti* (image) of the Damodar temple. Damodar's image was brought in a cart from Margao, when the old temple there was destroyed by the Portuguese. One untouchable had a cottage there, and so they hid the *murti* in his cottage, deceiving the Portuguese who just went by. After that, Lord Damodar stepped out in the middle of the river and said, 'I will have to ask permission of Ramnath – (to install myself in his temple)'. (There are in all eight deities in the temple. Even now Damodar is worshipped on the second day, while Ramnath, who is a form of Shiva and another important *kuladevata* among the GSB, is worshipped the day before.) The name Damodar, says Prabhu, comes from *dama* (rope) and dare (belly). He does not comment further on this etymology. Damodar is a *lingam*, Shiva's symbol, but he is really a form of Krishna: the latter was tied to a capstan, which then turned into the *linga* Damodar, says M.M. Prabhu. Thus Damodar is a perfect example of the confluence of Shaiva and Vaishnava symbolism so typical of the GSB deities.[44] Damodar is a *mukhalinga*, a *linga* with a face. In the morning he is just a *linga*: for the day's worship, his mask is put on. This was told to me by a member of the Ammunje Nayak family – Damodar is his *kuladevata*, too. But his family is also attached to Mahalasanarayani at Jamboli. This was, he says, the older of the temples, in the forest and quite close to the river Fanta. You have to bathe in the river before you can worship, he says. He goes once or twice a year to Jamboli, though it has happened that he has gone only once in two years.

The Jambovali – the title of the Calicut lord which became the Zamorin in European sources – also had Damodar as his *kuladevata*, says M.M. Prabhu. Evidently we may speculate on the possible ties to the GSB community implied here, though Prabhu does not say so. Damodar is among the most highly regarded of the GSB *kuladevatas*. Mangesh may be richer, says M.M. Prabhu, but Damodar is held in highest esteem. It is, incidentally, his own lineage deity: we see there is a tendency to stress the importance of one's own *kuladevata*.

The eight deities in the Damodar temple, continues M.M. Prabhu, are Ramnath, Damodar, Lakshminarayana, Chandi, Mahadev, Marangana (the untouchable who gave shelter to Damodar's *linga*) and Gramapurusha, the founder of the village and finally Mulupurush, the one who brought the image. This list contains both Vaishnavite and Shaivite deities. Prabhu's family, before auspicious occasions, present foodstuffs on a winnowing fan to an untouchable in honour of Marangana. This will be the food later served to the gods. In Goa, there will be toddy and rice cakes. The toddy is for them, not for us', explains Prabhu, for as a caste, the GSB do not use alcohol. We may choose to see, here, a tendency for the GSB cults to grow away from an earlier, more Shaktist and less purity-oriented, Vaishnavite form. As we shall see, a similar tendency may be observed with regard to animal sacrifice.[45]

Once a year, on the full moon following Navaratri, the Gaurava (the officiating priest) and a member of the original family will be presented as Gramapurusha and Mulupurusha, respectively. At the Damodar temple, the impersonator of Mulupurusha must come from the Bharadvaja *gotra* and that of Gramapurusha from the Kaushika *gotra*. At Navaratri, there will traditionally be possession in all the *kuladevata* temples at Goa, says Prabhu: the oracular idea is very deeply entrenched in GSB tradition and culture.[46]

Mahamaya temples are typical of Saraswats and in Rajasthan, says M.M. Prabhu, there are many Mahamaya temples. One such temple is at Dongarkeri, in Mangalore. The icon could not be brought from outside to this Mahamaya temple, so, we understand, it had to be made anew for the temple. This temple is also a *kuladevata* temple. It was the original temple in Dongarkeri – the main GSB quarter of Mangalore – older than the Venkatarama Temple, and it belonged to the Vaishya community. Earlier, says Prabhu, 'we had to go to the family who owned the temple to "borrow" the key'. The Mahamaya temple is about 250 years old, the VT[47] about 200 years. The other VT at Dongarkeri is a later one, and that also belongs to Vaishyas only. Now, the older VT is richer and more powerful than the recent one which is just a 'family temple'.

Recently, a Navadurga temple has been built in Nandiguddi, with several *kuladevatas*. There is also a Mahamaya temple at Ankola, and of course the Mahalasa temple at Basrur, which I shall describe later.

Mahamaya's image is a golden one. 'Temple dancers – devadasis – also performed at the Mahamaya temple at Ankola', says M.M. Prabhu. 'In fact they once did so at all the *kuladevata* temples. They were given houses and a little land, to perform at the temple. In Goa, they were called Naikins: in Kannada they are called Devadasis.' The custom of maintaining Devadasis has now disappeared. Again, we may see here a quest for a purer form of religion. As we shall see later, Basrur had at one time a reputation as a centre of prostitution, and it is not improbable that the Devadasis contributed to that image. The British, certainly, used their influence to curb the Devadasi institution.

'At the Mahamaya temple there is also a dancing oracle,' continues M.M. Prabhu 'dancing with only small up-and-down movements. Each of the *kuladevatas* originally had oracles impersonating the deity, and they all danced differently: thus Kalabhairava, Mahalasa, etc. At Manjeshwar – which, as we remember, was originally a Nag temple – the oracle imitates the movement of a snake: he walks on tiptoe.'

In the company of Ganesh Nayak's son Shailesh I had an occasion to go to Ponda to visit some of the lineage temples. His family – the Gundu Nayaks – are followers of Shanteri Kamakshi. She shares her temple near Ponda with Ramnath. With them is also Lakshminarayana. Standing in front of the altars, you will find Lakshminarayana in the middle shrine: in front and sharing the same shrine is Ramnath's *lingam*. They are looking east. To the left of this central shrine is the one to Kamakshi, while to the right we find a shrine for Shanteri. Though they are spoken of and treated generally as one, they do in fact have separate images. All these images are under a single dome, however. Like the other lineage temples we visited, the Ramnath/Shanteri Kamakshi temple is recently renovated, impeccably clean and well kept: it is surrounded by lawns which bear witness to continuous mowing and care, and the temple compound houses an excellent *dharmashala*[48] for pilgrims, a large canteen/marriage hall probably used mainly during festivals, a smaller 'snack bar' open at all times of the year, and clean and modern offices. Against the compound's southern wall, looking north, are the twin shrines of Betal and Kalabhairava. Apparently, there is no longer any *darshan* (oracular seance) to Kalabhairava here, though there would probably have been at an earlier time.

The Partagallo *math* – linked to the Gokarna *math* – is situated close to this temple. Very near, too, is the Shantadurga temple, with the Kaoli *math* just behind it. This temple is said – by some – to be the biggest of the GSB lineage temples in Goa: it is certainly bigger than the Ramnath/Shanteri Kamakshi complex. The Goan branch of the Kashi *math* is some distance away, close to the Mahalasa temple.

From there we take a short bus ride to the Nagesh temple, which is somewhat smaller than the other two, and less recently renovated. Yet this temple, too, is a model of cleanliness and order: it may not have been enlarged recently, but it certainly has been painted at most a couple of years ago. It is a very pleasant building, overlooking an old and beautiful tank. Beyond the tank there is an old and equally beautiful coconut garden – rather like a park – which belongs to the temple.

Here, Nagesh is alone in the central altar, flanked by a smaller shrine for Lakshminarayana to the left and another for Ganesh to the right. Nagesh is another form of Shiva, but his image is anthropomorphic, not a *linga*. There is, however, a *linga* outside, in front of the temple. This temple is also particular – and probably shows its age – in that there is no corridor inside for circumambulating the shrine: you have to make the tour of the whole temple building. Unlike most temples where the images look eastwards, Nagesh is looking towards the west, and the tank is on the western side of the temple. Conventionally, this might be taken to indicate that Nagesh is of a fierce nature – like some of the Goddesses elsewhere in India. Yet the main entry to the temple compound is from the east, as is common in Hindu temples. An interesting pillar outside the temple is sculpted with the images of the gods of the eight cardinal directions: Soma for the north, Ishandopati or Ishwar for the north-east, Indra for the east, Agni for the south-east, Yama for the south, Varuna for the west and Vayu for the north-west; neither our informant nor Shailesh or I was sure about the god of the south-western direction, where the inscription was partly effaced.

A much longer bus ride – through very beautiful hills – is needed to get to the Mahalasa temple at Mardol. This is the most beautiful of the lineage temples I have seen, and though the actual temple may be smaller, its compound is bigger than that of Shantadurga's sanctuary. This is the original temple built 'some five hundred years ago' when the original temple was destroyed, and the inner sanctuary has very heavy, beautifully sculpted pillars, like those that are found in the Venkatarama temples at Mulki or Karkala.[49]

Mahalasa looks eastwards, towards the main entrance to her compound. She is alone in her shrine, but a separate, smaller temple in the south-western part of the large compound houses the shrines of Shanteri (to the right) and Lakshminarayana (to the left). Behind the main temple, against the western wall of the compound, we find six small shrines. From left to right, there is a shrine to Gramapurusha,[50] Samonar Bhairava,[51] then there is a shrine which is now empty, then Chaturti Yogini, Kalabhairava, and finally Dhad Prasanna. In front of the temple there is a silver-covered lamp-stand which has been donated by one prominent Udupi family, the Airody Pais. In a small lane which branches off northwards from the compound, there is a small temple to Vadai Shanteri, which is a 'private temple' and 'entirely separate' from the Mahalasa temple, and another slightly bigger temple dedicated to Simha Purusha, which, I am told, is another name for Narasimha.

The Mahalasa temple, like the temples to other *kuladevatas*, is clearly both rich and flourishing, but it may soon have some competition for the devotees' attention. In fact, there are plans to reconstruct the original Mahalasa temple, situated at Verma in the 'old conquests', which, like the other temples to the *kuladevatas*, was destroyed by the Portuguese in the sixteenth century. Most of these temples have disappeared entirely: not only were they razed to the ground, but usually the Portuguese took care to build on the spot often a church or a monastery. But according to my informants any attempt to build on Mahalasa's site has been unsuccessful: such efforts have been regularly destroyed, and the destruction is, of course, ascribed to the Goddess' fury. Thus hers is the only one of the original temple sites still available for building, and a committee has been formed to build a new temple to Mahalasa there.

But in addition to the lineage temples in Goa, sanctuaries to some of the lineage deities have also been built in South Kanara. I shall describe one such later, the Mahalasa temple at Basrur. The establishment of temples to the *kuladevatas* on the Kanara coast testifies to a process by which the GSB have made this region their home. Indeed, when referring to their 'home place', a majority of the GSB will refer to a place in one of the Kanara districts. This also seems to be true of most of those now living outside the area. Thus, the

Kanara coast has become the 'home' of the caste, but this identification coexists with and in no way replaces the identification with Goa. The two places fill different functions in the complex of GSB identity. Goa stands for the unity of the caste, its ability to build and dominate its own region, its appearance as an integrated system symbolized by the lineage deities and the attachment to a village within one of their traditional regions of Goa. 'We are from Goa' relates to all this, as well as to the Konkani language as an identity marker. Further, Goa stands for the link to the north, with all that implies in terms of a continuous link to the northern Brahmanic culture.

The Kanara coast stands at once for dispersal or diaspora, and for the successful maintenance of identity among strangers in a new land. Saraswats did not have *agraharas*[52] in this area. Only when there is both a Shiva and a Vishnu can there be an *agrahara* of GSB,[53] explains M.M. Prabhu, a statement which is highly significant since, as we shall see, GSB religion does indeed conjugate the two gods. It also means, of course, that the GSB were not brought to the Kanara coast as officiating priests responsible for, and making their living from, temples of the area.

What is implied by the reference to Goa is that though Goa was lost, the achievements of their settlement there were not: they were transformed and applied to new tasks. Success in commerce and the strong position that the GSB occupy in the culture and economy of their new, chosen land, testifies to precisely the same innate qualities that made a success of the Goa settlement. Thus attachment to the two regions, each corresponding to a period in the caste's history, strengthen each other in the common view of the caste and its qualities. And, we may add, the present diaspora, from the Kanara coast to new places in and outside India, adds to the demonstration of the adaptability of the caste. By this combination, migration and new settlement becomes a positive trait, a demonstration of capabilities. This implies, of course, that the transition from settlement at Goa to the migratory phase must be imposed by external forces, and so the image of the Portuguese needs to be a negative one, for which there is ample justification in the circumstances. The necessity of 'vilifying' the Portuguese explains, to a large degree, the absence of any explicit discourse on the opportunities offered by the Portuguese trade system. Similarly, while it is common to stress that the British found the GSB by far the most progressive and lettered group in the Kanaras, the rather obvious advantages of British rule to a merchant community (at least till the 1920s) is obscured.

The GSB identity, then, refers to three stages in a successive construction of the present: their Saraswati Valley origins, their settlement and consolidation in Goa, and their subsequent migration to the south. The concomitant roots in Goa and the Kanaras – and the links further back to the Saraswati River and the north – can only fit together in a historicist mode, and so the historicity of GSB identity construction is a logical implication of their various identifications, or, indeed, vice versa. The two aspects – time and place – in this construction cannot really be separated from each other.

NOTES

1. V.S. Kuduva wrote the book *Tuluvarorum* about Saraswats long ago. This, I was told, could be found at MGM College, but I was not able to consult it and have it translated. He has also written *Saraswata Samaj*, dealing with the history of the GSB of South Kanara, and *Tuluvara Charitra* or *Dakshina Kanadar Itihas*. He has also written articles on the Kashi *math*, the Gauda Acharya *math* and on the Gokarna *math*, which I was unable to consult. Krishna Bhat mentioned that Santosh Kumar Gulvadi, a Chitrapur Saraswat who was editor of *Taranga*, wrote a book on Chitrapur Saraswats. He had the book and tried to find it so I could photocopy it, but this did not come about. S.S. Talmaki's work, cited by M.M. Prabhu, is another major work I have been unable to consult. V.M. Dubashi's book, cited by M.V. Kamath, is another such source.
2. The return from captivity started in 1800, when the British took control of South Kanara.
3. My approach here corresponds, in many ways, to that of Simpson (2006: 26-54), but his Kacchi Muslims were not in control of the 'standard narratives' of the region's past: the GSB to a much greater degree control their own narratives, which, as migrants, they consciously detach from those of surrounding peoples.
4. See Lobo (2000 and 2002); Machado Prabhu (1999). This paragraph also refers to personal information from Michael Lobo.
5. As noted, there are several theories. There are at least three regions known by the name Gauda: the main concentration of present-day Gauda Brahmins is in Haryana, around the old battlefield of Kurukshetra; North-

western Bengal, with eastern Bihar, and finally, Gondwana in central India which was often Sanskritized Gauda. As for the Saraswat country, there used to be two possibilities: Punjab or northern Gujarat. Recent research on the lost river Saraswati links the two by way of Rajasthan, and also links the Gauda country in Haryana to them. All the Saraswat countries would thus have been named from the same river. As the river dried out in Rajasthan, two Saraswati rivers resulted: one in Haryana and Punjab, and one in northern Gujarat. All this indicates that the GSB tradition of origin from 'the banks of the Saraswati River' is basically true. There is no obvious link to Bengal, however, far less to Gondwana. Since GSB Konkani is closer to Gujarati than Punjabi, the most likely theory seems to be that the ancestors of the GSB moved westwards into Gujarat when the river dried out and came to Goa from there (see Saraswati, 1977: 46-9).

6. This, too, corresponds generally to Saraswati's opinion (1977).
7. This of course corresponds with the upper course of the Saraswati River; see n. 1 above. Yet it removes his ancestors from the heartlands of the Indus Valley Civilization, and also puts their exodus at a date when that civilization had been gone for somewhat more than a thousand years.
8. This is yet another interpretation of the Gauda country, more or less contingent with the Bengal interpretation, but in Bihar.
9. The location of the legendary battle of the Mahabharata, in present-day Haryana. No reference was made by Prabhu or any other informant to link this battle with the Saraswat exodus.
10. Corresponding to Gauda, i.e. (in Prabhu's opinion), north-western Bengal and eastern Bihar.
11. The southern side of the Godavari River, in present-day Andhra Pradesh.
12. In Goa.
13. Machado Prabhu dates the Mangesh temple at Cortalim, ascribed to Saraswats, to 400 BC (1999: 245).
14. Saraswati is of the same opinion. There is no mention of this distinction in the Sutra literature. He notes that the *Skanda Purana* (ninth or tenth century AD) seems to be the earliest scriptural source for this division, and notes the tradition that it was created by Shankaracharya (ninth century) (1977: 49-50). Other sources locate Shankara in the eighth century.
15. P.R. Kuduva says of his own activities as a historian: 'You see, I am just a petty merchant. I have no time to go out and really do research. So, when I write from time to time, it is under pressure, to please my

friends . . . every time there is some celebration, they will come and ask me please to contribute an article. . . .'

16. Old Dwarka was engulfed by the sea, and never recovered. Recent archaeological research has dated the submarine remains at Dwarka to around 1500 BC, but Klostermaier feels that they pertain to the 'Vedic' period as the palaces and temples are 'constructed of solid stone', and not the bricks used in the Indus Valley Civilization. The present pilgrim centre came into prominence much later, see, e.g. Tambs-Lyche 2004: 104-6.
17. A *yagna* or *yajna* is a fire-sacrifice.
18. These would be GSB.
19. Thus an alternative to the descent of the GSB from the Indus Valley Civilization, making the GSB ancestors part of the 'Aryan' immigration.
20. The region created by Parashurama: see above.
21. 'The present districts of Champaran, Dharbhanga, Murattarpur and Saran in Upper Bihar' (Kamath, 1983: 3).
22. The low earthen walls separating one field from another.
23. Of these communities, Fonseca says: 'In the Velhas Conquistas a great portion of the lands is held by the village communities, which, after paying the usual rents and other Government taxes, divide the annual produce amongst themselves; while in the Novas Conquistas the lands are distributed among the *vangors*, who cultivate them and enjoy their net produce' (1878/1986: 22).
24. 'Maker or builder of the village.'
25. But we should note that many Brahmin castes have a tradition of descent from mixed marriages, usually with other Brahmin castes (Saraswati, 1977).
26. By which is meant here the converted Jews.
27. There are now some 250 temples at Goa: at least a similar number were destroyed by the Portuguese. These were in central Goa, in the 'old conquests': almost all the GSB lineage temples have, however, been rebuilt in the 'new conquests', to the south.
28. The temple is described in the 1999 Kerala Census publication, *Temples of Kerala*, pp. 57ff.
29. A form of Shiva.
30. As noted (n. 14 above), the *Skanda Purana* has been dated to the ninth-tenth century. Thus M.M. Prabhu takes the existence of the temple at least 200 years farther back than does Kuduva. It is not clear, however, whether the Konkani Brahmins were there at this earlier date.
31. There were three Kulashekharas in the Alupa dynasty, which ruled what

is now known as the Tulu country. According to S.U. Kamath, they were Kulashekhara I (*c.* 1160-1220), II (*c.* 1335-46) and III (*c.* 1355-90). (Kamath, 2001: 96). The inscription probably refers to Kulashekhara II or III.

32. Their southern seat was at Mangalore, then Udyavara (near Udupi), while their northern capital was Barakuru.
33. Prabhakar's history of Vitthala: K.K. Kuduva: Dakshina Kannada Itihasa; Aiggal: Dakshina Kannada Pratihasha Itihasa.
34. This was learnt on a field trip to Vittala with the folklorist Ashok Alva as our guide. I later had occasion to discuss the role of the GSB at Vittala with the historian Vasantha Madhava.
35. Kochikar means from Kochi, i.e. Cochin. P.R. Kuduva, however, now uses the name Padubidri, from the town where the family stayed for some time.
36. This may have been due to the annexation of Mahé by the British in 1793: much business moved to Tellicherry at that time.
37. The RSB – Rajapur Saraswat Brahmins – may indeed have been one such group, settled at Rajapur on the coast just north of Goa.
38. There were some good roads, but they were few. The bullock cart, otherwise ubiquitous in India, is practically absent from South Kanara. The traditional means of transport for high status people was the palanquin, as late as the 1920s (P. Suvasini Heggade, 1999: 2).
39. Parashurama can hardly be dated historically, yet the reader may well feel that there is some inconsistency between this statement and P.R. Kuduva's general account of GSB migration.
40. We shall return to these donations later.
41. In North Kanara, some 50 km north of Udupi.
42. As will be noted later, *kuladevatas* are linked to *gotras*, not surnames.
43. The main altar, the *sanctum sanctorum*.
44. We shall return to this theme in Chapter 10. Damodar does not need a compound name since he himself represents the unity of the two gods.
45. As for the combination of Vaishnavite and Shaivite images, we shall return to this theme in Chapter 10.
46. In today's South Kanara, the Kalabhairava oracle at Mulki is now the only one of its kind, but formerly, most of the important Venkatarama temples had such oracles. Though other Kalabhairava oracles in the region are now defunct, the GSB go to the *bhuta* oracle at Gurupur, where the medium is a GSB. And there are a number of other oracles not attached to the temples. I shall have more to say of these oracles in Chapter 10.

47. I shall use VT henceforth for Venkatarama temple when the context is clear, as the GSB themselves do.
48. A resthouse where devotees may lodge at a very moderate price.
49. These temples will be described in the next chapter.
50. I return to him later in this chapter.
51. We shall return to the different Bhairavas in the chapter on religion.
52. The living quarters allotted to the priests of a temple. In common parlance in South Kanara, the landholdings of the temple – and thus of the Brahmins attached to it – is often also implied by the term.
53. G. Pfeffer notes in his description of villages donated to Brahmins in the coastal area of Orissa that they invariably have both Shiva and Vishnu shrines. All also have a Shakti shrine, to a goddess (1976: 41).

2

Arrivals

As we have seen, the GSB were established as traders along the Kanara and Malabar coasts by the time the Portuguese arrived. Though present at Manjeshwar in the thirteenth century, they probably came to the Kanara coast later, but they seem to have arrived in Karnad during the fourteenth century. Karnad's port, of some importance at the time, later shifted to Mulki, as the rivers changed their course. The GSB probably came to Karkala a little later, in the late fourteenth or early fifteenth century. It was a Jain kingdom then, and the town must still have been controlled by the Jains. Still, the GSB soon took control of cashewnut production and trade. Gradually, they were to take over most of the trade of Karkala, and even today this is perhaps the most prestigious of the GSB settlements of the region. Kallianpur, also a port then, was another early GSB settlement: its temple is said to have been founded in the sixteenth century. Most authorities assume that 'Arab' traders – which must have included the Mapila or Moplah community – dominated the export trade of the Kanara coast at this time. It is likely that most of the GSB trade was regional, and we have seen that they played a crucial role in the expansion of rice cultivation in the area. Rice trade and export then is likely to have been the main base of the GSB community in the ports, from the fourteenth or fifteenth century onwards. But gradually they came to dominate commerce in general.

MULKI

Mulki, a small town on the coast south of Udupi, is generally seen by the caste's historians as the oldest GSB settlement still extant in South Kanara, dating from the fourteenth century. Strictly speaking, Mulki did not exist yet: the port was at Karnad[1] till the late seventeenth century, when the Shambhavi River changed its course (Vasantha Madhava, 1991: 143). It was then one of the two main ports of the area.[2] Here, the Portuguese used to buy rice, sugar cane coir and coconuts.[3] The port was the obvious reason for the GSB to settle here, well before the expansion in rice culture in the fifteenth to sixteenth century.

Mulki forms a kind of island between the Pavaje and Shambhavi rivers (Fig. 2). The Venkatarama temple is in a quarter of the town called Vallalankar Kasbah,[4] which lies well inland from the modern centre of Mulki. Surrounding the temple square are old houses in the Konkani style. According to P.R. Kuduva, the old port was here, at the end of a short street lined by old GSB houses, leading north to the river from the Venkatarama temple. It ends abruptly before some low-lying fields, over which the river must once have flown. If P.R. Kuduva

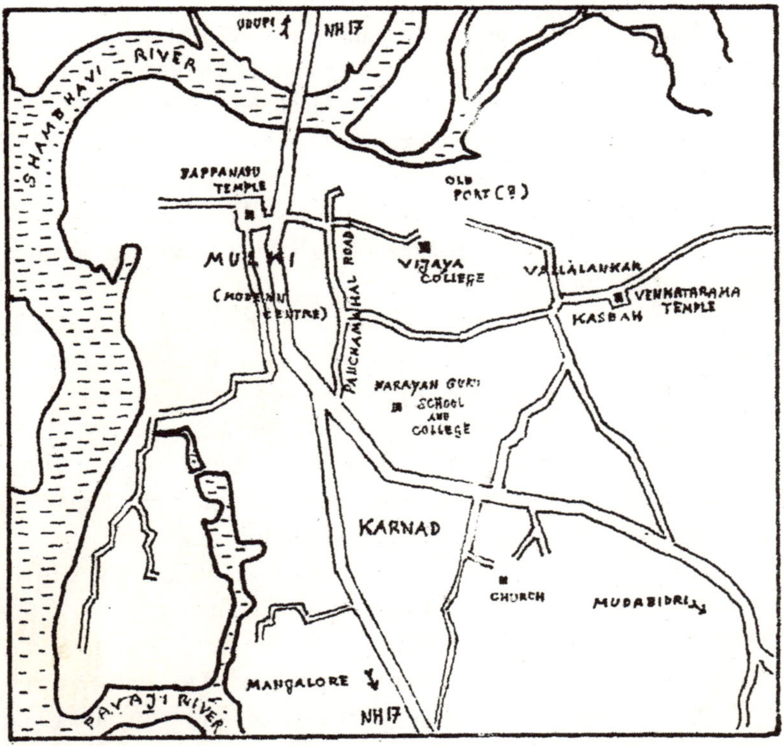

Fig. 2: Sketch map of Mulki with Karnad and the quarter known as Vallalankar Kasbah.

is right, which seems likely, the river must have been navigable up to this point: like many rivers in South Kanara, it has silted up since.

This then was once an important GSB centre. There were many shops, but they are closed now, says P.R. Kuduva. I saw only one still active. There is still a port near Mulki, but now it lies on the northern bank of the Shambhavi River, and caters only to local fishermen. The modern centre of Mulki did not exist then as the low-lying land where it is located was under water. Slightly inland from there is the Panchamahal Road, which was the mercantile centre until the bridge on National Highway 17, which crosses the river here, was built. The modern centre, like the Vallalankar Kasbah, is on the island formed by the two rivers. On the south bank of the Pavaje is Karnad, but here the river is gone and there is no harbour now.

Five families, known as the Panchamahal families, are said to have been the first GSB settlers at Mulki. Thus, it is said, the area they settled became known as Panchamahal – the five manors or palaces. Tradition has it they were brought here by the Vijayanagara kings to establish trade and as a gesture of goodwill, and that they settled in the present Panchamahal Road area which, indeed, was once dominated by GSB families. In the centre is a big 'villa' bearing the plaque of one Kamath, accountant, a house which is said to be the 'Barkera' or 'Borkera' – one of the five 'palaces' of the GSB. Or rather, it occupies the site of the 'palace'.

There are, then, two distinct poles of GSB settlement at Mulki: the Panchamahal must be the later one, for it lies lower than the modern centre, once covered by the sea, and could only have been settled towards AD 1700. The original five mansions must have been further inland. Panchamahal Road was for some time known as the Mulki Main Road. Clearly, this road once led to the ferry. The name Panchamahal has since been transposed to this street.

On the bus in Udupi, I met Mulki Dayanand Rao, whose grandfather was an important man in Mulki, chief trustee of the Venkatarama temple. 'His portrait is still there in the temple office. He wears a turban and looks very important.' Rao's father was a cashewnut exporter in the Mangalore Bandar (old port) area, and very rich. But then he lost Rs. 10 lakh. 'Some people took it and never returned it', says his son, who spent 28 years in Kuwait: he retired and returned to India in 1993, just before the First Gulf War. It is typical of India, and of the GSB, to tell such potted family histories at a chance meeting: our talk lasted only the short ride from the suburb where we stayed, and into town. Such stories may go from 'rags to riches', or the other way around, in the course of a few generations: there is not always a specific reason given for getting rich, but very often one for losing the wealth.

Rao well knows the large villa of Kamath, the accountant, in Panchamahal Road. Kamath's father was a well-known figure, a Gandhian, and even untouchables would be allowed into his house. 'That was the kind of man he was.' Now most of the family is in Hyderabad, while some are in America: only the old accountant remains in Mulki. This is typical of the old Mulki families. They settled there when Mulki was a port of importance, serving Mudabidri and other places inland. Since the National Highway came, most business moved to Mangalore, and Mulki is no longer the busy place it was.

Not far from Kamath's villa is an equally imposing house at the lower end of the road going east to the old port, which belonged to Sundaram Shetty, the founder of the Vijaya Bank.[5] The house symbolizes the period when Bunts began to challenge GSB monopoly on finance and banking in South Kanara. Now it is empty, like many houses in this part of town. 'Since the bridge came, everything is falling down here,' says a shopkeeper whose shop is opposite the big house. 'In the old days, Mulki was a very important port. Now it is nothing. All the business has gone to Mangalore.'

This road continues past Vijaya Hostel and College, another symbol of Bunt challenge to GSB dominance. The founder of the bank, or his family, must have been important in this venture. The road, called the Vijaya College Road, passes an ITI, changes its name to Kotekeri, and arrives in the area of the old port. A sharp turn and we enter the built-up lane leading to the Venkatarama temple, about 2 km from Panchamahal Road.

In this lane I meet Palimar Ganesh V. Shenoy, a young priest at the Venkatarama temple. The port, he says, is now at Hejekady, on the other side of the Shambhavi River. This refers to the modern fishing port, not the fourteenth century one nor its eighteenth-century successor. He, like the medium of Kalabhairava's oracle,[6] is from Palimar, the 'home village' of the Palimar *math*, one of the *Ashtamaths*[7] in Udupi. It is the village 'after Hejekady', to the north. Ganesh lives in a room at the temple complex: the senior priests live in four newly-constructed houses behind the new *dharmashala* for pilgrims. There is no traditional *agrahara* here, he says. The temple priests used to live among the GSB merchants, not in a separate quarter. He is a GSB, but does not come from the traditional, priestly Bhat family. Today at least, priests are also recruited from ordinary GSB families.

The trustees of the Lakshminarayana Venkatarama temple confirm that the area around the temple is inhabited by GSB families, but say the original five families were at Panchamahal. The old Jain Basti is on a hill in between.[8] If the old Jain quarter was close to the Basti, it would have been on high ground, and this may well have been the 'original' Mulki, predating the GSB settlement. Probably the Jains here were exporters of plantation crops coming down to the coast through Mudabidri.

The Venkataraṃa temple itself is not as big as some, but the outbuildings are large and in good condition. Most are clearly modern. Inside, the *garbaguddi* is profusely decorated in silver and very beautiful: even the wooden pillars of the verandah are silver-covered. This central part of the temple probably dates from the seventeenth century. The auxiliary shrines are traditional for a Venkatarama temple: Hanuman, Ganesh, Lakshmi and Garuda, one in each corner of the yard, going around clockwise.

Four main deities are worshipped at this temple: Venkatarama, Ugra Narasimha, Bindu Madhava and Vira Vitthala.[9] The temple has been enriched by the donation of several beautiful cult objects. In the Vasanta Mantapa is stored the *utsavamurti*, the silver idol used for processions. Here is also the golden palanquin, more than one hundred years old, used on such occasions. The temple thus, is very rich. This is due not only to the generosity of the GSB community. Known as Mulki Balaji – a pendant to Tirupati Balaji[10] – Mulki is a place of pilgrimage for Gujarati Vaishnava Banias, coming from all over India. Thus, there is a steady flow of pilgrims – including GSB from Mumbai and elsewhere. At Moghasira Sukhtar Passima, when the idol of Gramareshama is brought to the temple, over thirty coconuts are used for *abhisheka*,[11] and twenty to twenty-five thousand devotees will attend.

To the south of the main court, there is another one, facing a hall called *Bhojana Shala*. There is also an enormous, traditional kitchen. The new Shri Nivas complex, a guest-house, was opened in 2004, as well as the Annapoorna Hall for functions. The latter serves free – and excellent – meals to visitors.[12] The Navagraha Park, dedicated to and depicting the nine planets[13] was also opened in 2004, and new lodgings have been constructed for the priests. All this has been done these last few years. But during the great festivals, mass feeding is still done in the south-eastern court, with the food being prepared in the old kitchen.

On Saturdays, the temple receives offerings from Tirupati's Venkateshwara temple and from Dharmasthala.[14] Acknowledging these offerings constitutes the first part of the oracular ritual on Sundays. At Dharmasthala, much farther inland near Belthangadi, Shaiva and Jain worship is combined with that of Annappa Panjurli, the boar *bhuta*, connected with the fertility of the fields – all presided over by 'the Hegde', a Jain chief. M.M. Prabhu says:

> After making an offering (at the Mulki temple) they will make a *prasna* (questioning, interrogation). To see if the offerings have reached. Five generations ago the Hegde came to the Venkatarama temple with Annappa Panjurli to check. But the *bhuta* was so pleased that he chose to stay. The Hegde protested that he would no longer be protected in Dharmasthala. So Annappa Panjurli said he would stay partly here, partly there. Finally the Hegde gave a silver platter to the temple – the date is still on the plate.

Since then the Venkatarama temple is connected to the *bhuta* who controls the fertility of the land, a link, then, to the religion of the Tulu speakers.

K.R. Kuduva agrees that the temple is the oldest Venkatarama temple in this area, older than the one in Karkala, which is some four hundred years old. Vijayendra Tirtha Swamiji of Kumbakonam *math* – a Madhava *math* – instituted Yaduvendra Tirtha Swamiji, the first Madhava Swami of the Kashi *math*.[15] It was Yaduvendra Swami who consecrated the Mulki temple, or rather the Venkatarama and the Ugra-Narasimha images, in the fourteenth century.

The Vijayanagara king donated the place in Vallalankar Kasbah for the GSB to 'start their dharmic activities' in the thirteenth century, continues K.R. Kuduva. The five original Konkani families brought two idols of the god Vitthala and established them in a thatched shed. They were the Navelkars, Prabhus, Kilpadikars and Shenoys, and one more, whose name he could not remember, perhaps the Kamaths. The temple trustee stresses that the land was given by the Vijayanagara kings, and not as some say by the Savantar of Padupanambur, a local Jain chief. But he acknowledges the role of the Savantar: some, he says, hold that the Vijayanagara rulers were of the same family as the Savantars. On the day of Pratishta Unami,[16] the GSB offer *prasad* at the Savantar's house as thanks for his gift of the land. The relation between the GSB of Mulki and the Savantar then are still structured ritually as that between an immigrant community and a king.[17] The present Savantar certainly claims it was his ancestors who gave the original GSB families land to settle here.

M.M. Prabhu tells me the following tradition: The Swami of Kashi *math* was travelling to Udupi through Mulki. He asked for shelter but the Savantar did not wish to give shelter to 'a Konkani Swami'. So the Swami by his powers lighted such a fire that he could go straight to Mulki. The fire convinced the Savantar of the Swami's powers. The Savantars, continues Prabhu, were not really kings – there were so many petty chiefs then, all wanting to be 'real kings'. Here Prabhu gives a very different account of the relationship between the Savantar and the GSB community.[18]

In the fourteenth century, says Prabhu, Mahmud took Goa and three groups of GSB left. Some of them settled at Mulki; they were Vaishyas.[19] 'We come across so many Konkani names during this period', says Vasantha Madhava of the fourteenth and fifteenth centuries: 'Prabhu, Kamath, Shenoy, etc.' This, he feels, implies that there was a major incursion of GSB to South Kanara at the time. The Konkani merchants who came were generally Hindus, while Christians tended to be agriculturalists. The farmers were quite distinct from the merchants, though some GSB merchants later became landlords and some converted later. He feels the Christian influence came later, as in the case of the Aranha Shenoys, another prominent GSB family in the Mulki area.[20] They came into prominence in the sixteenth century, due to the Portuguese trade. According to Lobo, the father Anthony (Anthappa) and the son Manuel (Manu), born around 1710 and 1740 respectively, converted to Christianity around 1750. Two brothers of Anthappa remained Hindus. Manuel's sons founded the three major houses at Gazni, near Mulki – the middle, the north and the south house. The Aranha Shenoys have remained the leading Catholic family in Mulki for more than two hundred years (Lobo, 2000: 121). They had a lot of land, and are still big landowners in Mulki.

The best-known GSB mansion in Mulki is Mundkur, where Gandhi once stayed. The family has left, however. Among other important GSB families are the Kamaths and the Bhats. Deodar Kamath, says Vasantha Madhava, was for a long time the main trustee of the temple. He was probably related to the one who owns the large house at Panchamahal Road.

KALLIANPUR

Mulki is a quiet place today, but Panchamahal Road and the Vola Lanka area are urban in character. We can still imagine the lively little town it must have been when its port was still active. Such nucleated settlements may not have been typical of the area, however, and a better impression of what South Kanara was like when the GSB arrived is perhaps found in a cluster of villages I shall call the 'Kallianpur complex' (Fig. 3). Kallianpur, the centre of the district in early British days, is central to the cluster. Dominated by the Catholics, it is a very old Christian settlement, says Vasantha Madhava, who feels it is the one referred to by Cosmos. Certainly, it was Christian by the middle of the sixteenth century.

Oliver Lewis, a bookseller in Udupi and a leading member of its Lion's Club, comes from Kallianpur. Stressing the age of the village, he says there were at least three batches of Christian immigrants from Goa. Kallianpur was settled by the first batch: its church dates back to at least 1580.[21] Lewis' ancestors reclaimed an island from the seabed 'very long ago' though he cannot fix the date. It is still almost exclusively settled by members of his family.

Kallianpur, like Shirva – another old Christian settlement – was under the Ikkeri Nayaks, and both oral and written history indicates[22] that the Christians were welcomed or even invited as able agricultural-

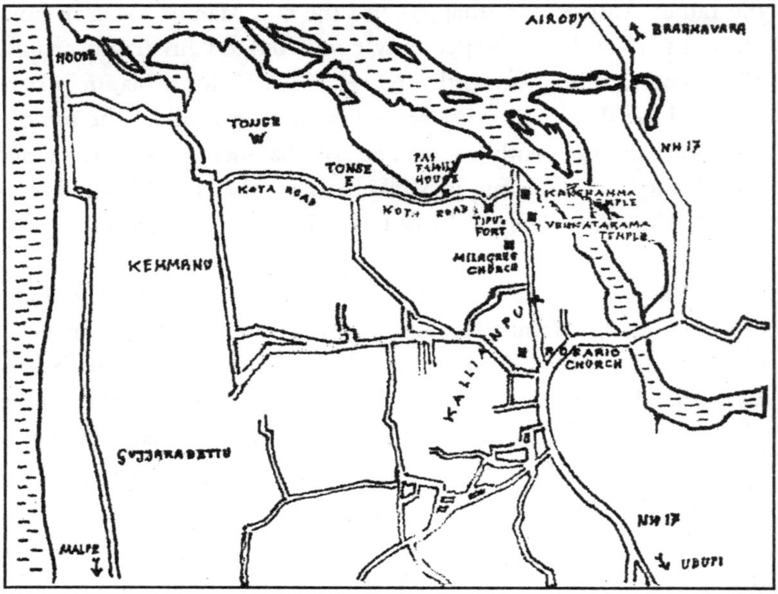

Fig. 3: The central villages of the Kallianpur cluster. Among other important villages from where Udupi GSB families have originated, Ammunje is to the right of this map, north of the river.

ists by the Ikkeri rulers, to cultivate waste land. Much of the Kallianpur area may indeed have been marshland then. Kallianpur itself was a port, but has silted up since. John Fernandes, who makes Ayurvedic medicines in Tonse, west of Kallianpur, showed me where, he said, Tipu Sultan had built his fort. The place is called Kota Road.[23] Nothing is left of the fort, he says it was pulled down by the British.[24] 'But at that time', he says, 'ships came up to here – the river is quite nearby and all this' – he points to the plain where his own house, that of the Tonse Pais and most of Tonse village is located – 'was only marshland then. Since then, the river has silted up and lands have been drained.'

If he is right, much of what is now Tonse must have been settled after 1800, yet the Tonse Pais, for example, are supposed to have come in the eighteenth century. But there may have been islands on what is but slightly higher ground.[25] What is clear from Fernandes' statement, however, is the changes in the coastline of South Kanara, especially near the river deltas: we have seen how the area around Mulki has changed. The Kallianpur area, which straddles a wide and complex delta, is a prime example of this. Any historical consideration of places such as Kallianpur, or indeed Mulki must take these changes into account.

It is clear, however, that Kallianpur's location was strategic. As a port, it was certainly important enough to fortify. Kallianpur Ferry, to which the old main road through the settlement leads, was a main link on the north-south road from Udupi to Kundapur, and the ferry only lost its importance when the bridge was built slightly further upstream. The ferry is still there, a shortcut for local people to Sansthan (Airody), north of the river.[26] The bridge was built inland to avoid the tides, which are very strong here: Fernandes told me his own and his neighbours' land has been flooded several times. The ferry for Uppar, another village on the north bank, is further upstream. The ferrymen are a Moghavera[27] family, using a traditional dugout. Such ferry services, common along the coast before the bridges were built, are still useful for crossing by the bridge may mean a considerable detour. At Uppar, there is a new dyke[28] as the coconut plantations were subject to flooding.

Karunakaran[29] says the Milagres church was built 325 years ago (1680), on land donated by Hindus. They fled from Goa and 'ran away to this place – at that time there was no population here'. The Christians 'came from Mulki and Kundapur'. Yet in Hoode, where Karunakaran used to live, the Lakshmiganapati temple is some five hundred years old, predating the Christian settlement.[30] It belongs to Jains, once masters of the area, whose manor[31] is at Suralu,[32] and the family is still there. Kallianpur too may have been an outpost for exporting their plantation products. Now the Bunts, once their tenants, control the land.

The *gramadevi*[33] of the whole Kallianpur complex is Kanchamma, whose temple stands on a hill which was once an island. It is quite modest in size but believed to be the oldest temple in Kallianpur, more than one thousand years old. Formerly, it was wooden with a thatched roof, now it is built from bricks. It must have been there when Barakuru prospered.[34] Kanchamma is a form of Durga, but she has Virabhadra at her side, with Bhadrakali and Nandi outside. The priest here is a Devadiga, not a Brahmin – 'a tantri priest'[35] – who used to be a photographer at Mumbai. When his father died, he returned to take over the *seva*.[36] The main festivals are in August and December. Goats, sheep and cocks are sacrificed here.[37] The *murti*, of wood, may well be five hundred years old, but there must have been another before that. There is no attendant *bhuta*, if Bhadrakali is not seen as such.[38] The temple is said to have served an area of seven villages (*gramas*).[39] The contrast between the renovated Venkatarama temple and Kanchamma's small shrine, quite close, is striking. One would hardly guess that the latter had once been so important, and the former just 'the temple of some immigrants'. The same point may be made if we contrast the Kanchamma temple to the large Milagres church complex or the smaller one at Mount Rosary. At Gujjarabettu, south of Kemmanna, there is another *gramadevi*, Durgaparameshwari. While Kanchamma is said to be the original *gramadevasthana*, the more recent temple at Gujjarabettu has 'moved with the times': it has grown and has abolished animal sacrifice, at least inside the temple compound.

Kallianpur still bears the marks of the schism of 1887, when those who wanted to be directly under papal authority through the Archbishops of Mangalore fought the partisans of the Archbishops of Goa, under the Portuguese king's authority.[40] Thus there are two churches: Milagres, the largest and today by far the most important, whose parishioners sided with Mangalore, and Mount Rosary, for those who wanted to remain under Goa. The community is still said to be divided, and I met people who were very proud of their forefathers' stand in the conflict – all I met being of the winning Mangalore party. It is said that the lowland part of the borough below the main road to Kallianpur ferry is inhabited by 'Mangaloreans', while the parishioners of Mount Rosary live 'uphill'. Some hinted at a difference in caste between the two parties, those converted from the GSB – referred to as Bamos or Brahmins – siding with Mangalore. The Lewis family, among the latter, has had a very important role in local affairs.

Kallianpur was once both a GSB and a Catholic centre. Today, most of the GSB have left for Udupi and elsewhere, leaving the Catholics more dominant than they may have been two or three generations ago. Still, in the middle of the Christian area lies the 'U. Sheshagiri Mallya Baug'[41] donated by descendants of that prominent

Congressman from Mangalore, with the T.M.A. Pai High School inside. Clearly, Kallianpur is still important enough to attract such investments, named after GSB personalities. A sawmill – Fancy Wooden Industries – was, I understand, founded by Christians but is now owned by 'Hindus', probably GSB.

Kallianpur's Venkatarama temple, say some, is three to four hundred years old, one trustee said five hundred years. It has been extensively rebuilt by U.M. Kamath, the 'builder' of Manipal, who says it dates from the seventeenth century. The old pillars around the *garbaguddi*, beautifully carved, give an idea of its age and former beauty. They do indeed seem to date from the same period as the interior of the Mulki or Karkala temples. Thus it is only a few generations later than the original church, and is situated a couple of 100 m downhill from the Milagres, with several houses of important GSB families around it. Perhaps the largest is the mansion of the Kallianpur Baliga family – one member was an important Congress activist in the independence movement.[42] In the temple committee we find a Tonse Pai,[43] among the few from that family to remain in Kallianpur. On my first visit to the temple, they were preparing a Bhajan Mahotsava[44] – a week of religious singing by invited artists. The programme was not restricted to Konkani songs but included all the 'big names' like Ramdas, Tukaram, etc. The first day, however, was dedicated to the songs of the Konkani poet P.N. Nayak. Krishna Bhat,[45] something of a religious sceptic, comments that the temple has few visitors these days, 'This is why they have to do special things like holding a *bhajan* festival to attract people. Now they have taken to feeding people – breakfast, lunch, dinner – in order to attract customers.' The temple was certainly built to cater for a much larger community than the GSB now living in the Kallianpur area.

'You will find that almost all the houses are surrounded by coconut groves,' said one of the temple trustees. Coconut cultivation is the traditional economic base of Kallianpur: not only Christians, but also the GSB are engaged in it. This is certainly true of Kallianpur proper. Krishna Bhat says the GSB, living at Tonse, are still landowners, though today most are businessmen. Tonse is about 1½ km west of Kallianpur and dominated by rice lands. Here is the Krishna Rama Pai Sabha Bhavan, the Tonse Pais' family house signposted as a local sight. It is a moderately sized house in a large coconut garden surrounded by rice fields. A simple *mandapa*[46] has been erected in the yard to house the family dinners that take place here every last Sunday of the month. Nearby, the area is mixed: Catholics and the GSB live side by side. I asked John Fernandes, who lives close by, how he saw relations between Hindus and Christians here. 'They have always been good,' he said, 'peaceful on the local level but the present government[47] is trying to make trouble between the communities. The Congress is better – anyhow, they may soon be back.' He turned out to be right.

This is Tonse East, Tonse West having a concentration of Muslims.[48] According to John Fernandes, the Muslim area is about 2 km west of his own house. M.A. Tonse, a Dekkani Muslim, is from Tonse West, His family came from the Bijapur area: they were 'under pressure' at one time[49] and 'so they came down here'. He is an Urdu speaker. Other Muslim groups here are the Navayyats of Bhatkal and elsewhere on the coast, who speak their own dialect of Konkani, and the Mapilas, whose language is a variant of Malayalam. Tonse West is largely on yet another island in the river. While Oliver Lewis' family comes from a Catholic island, yet another one, not far from the Pai family house, is entirely Hindu.

West of Tonse where the river joins the sea lies Hoode. The point where the river meets the sea is called Kodibangare.[50] Facing Hoode, on the other side of the river, is Hangarkatte, known for its beautiful beach, and at one time an important port. Hoode, which is part of Padutonse, has no port but formerly fishing boats operated from the beach. The sea is gradually encroaching. Karunakaran used to have 70 cents of land, but 10 cents have been lost to the sea, and his neighbours also lost land. Recently, the municipality has built a protective barrier of large boulders. This could not have been done earlier as it prevents the beaching of fishing craft. Most of Hoode's seaside population are fishermen[51] but nobody fishes from Hoode now. Karunakaran's grandfather was president of Hoode's fisherman's cooperative for thirty years (1952-82). Hoode has a *bhutasthana* to Bobbariya[52] and two *bhajanmandir*,[53] one belonging to the Moghavera, another to the Billavas. There is also a mosque. Another mosque is at Timmanna Kudru at Tonse West, catering to the Muslims of that island. In Hoode, Muslims account for some 90 per cent of the population, says Karunakaran. The fishermen live only along the beach. There are no Christians here, but they form the entire population of Kambala Tota, just south of Hoode. Further south, towards Kemmana, is Padutonse Bengara. Going south from Hoode to Kemmanna, you leave the Muslim area to enter a Hindu village: Shivalli Brahmins, GSB, Bunts, Billavas – the largest group – Moghaveras and some Harijans live here. There are also some Christians and a few Muslims. On the islands, there are different communities. Timmanna Kudru is Muslim, Parangi Kudru Hindu, while at Padugudru there are Brahmins only, and at Mudugudru a large Christian settlement – the Lewis family – as well as Hindus.

Quite recently, Kemmanna and Kallianpur were separated by jungle.[54] The Hoode bus passes through Kemmanna, named for its red soil. It has a large, recently constructed temple dedicated to Bhadrakali Mahamarakamba. It was discovered that there had once been a goddess temple there, and more than Rs. 50 lakh were spent to build a new temple. In Kemmanna a *kambala*[55] is held every year in December. It was started in the time of the Jains but the Bunts later took it over. They ignored it for some years, but then the people of the 'Kambala house' suffered a lot and decided this was due to a curse of the *bhutas*.[56] The house of K. Raghuvana Shetty used to be the local manor,[57] with Dhumavati as their royal *bhuta*,[58] so the family were 'chiefs', and the *kambala* part of their chiefly complex. It was this Bunt family that took the initiative to construct the Bhadrakali temple. Kemmanna is a sleepy place, says Krishna Bhat, whose ancestral house is between Kemmanna and Gujjarabettu. There has been 'no improvement'; as an Udupi man he considers it backward. There is a shrine to the fierce *bhuta* Babu here, which was restored in 1993.[59]

The Kallianpur complex presents us with the complexity of the many overlapping layers that constitute society in south Kanara. We find vestiges of a Hindu society having the Kanchamma temple as its centre, co-existing with a Jain chiefdom based at Suralu. It is striking that the Kanchamma temple has a Devadiga and not a Brahmin in charge – tradition has it that this temple was never run by Brahmins. The image that emerges then is of a low-caste Hindu society ruled by Jains, the latter forming the upper-caste element. Later, the Bunts became lords of the land as Jain power waned, and waves of Muslim, Christian and Konkani Hindu immigrants settled to farm the marshlands as they emerged from the sea. It is likely, however, that their settlements remained outside the effective domains of the Bunt chief.[60]

In spatial terms, we are far from the nucleated and often walled villages of northern India. Neither does the Kallianpur complex resemble the Brahmin-dominated villages, centered on the temple and its *agrahara*, that we know from Tamil Nadu. Instead of expressing hierarchy spatially within a common nucleus, the castes and communities that make up the Kallianpur complex are settled on separate but adjacent lands, a pattern which renders their successive colonization far more visible than their rank order. Here and there, a temple or a church marks a node, rather than a centre, since each node primarily concerns one of the communities.[61] This multicultural mosaic makes it easier to understand the place of the Konkani groups in the regional social pattern. They could become a presence while never having to integrate into a close-knit web of village relationships, generally taken as typical of rural Indian society, giving rise to a quasi-organic image of the 'caste system'.

KARKALA

Karkala is an old town south-east of Udupi where the rice land gives way to the arecanut and cashewnut plantations of the ghat foothills. Karkala bears the mark of former glory when it was the capital of a Jain kingdom, whose heyday seems to have been the fifteenth and sixteenth centuries. The famous Gomasta[62] statue was erected in 1432 by King Virapandya, and the well-known Chaturmukha Basadi[63] was consecrated in 1568. Apart from these monuments, little of the sixteenth-century Jain town is visible today.[64] The town plan (Fig. 4) does not resemble Mudabidri, still largely Jain, with its straight streets meeting at right angles. Instead, the centre of Karkala is the Car Street dominated by the GSB.

This is where we find the Venkatarama temple, said to date from around 1600, and it seems that the Car Street is the oldest part of the present town centre. Clearly, a considerable influx of GSB around that time created a new commercial centre in and for the town, as the

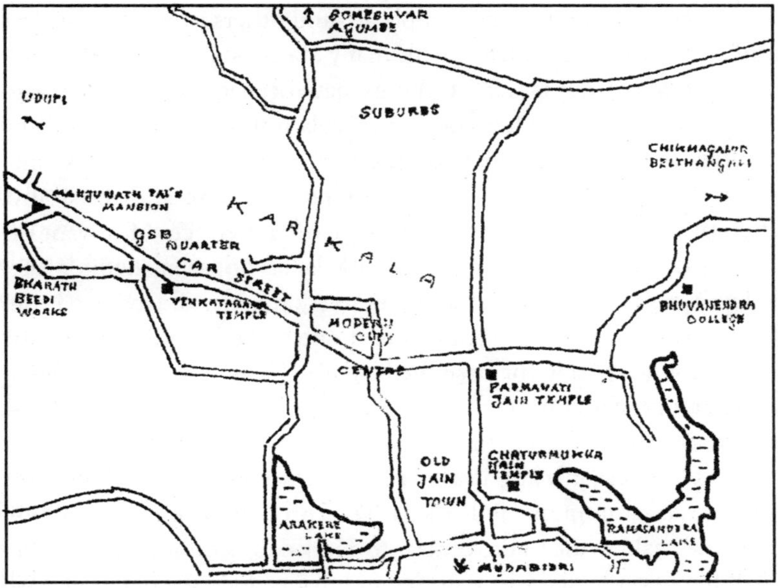

Fig. 4: Sketch map of Karkala, showing the location of the old Jain town and of the GSB quarter. The Bharath Beedi Works are just at the left of this sketch

Konkani merchants took over from Jains the dominant role in the town's economy. Most of the Jain monuments are now well away from the city centre, to the south or south-west. In the Car Street the predominance of the GSB community is clear from the old Konkani houses, some very large and beautiful. The Venkatarama temple, with impressive silver decorations, seems as rich as the one in Mulki. Comparing the temple and Car Street with Udupi's VT Street, one realizes that the GSB community has, historically speaking, been larger and richer in Karkala, a town of regional importance when Udupi was still just a centre of pilgrimage.

Most of the present GSB houses seem to date from the end of the nineteenth century or the beginning of the twenteeth, as in Udupi. The GSB community of South Kanara must have been particularly flourishing then. The housing fashion must have changed, probably due to colonial influence, and so most GSB merchants built new houses or rebuilt old ones on their old grounds. Though some houses have been replaced by new complexes, and others present a derelict aspect. Karkala's Car Street, with many shops still active, offers an image of what Udupi's Car Street must have been in the past.[65] Among many old houses, one stands out as particularly well preserved, recently painted blue with the pillars of the porch black and gold.[66] While many GSB families want to keep the family house and resist any attempt to pull it down, such houses are often neglected for want of paint and upkeep.[67] In recent days, Karkala has not seen anything like Udupi's growth, and so the Car Street still dominates the town, whose present centre – the bus station – is at one end of it. Richer than its Udupi counterpart in the past, the Karkala GSB seems to represent a more traditional community. My Udupi informants say it is more united and dense than their own.

The GSB certainly are, and have been for some time, the dominant commercial community in Karkala. They probably came here to take over the cashewnut trade, central to Karkala's economy, which the GSB have dominated for centuries and from which the big money in Karkala comes. They owned most of the oil and flour mills, and probably dominated the trade in grains. Export of rice to Goa was an important business when the GSB arrived in Karkala. We do not know how the cashewnut trade came to change hands, but the seventeenth century was a period of decline in Jain fortunes: the Nayak kings considerably reduced the power of the Jain chiefdoms. It is possible that this situation also hurt the financial position of the Jains, offering an opening for takeover by the GSB merchants. According to M.M. Prabhu, they came to Karkala from Shimoga district, above the ghats. He mentions a very rich Kamath family, probably that of B. Raghunath Kamath, whose factory – about 2 km from Karkala proper – employs some seven hundred people. He is currently regarded as the most important of the cashewnut merchants.[68] But there are other important families: at one time K.P. Mukundu Prabhu was the richest landholder in Karkala. All are not outright owners in the legal sense: there are both outright land grants and Bairavara and Mulugiri leases.[69] 'They say', says Krishna Bhat, 'that Karkala – and B.C. Road – Koṇkanis are very hard people, much harder than Konkanis elsewhere.'

The niche that attracted the GSB to Karkala was the cashewnut trade. But they soon came to dominate all branches of commerce, and to invest in new ventures. Beyond the Venkatarama temple and close to the end of Car Street we find a mansion, probably built in the 1920s, which differs from the traditional GSB villas. It is in a kind of Indo-Saracenic style: today, it houses the local branch of the State Bank of Mysore. This house is still the most impressive secular building in Karkala. It was built by B. Manjunath Pai, who branched off from traditional GSB trades to found the Bharath Beedi Works. The factory, large and impressive, is located down the lane that branches off from Car Street at Manjunath's house. Farther back, we find the B. Manjunath Pai Foundation's hall. Clearly his family, now headed by an elderly lady who lives outside Karkala, was important in Karkala for a long time.

In the early years of his Beedi Works, however, Manjunath seems to have been the 'nouveau riche', trying to establish his place among the established families. His mansion, outdoing the older houses, seems the perfect expression of his ambition. Even now, it is not his family but that of Bhola Raghunath Kamath which is first mentioned when outsiders refer to the Karkala families. Raghunath's family, too, came from a small village near Karkala, so perhaps the GSB families first settled in the countryside, moving into town as the cashewnut trade expanded and the Venkatarama temple was built.[70]

At any rate, Karkala's Venkatarama temple vies with that at Mulki as the richest and architecturally the most interesting of the Venkatarama temples in the region. The GSB at Karkala are proud of their temple, with its elaborate pillars carved out of a single block of basalt.[71] Other pillars in front of the *garbaguddi* are covered with silver plate, and the temple possesses a number of valuable ritual objects.[72] The group which showed me the temple, a couple of boys from the Bhat community and some workmen or volunteers who had been cleaning the pillars, were very enthusiastic.[73] The Karkala temple is known as Padu Tirupati – 'Western Tirupati' – and visited by devotees from well beyond South Kanara or the GSB community. Facing the temple, on the other side of the Car Street, is a portal that leads to the temple tanks.[74] A marriage hall lies along the southern bank of the new tank, and in the south-western corner looking north is a small shrine to Kalabhairava. Here, oracular sessions were held until the last medium died some five years ago. But unlike Mulki, Karkala has not been able to find a successor to the medium.

In Karkala, the Venkatarama temple is more than a caste temple. It has been for a long time the town's largest, richest and most prestigious temple, and people from other communities sponsor rituals there. This was the case of the *utsava* in which I participated on Sunday, 25 March 2006, financed by Giresh Banana, a Karkala businessman established in Delhi, where he owns five hotels. He also has a hotel in Karkala, to which he had just added a new building, and he held this *utsava* to celebrate its inauguration. Banana is not a GSB but a Gadiga from the oil-presser caste.[75] The measure of his success is precisely that he has risen from this humble background. By celebrating his success in the town's most prestigious temple, owned by the established bourgeoisie in town, he contributes to the temple's prestige and to that of the GSB community. This seems to be the how local GSB saw the event, and nobody seemed bothered being feasted by a member of a lower caste. They turned the occasion into a celebration and manifestation of their own community, as we shall see later.

Around 1900, the Basel missionaries tried to gain a foothold in this fief of Brahmin businessmen. The missionary G. Fischer describes the 'hard soil' in which the missionary tried to plant his religious seed in the years 1898-1904: 'The missionary must "listen to hateful arguments, clever turns of phrase, fine as well as coarse spite against his views . . ." from the Konkani merchants' (Fischer, 1906: 7). Yet in 1900 he managed to start a boys' elementary school, the first in town, near the mission station at Parpala, on a hill outside the town (ibid.: 9-12). It is typical of Karkala that the next school was started by the Venkatarama temple, followed by two high schools, one for boys, one for girls, established under the leadership of the temple (Menefee, 1967/84: 154). The temple, of course, represented the GSB community.

'These Konkani' continues Fischer, 'are our most determined opponents there.'[76] Christianity they hate with all facets of their hearts. May it be, because many of their caste-fellows were converted by force to Catholicism by Portuguese priests in earlier times…? When the news came to Karkala that a Brahmin youngster had handed over his holy thread in the Mission School, a general mobilization took place among the Konkani Brahmins. The citizens now decided to stop the spread of Christianity in Karkala by all means, to block any initiative from the missionaries and to keep to their old religion. A little later it was made known that their God had revealed to a temple priest, that he would, in the future, show himself to be stronger than all other gods or demons in the neighbourhood. There was a further rumour that this God had freed one family from the hold of a powerful evil spirit. A Shastri (learned man) now got young and old together, twice a week, in the forecourt of the temple and from eight in the evening till twelve at night he told, with great enthusiasm, stories of the wondrous doings of the said god. There was great uproar when one of their caste-fellows passed an advanced state examination. In recognition of this they held a great feast, where they praised their god for the victory achieved, and showered great gifts on the temple to embellish and enlarge it. True, this big and beautiful temple shows their riches and their faithfulness to the old religion' (Fischer, op. cit.: 13-14). Some of the GSB argued their case politely, says Fischer, others not. The same may be said of the missionaries.[77]

Clever, smart and thinking only of their profit, 'their money is more important for them than anything else. They are hated by others, just like the Jewish tradesmen among us. Nobody surpasses them in swindling.'[78] The Tulu says: 'Do not trust a weeping woman, and do not trust the friendly face of a Konkani.' He serves his clients with smiles[79] and outward friendliness, but he makes a big difference between his caste-mates and members of other castes. He uses two kinds of weights and measures: while selling, the smaller weights and measures are used; when buying, the larger ones. In his shop lies, besides the different goods, also an open religious book. As soon as he is serving a customer and has calmed his conscience with the thought that the world wants to be betrayed, he grabs this book and reads with much ceremony and a powerful, singing voice, in order to convince buyer and seller of his earnest piety. Much money flows from them into the temple treasure, for the more swindling and inequitable profit, the more money runs to the coffers, so that their god closes his eyes and does not see their unjust conduct (ibid.: 15).

We get a clear picture, here, of missionary prejudice. Fischer's view of the GSB should not be taken at face value. Few missionaries came from a merchant background: many were of peasant stock, in a country where the priests were officials of the state church. Often, they served in villages where peasants were their main clients and the shopkeeper an outsider. If he was a Jew, so much the worse: the blatant anti-semitism of Fischer's remarks was hardly unusual in the middle European countryside. Also, the missionaries were Evangelicals, with a healthy respect for hard-working farmers or artisans, but sceptical of the rich and of commercial ventures. The opposition between the missionary and the GSB here is not simply one of Christianity *versus* Hinduism. It is a class conflict. To the Konkani bourgeoisie, the missionaries must have appeared uncouth – people without culture, stubborn and fanatical. Elsewhere, some missionaries managed to assume something of the guru's role: here, the missionary did not resemble and was hardly the equal of the GSB community's own gurus. Yet Fischer's remarks were not only the product of European and class prejudice. Local people often make similar remarks, and there exists, particularly among the lower castes and groups active in the Tulu revival, a view of the GSB as usurers and 'exploiters'.[80] This is the symbolic aspect of class conflict, with an ethnic gloss, as in Fischer's anti-semitism.

The missionary's efforts to establish a girls' school in Karkala in 1901, and the response of its citizens, provides an insight into community politics at the turn of the century. 'Give up that idea', said one 'heathen,' 'the Konkani will destroy everything for us' (ibid.: 12). But

> precisely a member of this caste brought about the foundation of a girl's school and gave us access to the city. It was the postmaster of Karkala. He had shown us much friendliness in matters of mail and even came to visit us, with his wife. My wife showed the latter some of her handwork and came to know . . . that the still quite young lady had studied up to third class in the Mission's boy school in Bantwal, but that she knew nothing of sewing and was just dreaming of learning this art. My wife proposed that as soon as there were five ladies willing to come and study with her, she would be quite ready to come to town thrice a week to teach them, and she (the young lady) accepted gladly and promised to bring together not just five or ten but thirty. She soon had the agreement of thirty ladies or girls.

Now there was the question of rooms. We . . . let the postmaster and those who wanted to send their children take the responsibility for the accommodation. Very soon a suitable room had been found. . . . The School was to start on Monday, the 2nd April, 1900, at three o'clock in the afternoon. . . . At two-o'clock the cart was ready, we[81] had the tropical helmet on our head, the parasol covered in white in the hand, a basket of handiwork and materials was already in the cart, when a messenger arrived in full speed with a letter from the postmaster. It had been written hastily and contained the following: 'Please put off the opening of the school: the owner refuses to rent the room because of the teaching of the Bible'.

The Konkani, says Fischer, 'were true to their nature.[82] . . . With a sigh, we remained at home.'

In the evening we went to town to visit, at the postmaster's bidding, a renowned merchant, who owned several houses and big shops. 'This rich man can certainly let us have a house' opined the postmaster as we were on our way. The ample and well-fed man welcomed us with a friendly smile, brought forward chairs for us and assured us that it was a particular honour for him, that we should come just today, on their New Year's Day.[83] . . . 'Since custom forbids bringing up the purpose (of the visit) directly, the postmaster had to find his way around the issue. . . . At last we could bring up the purpose of our visit. The worthy man belched, spit out the chewed betel nut, smiled at us, looked about, sent forth a woman, who was standing nearby, to buy something, so that she could not overhear his speech, and then began: 'You are right, it is a problem that there is no school for girls here, it is not seemly that girls and boys should be taught together. I shall send my daughter to you, as soon as you start. But I have to say one thing: you must not lose courage, if people here are not grateful for the good work that a girl's school is; for here in Karkala people are like sheep, they look askance at anything new. What cries of shock there were . . . when somebody brought a kerosene lamp to his house. 'The house-gods will be driven away', they said, and today – who can manage without a kerosene lamp? You must be patient at least for a year. I promise one thing: when I send my daughter, then twenty-five other girls will come the next day, for people respect me and the people will take care that their children shall miss nothing that mine are enjoying. I am on your side, of that there must be no doubt. As for accommodation … I shall liberate a shop in the centre of town.' Then a stranger arrives, a friend of the house, 'who greets us in English, sits down stiffly facing us and lets himself be informed, in a detached manner, of what we were discussing. He responds curtly: 'When you give English education to the girls, it is a good thing:

otherwise the government school is doing very good work.' He is a lawyer and has a good income. We leave, as it is getting dark.

The very next day we hear, that the lawyer has talked (the merchant) out of any idea of sending his daughter to our school or to let us have rooms. . . . During the night the postmaster talked about this for him so important matter with his wife. 'Now and then even the women have good ideas', he opined, as he told us: 'Not I, but my wife had the idea that we might let out part of our own house for the school.' . . . A friend of the postmaster, an astrologist, advised that the school should start on Wednesday, or, if not, on Saturday, since both these days were auspicious. We insisted that Thursday should be the starting day, since our work depended on God, and not on the stars.[84]

How astonished we were when we were shown, by the postmaster and his beaming wife, the room, decorated with garlands, with a table, two chairs and six banks and even two inscriptions. Many curious people were assembled. Almost all asked the question that was so important to them: 'Will the Bible be taught here?' When we answered in the affirmative, they withdrew, shaking their heads. Even the postmaster tended to lose courage. 'Could you not introduce the teaching of the Bible at a later time? I fear nobody will be sending their children if you start Bible lessons straight away', he thought. But Fischer refused.

A Saraswat Brahmin[85] calmed the people with the words: 'Don't believe that Bible teaching is harmful. Look at me: I went to the Mission School for six years and it did me no harm, I am still a Hindu like you'.[86] Another defended the missionaries, saying 'You should not skip the Bible teaching, that is the condition, without which you may not start a school.' Others cried: 'Let us see if they ruin the caste of these girls[87] or not, then afterwards we may send them our children. Sewing is also taught in this school . . . the rest is useless to them.'

'No wonder that only six girls came in the beginning,' says Fischer. The girls would listen attentively to Bible stories, but none dared to answer the questions put to them.

Dumbly they shook their heads and looked fearfully at the others. . . . My wife told them of the many children who came to school daily at Mangalore, and how they listened gladly to the stories from the Bible, learned them and retold them gladly, answering the questions. But all was in vain. The girls followed in the strictest manner the advice of their elders, to give no answers to Bible lessons. It was impossible to make them repeat the Paternoster.[88]

It was with sorrow that we ended the first day at school (ibid.: 16-19).

The next day, however, a new girl, seven years old, arrived. She was an earlier pupil of Mrs. Fischer from Mangalore, come to stay with her married sister. She repeated the Paternoster and answered questions with enthusiasm, to the astonishment of the Karkala girls. Her example helped, says Fischer. Next day three more girls came, and the day after, most girls answered questions. Only six refused, and they were Catholics. 'I know the phrase,' said one, 'but my mother has forbidden me to learn the Bible or repeat prayers, since the Priest does not like it.' A month later there were fifty girls in the school. But one day, the owner of the house threatened to evict the postmaster, because of the Bible lessons. The postmaster refused, saying that there was no such clause in his contract. But then he was promoted to a post elsewhere. The missionaries had to build a new school, but when one Konkani official offered to sell them land, they had to act quickly. 'It happens,' says Fischer,

> that a house or a piece of land is offered for sale, only to drive up the price. The vendor goes from house to house saying that the missionary wants to buy. . . . People discuss, the vendor is besieged. The latter answers: 'If you pay me as much as the missionary, then of course I sell it to you.' Generally a buyer is found, only to block the missionary's acquisition. (ibid.: 19-20)

Seen with Fischer's eyes, all this proves how clever the heathens, and especially the GSB are: you cannot trust them. Reading the story backwards, however, we gain some insight into the local politics of Karkala at the time, and we see both willingness to try new opportunities and potential for resistance. The postmaster and his wife stand out as allies of the missionary, true to one of the acknowledged roles of the GSB in South Kanara: advocates of 'enlightenment', 'progress' and 'modernity'. There is no hint that they are potential converts. They are GSB, but not merchants, and probably not locals. As a postmaster the husband represents colonial bureaucracy; values of 'progress' are expected from a man in his position, and encouraged by his employers. Similarly, when the missionary seeks land to build the school, it is an official who comes forward, and who, despite

Fischer's remarks, earnestly wants to sell to the missionaries. This GSB, too, seems to be an 'advocate of progress'. A third person supporting the school is a Chitrapur Saraswat. We know nothing else of him, but Chitrapur Saraswats were scribes or administrators for the British or indigenous organizations.[89] Here is another high-status person, educated,[90] and outsider to the network of merchant GSB families that were the node of civic power in Karkala. He too is no convert. These three men want a school – an obvious symbol of progress – and, as an unidentified fourth person says, you can't have this school except on the missionary's conditions. In their view, the school is a greater good than the 'cost' of some Christian propaganda. But the postmaster is clearly conscious that for many citizens this is a high price to pay.

The merchant Fischer visits at first shares these progressive views. A girls' school is a good thing, avoiding the promiscuity of teaching the sexes together. Then his friend the advocate turns up. We do not know the advocate's views, but his reference to the government schools give some indication. He too, a learned man, is positive to schools. But he probably feels there is no rush to have a missionary school if a government school may be built soon.[91] Moreover, a mission school in Karkala might be an argument for locating the next government school elsewhere. He is against the missionary influence and he too may be a GSB, a Chitrapur Saraswat, or possibly a Jain. Most of those concerned are likely to come from these three castes, or from the Catholic community. The latter seem as sceptical to Bible teaching as the GSB, and they too may have an alternative in mind: the Catholics were expanding their own school system at the time. Even the GSB, latecomers in the race for community schools, were starting their first schools in Mangalore by then.

Thus, we get a picture of 'public opinion' in Karkala at the time. Schools are in; but is it necessary to accept Bible teaching? Fischer is playing a gamble which paid off a generation earlier, when the Basel mission was able to monopolize schooling in many places. He may know that he is involved in a race against time: he does not tell us, as he certainly would not tell his readers at home. To build schools in a school-less area would be an obvious act of progress: to involve his supporters in a battle for pupils between government, Protestant,

Catholic and Hindu schools would be a different proposition. Most of the actors in the civic sphere in Karkala – and not least the GSB – must have known this.

Officials owed their career to schools, and other communities – notably the Catholics – may have held hopes even then of mobility through education. The GSB merchants were in a different situation. Commerce is learnt in the family firm. They, therefore, could look at education as a symbolic option rather than a utilitarian need.[92] What they could get from schools was 'culture' which they already had as a cultured bourgeoisie, as Brahmins, and through their system of temples and *maths*. For them, there was less reason to 'buy' schooling at the cost of Christian propaganda, threatening the very values on which their cultural superiority[93] was built. Perhaps even less when the missionaries were people of much lower social standing, far less refined and cultured than they themselves were.

The picture Fischer paints of Karkala in 1901 shows us a small town with a healthy public sphere where citizens debate the missionaries' propositions. The 'heathen' were not simply responding to Protestant influence, but were trying to get what they wanted, while rejecting what they did not want. They acted just like we would expect from small town citizens of a fundamentally democratic country, which India, as Kipling[94] would have agreed, was even then. Of course, those who participated in this civic sphere were the small-town elite in which the GSB held a central place: as in most democratic set-ups, participation was not for all.

THE GSB SETTLEMENTS IN SOUTH KANARA

Still, the position that the GSB hold in South Kanara, is ambiguous. We have seen how in a local setting like Karkala they came to occupy a central position. In a similar way, they once dominated the small port of Mulki, which seems to have grown mainly around their trade and their temple. And yet, as the panorama of the Kallianpur cluster shows more clearly, their settlements were enclaves, surrounded by rural areas dominated by other groups such as the Bunts and by the enclaves of others, such as the Catholics. In a sense, then, South Kanara resembles Furnivall's plural society (1939) where ethnic groups live and pursue their cultural concerns separately, meeting at the market-place. Dominance in such a society, save for that of king or state, is necessarily partial. The particularity of the GSB position in Furnivall's terms, however, is that they dominated – and still largely dominate – a sector that integrates the various groups, namely, the market-place and the market economy.

Culturally, the position of the GSB came to resemble that of a colonial elite, controlling the cultural nodes that the small towns constituted but not really penetrating the culture of the surrounding countryside. They were immigrants, but they were not integrated, as most immigrants are, at the bottom of the local hierarchy. They came to occupy, instead, a particular and important niche at or near the top.[95]

The position of the GSB clearly relates not just to the particularities of their own history and character as a community, but also to the nature of society in South Kanara. Here, the nature of the Kallianpur cluster is revealing. In Saurashtra (Tambs-Lyche, 2004) and to some extent elsewhere in the north, village stratification tended to form either by conquest – at the top – or provision of services, at the bottom, in a habitat of nucleated villages which in Saurashtra were defended by a common, village wall. Interstices of pastoral and peasant hamlets existed, but were generally a feature of the less fertile periphery (Tambs-Lyche, 2003 and 2004). In South Kanara, the habitat was more dispersed, and new groups tended to settle on their own lands, sometimes adjacent to but separate from that of established groups. Though these different groups may be ranked, they were not necessarily integrated in the kind of village hierarchy we know from many other parts of India. The peculiar mix of superiority and separateness that characterizes the GSB position is partly a function of this particularity of the social landscape of South Kanara.

NOTES

1. Known as Carnate in Portuguese sources.
2. This is the opinion of one of the main trustees of the Mulki Venkatarama temple. Gangoli, the port of Basrur, close to modern Kundapur, was the other main port of the area then.
3. Vasantha Madhava, 1991: 143, who refers to the account of the visit of Saint Catherine to this place in 1656.

4. A name said to be derived from Vola Lanka, 'Inner Lanka'.
5. An important bank regionally, founded and largely led by the Bunts.
6. We shall meet this man later: see Chapter 10.
7. The eight monasteries of the Madhava sect, of which I shall say more in Chapter 4.
8. It is not far from Vijaya College, though its entrance is from the road leading directly from the Panchamahal to the Venkatarama temple. Along the road, there are both Christian and Bunt houses.
9. We shall say more of Venkatarama later. Narasimha is the lion-headed form of Vishnu, who plays a role in Venkatarama's myth. Ugra Narasimha is the 'ferocious' form of this god. Bindu Madhava seems to link the temple to the powerful Madhava sect based in Udupi, and Vira Vitthala – 'the hero Vitthala' – to the popular god Vitthala of Pandharpur in Maharashtra, which was one of the original deities of this temple.
10. A name used for Venkatarama at Tirupati in Andhra Pradesh: see Chapter 10.
11. *Abhisheka* may be described as a ritual bathing of the idol. It is an important part of the installation rite, and sometimes used as a synonym of installation. Here, however, it refers to a rite which is repeated annually.
12. Here, I am told, there will be 'mass feeding' on 4 Febuary, to inaugurate the building.
13. Such parks are becoming more and more common all over India.
14. Dharmasthala is now probably the most influential religious institution in South Kanara. At its head is 'the Hegde', descendant of a minor Jain chief, and guardian of an important Shiva temple, as well as the main sanctuary of Annappa Panjurli. The latter is the 'peaceful' version of the sacred boar, symbol of fertility and autochthony. Dharmasthala thus stands at the confluence of Jain, *bhuta* and 'Sanskritic' Hindu cults. But the Hegde also owes his particular position to the political acumen of his ancestor, who, during the British conquest in 1800, aided the colonial army with his own force against the ruler of Vitthala. The British rewarded him with the right to judge in civil matters. Though this right is no longer formally recognized, the Hegde still holds court and his decisions are widely respected.
15. This *math* has its headquarters in Varanasi (Kashi), but caters to the GSB community.
16. A full-moon day in December.
17. The ritual still exists, but the trustees stress that the Savantar's seat at Padupanambur dates only from the fifteenth century. Earlier it was at Shivaru, further inland, only 4 or 5 km from the Venkatarama temple.
18. He says the temple is from the sixteenth century, but he may refer to the oldest parts of the present building.

19. That is, *panchavanga*. M.M. Prabhu feels 'Panchamahal' may refer to 'fives', not necessarily to five families.
20. He says they converted only 3-4 decades ago. Apparently, however, they converted much earlier than that.
21. Some Christian settlements came much later. Thus Shirva, between Udupi and Mudabidri, says Oliver Lewis, dates from the eighteenth century. The land there is dry and its settlers have been much poorer than at Kallianpur. This would seem to be confirmed by Lobo's work: very few prominent families come from Shirva.
22. The Nayaks welcomed the immigrants (Machado Prabhu, 1999: 137; Vasantha Madhava, 1991: 52).
23. From *kot*, measing fort.
24. Buchanan, however, says Tipu destroyed all the forts he had built along the coast before the last Mysore war, due to the ease with which the Mangalore fort was taken by the British (1807/1999: 21).
25. It is possible, however, that the fort was built by Haidar, perhaps at the time of the 1778 war. This would fit with the date given for the Tonse Pais. We know there was an influx of Christians from Goa in the eighteenth century.
26. This is the place of origin of another important Udupi GSB family.
27. Fisherman's caste.
28. Built at Karunakaran's instigation, he says.
29. Karunakaran is a Moghavera, who runs a marriage agency for disabled people.
30. This temple must once have been on an island. Its special name is Kandige Matha, *Kandige* meaning 'one piece of wood'. It is said to have been built from a single log, though it has been rebuilt recently. A Jain couple used to visit the Ganapati temple. But one day they arrived too late for *puja*, and were very unhappy. They stayed the night there, and the wife dreamt that she found a *murti* of Lakshmiganapati in the river. The husband dreamt that somebody told him to go to the seashore, where he would find a log, from which the temple would be built.
31. 'Arasu'.
32. Near Barkur.
33. Village deity.
34. Barakuru was one of the capitals of the Aluva kings.
35. The term would imply that the ritual is 'tantric', i.e. not Brahmanical.
36. 'Service', here, taking care of the temple.
37. There was quite a discussion between Karunakaran, a staunch vegetarian, and the Devadiga priest on the subject of animal sacrifice. The Devadiga said he felt obliged to continue the traditional practice of the temple.

38. A ferocious goddess, Bhadrakali is sometimes present in the pantheon of the *bhuta* cults of South Kanara.
39. They are Mudutonse (Tonse East), Padutonse (Tonse West) or Kemmanna, which includes Hoode, and Padutonse proper, then Bengere and Gajjarabettu, Uppar, Bhadragiri, Nayampalli and Puttur. 'All these places around the Suvarna River are supposed to worship at this temple.'
40. 'Padrazgo.' This schism among the Catholics has marked most of their settlements in South Kanara.
41. *Baug* or *bag*, garden or park.
42. The mother of T.M.A. Pai, who founded Manipal, came from this family.
43. A very important Udupi family, of whom more later.
44. *Bhajan* means religious song; *Mahotsava* (*Maha Utsava*) means big festival.
45. A Shivalli Brahmin, at one time my wife's assistant, who has helped us greatly in our work. His family comes from Kemmanna, a village of the Kallianpur cluster.
46. Canopy.
47. Vajpayee's Bharatiya Janta Party (BJP) government.
48. As Krishna Bhat puts it, Tonse East is the GSB area, while Tonse West is 'different'.
49. Probably during the Maratha expansion around the eighteenth century.
50. End point.
51. Moghavera.
52. Bobbariya is the *bhuta* of seafarers and fishermen. Born from a Muslim father and a Jain mother, he was a giant: it was he that cleared the 'road' which *bhutas* follow from the mountains to the sea. Bobbariya took a tree of every kind from the forest to build his giant ship, and set out on a merchant expedition. There, his ship was sunk by a 'stone ship'. Bobbariya drowned and became a *bhuta*. He is the protector of those that are drowned.
53. A hall built for groups that meet to sing *bhajans*. They cater mostly to low-caste people, such as Moghaveras or Billavas. There seems to be little contact between these groups and the *bhajan* enthusiasts among the GSB, though both groups sing the *bhajan* classics, such as those of Tukaram.
54. Karunakaran says that between Kemmanna and Kallianpur there was some garden land, but no houses, when he went to school. He was born in 1952, so the houses must have come up since the 1960s. Many of them belong to Christians. Krishna Bhat says that this area used to be waste – grazing land, rather than jungle.
55. A ritual buffalo race, closely connected to the *bhuta* cults, especially to the annual *Nema* of the royal *bhutas*.

56. *Daivas* – 'demons' – is another term for the *bhutas*.
57. The *gutu* house. *Gutu* families were once vassals of the Jains, becoming chiefs when the latter lost their power under the Ikkeri Nayaks.
58. *Rajandaiva*.
59. Babu is a *bhuta* of the lower castes, but he is very powerful in exorcism, and so has a clientele from many castes. He is 'under the influence' of the seafaring *bhuta*, Bobbariya (Marine Carrin, personal information). There is another, well-known *babusthana* at Manipal.
60. Probably the Bunt chiefdom included the lands of the Billavas and other low castes, while Christians, Muslims and GSB settled on waste lands donated by the Nayak kings.
61. Kallianpur proper has certain central functions such as shops, but this seems due to its being on the old coastal road, and presently, its junction with the new National Highway 17. There are some shops elsewehere, such as at Kemmanna.
62. An enormous statue of a Jain *tirthankara*, hewed from a single block of the black basalt rock found in the area.
63. A Jain temple known for its sculptured pillars which bear witness to the widespread commercial ties of the town at that time. It is said to have taken thirty years to build.
64. I speak here as a visitor: certainly an archaeologist would be able to see traces of the old street pattern. I have not had the occasion to examine the south-western part of the town more closely.
65. In 2004, the inscription of 'G. Nayak, general merchant and money-lender', could still be seen on the house that now serves as the family's driving school: by 2006 it was no longer legible. The inscription must date from the days before the word moneylender got its present negative value.
66. This is the house of B. Sadashiva Shenoy and his brother. It is not big, but the pillared porch and heavy woodwork give it a distinctive character. One climbs the stone steps sheltered by the porch to enter the visitor's room, behind which is another, used as a visitor's bedroom or quite often as an office. Behind this is a small court, surrounded by a verandah with wooden pillars. The rear part of the house is reserved for the family, with another bedroom and the kitchen. A steep staircase leads to the first floor: there is a bedroom opening to a balcony above the front porch, and a large storage space where the Shenoys keep old household objects. Behind it is the granary, with a slatted floor which lets in air from below. A hatch leads to the loft, used as storage space. Many houses are to a similar pattern, with more rooms if the frontage is longer. This

house differs from the typical Konkani farmhouse, but is typical of GSB town houses from the late colonial period. The earlier houses did not have the central court. In spite of the fondness of the GSB for their traditions, it is rare to find an old house freshly painted and done up in this way.

67. The 'heritage village' in Manipal, where another Shenoy has assembled and renovated a number of old GSB houses, remains an isolated example. Will the trend to return to old town-houses, noticeable in the West, arrive in time to save the old houses in South Kanara? One would hope so.
68. This is certainly the opinion of Krishna Bhat.
69. Mulugiri leases are for 99 years. I have found no precise information on Bairavara leases, but I understand they have no fixed time limit.
70. If so, they may have been in the region before 1600, but this is conjecture.
71. The carvings are very fine and detailed. It is said that the sculptor spent eight years carving each pillar.
72. Among them is the 'golden *mantapa*', a gift from the temple at Tirupati. It was donated in 1906, a year of drought, in reconnaissance of the prayers for rain that the Karkala community had staged. Garuda finally brought the rain. There is also a silver *mantapa*, a silver-covered *utsavamurti*, and other impressive paraphernalia.
73. A touching point was when one of the boys tied a *rakhi* to my wrist, thus according me priestly protection.
74. There are two: clearly a smaller and older tank, at a lower level, has been replaced by a new one. They are slightly differently orientated, no doubt due to a revision of *vastu* (prescriptions for the orientation of a building) when the new tank was built. A tunnel under the walls surrounding the new tank connects the two. It may be noted that the tank of the Chitrapur Saraswats' Shirali *math* was similarly made 'ritually correct' in the last quarter of the nineteenth century (Conlon, 1977: 142).
75. The Gadigas also call themselves Somakshatriya, implying a claim to Kshatriya status. They were, says P.R. Kuduva, soldiers to the Nayaks and the local chiefs, but the British abolished the chiefdoms and the Gadigas had to find another niche. They became oil-pressers. Similarly, the Kote Sheregars claim ancient Kshatriya status for the same reason, calling themselves Ramaraja Kshatriya.
76. 'Widerwärtigsten Gegner'.
77. Asked why he no longer came to discuss with them, Fischer answered: 'You know that we follow the words of Jesus closely. One of his sayings runs that you should not throw pearls for swine. As a follower of Christ I must follow that saying' (Fischer, 1906: 14).

78. Betrügen.
79. Müsse.
80. Compare Hardiman's remarks (1996) on the position of the Bania.
81. Here, the missionary uses the honorary 'we' for himself.
82. He continues: 'a Tulu proverb says, succinctly: 'eighteen words has the Konkani'. That is to say, not one man, one word, but many words and no man!'
83. On 2 April; this cannot be Diwali, the 'New Year's Day' here probably refers to Holi.
84. Fischer continues: 'For the Hindu never marries, builds not, studies not, does not conclude any deal, without looking to the position of the stars. What the astrologer sees in the stars, is for him the decisive factor.'
85. Since Fischer refers to the GSB community as Konkanis, it is likely that this person is a Chitrapur Saraswat. In Udupi, many people, though not GSB, refer to the GSB as Konkanis and the Chritrapur Saraswats as Saraswats.
86. The Saraswats had gone in for education since 1838, when the Basel missionaries established a school in Mangalore, aiming at posts in the British administration. There were at least two cases of conversion, the first in 1843 when two GSB were also converted. They 'caused immense shock and stir' in the two communities. But since then, many Saraswats had gone to mission school without being converted (Conlon, 1977: 78-84).
87. I.e. convert them to Christianity.
88. 'Our Father, who art in Heaven …'.
89. By 1870, Saraswats held 37.5 per cent of the administrative appointments in South Kanara 'below posts reserved for Europeans and above menial ranks that paid under Rs. 10 a month'. The median income for the 189 Saraswats employed was only Rs. 15, however, so most were clerks or had similar junior positions.

    The caste constituted only 0.4 per cent of the district population (Conlon, 1977: 93-4).
90. Six years at school was quite something in Karkala in 1901. In Mangalore, the situation was different, but Chitrapur Saraswats were well ahead of the GSB in education. Thus by 1892, 94 students from South Kanara had passed the B.A. exam at Madras; 48 were Saraswats, 15 were GSB (Conlon, 1977: 92, citing *History of Higher Education in South India*, 2: 48, 70).
91. Saraswat pressure led to the establishment of a government school in Mangalore in 1866 (Conlon, 1977: 83-4).

92. This may explain why the GSB were behind the Catholics in starting their own schools.
93. Cultural capital, in Bourdieu's terms.
94. India is the only democracy, says Kipling on the opening page of *Kim*.
95. In this, the GSB's position resembles that of the immigrant bourgeoisie that dominated urban and political life in Norway for a long time after 1814, when its members were the main architects of a democratic constitution.

3

Udupi becomes a Town

Udupi was not among the early GSB settlements in South Kanara. Today, it has become the centre of Udupi district – the northern part of the former South Kanara district – and a very convenient centre of communications. It was largely by chance that I chose Udupi for the present study: we had used it as a base for an earlier fieldwork and were well connected there. Udupi's GSB community is now among the most important in the Kanaras, and so it seemed both pertinent and convenient to make a study of it.

As a centre of pilgrimage, Udupi dates from medieval times, but as a town it is relatively recent. It was largely the GSB who effected the transformation in the last decade of the nineteenth century. They developed the commerce around which the town grew. This chapter tells the story of that transformation, but also looks briefly at earlier developments.

Udupi is best known as the centre of the Madhava branch of Vaishnavism, with its Krishna temple and the eight *maths* or monasteries that surround it. It was Madhavacharya, the founder of the Dvaita or dualist variant of Vedanta philosophy, who established the cult of Krishna here in the thirteenth century. In the sixteenth century Vadiraja, then head of the sect, instituted what is known as the *Ashtamath*[1] system and laid the foundation of the present religious organization. The system, briefly, consists of the Krishna temple, surrounded by eight monasteries which are in principle equal and independent of each other. By a system of rotation, the *mahant* (chief ascetic) of each monastery is in turn responsible for the rituals of the Krishna temple, as well as its upkeep and development.

But long before Madhava came to Udupi, two temples had been established in what is now the middle of the temple square, around which the Madhava institutions are grouped. One is dedicated to Chandramauleshwara, a form of Shiva.[2] Several people, including Krishna Bhat, maintain that both this temple and the Ananteshwara temple, close to it, were originally Jain *basadis*. Tradition has it they were abandoned – or at least decaying – towards the seventh or eighth century, then taken over as Hindu temples towards the tenth century. Gururaja Bhat dates the Ananteshwara temple to the eighth century (Bhat, 1975: 408). Based on architectural evidence, he says it is anterior to the Hoysala period. Some say the Kadiyali temple, on the road to Manipal, is even older – as a Hindu shrine – than the two centrally located temples.

One day, it is said, a *swami* was bathing in the tank before the Ananteshwara temple. The god appeared, but the *swami* had but little to make homage to the deity. So he beat his razor against his begging bowl to imitate the sound of *puja*. The god was pleased, and so the Chandramauleshwara temple came into being. It is not as old as the Ananteshwara temple, which has an ancient and handsome roof, but the Chandramauleshwara image is also very old, and beautiful. Certainly, both were dedicated to their present deities before Madhava came to Udupi to establish his *ashram* in the thirteenth century. The Krishna temple at first was but a wooden *mandapa*, says M.M. Prabhu. If so, this was still a small establishment far less important than the original shrines. Yet this event was the beginnings of Madhava Vaishnavism, with Krishna as its central deity.

Several inscriptions relate to Madhava's Krishna temple in the following centuries. Inscription 296,[3] of AD 1437, says M.M. Prabhu, tells us that, Annappa Wodeyar raided Shivalligrama (Udupi) and destroyed the shrine. The Krishna idol was taken out of the temple, and the people from Barakuru came and consoled the Shivallis'. The Shivalli Brahmins then were associated with the Krishna temple from the beginning. 'Then Devaraya sent some compensation to restore worship,' continues M.M. Prabhu.

Why? When Pratapa Harihara was ruling in Vidyanagara (AD 1399) the Barakuru kingdom was ruled by Nagara of Muduni; then Nagappa Nayak came from Vijayanagara with his troops on royal order to destroy the two *devasthanas* of Mahadeva.[4] To restore these two temples, he donated two fields to be used for services at the temple. The figure on the pillar of the

Ananteshwara temple, who is wearing a conical cap, must be the general who restored the temples, pictured as a devotee.

In fact, reflects M.M. Prabhu, 'there may have been two raids'.

'There was considerable opposition to Madhava in his own days', M.M. Prabhu continues. 'He was considered a heretic then. The opposition continued up to Vadiraja but the latter was a powerful pontiff and it was in his time that all the temples in the area were given Shivalli priests. Vadiraja, it should be understood, is a title rather than a name.' Thus, if M.M. Prabhu is right, the Shivalli Brahmins owe their present position in the area to their alliance with Vadiraja.[5]

In the seventeenth century, Udupi became a major centre of Krishnaism. It was then, says M.M. Prabhu, that the *maths* started to place Shivalli Brahmins in all the major temples of the area, replacing, I understand, Sthanikas and/or Devadigas, who are still officiating in the Kanchamma temple at Kallianpur. Thus was established the supremacy over other, non-Madhava, temples in the area that the *maths* have enjoyed up to the present time.[6]

The Madhava *maths* came to own a lot of land around Udupi, elsewhere in south Karnataka, and also in other parts of India. Most of the land was lost during the land reforms of 1967-73.[7] Traditionally, these lands formed an economic base for their operations, and also furnished the vegetables, spice and coconuts necessary for the ritual and for the sustenance of the *sadhus*. When the land was confiscated, the 'government paid to the *maths* the amount of tax they used to pay for the land multiplied by approximately ten (depending on dry, wet or garden land) as yearly annuity' (Rao, 2002: 60). Some *maths* manage to function on this economic base, others have had to find other funds. One *math* runs a cinema in Udupi. Others still make some money from the sale of surplus agricultural produce of the land that is left. The *maths*, therefore, are largely independent of the merchant economy of the town, while they run schools and a college, a hospital, and a number of charitable institutions and so still wield considerable power at the local level (ibid.: 59-61).

By the thirteenth to fourteenth centuries, the GSB were present in the region, at Mangeshwar and Mulki. In the fifteenth to sixteenth centuries, there was, as we have seen, considerable expansion of agriculture (Vasantha Madhava, 1991), and of the export trade in rice, and the GSB were active in this trade from the start. According to some, the Kallianpur Venkatarama temple was built then. Some of the GSB families in Udupi, such as the Ammunje Nayaks, may have been active in the rice trade since this period. The role of the GSB was financially important. They already had their own *maths* and temples though not yet in Udupi. This was when the Venkatarama temple was built at Karkala, with the presence of a strong community of GSB in the town. Even as they were settling there, we begin to find traces of them at Udupi. M.M. Prabhu describes various inscriptions at Udupi which relate to this community. One inscription, no. 301 from AD 1614 says: 'Chinnavaradha – (woollen merchant) Lingappaya son of Nanappaya gives 100 gold coins from the interest of which the services of the temple are to be conducted.' Nanappaya is described as coming from Sankawalia *agrahara* (in Goa), a Brahmin of Konkani class, Bharadvaja *gotra* and Ruk *shakha*. He must have been a member of the community that became the GSB caste. Inscription 302 is also from 1614: 'During the *pariaya*[8] of Vedavidyatirtha Ashtapura in Sahashtigrama Muhadshyapura and leader Mathagama, of Kaushika *gotra*, Ruk *shakha*, Damasa Prabhu, son of Dam Prabhu, made this donation for the benefit of his uncle, may imperishable merit accrue to him . . . 160 big *gadyamas* (a gold coin of 4.3 grams) – for the interest of which the rites should be performed. . . .' These donors, then, were Prabhu of Kaushika *gotra*, like M.M. Prabhu himself. The inscription continues: 'Govinda Pai son of Dasasidam Pai, for the . . . of his mother and father, and for the prosperity of his children and grandchildren; Shri Krishna's *garbaguddi* to be completely made anew; the base stone, the *pashupitha* (pedestal), the walls, the door frames, beams and corners of the roof, the cost of making it in stone, and the amount to be expended on that (to be borne by the donor). Over and above that, for the offerings to the *acharyas*, 55 gold coins are given, from the interest of which these expenses will be paid.' Again, the donors are definitely GSB, and clearly they made an important contribution to replace the wooden *mandapa*. This is clear from inscription no. 297, again from AD 1614 which was made for Vedavidyatirtha himself. He was the direct disciple and successor of Vadiraja. The idol of Krishna seems still to have been inside the old structure – it was moved outside under the *mandapa* and the *puja* conducted there, in front of the *garbaguddi*. The *mandapa* was now remade in stone with a two-level roof of copper sheet on which the *kailasa* was placed. Apart from the money received, Vedavidyatirtha spent 145 *varahas* of his own.

What emerges from these inscriptions is the important role of the GSB in relation to the Krishna temple at Udupi in the first part of the seventeenth century. M.M. Prabhu feels that by then the GSB were rivaling the importance of the Shivalli Brahmins in the temple.[9] As I read the evidence I feel there was complementarity rather than rivalry. The Shivallis were probably the temple priests, as they had become by the fifteenth century and as they still are today. The GSB donors were more likely businessmen. Both Brahmin groups certainly had real influence over the growing pilgrimage centre at Udupi by the seventeenth century.

The *murti* of Krishna at Udupi is in fact an idol of Skanda, says M.M. Prabhu:

> The original idol was lost. Vadiraja had ordered Vedavidyatirtha to do the *puja* in his absence, while he himself was at Sode,[10] But the *shishya*[11] was not allowed to do the *puja*, and the caretaker refused. There was a conflict, and . . . the *murti* disappeared. So they had to find a new one. The GSB had quite a stock of *murtis*, saved from their destroyed temples at Goa. So they said, please come and find one. But Vadiraja was almost blind at the time, so he found a *murti* about the same size, placed it in a wooden box and sent it by ship to Malpe. But it was the wrong *murti*![12] Vadiraja then created a *ganasloka* – verses praising the image – which corresponded to the Skanda image. Before, it was called Vadiraja's *sloka*. The earlier one must have corresponded to the other image; Vadiraja himself described the image as dancing.

There is a story about finding the *murti* in the water, or bringing it by ship, but it does not exist before Vadiraja. 'In the contemporary biography this important event is dismissed, receiving two lines only', says M.M. Prabhu. If his own interpretation is correct, not only did the GSB contribute heavily to build the Krishna temple, they also provided the *murti*.

The period in question – when the Krishna temple was rebuilt and the *murti* changed – corresponds roughly with the time of the building of the Karkala and Kallianpur temples, and there was a sizeable GSB settlement at Mulki. The role the GSB played in the Krishna temple was perhaps the reason why no Venkatarama temple was built in Udupi then. Another GSB temple, the Lakshminarayana, was in fact built near the later Venkatarama temple, in VT Street. This is private, kept by a GSB Bhat family. It is more than 400 years old, and the Acharya Math – one of the *maths* in Udupi that do not belong to the *Ashtamath* group – is attached to it. The *math* is some five hundred years old, says K.R. Kuduva. There were some GSBs in Udupi, then, before the great influx of the late nineteenth century, and they would seem to have been living near the present VT Street.

There was an important new influx of GSB, as well as Konkani Catholics, to South Kanara in the eighteenth century. Mangalore's Venkatarama temple was established at this time, and the Dongarkeri settlement – the GSB quarter of the town – probably dates from this period. This implies that Konkani Christian and GSB settlements at Mangalore are roughly contemporary, and Mangalore must have grown considerably in this period, an expansion possibly related to its role as Haidar Ali's main port. We know that Ali was liberal, and his relation to the Tranquebar missionary Schwarz[13] indicates a positive attitude to Christians.

In the early nineteenth century, Udupi seems to have remained mainly a ritual centre around the *maths*, as only a few GSB families were settled there by 1860. K.R. Kuduva gave me a short list of what he thought must be the oldest GSB families in Udupi: The Padiyars; the Yogapashanai (Shanbag) family;[14] the Kuduvas;[15] then there were the Udyavara Pais, the Udupi Baligas and the Udupi Bhats.[16] The latter are the owners of the Lakshminarayana temple. All these families, according to Kuduva, were settled in Udupi before the main influx of GSB families around 1890. What is now the centre of the town was uninhabited in the mid-nineteenth century. Down by the river, however, there were the temples and monasteries of the Madhavas, an important centre of pilgrimage. Part of VT Street, near the Acharya Math and the Lakshminarayana temple, may also have been built then. Before the great influx of 1890s, the Basel Mission (1855), the British ditrict administration and court (1870s) and the Catholic Church (1880s) had established themselves at Udupi, but at their present locations, quite far to the west of the *maths*.

It is said that the *maths* did not want either of the Christian institutions at Udupi. When the Basel Mission established their out-station and school at Udupi in 1855,[17] they met with considerable resistance. Among other events, the missionary bungalow was burnt down. Next year, it was the Church that burned (Hartenstein, 1935: 83-4; Ammann, n.d.: 41-3). According to Hartenstein, the main resistance against the missionaries in Udupi came not from the GSB community but from the Shivalli Brahmins. The difference from Karkala is important: Karkala was a real town with considerable trade in cashewnut, monopolized by the GSB. In 1855 Udupi was hardly a town yet, and the GSB community was still quite small.

The Basel Mission, however, gradually gained a foothold in Udupi, and this was where the 'Tulu movement' of conversions in 1869 was strongest, says Hartenstein (1935: 84). These conversions continued in the 1870s, and the Protestant community grew till the 1890s. By then, reconversions to Hinduism outnumbered new conversions, partly because ex-Christians were freely welcomed back to their former castes (ibid.: 85). They were mainly Billavas and Moghaveras. Yet Udupi continued tc be an important centre of education for the Protestants: their 'middle school' was moved to Udupi in 1868. It prepared the youngsters for the seminar in Mangalore, where pastors were trained. The institution for orphaned boys was also relocated here, and a small school for teachers was also started. One of the problems that the missionaries faced, was that school reform in the 1890s called for the transformation of their Tulu-language middle school into an English medium high school, and the new plans left less time for teaching the Bible, to the regret of the missionaries.

It was largely the 'heathen' who financed their mission school in Udupi. Even the *swamis* of the *maths* took part (Ammann, n.d.: 45), and the school reforms strengthened the schools' appeal to non-Christian pupils and parents. This period, which saw many GSB and other Hindu pupils graduating from the school, was in many ways its heyday. Later, Hindus and Catholics established their own schools.[18] Hospitals for women and children were added to the mission compound in these years. By 1935 there were some three and a half thousand Protestant Christians in the area of the Udupi Mission Station (Hartenstein, 1935: 86).

In the second half of the nineteenth century, Udupi was still dominated by the *maths*. They owned most of the land around the temple, and each *math* also owned one or several villages in the countryside. As Ammunje Babu Amin, a Billava author and activist put it: 'When they constructed the *Ashtamaths*, people voluntarily gave a lot of land to the *maths*. The piously-minded people gave land for Bhagavan. There is a lot of land in the countryside, but the *maths* still have very valuable property in Udupi city. Even the (Catholic) Church land was bought at a very high price from the *maths*. The land around here,' he points to the surrounding land,[19] 'all belongs to the *maths*. So here it is business: to other parts of India they preach religion.' The *Ashtamath* lands originally included all of the Car Street–VT Street axis. At the southern end of VT Street stands the Poornapraja (PP) College founded by the *maths*, indicating that their lands stretched further south. 'In the beginning the Konkanis leased the land from the *maths*', says Borkar, who, as an estate agent, knows well the distribution of property in the town. 'Then, little by little, they bought the plots outright.'

Near the temple, between the river and the present Car Street, was the *agrahara* of the Shivalli Brahmins who served the temple, some of whom no doubt engaged in commerce to serve the pilgrims, as is common in pilgrimage places in India. The town as such, however, did not yet exist. Today, between the *maths* and the river, are what must once have been the gardens of the *maths*, but now we find a big portal through which cars enter an enormous open space used as a parking lot and – occasionally – for large open-air meetings. There is also a *dharmashala* for pilgrims here, and a girls' school, probably belonging to the *maths*. They also controlled the coastal lands west of Udupi, such as at Udyavara. This is why, says Jayashankar Kuthpadi, a Billava teacher and social worker who lives in Kuthpadi west of Udyavara, there are very few Bunt landlords there. The Billava coconut-growers were tenants of the maths until they became owners through the land reforms of the 1960s and 1970s.[20] Borkar confirms that the *maths* owned a lot of land in and around Udupi. All the land around Chitpady[21] belonged to them, and the local population was their tenants. Only after the land reforms of 1972-3[22] did they become owners. Unlike many of the landlords inland from Udupi, the *maths* did not openly resist the land reforms. Instead, says Jayashankar Kuthpadi, they incited or encouraged people to give their lands back 'to Krishna' and in fact many religiously minded people did so.

But at the Budnar *bhutakolla* to Jumadi and Kotichennaya[23] we met Shambhu Shetty, a Bunt who has been working for five years in Mumbai. His uncle is the *jajman* of this *bhutakolla*. Another uncle is the leftist writer Gopala Shetty, now about seventy years old. There is no committee of trustees at this *bhutasthana*, 'the *garudi*[24] is run by the Billavas and administered by the Shettys' as Shambhu Shetty says. Budnar was the *magane* – the fief – of his family. Mostly, the tenants and workers were Billavas. Budnar was the *garudi* of Billavas of the area, while the *nema*[25] for Jumadi, a royal or chiefly *bhuta*, was separate. Now it is apparently held in the *garudi*. The *bandara*[26] of Jumadi is kept at Shambhu Shetty's own house.[27] 'All this land was ours,' he says. At that time, Udupi town was still very small, and the Shettys owned the land up to Kalsanka, which lies beyond the temple square. Around Udupi, Ambalpady, Katpady and Budnar (Chitpady) were all *bidus* or manors.[28] Later, when I remarked to Borkar that Shambhu Shetty had claimed that all the land 'around here' belonged to his family's *magane*, he was doubtful. 'What we have heard,' he said, 'is that all the land around here belonged to the *maths*.' We discussed how this could fit what Shambhu Shetty had said. We felt that if the Shettys owned land up to Kalsanka, it must be on the other side of the river, opposite to the *maths*. Borkar did not think it could be a case of 'double ownership', for example, that the Shettys were formally tenants of the *maths*.

Shambhu Shetty made several remarks on the economic transitions of this area. At that time, 'everybody' lived from agriculture. 'But in fact, this zone was not very good for crops. The soil here is not good,' he says, 'and irrigation facilities are also lacking. Coconut is the best crop here, but even that is not outstanding. So today, agriculture here is simply not profitable.' Only some fields here and there are left in their *magane*. Labour costs have contributed to make cultivation unprofitable. So the Shetty family now get their income from other sources – he himself has been working in Mumbai. But we understand that the diminishing importance of agriculture made the land reforms rather less controversial here. This was borne out, we feel, by the atmosphere at the *bhutakolla* at Budnar in 2003. There was no obvious animosity between Billavas and Bunts. The *jajmans* seem to take a serious but good-humoured interest in the proceedings, and to know well most of the people present. The only area where we felt some animosity between high and low castes was in the attitude of the Parava[29] dancers.

The crowd was not big, and must have represented only a small proportion of the Billavas – let alone other castes – in the area. The ceremony seemed to be done for and by the participants for their own pleasure in maintaining tradition, rather than to attract a following or stage a show.[30] Yet the decorations of the 'altar', of the *garudi*, and the duration of the dance indicate that considerable money is being spent. The woodwork had in fact been done by our landlord, Acharya, a well-known artisan who specializes in elaborately carved doors and pillars. As far as I could see, no GSB were present at this *kolla*.[31]

Basically then Udupi and its surrounding lands were dominated by the Madhava *maths* till the second half of the nineteenth century. Their lands bounded on the various surrounding *magane* of the Bunt chiefs. There was no town yet.

It was an administrative decision by the colonial power which gave the impetus for change. When the British took South Kanara from Tipu Sultan in 1800, they established the district administration at Kallianpur, then far more important than Udupi. Kallianpur was a port then, in a system of meandering river branches and backwaters that harboured several other ports. Ammunje, Tonse and Airody, villages from which hail some of the most important GSB families in Udupi, are all situated here, and Kallianpur's old Venkatarama temple is emblematic of the existence of a GSB community. Kallianpur was and is above all, however, a Catholic village, and it is said that the British were not too happy about the close association of their administrative centre with the Catholic minority. Thus, when the Basel missionaries came to Udupi, the British administration and court followed. Due to resistance from the *maths* and the Shivalli Brahmins, the missionaries had settled on the stony high ground to the west of the pilgrimage centre, about 1 km away, on lands which – probably since they were barren – were not part of the temple estate. The British then established the court and administrative centre in the same area, though a little closer to the temples.

The influx of GSB merchants[32] in the 1890s followed the establishment of the court. There seems to have been a major relocation of business from several villages to this new centre at the time. In general, the years from 1870 to 1913 saw considerable growth in the Indian economy. This was mainly in the textile industries – cotton in the west, jute in the east – but in general, these were years of expansion for Indian capital after the 'de-industrialization' of the early colonial period (Tomlinson, 1993: 137-43). Certainly, the view from Udupi indicates market growth at the local level, and the GSB community was the dynamo of this growth.

It is useful to note some particularities of the Indian economy in colonial times. 'In the difficult and disturbed conditions that were endemic in colonial India,' says Tomlinson, 'it is hardly surprising that business behaviour was dominated by considerations of risk, uncertainty and imperfect knowledge.' This led to a division of labour: British firms were well connected to important export markets, while Indian firms knew the hinterland better (ibid.: 146). Exceptions were old and substantial Indian firms like the Tatas, who built an export network in China for opium in the nineteenth century. From 1873 to the 1890s the value of the rupee fell, which made British firms wary of investing in India, and when the exchange rate stabilized after 1900,[33] 'the forces of foreign and indigenous capitalism were too weak to break the hold of small-scale producers and petty traders on the supply of agricultural goods' (ibid.). 'The colonial firms,' says Tomlinson, 'were strong enough to prevent local entrepreneurs creating autonomous marketing networks from the bottom up, but were too weak to impose their own from the top down' (ibid.). This situation offered some room for the small-scale entrepreneur, as the GSB families of Udupi were on an all-Indian scale.

Around Udupi, there were already some other villages – there seems to have been one around the Kadiyali temple, for example, which is now a south-eastern suburb of the town, close to the Udupi-Manipal road. This was then part of the main road from Kallianpur and places north, passing close to Udupi, and continuing by the hills where Manipal was to be built, south-east to Karkala, before turning south-west towards Mudabidri and Mangalore. There was no road then along the coast, where the wide rivers had to be crossed by ferries.

The main roads of the area followed the dry ridges, intersecting the rivers inland, where they were narrow and could be bridged.

There were not many bridges, however. But one was at Kalsanka, where the main road intersected with the branch going to the pilgrimage centre at Udupi. Kalsanka literally means stone bridge, but my informants say it was still wooden, so one wonders whether the name itself is more recent. It was at Kalsanka that the first of the new GSB families established themselves when they moved from the Kallianpur area to Udupi. It must have been a strategic location. Among the first GSB settlers here were the Ammunje Nayaks and the family which became known as the Kalsanka Pais. The Kalsanka settlement stretches north along Gudialbail Road, which leads to Kallianpur, and was to expand southwards along Badagupete – Car Street – towards the temple square.

The leading family among the early GSB in Kalsanka were the Ammunje Nayaks. They were, for a long time, the largest and most important GSB business family in Udupi. They came from the village Mukde (Mukte) north of Kallianpur, on the north bank of the Suvarna River, about 10 km from Udupi. But they take their name from Ammunje, another village in the same area, on the north side of the Kallianpur bridge.[34] Ammunje, a peaceful village today, was then a trade centre. Barkur was then the main port of the whole area. One member of the family explained how the rivers and backwaters around Kallianpur formed a centre of trade in the days of country craft, sheltering numerous little harbours – of which Hangarkatta was the most important. There were places of transit from ship to shore. The Ammunje Nayaks were then in the rice trade, exporting to Goa and other places, and K.R. Kuduva feels that this is one family which may have been active in this export trade since early Portuguese times.[35] One family member says he does not know when they came to Ammunje, but he never heard about any other place of settlement since they came from Goa: he feels they settled at Ammunje when arriving from Goa. Thus, among all the Udupi GSB families, the Ammunje Nayaks seem to have the longest and most continuous history as traders in South Kanara, and this certainly corresponds with the image others have of them.

Trivikram Nayak's grandfather came to Kalsanka in 1889. Thus their present business goes back more than a hundred years. Trivikram's was then the main concern exporting rice and other grains from the Udupi area. He bought a lot of land and the family seems to have owned most of the property at Kalsanka. Their business was known as A.G.S. Nayak and Sons, still the name of the original shop located on the north side of Kalsanka bridge. The family stayed united – and powerful – till the death of Trivikram Nayak in 1975. Then they divided, but taken together they are still one of the most important families in the town.

As their name indicates, the Kalsanka Pai family, too, first established themselves at Kalsanka. Their ancestral house is on the eastern side of the road, towards Kadiyali. This house is owned by K.K. Pai, the present head of the family who also used to have his office at the Kalsanka crossroads: the office entry was from the Gundibail road-side. Possibly the property still belongs to K.K. Pai.[36] The shop of the Kalsanka Pais was at the north-western corner of Car Street, facing the bridge. This shop was sold by K.K.'s father to the Ammunje Nayaks, and now houses a wholesale grain shop of a member of that family. The sale took place before 1937, and the Pai shop then moved to the temple square, where it is still located.

Another branch of the Kalsanka Pai family is strongly established in the cloth business, especially silk. They use the name Kalsankar, and their most important sub-branch owns two of the biggest cloth shops on Car Street, and three others towards the newer parts of the town. There are two other sub-branches, all in the cloth trade, with two and one shop each. The branches are seen as one family, though they do not constitute a single 'family firm'; the Kalsanka Pais and the Kalsankars are also separate in this respect. Taken together, however, they form one of the most powerful business families in Udupi.

There were other GSB communities established at around the same time: one was at Kadpet, then outside Udupi proper. Kadpet is behind and to the west of the Court Road area. It may well be, as was the case for the Basel Mission, that this place was chosen since it was outside the *math* property, so that the GSB families could become outright owners of their house plots. Even now, this is a residential quarter sheltered from the main thoroughfares of the town. The Catholic church and compound lies just east of it.

One immigrant who built his house at Kadpet was Sheshagiri, the founder of the Kadpet Nayak family. They were then known as the Gujjadi Nayaks, from the village Gujjadi near Gangoli in Kundapur district. Gujjadi is a small fishing harbour today, but was of some importance as a port then. They settled there when they arrived from Goa, at a time they are not able to specify. Since Sheshagiri settled in Kadpet, the family has been known as the Kadpet Nayaks. Their shop in VT Street, established in the 1880s, sold provisions, but the family was also lending money against security in gold. Sheshagiri's two sons, Sabbana and Narasimha, were also residing there in the 1890s. Narasimha was the father of Vasudev, the founder of Ideal Studios, which we shall discuss later. Sabbana had three daughters, so the line was continued by Narasimha's three sons. Another branch of the family, also present in Udupi, is still known as the Gujjadi Nayaks.

The Kadpet Shenoys also settled in Kadpet at about the same time and opened an Ayurvedic shop on VT Street using the name Shanbag.[37] The founder of the shop, the great-grandfather of my informant, came from Karkala, and one sister is still living there. They were not among the families involved in Karkala's cashewnut trade, however – which tends to indicate that they were not among the 'big' Konkani families of the town. In Udupi, their Ayurvedic concern is well established and widely known. They also have a couple of other shops on VT Street.

On the axis from the courts to the Venkatarama temple, the British built Udupi's first post office, and the road is still known as Old Post Office Road. Near the Venkatarama temple the Old Post Office Road joins what had then become the main axis of what the British must have seen as the 'native bazaar'. This consists of Car Street (Badagupete), almost entirely settled by the GSB and where many of their shops are still located, which runs straight from Kalsanka bridge to the temple square. Straight on from there, again almost entirely settled and built by the GSB, the VT Street (Tenkapete) runs south to the temple in question, and on towards the PP College. Between Car Street and VT Street is the temple square, where the Krishna temple and the eight Madhava *maths* surround the Chandramauleshwara and the Ananteshwara temples.

On the corner of temple square and VT Street, Kesho Kuduva, ancestor of the Udupi branch of the Kochikar Kuduvas, had established his general store in or before the 1850s, well before the influx of the GSB community. This is certainly the oldest extant GSB shop site in Udupi, but the shop was sold to the Gundu Nayaks in the 1920s, when Ramakrishna Gundu Nayak built the present, large building there.

Apart from this shop, the oldest GSB concern still active in the temple square is one shop of the Airody Pais, in the narrow lane separating the Ananteshwara from the Chandramauleshwara temple. Even before the Ammunje Nayaks, the Airodys established a shop at Kalsanka in the 1850s or 1860s. They moved to the temple square in the 1890s, however, and it is this shop that they now see as the original one.[38] Before the family came to Udupi, they lived at Airody or Sasan, just north of Kallianpur and quite close to Ammunje. But they came from a background very different from the Ammunje Nayaks. The Airody family has 'always' been dealing in hardware, but before they settled at Udupi, in 1895, they were itinerant traders, going from one village to another. They continued this itinerant trade for quite some time after establishing themselves at Udupi. The Airody Pais are remarkable for their family unity, making them today probably the strongest single family firm in town. They are still active in the temple square area, but have a number of shops elsewhere in central Udupi, covering a large variety of merchandise. All their shops carry the 'Airody' logo, making the corporate nature of the family enterprise more visible than is the case for most other family firms in town.

Specializing in metal images of gods and *bhutas*, made in the family's own workshop in Kalsanka, their 'original' shop is kept by the oldest son of Radhakrishna Pai. Opposite, in the same lane, is a large hardware shop, run by another of the brothers. This is said to have been their second shop. More recent is the hardware shop – differently stocked and arranged, with a much more modern appearance – situated at the south-western corner of the temple square. Here 'sits' the second brother. Next to it is a gold and jewellery shop, a recent development, owned by the present head of the family, Airody Ghanshyam Pai, but run on a day-to-day basis by his nephew Anant. This shop is a point of pride for the concern: clearly the expansion into gold was seen as a major step in terms of family prestige, as well as commercially. Two shops, in or near Car Street, deal in kitchen appliances and other modern hardware. The fourth son 'sits' in the shop in Car Street, which houses their 'museum' on the first floor. The cult objects found there are partly samples of their own production, and partly old objects collected by Airody Ramanath Pai, Radhakrishna's brother, who was a very religious man. A four-story complex in the more recent part of town, between Car Street and the bus stations, includes the only real supermarket in Udupi town. It is called 'Little Pai' – clearly an allusion to those other and 'bigger' Tonse Pais – and a large shop of cult objects, handicrafts and souvenirs.[39] This complex is run by the fifth son. Another modern building, called 'City Camp' – an allusion to the family's past as itinerant merchants – is mainly used for offices with the ground floor rented out to other merchants. Yet another building, the 'ARP Sadan' is also mostly used for offices, but the ground floor is occupied by another branch of the Airody Radhakrishna Pai hardware stores. Like the modern hardware shop on the temple square, the supermarket and the craft shop are run by the younger generation. While they have expanded along several lines, they still keep their old, traditional shops going. This is also true of their production of copper and brass ware. Though manufacture is on a small scale, it is still done at Kalsanka. They have donated many important objects not just to the temple of their *kuladevata* in Goa, but also to many of the local temples in and around Udupi.

The family still controls all of the Airody shops. They have gone into diversification, says Ghanshyam, the present head of the family, since the market is always developing. But they have followed a conscious strategy to maintain the old lines while developing new ones – a strategy which ensures resilience in case one of the new lines fail. Thus the gold shop was started in 1995, while the 'superstore' is even more recent. It is his nephews, Ghanshyam and Anant, who run these new branches. They still manage, says Ghanshyam, the head of the family, to employ all the family in their own concern. Two sons are currently studying for their degrees (B. Com.), but 'they will come back to the business'. The family, he says, will study further possibilities for expansion, but they do not want to expand beyond Udupi. 'If you do that, you tend to lose control', he says.

Ghanshyam tells me the Airodys are, in fact, from the same original family – 'same *gotra* and everything' – as the Tonse Pais of Manipal, of whom more later. They also come from the same area in Goa. They separated some two hundred years ago, around 1800. One branch went to Sasan, also called Airody, the other to Tonse – both villages near Kallianpur.

He gave me a booklet they produced in 1995, on the hundred years' jubilee of their establishment at the temple square, dealing with the history of the firm. He assures me they have everything necessary – from about 1940 onwards – to study its history. I quote this pamphlet extensively, since it provides not only an insight into the history and growth of the firm, but also shows the way the family wants to present itself to the public.[40]

After a brief presentation of Udupi, the brochure states:

> Our family is very prominent in Udupi – the famous pilgrimage centre – whenever you think of gods and deities, or matters connected with worship, such as household utensils, you will definitely remember the name Airody. Recently we have entered the field of Goldsmiths also, and we have a history of more than one hundred years.
>
> From Airody the family came and settled in Udupi in 1890. The late Airody Radhakrishna Pai's grandfather, Panduranga Subramaniam Pai, started his business at Kalsanka, Udupi. His son, the late Subbarna Pai, established this enterprise in 1893. He and his sons organized and assisted the bronze and brass industry, using artisans of Udupi and places nearby, making them manufacture icons and *puja* implements which they sold. They were also doing some business in such objects during the annual festivals at places like Gokarna, Shirali, Sirsi, Kumta, Sringeri and Banavasi, and along with this business they were supporting the home industries, too, with loans, etc.

We shall return to the Airodys and their brochure later. For the moment, let us take stock of the GSB community, as it existed in Udupi around 1900. By then, the Kochikar Kuduvas, the Ammunje Nayaks, the Kalsanka Pais, the Airody Pais, the Kadpet Shenoys and the Kadpet Nayaks were all active in business at Udupi. Of these families, only the Kochikar Kuduvas and the Airodys with their one shop at Kalsanka, had been present before 1889. All the others came during the great influx of 1889-1900, with the Venkatarama temple being established in 1896. Apart from the Kochikar Kuduvas, whose shop was sold,[41] all these early settlers are still important business families in Udupi, and there are no doubt others, less known today, who came at the same time.[42] This, then, was the period when the GSB established themselves as the dominant business community in Udupi, and their houses and shops effectively constituted the town centre and commercial quarter, the Kalsanka to VT Street axis, north and south of the temple square. This was also a period of cultural and economic expansion at Mangalore, with the foundation of the Canara High School and, later, the first GSB banks. It was the period when the GSB really started to take to education. From then onwards the history of the community is better known.

Another axis was established in Udupi around this time, not by the GSB but by the Chitrapur Saraswats.[43] Popularly called Saraswats, they were not merchants, but scribes and bureaucrats, and there was probably a small settlement of them in Udupi before the court came, serving the temple and *maths* in an administrative capacity. Their caste shrine, the Shankaranarayana temple, is certainly older than the Venkatarama temple of the GSB. The court must have attracted further immigration, however. Their area, along the road from Kalsanka to the port of Malpe, is known as Siribettu.

'The Saraswats dominated Siribettu: they owned all the land – and houses – from near Kalsanka up to beyond our house,' said U.A. Kamath, the GSB engineer responsible for building Manipal, who lives in an old house just north-west of the present bus station.

> It was the Saraswat street, which is why the temple is still there. Now there are only three or four families left in Udupi, but the temple is three to four hundred years old. The Saraswats were bureaucrats, scribes, but not generally businessmen. In the British period, they were definitely a cut above the GSB. It is said they had taken a vow not to touch business.

It is not clear why the Saraswats came to Udupi. If we go by the age of the Shankaranarayana temple, they must have come by the late seventeenth or early eighteenth century. If they were already scribes at the time, the only employment for them in Udupi would seem to have been the *maths*. With their lands to administer and with plenty of money to account for, the *maths* may in fact well have been an important employer of clerical and administrative staff. Today, most Chitrapur Saraswats are in Mumbai; very few are left in Udupi.[44]

They originally came from the Ratnagiri area, says the Ammunje Nayak who keeps the oil mill. This is interesting, since it contrasts with Conlon's conclusion (1977) that there was no difference between Saraswats and GSB before they split around 1700. The remark increases the distance to the Saraswat 'break-aways', underlining their difference from the GSB. It contrasts, too, with other remarks that there is no 'real difference' between the two castes, since they were once one. We may note that the Rajapur Saraswat Brahmins (RSB), too, who split from the common caste some time in the past, are distinguished by their geographical origin. Did the geographical marker precede or follow the split? Whatever the sequence, the marker points to a consciousness that different historical itineraries are responsible for the difference. This implicit reference to the vagaries of history may be seen, then, as another example of the historicity of GSB thought – and that of the other Saraswat Brahmin communities.

Nevertheless, the Saraswat settlement could hardly be seen as the germ of a town, in the sense that the GSB's establishment of the Car Street and VT Street axis clearly was. In the middle of this area, however, is an old Virashaiva *math*, founded some 350 years ago during the rule of the Ikkeri Nayaks but probably inactive by 1900. It has now become an art school. Its lands stretch down towards Kalsanka – clearly the old entrance to the *math* was from the Kalsanka side since the grand reception verandah turns that way and marks both the limits of the present town centre and, certainly, those of the *Ashtamaths*' lands in former times. At the southern end of town, another axis developed from the turn of the nineteenth and twentieth century onward. This road – now called the Old Post Office Road, led from the southern end of VT Street towards the courts. Here, as the name indicates, one of the main buildings was the old post office.

Around 1900, then, the budding town of Udupi was shaped like a broad U, the bottom line in the east consisting of Car Street and VT Street, with the *Ashtamath* and the Krishna temple in the centre (Fig. 5). The Old Post Office Road and Siribettu formed the legs of the U. Behind Car Street, on its eastern side, was the *agrahara* of the Shivalli Brahmins. The southern leg of the U was Old Post Office Road, leading to the courts and the Protestant Mission; the lower part of

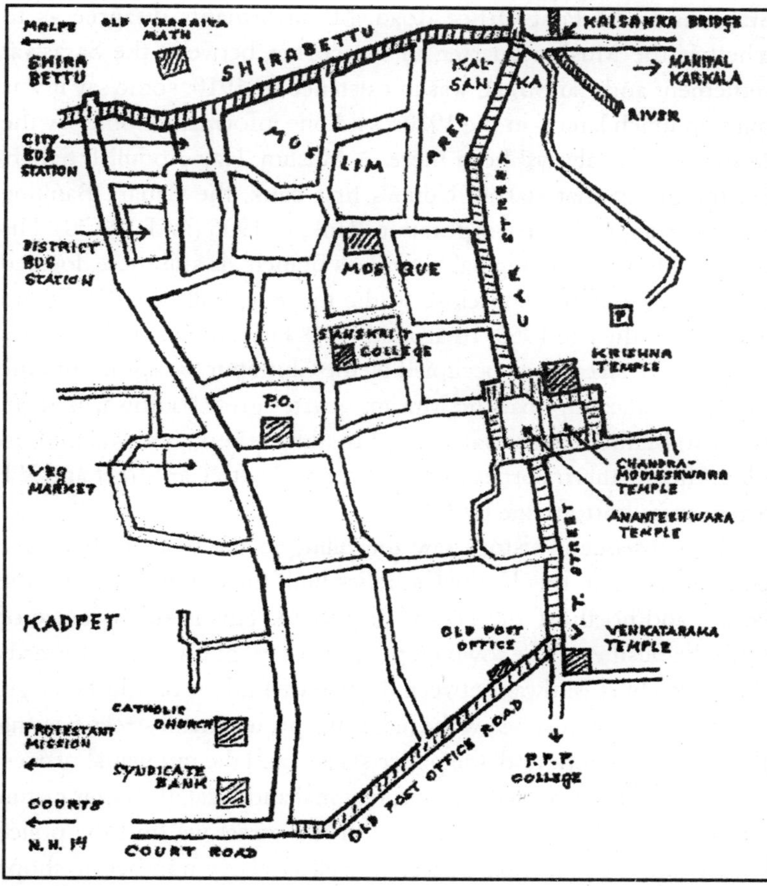

Fig. 5: Sketch map of Udupi. The three axes of the 'U' that formed the town centre around 1900, are stippled.

this road was also, judging from its architecture, built by the Konkanis. The northern leg was the settlement of the Chitrapur Saraswats. The town had about 15,000 inhabitants at the turn of the century (Kamath, 1983: 11). It must have grown very fast indeed in the preceding decades.

By 1910, Udupi had become a centre of commerce; 'it was here that farmers brought their produce and bought their bare necessities: kerosene, salt, soap, clothing' (Kamath, 1983: 19). The town consisted of the Saraswat quarter, Kalsanka, Car Street, the temple square, VT

Street and Old Post Office Road. My informants disagree as to whether the Muslim quarter, in the corner between the Saraswat settlement and Car Street, was in existence by 1910: some say it was built up much later – in the 1920s, said one informant. Some say the Muslims have 'always' been there. A Muslim, Haji Abdullah Saheb, led the group that started Udupi's first bank, the Canara Banking Corporation, now the Corporation Bank, in 1906 (ibid.: 19-20). His beautiful house, the original 'founder's branch', is still there, located in the bank's compound close to the mosque, built in 1936-7, and enlarged in the late 1960s or around 1970. Haji Abdullah's house lies between the street then occupied by the Chitrapur Saraswats and the mosque, indicating that the Muslim quarter grew southwards from the established Saraswat area. Muslims, then, had started to fill in the northern corner of the U formed with Car Street and VT Street as its bottom line by 1906.

The subsequent history saw the filling in the rest of the space contained within this U: the Catholics built their church east of the courts and north of the Post Office Road. This is still a centre of Catholic business. The town crept upwards from Car Street towards the barren hills. Midway between the two we find the Sanskrit college, started in 1934.[45] Just below the hills is the present main street, passing the Catholic compound, the police station and the municipal offices, to end up at the two bus stations, regional and local, the latter just in front of the old Virashaiva *math*. On this street we find the police station and the municipal offices, as well as a large number of shops and other commercial establishments. The vegetable market is also situated on this axis, while the fishmarket – an unclean occupation – is 'beyond the walls', to the south of the Old Post Office Road, and downhill from the courts. Mitra Hospital, at the top end of Old Post Office Road, is the hospital run by the *maths* which bears their insignia. The shop now occupying the Old Post Office building was started in 1959, so the post office must have been moved just before that time. This corresponds with the style of the New Post Office building, which is close to this new, upper axis. Basically, the northern half of the space within the old 'U' is now commercial; the southern half, south of the Sanskrit college, still has gardens and empty spaces, giving it a much more suburban look. Beyond Old Post Office Road, along Court Road and to the south-west, the town has expanded, so Court Road is also now a commercial area, though in no way comparable to the centre. Behind the barren hills, west of the town proper, the area – of which Kadpet is a central part – is largely residential. These are suburbs built, mainly for the GSB and the other high castes, in the twentieth century. Lower caste populations, like the Billavas, generally live north and south of these suburbs, on the fringes of the town. Some must have been present earlier, but I have not found any reminiscences of where their earlier living quarters were. Either, the high castes must have pushed the lower gradually outwards – which seems likely – or low-caste people tended even at that time to live some distance from the centre.

It will be clear from this description that Udupi, like most Indian towns, shows a relatively clear-cut pattern of location by communities. In the areas built up since the Second World War, this is less evident. As is so often the case in India, commercial buildings, often called 'complexes' – buildings housing several shops and offices – tend to be built and owned by members of a certain caste and most of the shops in it tend to be owned by its members. The name of the complex is often an indication of the community from which its owner comes. Thus we find complexes dominated by Muslims, by Bunts, by Catholics, but above all by the GSB. These four communities between them share most of the business in Udupi, with the GSB easily being the most important group. Still, renting locations in such a complex is a matter of business, so other communities than the owner's will be present. Such complexes dominate the modern centre.

As in most towns of South Kanara, there is nothing corresponding to the clearly defined *mohallas*[46] of north Indian towns. Yet again, some geographical differentiation by community is common to the Kanara towns also, and quite noticeable in Mangalore. As in Udupi, this pattern is generally more pronounced in the older parts of each town.

The pattern of Udupi's growth was heavily influenced by changes in the regional road system. Though still important, the road through Kalsanka, from Kallianpur to Karkala, is no longer the trunk road. The National Highway 17, which runs all the way from Mumbai to Kerala along the coast, is now the main thoroughfare, well to the west of the city centre. Some business – a hotel, a large petrol station, several capital-intensive shops such as car dealers and furnishers of sanitary equipment, are located here. In general, the highway has contributed to drawing the centre of town westwards.

The recent urbanization of Udupi makes the town very different from old towns like Karkala or Mudabidri, as well as from the older centres like Kallianpur and Mulki, which have now been 'ruralized'. The position of the GSB community is also very different in these places. In Karkala, the caste has a very strong position, dominating the cashewnut trade and thus being preeminent in the town's economy, in spite of the strong Jain element. In Mudabidri, where there is no such trade, the GSB have not displaced the Jain elite: Mudabidri remains very much a town dominated by the Jains. In Mulki, the GSB were clearly the dominant community at one time. But now most of the important GSB families have left Mulki, no longer a port or an important business centre. At best, the GSB families have kept their ancestral houses in the village, while their business interests and main sources of income are elsewhere – in Udupi, Mangalore, or farther afield. Much the same may be said of Kallianpur and its surrounding villages, yet the situation is somewhat different here, since in Tonse – a satellite village of Kallianpur – the GSB had and still have considerable landholdings, so that at least one member of the family is often present to look after the land. GSB commerce, however, is not a strong presence in Kallianpur, and most such enterprises are small. It is the Catholics, rather, who dominate Kallianpur's commerce.

Similar trends are visible elsewhere; the important GSB trading families have left the small ruralized centres, leaving the field to the local petty bourgeoisie – of which the Catholics represent one of the strongest components. Other businesses belong to castes that were not previously inclined to business, such as the landowning Bunts or even the low-caste, but numerically important, Moghaveera fishermen and Billava coconut farmers.

It was, we have seen, the British who gave the impetus to the growth of Udupi, the pilgrimage centre, into a town, by moving the district administration from Kallianpur in the 1870s. But this did not immediately promote the new administrative centre to a commercial one. It was in the 1890s that the centre began to expand, with the

GSB establishing their shops along the Car Street-VT Street axis. The plots along these streets, owned by the *maths*, were leased or rented by the GSB and gradually became their particular territory. It also became the nucleus of the town, growing up separately from the British administrative centre around the Court, the Catholic Church, and the Protestant Mission compound. Though some GSB built their houses on the high area behind the courts and the Christian centres, these became suburbs: what the British may well have called, then, the 'native bazaar', gradually became the city centre. In this sense, the GSB may well be seen as the group that 'made Udupi a town', and this is certainly how they themselves see it.

But we also see that in this early period Udupi retained some of the dispersed character of the Kallianpur cluster, structured by separate though adjacent territories having different groups as their nucleus. In Weber's terms, then (1958b), Udupi is a town of several origins: the temples and their institutions of pilgrimage, the ritual and administrative loci of Catholics and Protestants, and the GSB-dominated market. But it was the latter that came to grow in such a way as to integrate the various centres into a town.

NOTES

1. 'Eight monasteries'.
2. The name is derived from *Chandra* – moon. It is said that Udupi is cool because of this temple, relating the place to the coolness of the moon.
3. This and other numbers for inscriptions refers to the *Epigraphia Indica*, vol. 7: South Indian Inscriptions.
4. I.e. the two Shiva temples.
5. Shivallipura, the name then used and which gave its name to the Shivalli Brahmins, was a much bigger unit than Udupi, not simply a name for Udupi, explains Prabhu.
6. This would explain the present situation where most important temples in the area are served by Shivalli priests, whatever deity worshipped there. Important Madhava ascetics often preside over ceremonies, with no obvious link to Madhava religion at these temples. This dominance is now challenged by the Hegde of Dharmasthala, of whom more later.
7. Some land was returned 'to Krishna' by their new owners, the former tenants of the *maths*. It has not been possible here to form a concrete idea of the amount of land so returned.

8. The term Pariaya designates the period of leadership of a particular *Swami* in monastery history. See Rao, 2002.
9. It may also be a point made in Govinda Pai's 1945 article, which I have not been able to see.
10. The village *ashram* of one of the *maths.*
11. Apprentice.
12. M.M. Prabhu shows us an image of Skanda from Gururaja Bhat's book (1975), which is very similar to the Krishna image at Udupi. He has sent a photo of the *murti* of the Krishna temple to museums at Delhi, Kolkata and Ahmedabad. All agree that by its iconographic features, it is a Skanda. 'As for the Vadubandeshwara temple at Malpe, the port close to Udupi, the traditional *archakas* (officiating priests) at that Skanda temple, say that the image in the Krishna temple is Skanda.'
13. Schwarz was based at Tanjore in Haidar's time, and was very close to the Tanjore rulers. But he became a friend of Haidar, and his relations with Mysore made him a very useful diplomatic link between the British and that state (Peterson, 2003).
14. They are the Kadpet Shanbags mentioned below.
15. His own family descended from Kesho Kuduva, who had a hardware shop on the corner of VT Street and the temple square, the site now occupied by the shop of the Gundu Nayaks. Kesho's shop was certainly there more than 150 years ago, that is in the 1850s.
16. The latter were the first *archakas* (priests) of the Venkatarama temple, which was inaugurated in 1897.
17. Hartenstein, 1935: 82-3. The Basel Mission, theologically close to the Calvinist-inspired Protestants of Württemberg, established its first station in Mangalore in 1834. South Kanara remains their main field of activity, and theirs was the first 'modern' school in Udupi.
18. As Hartenstein comments (1935), 'today the school is suffering from the competition of the Brahmins' (ibid.: 86).
19. We were at the shop of his friend, at a corner opposite Sanskrit college.
20. The final and most important reforms were declared in 1973. In general, they were effective in the coastal area, which was not the case inland. There, landlords often barred their tenants from claiming their rights. It is not by chance that inland parts of Udupi and Karkala districts have now become a base of Naxalite operations.
21. Where we stayed close to his own house.
22. When Devaraj Urs was the chief minister of Karnataka.
23. Budnar is the *bhutasthana* close to Chitpady, not far from the railway station. A *bhutakolla* is a ritual where dancers impersonate the *bhutas.* A *bhutasthana* is the shrine of a *bhuta.* Jumadi is one of the royal *bhutas,*

from whom the chief's domain is held in fief (Brückner, 1995). Most such chiefs are Bunts. Koti and Chennaya are the *bhutas* and cultural heros of the Billava caste. While their cult has often been controlled by the Bunt chiefs, there is today pressure from the Billavas to control this cult themselves (Carrin, *forthcoming*).

24. See above. *Garudi* is a term specific to the *bhutasthanas* of the Koti-Chennaya cult.
25. A *nema* is the ritual of a royal *bhuta*, more elaborate than an ordinary *bhutakolla*. Establishing and manifesting the chief's position, it is a highly political affair even today (Carrin and Tambs-Lyche, 2003).
26. The *bhuta's* paraphernalia, of which the mask is the most important single item. Housing the *bandara* implies patronage – being the *jajman* – of the cult.
27. At Indrali temple road.
28. Budnar is not on the coast, and might have been outside the domain of the *maths*. But Ambalpady and Kuthpady are in the very areas said to belong to the *maths*. Hence the contradiction discussed in the following paragraphs.
29. Paravas are one of the untouchable communities which specialize in impersonating the *bhutas*.
30. Sometimes, such ritual is staged in a way where ostentation and a political message are evident.
31. The non-participation of Konkanis in the *bhuta* cults will be discussed later.
32. And probably others, like the Pandya family of Gujarati Shrimali Brahmins. The importance of administrative posts for the Chitrapur Saraswats (Conlon, 1977) indicates that many of them too must have followed the court at this time.
33. With the establishment of a *de facto* gold standard.
34. There is a big chariot at the Ammunje temple, one of the sights of the area.
35. P.R. Kuduva feels that the Ammunje Nayaks must have been in the rice export business for 'at least some 300 years', which takes us back to around 1700.
36. This, says one informant, is one reason why the municipality has not been able to widen the road, which takes all the traffic from Udupi to Manipal and which is extremely congested. K.K. does not want to have his ancestral property pulled down, and he has a lot of influence in Udupi. The same informant says K.K. has asked others to give land for the road, but 'he himself will not give'. The plans to widen this road have all come to naught.

37. Shanbag is simply an alternative and more archaic form of the name Shenoy.
38. One brother told me they had records of their business dating back to the 1850s or 1860s. At that time the shop was on Car Street close to the Kalsanka end. He thinks the move to the temple square was made in the 1890s. The first shop there was the one selling religious figurines. The other shop, where I talked to him, was added, he thinks, around 1940, when his uncle, Airody Radhakrishna Pai, headed the firm. The uncle's picture is found, for example, behind the counter of the gold shop. Radhakrishna had no issue, but was one of six brothers. In the present older generation they were again six brothers, all nephews of Radhakrishna.
39. These two branches are led by Airody Sudishyam Pai, younger brother of Ghanshyam Pai.
40. The translation that follows is by our friend and helper, Krishna Bhatt.
41. Kesho Kuduva's firm disappeared, but his relatives are still present in Udupi.
42. Conlon (1977: 171) refers to reduced profitability of landed estates from the revenue reforms of 1902. This is too late to explain the GSB influx to Udupi in the 1890s, but there may of course be a link to later migration.
43. A caste which had separated from them – or vice versa, according to whose point of view one adopts – in the eighteenth century. The actual circumstances of the division are complicated, says Conlon, and he refers to three different stories (Conlon, 1977: 37-9).
44. A 1971 census showed that more than half of the 21,000 Saraswats lived in Mumbai (Chitrapur Saraswat, 1971 Census: 6).
45. It is not entirely clear when the building itself was built, but judging from its style it is likely to have been built in the 1930s. It is possible that the building was in fact ready for the opening of the college.
46. *Mohallas* are the quarters of a town, the term widely used in parts of north India. It seems to be associated with areas ruled by the Mughals. Elsewhere, other terms are used, as in Bhavnagar, where such areas are called *wad*. These areas tend to be populated (at least originally) by a single caste or by a cluster of closely related castes. Unlike the *pols* of Ahmedabad, the *mohallas* are not walled in, and do not ususally have a gate. Houses in the *mohallas* tend to be 'back-to-back', not opening towards a closed yard as the Ahmedabad *pols*.

4

Udupi Grows: From 1910 to 1947

Though Udupi had clearly become a town by 1910, it was still a small place. But from 1910 to 1947, Udupi and its GSB community grew quickly. New families arrived from the countryside to establish businesses in Udupi. Some agricultural land was left or sold, but in other cases, one branch of the family stayed behind on the land. This development seems to be quite parallel to what happened among Christians in the same period.[1]

Meanwhile, the established families branched out into new fields of trade. Some of this expansion followed a demographic logic, to find room in the family business for several sons. The Airodys divided their forces between their shop in Udupi and their itinerant trade, an intrinsically elastic type of activity, and this may have helped them build a family tradition of unity. Others, like the Ammunje Nayaks, expanded by opening new shops. In some cases, like the Kalsanka Pais, this expansion led to division, with new family branches being formed. Others again invested in education: during this period, in Udupi and elsewhere, the GSB entered the professions on quite a large scale. A special but significant case is Ideal Studios, the photographic studio started in 1925 by Kadpet Vasudev Nayak – a nice case of entering education to open up an entirely new line of business. Similarly, V.S. Kuduva started a spring factory in Mangalore and took to running buses, profiting from the introduction of motor transport as an opening for business in these years.

It seems that the business scene became more dynamic from the second half of the 1930s, as one would perhaps expect from developments in the Indian as well as the world economy. Rothermund notes the opposition, in the 1930s, between stagnating agrarian prices and agricultural credit on the one hand, and investment and consumption by the urban and rural middle classes on the other. Rice and oil mills proliferated, as did investment in local transport: these investments 'were certainly not backed by a few large entrepreneurs, but by a host of small ones', comments Rothermund (1993: 113). In textiles, power looms and similar equipment for the small-scale sector were imported, rather than machines for the big mills. Even the import of alcoholic beverages increased strongly (ibid.: 114), not necessarily relevant for the GSB but certainly indicative of an expanding consumer market among the middle classes, which must have benefited small-scale entrepreneurs in country towns like Udupi. This was the period when Udupi town climbed the slope from Car Street towards the present centre and the bus stations. Several shops were opened, moved or expanded.

Ideal Studios is the oldest photographic studio in Udupi, built before anybody had opened such a studio in Mangalore, and, say the present members of the family, it was the first building in South Kanara to be expressly planned and built as a photographic studio. It has a glass roof, and one wall covered with matt glass, to give perfect lighting conditions in the days before modern studio lighting. Kadpet Vasudev Nayak opened his studio in 1925. His successors still keep an extensive collection of his photos of old Udupi, mainly dating from the 1940s and 1950s, though some are older. Vasudev was a real artist, says his son. On the centenary of Vasudev's birth, he and his son went to the temple of their *kuladevata* in Goa to celebrate the occasion.

The Studio was built as an extension of the family shop in Tenkapete (VT Street), which is about one hundred and twenty years old – built, then, in the 1880s, which makes it one of the oldest GSB shops in Udupi. The shop sold provisions, but the family was also lending money against security in gold. The two sons of Sheshagiri, Sabbana and Narasimha, also lived there in the 1890s. Narasimha was the father of Vasudev, the founder of Ideal Studios; his brother Sabbana had three daughters only, so the line was continued by Narasimha's three sons. The studio is now run by one of the younger sons. He is eager to stress that the moneylending business was 'long ago' and 'long since ended'. One felt that the reference to moneylending past was a touchy matter. Both Sheshagiri and Narasimha were very pious men, he says.

The shop is run by the two sons, Gopalakrishna and Tharappa, of Vasudev's elder brother Thommappa. Thommappa built his own house in 1926, not far from the shop at Kadekoppal, still on V.T. Street but further from the temple square, close to where the P.P.C. Road branches off from V.T. Street.[2]

Among other families who expanded their interests in Udupi in this period were the Airody Pais, whose first shop in the temple square had been established in 1896. Here, I cite their own account from their brochure.

Subbanna Pai had five sons: Madanmohana, Ganesharaya *alias* Panduranga Pai, Ramdas Pai, Radhakrishna Pai and Ramanath Pai. Among them, the oldest, Manmohan, was very active in running the business along with his father. Afterwards, they started manufacturing brass cradle and padlock keys, kerosene stores, etc. They were very conscious about the quality of their products. Till the end, they were RSS activists.[3] The second son, Ghanshyam (b. 1907 in Udupi), started (selling) the 'photos' of the gods and eight *maths* of Udupi. They were made in Bombay and sold here. For that work he started the 'Phoenix framing works' and moreover, he brought bicycles, then a new fashion, on the market, as well as wooden churns, and some wooden vessels from skilled carpenters. (Thus) they were helping the home industry. (But then) Ghanshyam came to a sudden end.

Ramdas Pai (b. 1909) was himself a skilled worker. He used to manufacture icons from *panchaloha*,[4] and other articles of worship. Further, he was attracted to social work and patriotic service. He was active in the Congress, in Arya Samaj, etc. He took part in the fight for freedom, and was imprisoned. He participated in the Bhoodan movement,[5] the prohibition movement, and welfare work for Harijans. A man of immense courage, he was a strong pillar of the firm. He is mainly responsible for its growth in the handicrafts industry, and has contributed to family as well as social life.

. . . like the Rama-Lakshmana brothers, in 1930, when the father Subbanna Pai retired at 68, Radhakrisna and Ramanath – the 4th and 5th son respectively – entered the business. They were good businessmen, being very generous. Ramanath was a very inspiring force till the end; with the elder brother, he strived for the progress of the firm. That the firm has grown to the extent we see today, is mainly due to the efforts of Ramanath Pai.

Radhakrishna Pai was, in the beginning, selling the items for worship and the brass utensils. He was mainly working in the shop at Udupi. Manmohan, the elder brother, and Ramanath were mainly looking after the (itinerant) business at festivals. Within a short time Ramanath Pai obtained copper sheet and started manufacturing copper utensils. They were selling copper and brass vessels. They also bought and repaired old vessels. Old vessels were exchanged for new, and as time passed, they also brought in aluminium, german silver and steel utensils from Bombay, Calcutta and Madras. Bronze vessels they got from Kerala, selling retail and wholesale.

The Ammunje Nayaks, then probably the leading business family in Udupi, also expanded their activities in this period. What is now their oldest shop was established near Kalsanka bridge about seventy-eighty years ago – in the 1920s. It bears the name of the then family head, Ammunje Vittaldas Trivikram Nayak. The family had been in the grains business for centuries, but the new shop was a grocery and general merchant concern. The grains business is now opposite the shop, on land bought from the Kalsanka Pais around 1937, when that family moved into their present locale at the Temple Square. The Ammunje Nayaks started another shop in these buildings, but this was no longer active when the present owner took over. A third family shop at Kalsanka may also date from this period.

New families also came. Pannalal Govindjay Shenoy, a cloth shop in Car Street, was founded around 1913. This was apparently the first shop of this Shenoy family in Udupi, but they also own Gajanana Cloth Stores, one of the few remaining cloth shops in V.T. Street. It is relatively recent, in spite of its traditional appearance: it was founded in 1948. Elsewhere, the family has other shops, run by 'uncles, brothers, etc.'. Thus they have shops in Mangalore and Bangalore. They came from Katpadi, a village some 6 km from Udupi.

As I began looking for the old GSB firms of Udupi, the P.R.R. Nayak shop was my first stop. Looking very traditional in every way, it is located about midway down Car Street. 'I don't know', said the elder of the brothers who now run the shop, 'whether this is the oldest of the General Merchant shops of the Udupi Konkanis. I only know it is about eighty-five years old'. It was founded about the time of the First World War by Parempali Ramesh R. Nayak, the great-grandfather of the present generation – the elder brother may be in his forties. Before coming to Udupi, the family owned land in the village of Parempali, near Manipal. Now there is nobody left there – all have moved to Udupi. The shop has been in the same location ever since the First World War, and an observer may well feel that little has changed since. As in other traditional stores, much of the sales are in bulk: there is also packaged goods, but the big metal boxes and bins of grains, spices, oil, ghee and similar goods dominate the scene. Their *ishtadevata* is Ganesh or Vinayaka, and like the Katpadi Shenoys, they stress he can be propitiated in any temple. The Parempali Nayaks, however, particularly venerate the image they keep at their own house. Their *kuladevata* is Shanteri Kamakshi, whose temple is near Ponda, in Goa. They, 'do not really' go there, however. 'At Goa, the Portuguese destroyed everything. So our proper *gam*[6] is Parempali – our home place. That is the main point of identity. We are known as the Parempali Nayaks'.

Among the new arrivals these years, no family was to have a stronger impact on Udupi's development than the Tonse Pais, descending from Manja, a merchant at Tonse in the Kallianpur cluster, who moved to Brahmavara in the late nineteenth century as a result of 'some differences' with his father (Kamath 1983: 10-11), and of his son Ranga. Here, they had some 20 acres of good paddy land, then a sizeable holding. The joint family grew till the household had some fifty members, and the holding was kept undivided till 1926 (Menefee 1969/1984: 6-7). Tonse is still regarded as the family's ancestral home, and the descendants use it as the first part of their name (Kamath, 1983: 15). At that time, says Kamath, Brahmavara had about a thousand inhabitants.[7] Ranga's was a large two-storey house, with several out-buildings. He was a 'model agriculturalist' who 'set a stern discipline for himself and his regular labour force'. He was a religious man, observing all the rituals – like all GSB, as Kamath, himself a member of the caste, puts it (ibid.: 11-12). 'For a Brahmin family to have illiterate sons was unthinkable, but higher education was still beyond the means of most families . . . Ranga Pai was well off, but by no means rich' (ibid.: 13). He 'ran his family with an iron hand', says Menefee.

> All his seven sons – but not the three daughters – went through fourth standard of primary school so they could read and write. Only one got higher education, since the family's income was small: Mukunda Pai got his B.A. from Madras University, and became an advocate in Udupi. This was a great help to the next generation, for 'Mukunda's house in Udupi was open to his nephews'. (Menefee, 1969/1984: 7)

Of the seven sons, it was Ananth, the fourth, who became the ancestor of the Udupi branch of the Tonse Pais. He is said to have been a very religious boy, fond of listening to the priests and *sadhus* telling stories from the Puranas. At about 19, he was married to Yashoda, from the Baliga family of Kallianpur. Members of the Baliga family still live in their big family house, almost facing the Venkatarama temple. They must have been one of Kallianpur's leading families. Yashoda was 11 when married: this was when child marriage – at least of girls – was the general rule among Brahmins.[8] She, of course, stayed with her family until she reached puberty. Then the couple settled with Ranga's joint family in Brahmavara. Three sons, Purushottam (P.A.), Upendra (U.A.) and Madhava (T.M.A.) were born one after another, Madhava in 1898. A daughter, Marthi, followed after two or three miscarriages,[9] and in 1907, the youngest of the sons, Raghunath (T.R.A.) was born (ibid.: 7-8; Kamath, 1983: 14-15).

Yashoda often visited her father's house in Kallianpur, staying two or three months at each place, and her sons 'much preferred his mother's house because it was less crowded' (Menefee, 1969/1984: 8). Kallianpur is an old settlement of Konkani Christians, and one-fourth of its population is Christian. Madhava joined the Catholic primary school. But 'the Hindu parents objected when their children were required to kneel and join in praying to the Christian God, and withdrew all their children from the school' (ibid.: 8). Next year a Hindu school was started. These were the years – the turn of the century and just after – when Hindus, in practice mainly the GSB, took to education in a big way, duplicating the Christian schools which had for some time held a monopoly.

Ranga Pai died around 1905. He left a building and some property to six of his sons, but nothing was left for Ananth. He took care of the common property, but died of pneumonia in 1907, only 39 years old. Yashoda moved to her father's house in Kallianpur, and the children went to school there (ibid.: 9-10; Kamath, 1983: 16-17). To live with the maternal grandfather was not easy, but Yashoda was a strong woman. 'She was in her twenties when her husband died.[10] She was still in her early thirties when the Baliga family fortune was gone and she was left to fend for herself' (Kamath, 1983: 17). We are not told what happened to the Baliga fortune.

After three years there was no money left, so around 1910 Purushottam, the eldest son, moved to Udupi and started a small shop, selling cutlery, stationery and books. The firm, P.A. Pai Brothers, was clearly intended to include the other boys. They lived with their father's brother Mukunda, in his house Mukund Nivas. Mukunda moved to Cochin in 1916, where he had been chosen as manager of an important temple, so his sister-in-law and her children took over the house (Menefee, 1969/1984: 10-11; Kamath, 1983: 19).

The 'brothers' of the firm really included only Purushottam, Upendra and Madhava, for Raghunath was still very young (Kamath, 1983: 19). Purushottam ran the shop and did not continue his schooling. Their shop, says Kamath, was

> where the town's *literati* would come to buy their copies of the weeklies – *Swadeshabhimani*, started in Mangalore in 1907, the *Kannada Kesari* from Manjeshwar, the monthly *Suvasini* from Mangalore, or even a few copies of Tilak's *Maratha*. They must have been reading the patriotic poetry of Panje Mangesh Rao. Purushottam came to identify himself with the budding nationalist movement, which had become more active since 1920, and published 'pamphlets on the Gandhian movement, a booklet of nationalist songs (in both Ḳannada and Hindi) and other nationalist publications'.
>
> (Kamath, 1983: 20)

But he died early, during Second World War.

Upendra, the second of the brothers, finished his middle school in Udupi. Then he went to Mangalore for his first year of high school, changed to Kumta, in North Kanara, for the second, and finished with a third year in Karwar. He spent his first pre-university year at Baroda, but then moved to Elphinstone College, Bombay. He did not go to university, but returned to Udupi in 1919, to help in the business (Menefẹe, 1969/1984: 11; Kamath, 1983: 22-3). Meanwhile, he had married a girl from the Mulki Kuduva family. On his return he became the secretary of the National School set up in 1920 for those who followed Gandhi's call to quit British-controlled schools and colleges. He set up Udupi's first *khadi*[11] shop and started wearing *khadi* himself. He was a follower of Ramakrishna, and often acted as host to visiting *swamis* of the Ramakrishna Mission.

It was the maternal grandfather, Krishnaraya Baliga, who predicted, from Madhava's horoscope, that he would become an educated man

(Menefee, ibid.: 9). Madhava finished his middle school in Udupi, and developed a strong interest in medicine.[12] He then went to Mangalore with a friend to get a seat in the Government College. But his friend was turned down since his record referred to his 'rebellious spirit', and so they went to the Catholic St. Aloysius College instead. Its principal, father Peraje, is said to have read the same record, saying: 'Here is a boy with spirit. Give him a five rupee scholarship!', which represented half the tuition costs. Madhava himself was the 100th boy registering that year, which earned him free tuition (ibid.: 14). He never regretted the choice, and his interest in medicine was further strengthened during his years at St. Aloysius.

> 'I was wonderstruck when I saw all these people leaving their homes and coming to such a far-off place to help us with their teaching and social work', said T.M.A., later, of his Italian Jesuit teachers. Six years of Christian education, says Menefee, himself a contributor to the Christian Science Monitor, 'were probably a factor in young Madhava's developing interest in social service and education'. (ibid.: 16)

One year before graduation, in 1919, Madhava learnt that the Hindu Higher Elementary School in Kallianpur, which he had attended, was closing for lack of funds. He got four 'old boys' of the school to join him in teaching there, acting as headmaster (he was 21) and even wrote texts in Kannada for the mathematics course, since there were no such books. He got timber cutters to donate logs and carpenters to make school furniture for free, but the school was still short of cash. He went on a fund-raising spree, but 'money was tight that year and the highest individual donations were only 25 rupees' (ibid.: 16). Yet with his friends he got enough money together to stave off an auction of school property. Still, they needed some Rs. 5,000 to put the school's economy on a sound base. Through a Gujarati businessman in Hangarkatta he was tipped about possible donors in Bombay. Here, he got aid from a Muslim businessman, Omar Sobani, and returned with more than Rs. 4,000, enough to save the school (ibid.: 17-19). Kallianpur's Hindu school is still active, situated just across the road from its older, Catholic counterpart, where Madhava had spent his first year at school.

In 1920, Madhava was admitted to study Medicine at Madras University. Next year he was married to Kamakshi Shenoy of

Mavinkurve, near Honavara, the daughter of a retired sub-registrar. As is usually the case, his mother's family, the Baligas of Kallianpur, had taken the responsibility for finding him a bride. She was 13, and illiterate, but Madhava later taught her to read and write. There was a dowry problem,[13] but the wedding went ahead, and they seem to have been a very close couple. Sharada – the name given to Kamakshi after the wedding[14] – stayed with her parents while he continued his studies, though he took her to his family in Udupi in June every year. As he returned to college, she would stay with his mother three months, then return home. When Madhava graduated in 1925, she was 17, and they could start living together (ibid.: 21-7).

Encouraged by one of his professors. Madhava wanted to work in Hong Kong, but his mother was against it. 'You must stay with us', she said. 'You must serve your own country: you must serve your kith and kin. You have been away for years. I am growing old now. I must see your greatness with my own eyes'. He stayed. (ibid.: 29).

Raghunath, the youngest brother, had just started high school in 1920 when Gandhi called for students to strike against British-run schools. He was then at the Christian High School in Udupi, run by the Protestant Basel Mission. He left the school, but attended a 'National College' set up by the independence movement and passed his exams for entry to college. Then he, too, joined the business (ibid.: 11-12).

The family house in Udupi was Mukund Nivas, Upendra's house, on the plot now occupied by the 'Syndicate Towers', the main town offices of the Syndicate Bank. This is outside the old town, quite close to the Catholic compound, and not far from the Court buildings, which lie beyond. Upendra was, as we have seen, an advocate.

Historians of banking in the South Kanara area stress the absence, for the region, of the traditional banking facilities we find in Gujarat and Rajasthan. The Gujarati bankers greatly impressed the Portuguese and later European merchants: the long-distance transfer of funds by letters of credit (*hundi*), for example, seems to have developed much farther, by the sixteenth and seventeenth century, than in Europe. The role of Gujarati and Marwari bankers remained essential for the East India Company till the end of its rule (1858), and some of these banking families later developed into modern business houses.

The GSB did not form part of this indigenous banking system. They were moneylenders, but their financial activity was generally of a local or regional character. Still, we must assume it was they of who financed the agricultural expansion of the sixteenth century, and by the late nineteenth century their financial role was important in South Kanara. They shared this role with the goldsmiths: loans were often given against security in gold jewellery. Still, at the turn of the century the Bank of Madras,[15] more or less a government undertaking, shared with a couple of British-led commercial firms most of the modern banking of the area.

The first two indigenous banks of South Kanara were started in 1906. One, later to become the Corporation Bank, was started by Haji Abdullah, an Udupi Muslim, and his associates. It grew slowly, however. By 1926 the founder was in difficulty and was bought out by his GSB co-directors. The other, created by a Mangalore GSB, grew into the Bank of Canara, today a major bank and the 14th in India in terms of its deposits when nationalized in 1969. Largest of the banks founded in the area, however, is the Syndicate Bank, founded in Udupi in 1925, which was the seventh Indian bank by size at nationalization. This was the bank the Tonse Pais founded.

Kamath, in explaining the early emergence of banking in South Kanara, stresses the compact and distinct character of the area. Social tensions, he says, were 'at a minimum', and literacy was high. The district 'had a large middle class aware of the needs to save for a rainy day'. Mangalore was linked to the South Indian Railway by 1907, and by the 1930s many villages had been linked with roads.

> Kanara always had a flourishing business community; in the past coastal trade had been carried through *machwes* – country craft that plied between Mangalore and Bombay and Arab ships frequently docked in Mangalore harbour. In 1887 a direct Bombay-Mangalore passenger ship service had been opened giving an additional fillip to trade and commerce. For the smooth functioning it was necessary that adequate banking facilities be available....
> (Kamath, 1983: 73-4)

The GSB were to dominate this new sector. Till after the Second World War, all directors and members of the managing committee of the Bank of Canara came from their community. The GSB took over the Corporation Bank, and dominated the Syndicate Bank, though it had some officials from other communities. The Bunts later founded their own Vijaya Bank, which has grown to an important stature, while the first Billava effort, the Pie-Money Bank, remained small till it was absorbed by the Syndicate Bank. The Catholic Co-operative Bank remains a minor and regional institution. Another local bank, remaining a small-town concern till absorbed by the Syndicate Bank, was led by, and mainly catered to, non-Konkani Brahmins.

The banking history of the area, then, is typical of a pattern also found in Bombay, where each bank was founded by one of the trading communities of the city.[16]

The committees of the Venkatarama temples provided an important infrastructure for the expansion of the GSB banks. Kinship, as well as established business connections within the caste, were also crucial. This structure is repeated in education. The founder of the Bank of Canara also founded Canara College at Mangalore, and several schools. Upendra Pai started the Syndicate Bank, while his brother Madhava built a whole empire of hospitals and colleges, now the 'deemed university' at Manipal near Udupi, known for its excellence in medical and engineering studies. No wonder the GSB see themselves as the main promoters of 'modernity' in South Kanara. They played a major role in creating educational institutions, and are – with reason – proud of the level of education of the caste.

What was to become the Syndicate Bank had a small beginning. U.A. wanted to provide finance to weavers and farmers, and in 1925 registered the Canara Industrial and Banking Syndicate. The stated purpose of the Syndicate was 'to help cottage industries such as weaving and spinning by supplying yarn and cotton at moderate price' (Menefee, 1969/1984: 47). Upendra wanted to introduce banking to a new kind of customer, who had never had the money to think about dealing with traditional banks. The bank was incorporated with a capital of Rs. 100,000 in hundred-rupee shares, of which Rs. 20 were 'called' for initial payment. T.M.A. came in to help him. P.A. Pai Brothers was the managing agency. U.A. and T.M.A. were two of the three directors, with T.M.A. – informally – as managing director and, from 1927, chairman of the board (ibid.: 46). T.R.A. also joined the bank, managing its Udupi head office, then left to head the insurance company the brothers started.

'Three men started (the Syndicate Bank)' says Kamath, 'and two men pushed it forward to greater heights' (1983: 63). The third founder was V.S. Kudva. He was 26, a nationalist and a 'freedom fighter'. He founded a number of concerns, and later left the bank to look after his own enterprises[17] (ibid.: 63-4).

But, says Kamath, 'the three of them could not have chosen a worse time to start a bank. The district had, by then, a food deficit and after the rains, floods were a problem. Menefee also stresses how these were hard times to start a bank. Yet in reality, the second half of the 1920s saw quite a rush to start banks – most of them small and local – all over South Kanara. As noted, the Corporation and the Canara banks had been started in 1906. In 1924 the Karnataka Bank was founded in Mangalore. Competition was hard, and Udupi was a poor town. The Syndicate shares found few takers: T.M.A. promised investors that he would buy back any stock whenever they might want to sell, guaranteeing to pay the price they had paid. Yet it was 1930 before the initial shares were sold. None of the founders had any experience in banking. And then, the purpose of the bank was to help the weavers: banks, in principle, were there to make money (Menefee, 1969/1984: 47, Kamath, 1983: 64-5).

The bank's first office was a single room adjoining the P.A. Pai shop. There was only one employee. K.K. Pai, later chairman of the bank, has said that 'Krupp Steel might have been built on slave labour, but the Syndicate Bank was built on voluntary sacrifices'. Employees were told to be frugal – 'a wholly unnecessary piece of advice considering how poorly the early staffers were paid', says Kamath (1983: 67).

They dealt in chit funds,[18] opening 'prize chit fund' accounts for groups, and taking a small percentage for managing the fund. In 1939, lotteries were banned and this included chit funds, so the practice had to stop. Chit funds are still popular in India, however, in spite of formal legislation.

'Although not a 'joint family' in the legal sense' says Menefee of the brothers, 'they behaved like one. They worked as a team on all matters of business and civic enterprise. The family solidarity was responsible for the success of many of their projects'.[19] They discussed the bank's policies and problems daily.

'It is hard to say where some of the ideas we used originated', said T.M.A.

later. They looked to me to make business decisions, but it was always on the basis of a family consensus. We seldom raised our voices on any issue, and if we did, my mother would come into the room and say my eldest brother's desires had to be respected.

T.M.A.'s love of maths came in handy for banking: 'he could look at a set of figures and estimate the potential in compound interest'. Menefee cites a number of examples of how the brothers helped each other – as if they were really a joint family. P.A. Pai helped Madhava with money for his studies and to set up his medical practice and nursing home when he graduated. The brothers several times had to find money to save the Mukund Nivas from foreclosure. Here, the Syndicate Bank built its headquarters in 1950, which still serve as their main city branch (Menefee, 1969/1984: 36-38, 47-8).

P.A. Pai Brothers was selling yarn and dyes to the handloom weavers and marketing their produce. The material was sold on credit and paid for in finished goods, which could well make the weaver dependent on the merchant. This, of course, was the traditional moneylenders' role in manufacture; a role not always popular. But Purushottam, says Kamath, 'came to be known as the friend of handloom weavers' (Kamath, 1983: 21).[20]

The bank was unusual in making loans without any security, when the lender's character and reputation was known. They dealt in very small loans, from five rupees onwards, so the bank became a real competitor to the local moneylender, in a way that more conventional banks were not. Indeed, the Syndicate Bank is said to be largely responsible for the demise of the traditional moneylender's role in South Kanara, undermining a main commercial base of many of the Pais' caste-fellows. In fact, the demise of the rural moneylender may have been due to other factors. Before 1929, says Tomlinson,

> the profits of agriculture had tended to remain in the rural economy. Some expansion of small-scale industry for processing agricultural produce had taken place, but, in general, the agrarian surplus was ploughed back into land-owning and rural moneylending. The decline in agricultural profits and the disruption of established capital markets and marketing networks during the depression provided an incentive to diversify investment. In particular, the liquidity crisis of 1929-30 pushed many rural bankers out of business. (1993: 138)

It must have been hard times, then, for the traditional rural moneylenders, and the Syndicate Bank may have expanded into a gap left open by their decline.

As for the traditional moneylender, small loans were profitable for the bank, since they carried a high interest: yet the 12.5 per cent the bank charged was much less than the traditional moneylender's rate. Upendra felt the large number of small loans spread risk. Also, you could help more people this way (Menefee, 1969/1984: 48). This combination of social involvement and a sound sense of profit is typical of the Tonse Pai enterprises, and makes it hard to criticize the bank: such criticism would go against the grain of a dominant idiom of discourse, since the moneylender has become 'the villain of the piece'. Few GSB identify, today, with this practice of their ancestors. 'That was very long ago', as the Kadpet Nayaks say, referring to this past aspect of their business.

The Syndicate was probably the first Indian bank, it is said, to go in for rural banking as a main line. Yet we must note the particular structure of South Kanara: branches were opened, not in agricultural villages, but rather in the small country boroughs that still formed local nodes of trade. The first branch was in Brahmavara, where a relative, T.V. Pai, was a director of the bank. Next was Kumta, where T.M.A.'s wife's brother lived; then Payyanur in North Kerala, where the link was the family of T.R.A.'s wife. Then followed Honavara, the hometown of T.M.A.'s wife Sharada,. 'We followed the line of least resistance', said T.M.A. later (ibid.: 48-9; Kamath, 1983: 68) – which seems to have been the kinship network. Later, the expansion in rural areas continued. It could have been very costly, but instead of appointing salaried managers, 'a prominent citizen of the village known and acceptable to the rural community as leader and who enjoyed their confidence was appointed as Rural Representative in charge of these branches', with limited powers of accepting deposits, making loans and advances, issuing drafts, collect bills, etc. They were paid a commission on the deposits. Such representatives, when not kin, often seem to have been members of the Venkatarama temple committees. The premises of such rural branches were kept as simple as possible (Kamath, 1983: 97).

'No man is too small for a bank account', was the bank's motto, and in 1928 they announced the 'Pigmy plan', one of T.M.A.'s ideas. 'Runners were hired to pick up deposits as small as two annas (an eighth of a rupee) daily. It was a time deposit scheme, repayable at the end of seven years with interest at $3^1/_8$ per cent.[21] By saving two annas a day a Pigmy depositor would have Rs. 350 at the end of seven years – a small fortune to a poor man then' (Menefee, 1969/1984: 49). That runners came after working hours to pick up deposits was an advantage to working people, and the plan was a great success. By 1967 there were over 120 million rupees deposited with the bank under the Pigmy plan (ibid.: 49).

The bank, like several others in the district, also accepted gold jewellery as security, thus tying in with the old practice of storing wealth in this form. In 1937-8 several Indian banks failed. But Madhava felt that with its base of small deposits, the Syndicate stood on firmer ground. It was, he said 'like a boat which requires only little depth to float on water unlike a steamer which requires greater depth' (Kamath, 1983: 71). He was right, and the profile of the bank – based on a very large number of small accounts – proved resilient: profits rose each year except 1934. By 1939 the bank was well established, with 35 branches spread over Madras, the Malabar Coast, Bombay and Hyderabad. That year the system of managing agents was banned by the government and the link with P.A. Pai brothers was severed, but T.M.A. became the managing director (Menefee, op. cit.: 50).

It may have been P.A.'s enthusiasm for Gandhi and the Independence movement which influenced him to start a weaver's cooperative. Sceptics might infer it was a question of capital: by transferring the lending business to a cooperative the weavers not only financed production themselves, but the founder's link with the cooperative might gain him a higher share of the trade than he would have been able to finance. Still, 'no one was doing anything' about the expanding cooperative movement in Udupi (ibid.: 31) and P.A.'s initiative was a pioneer effort locally. The Udupi Weavers' Cooperative Production and Sale Society started in 1939, and it may be no coincidence that this was when the management agency system was abolished. P.A. 'advanced money to about 100 members to pay for their memberships'. Menefee's account of what then happened is not entirely clear: P.A. was elected president of the cooperative society, and so 'the business the P.A. Pai Brothers firm had hitherto done with the weavers was cut-off; he could not, as president of the co-operative, buy from his firm in good conscience. Even so, when there was a slump in sales the firm continued to assist the weavers by taking over surplus stocks and sending a salesman out to dispose of them.' This seems clear, but the following blurs the image: 'Despite losing the weavers' trade, however, P.A. Pai Brothers did not suffer too much because the outbreak of war brought an increase in prices of yarn and cotton goods, and the firm had a large stock of both on hand' (ibid.: 31). How could they deal in such goods if the trade with the weavers was cut-off ?[22]

Neither Menefee nor Kamath mention another factor which may have helped the Syndicate grow. This was the growth of handloom manufacture. In the late nineteenth century this sector had receded under the onslaught of the cotton industry: from about half the domestic production around 1880 its share had receded to 31 per cent of the market by 1900. The share continued at about the same level till the mid-1930s, then fell to around a fifth of cotton cloth production. But if silk and rayon cloth is included, the share of handloom production actually increased, to 30 per cent by weight and 40 per cent by value (Tomlinson, 1993: 108-9). During the inter-war period, the Bombay mills lost market share to new industrial centres such as Coimbatore and Kanpur, but also to the handloom sector, spread out in many parts of the country. 'Many of these producers were diversifying into higher-value non-cotton textiles, especially silk and art-silk (rayon) products where powerlooms were beginning to be used quite widely, but even in purely cotton textiles handlooms had a market share of 24 per cent by volume in and 36.5 per cent by value in 1937-38', says Tomlinson (ibid.). The handloom weavers were 'actually the pioneers of import substitution', adds Rothermund. 'Whenever there was sufficient demand for cloth and a surplus of raw cotton, the handloom weavers increased their output very quickly and reduced it again when there was a glut in the market' (ibid.: 107). Thus the Syndicate, with its links to the handloom weavers, was in fact riding on the top of an advancing sector.

This advance seem to have accelerated during the war, when the production of the large mills was largely absorbed by the demand for uniforms and other war-related products.

I have not seen statistics for the handloom sector during the war, but production of yarn from the mills increased considerably more than that of cloth, and Rothermund concludes that 'there was a greater demand for industrial yarn from handloom weavers, who could step up their production more easily than the mills' (ibid.: 118).

P.A. Pai was active in the Congress, receiving freedom workers at his house, publishing pamphlets including a history of the Congress movement, and active in the 'Quit India' movement which he talked about even as he died, in 1942. This engagement was not unanimously shared among the brothers. Upendra was enthusiastic, but less active than Purushottam, and Madhava, alarmed at the 'extremism' of the independence movement during the war 'felt the family should stay out of politics'. These differences, however, never affected the solidarity of the brothers in business and 'civic affairs' (Menefee, 1969/ 1984: 31).

Upendra always had a building project going. He was an art enthusiast, and built Udupi's first theatre, the Ramakrishna close to the Mukund Nivas, in 1932. He leased it to travelling theatre groups, then changed to films, but both rarely paid their rent so he became his own theatre manager. To promote the venture he offered free tickets to deserving students, as a reward for high grades, to make the youth theatre conscious, then extended the system to workers in local industries. He started a local film monthly, the *Chitrakala*, which soon became popular. After some time, he printed a coupon in each issue, where people could declare their inability to buy a ticket: the coupon duly filled bought a ticket at the reduced price of ten paise. Attendance and box receipts rose. For another five years, however, the theatre lost money, but by 1940, it was in the black. In 1941, it became a limited company, and the issue of shares at ten rupees each was a great success. By 1962, a second theatre was needed, so the Alpana was built and the Ramakrishna changed its name to Alankar (ibid.: 33-5). Still, when U.A. died in 1956 he left little money. He did, however, leave property in Manipal to a foundation he had created, the Gram Seva Pratishthan.

T.M.A. became a successful doctor in Udupi, and his nursing home, too, was an immediate success. It is said that his treatment saved the life of Roque Fernandes, father of Oscar Fernandes the M.P., when he was down with dysentery. Dr. Pai was also known for his efforts at vaccination against smallpox, cholera and typhoid: he would tour the villages to do the injections, always trying to convince the headman first of their utility. He performed simpler operations, but more complicated cases were referred to Dr. A.V. Baliga of Bombay, of the Kallianpur family of his grandmother. He charged top prices for surgery when the patient could pay, but 'he never put pressure on the poor to pay up. Many in poor circumstances never paid anything' (ibid.: 39-42).

T.M.A. started a training course for nurses at his nursing home, and trained his own compounders. He founded a chemist's shop which is still active, though no longer run by the family. A tuberculosis sanatorium built on the Manipal Hill in 1934 never became popular, but the building was soon used for other purposes: a nursing home, a higher elementary school, physiology block for the medical college when that got started, and, as by the late 1960s, a pharmaceutical lab producing drugs for the hospital. The Pais always found some use for any building they put up. T.M.A. also found time to lecture on banking and its social objectives to employees of the Syndicate Bank, from 1927 (ibid.: 43-4).

In 1943, he moved to Kadekar, some 3 miles from Udupi on the coast, working half-days at his practice and the other half at banking. Gradually, the bank took more and more time, and by 1949 he handed over his medical practice to K. Mohandas Pai, who had married one of U.A.'s daughters. Kinship was clearly important here, too. Sometimes T.M.A. felt guilty of leaving his practice, but then he thought: 'If some day I can educate 100 new doctors a year in a medical college, that will make up for my defection a hundred times over' (ibid.: 44-5).

T.A. Pai (Anant), Upendra's eldest son and T.M.A.'s nephew, took over as general manager of the Syndicate Bank in 1944.[23] He was then 21 (ibid.: 148). T.A. was Yashoda's favourite grandson. Ramesh, his younger brother, recalled how, once Anant misbehaved and was beaten by his father, the father was in turn spanked by Yashoda (Kamath, 1983: 15-16). Yashoda seems to have been quite a personality.

Anant grew up in the Mukund Nivas. He went to the public Main School, avoiding the costly Mission Schools. Though his uncle was a doctor, the world of Anant was that of small business. 'Udupi has its Saraswat Brahmin aristocracy', says Kamath, 'but its leaders lived apart and did not form a ghetto'. Next to the family lived the Prabhus, who owned Udupi's leading printing press. But Anant's school mates were lower middle class, from families much poorer than Anant's. Later, he went to Jaganath Nayak's Modern Higher Elementary School, run by a GSB but one mile's walk away. 'Everyone in the small town walked. Affluence had not yet come to Udupi though the well-to-do could hire a *jutka* – a two-wheeled, heavily adorned horse-drawn vehicle – to travel long distances'. Some few, doctors among them, rode bicycles (ibid.: 34-6).

When Anant had just entered high school, the family invited the astrologer Baburao Joshi to tell the future of the children. 'This boy', he said of Anant, 'will not study beyond high school.' Ramesh, his brother, has told that Anant changed completely from that day, as if he was determined to prove the astrologer wrong. He became an avid reader: by his death he owned a library of some five thousand books. By 1938, when he was to pass his SSLC exam, he was struck by pleurisy, and the examination had to be postponed. Roque Fernandes, the headmaster of the school, gave him a splendid certificate: he had been very ill but was saved by Anant's uncle.[24] Anant finally passed his examination with credit, and went on to study Insurance and Commerce at Sydenham College, Bombay (ibid.: 36-42). The Bank was growing, and the family had founded the Canara Mutual Assurance Company in 1935, so the choice was logical. As a graduate of India's premier commerce college, Anant 'would be a marvellous acquisition to the web of the Pai family enterprises', says Kamath (ibid.: 44).

As a student in Bombay, he first shared a room with a distant relative, H.V. Kamath, later a manager in the Syndicate Bank. But their room in Lohar Street was dingy, and Anant shifted to the Modern Hindu Hotel, until Dr. Baliga, of the Kallianpur family to which they were allied by marriage, insisted that Anant move in with him. Baliga was a successful doctor, well connected in the Bombay elite. He was a partisan of the Independence movement from his youth: at one time he was hawking *khadi* in Udupi taluka. He was a socialist, and his house in Bombay was the headquarters of the 'Free India

Movement' – the left wing party to the Quit India Movement of 1942 (ibid.: 44-5).[25] Baliga, who founded the Indo-Soviet Cultural Society and visited the Soviet Union in the 1950s, may have had quite an influence on T.A. Pai, who soon took part in the underground activities of the Free India Movement, though he was never arrested. It is told that he sat for his final examinations in *khadi*, as if to test the patriotism of the examiners. K.K. Pai,[26] who later led the bank, was also at Sydenham: so was H.N. Rao, another later director (Menefee, 1969/1984: 148-50).[27]

In 1943 Anant came back to Udupi, as Deputy Manager of the Syndicate Bank. Next year, he became general manager. 'There were some murmurs of dissatisfaction' says Kamath, 'among senior officers in the bank that a callow youth just out of college should be named to the Number Two post'. This was, of course, natural. But the murmurs 'died down quickly enough' (1983: 89).

It was time for him to marry. Apparently, it was Pitre Rama Rau, Anant's music teacher, who suggested Prema Pai, one of his students. She was a Kochikar[28] Pai; her grandparents had settled at Brahmavara. Her father, Kochikar Padmanabh Pai, their elder son, like T.M.A. Pai, was an early graduate from Madras University. 'He was one of that early band of nationalists who actively sponsored the nationalist movement in its younger days in India', through the Bombay Life Insurance Co. In a crucial and difficult period in that company's history, Padmanabh was their agent in Madras Presidency and 'proved of great assistance in strengthening the position of the company'.[29] A Bombay Life building was later built in Udupi for their family firm, Kochikar Brothers (ibid.: 161-2).

The Kochikar Pais had become a name in insurance while the Syndicate Bank was still a small-town affair. Padmanabh was a man of standing in Udupi, sophisticated, a lavish entertainer, one of the first men in town to own a car (ibid.: 162). So Anant married up – the opposite of what one expects in a middle-class Indian marriage. The families were unrelated, so there was no question of repeating a marriage alliance. Anant's father Upendra was a friend of Padmanabh Pai, however.

Anant did not dare to approach Prema directly, nor ask his parents to raise the matter with the Kochikars. Instead, he approached another respected GSB in town, Vittal Kamath, a lawyer and social worker. He was married to a cousin[30] of Padmanabh and knew the family well. 'But nobody seemed particularly enthusiastic about the match'.

> The Tonse Pais were just one more family within the Gowd Saraswat Brahmin community that was making its presence felt. The Syndicate Bank was a good effort but in Udupi there was the older and more conservative Corporation Bank which had one of the Udyavar Pais (Dr. S.R. Pai) at its head. And the Corporation Bank (then known as the Canara Banking Corporation Ltd.) often loaned money to the Syndicate Bank and was known for its staid banking policies. (ibid.: 163)

Still, they were married in 1944. But there were troubles from the start. The Tonse Pais were a joint family, and the couple was expected to live with them: Prema wanted her own house.[31] She was not well liked by the Tonse Pai family, 'who felt she did not belong to their culture: the culture of the middle class, comfortable with old world values and social mores that would treat a husband as *patidevata*, husband as god and would permit no wife to create waves' (ibid.: 166). Anant was removed to Bombay for some months, so the couple could live separately, but the conflict continued. Dr. Baliga was often asked to intervene.[32] Anant decided to return to Manipal, and build his own house there. Prema was happy about the new house, but soon the conflict resumed. Prema would leave for her parents' house in Udupi, and Anant would have to come to fetch her after a few days.[33] Finally, Prema left, never to come back, and Anant sued for divorce, which he obtained in 1972.

In the meantime, Manipal, now a satellite town of Udupi, had come into being. It began as a bare and dry hillock with only a few houses.[34] 'Scrub jungle covered the steep south and east slopes; the plateau on top was barren and treeless, with outcroppings of porous laterite bed-rock everywhere, turned black by many monsoons' (Menefee, 1969/1984: 54-5). Leopards and cheetahs roamed there: farmers on the west side of Udupi had to keep their cattle in compounds (Kamath, 1983: 79). But the road from Udupi to Mangalore traversed the hill, going by Karkala in those days, since the rivers towards the coast were not bridged.

It was in 1933 that some land on the hill was auctioned by the district court, and T.M.A. saw a possibility for developing the land.

Others, in the midst of the economic depression,[35] thought the brothers must be mad to waste money on such unusable land (ibid.). But with his brothers' backing, T.M.A. founded the Canara Land Investments Ltd., in which he was the main shareholder. They bought 107 acres on the hill for Rs. 70 an acre. More land was added later. Their first building was a tuberculosis sanatorium, in 1934, but it never worked out. They thought of developing some land for agriculture, then discovered good clay and went into the roof tile business in 1935.[36] The factory is still running. A small sawmill followed. U.A. then built a commercial structure, and a house for himself next to it. When his wife Parvati had enough of the bleak hill, T.M.A. and P.A. moved to the hill, too. P.A. also moved his small dyeing and handloom plant to Manipal, where the family continued it till 'a combination of poor market conditions and labour agitation closed it down' around 1960 (Menefee, 1969/1984: 56-7; Kamath, 1983: 79-81).

By 1935 the curious from Udupi came to visit the budding community on weekends: U.A. installed benches on the hilltop, and the first radio in Udupi or Manipal to entertain the visitors. 'Soon U.A. was building still more houses for those who came to live and work there. The town was on its way' (Menefee, op. cit.: 57). In 1936, the Pais opened the first, single-room, school in Manipal. When the sanatorium closed in 1939, it became the higher elementary school. An orphanage was started in 1938, but closed after a few years. Canara Land Investments is still the main landholder in Manipal, but by 1969 shares had been sold widely and only some 15 per cent remained in family hands (ibid.: 58).

It was in the 1940s that the Tonse Pais got into education in a big way. An elementary school in Manipal had been started in 1939, but now a whole programme of vocational training was launched. Printers were trained from 1941, book-binders from 1942, and that year the Academy of General Education came into being, to 'organize such short-time vocational courses on a larger scale' (ibid.: 60). In 1940, he had discussed the possibility of a college at Manipal with important civic leaders. Now these plans began to take shape. A governing body of 31 members was elected to preside over the planning, including six of the eight *swamis* of the Ashtamath, the Catholic priest of Udupi

(Fa. Alexander Pinto), K.V. Subba Rao, a local man who had become an important businessman in Madras, 'most of the educational and business leaders of Udupi', and several prominent men from Mangalore, Mulki and Karkala (ibid.: 61). The first convocation address was held by B.V. Baliga, a Mangalore attorney: T.M.A. became the registrar. Day-to-day affairs were handled by Ramesh, Upendra's second son. The first year, there were courses in 'Practice and Law of Banking, Insurance, Motor Engineering, Chain Surveying, Nursing and Midwifery, Cinema Exhibition . . . , Printing and Photography'. There were fees, but concessions for those unable to pay (ibid.: 63). The number of paying members of the Academy had grown to 12,000 by 1967.

In 1925, Kesho Kuduva's old shop on the corner of VT Street and the Temple Square was taken over by K. Ramakrishna Gundu Nayak. It is possible that the Kuduva shop had failed, since it is said to have been sold at an auction. The K. in Ramakrishna's name stood for Kadpet, the suburb to the west of Udupi, where he built his house. But since there was already a Kadpet Nayak family in Udupi, Ramakrishna's family is known as the Gundu Nayaks. He had a brother, Gopalakrishna, who started a shop in the Old Post Office Road.

Ramakrishna tore down the Kuduva shop and built the impressive building which still stands. He was helped 'a lot' in founding his firm by his in-laws, the daughter of Achut Rao,[37] a sub-registrar in Mangalore. This was about the highest an Indian could hope to climb in the administrative hierarchy of the 1920s, and the family was rich and prestigious. Ramakrishna Gundu Nayak's shop became one of the most important firms in Udupi. They dealt in imported goods, in a period when the bourgeoisie and the market for luxury goods expanded. He liked to say he sold everything 'from pins to planes' – though there is no record of any aeroplane sold by him. As we shall see later, his business suffered from the war, then the austerities of the early Independence period, and went under after 1947.

Ramakrishna's success in the inter-war years reflects the growing consumer market, especially among the middle class, which characterizes the period in India as a whole. Similarly, around the time that the Kalsanka Pais sold their old shop to the Ammunje Nayaks and established their present premises in the Temple Square, a branch of the family set out to establish a shop for silk saris and other high-grade fashion goods in Car Street. It was also during the mid-war years that the Airodys branched out into such modern and expensive goods as bicycles, while the Tonse Pai's paper shop catered to the intellectual and political tastes of a middle class which now read widely. Kadpet Vasudev Nayak photographed them. The middle class had become important enough, in Udupi, to constitute an important market. The expanding local business in Udupi was part of a larger trend. 'After the First World War', says Tomlinson, 'a new breed of Indian entrepreneurs challenged the hold of the expatriates on the institutional structures of the organized economy very effectively, weakened it decisively in the 1930s, and destroyed it almost completely after 1945' (1993: 100). The slump of the early 1930s had opened the way for import-substituting industrialization (ibid.: 101), while the disinvestment in agriculture at the same time led many, Udupi GSB among them, to move into towns.

NOTES

1. I base this conclusion of my reading of Lobo's work (2000).
2. P.P.C. Road is named from the college founded by the Madhava *maths*, the campus of which closes off V.T. Street at its southern end.
3. RSS or the Rashtriya Swayamsevak Sangh, a right-wing nationalist organization. For a full analysis of its history and development, see Jaffrelot, 1993.
4. *Panchaloha* is the traditional material for icons in this area. It is an alloy of five different metals.
5. *Bhoodan* – gift of land – was a movement started by Vinoba Bhave in which landowners were invited to give away some of their land to the poor.
6. Literally 'village', but also used to designate the place of origin.
7. It was important enough to have a traveller's bungalow, and the 1900 gazetteer says it had a tiled roof, then a rarity in the countryside.
8. Child marriage among Brahmins increased in the nineteenth century. T.M.A. also married a child bride – she was thirteen. By the time of T.A.'s marriage in the 1940s the custom was defunct. It must have disappeared in the 1930s in the Udupi area, probably at least in part due to Gandhian reformism.
9. 'It was the custom then, after two or more children had been lost and a live birth was at last achieved, to name the baby Martha if a boy, and Marthi

. . . if a girl.' These names may be translated as he/she who will die (Menefee, 1969/1984: 8).

10. Yashoda must have been born during the first half of the 1880s.
11. *Khadi* is homespun cotton cloth, which through Gandhi's promotion became emblematic of the Independence movement.
12. Menefee (1969/1984: 13) presents several anecdotes to explain this interest, which must have been told to the author by T.M.A. himself.
13. I deal with this example elsewhere.
14. As is the case among most Brahmins, GSB girls change their first name on marriage.
15. South Kanara was administratively a part of Madras since the area had been conquered by Madras troops from Tipu Sultan in 1799.
16. In the princely states of Saurashtra, by contrast, the princes founded state banks to guard banking as a state monopoly, opposed, at least in principle, by the merchant communities. They, in their turn, continued to do financial business but largely refrained from banking to ordinary customers.
17. One was, apparently, the first company started in India expressly for passenger transport. He also founded the *Navabharat*, a Kannada daily published from Mangalore. One story about him is that, as its editor, he took care to write his own obituary in advance.
18. The chit fund is and was a very common practice in India. The members subscribe to pay in a certain sum, usually once a month. There is a monthly draw where the winner gets the accumulated funds, or an auction is held, where the winner is the member who will pay the highest interest rate for a loan. The interest goes to the common fund. The arrangement makes ready money available to people who have little capacity for investment. Most banks see chit funds as competing with conventional banking, but the Syndicate worked with, rather than against, these popular credit arrangements.
19. He cites H.N. Pai of the Syndicate Bank – not a relative: 'The four Pai brothers were an ideal team. P.A. (Purushottam), the eldest, was a great idealist and provided moral leadership. He was a quiet man who never thought ill or spoke ill of others. He was active in the Congress . . . and especially in encouraging handloom weaving in the villages. U.A. (Upendra) was a man of ideas, a builder and a practical politician. He was always a supporter of constructive projects. He built about 75 houses, not to make money so much as to keep people employed. T.M.A. (Madhava) was a healer, as a doctor and a business man, and a great leader. He was the dynamic force in the family: to him a problem was

something to be solved, an obstacle something to be overcome. He would not let any family project fail. He also had a national vision; he saw South Kanara as a model for India. T.R.A. (Raghunath) came along later. He was trustworthy and efficient in looking after details in the family businesses, which is indispensable in any organization. Put together, the four of them were hard to beat' (cited by Menefee, 1969/1984: 30).

20. Hardiman (1996) expands on this ambiguity in the moneylenders' role.
21. It was not withdrawable for the first three years, though it could be used to secure 85 per cent loans at the bank. It could be withdrawn after three years, but no interest would be paid for less than seven years.
22. In 1939, the firm had been transferred to P.A. Pai as his sole property. After his death, his widow Shantabai continued for two or three years, helped by her brother; then the firm had to close. Two of her children were struck by paralysis, and died. Then Shantabai herself was paralysed. She later committed suicide by throwing herself into a well. Her two older children struck out on their own, the son becoming a doctor in Mexico and the daughter married an engineer, to live in Bangalore (Menefee, 1969/1984: 32).
23. His biography has been written by M.V. Kamath, from a local GSB family. My copy was a gift from the headmaster of the Christian High School in Udupi (part of the Basel Mission organization), Mohan V. Kumar: Kamath had been a pupil of his school.
24. Roque's son Oscar later became Anant's election manager, finally to stand against him and beat him in the post-Emergency elections of 1980.
25. Kamath, in fact, claims the socialists were spearheading that movement (1983: 58-9).
26. K.K. Pai married Anant's sister Saguna.
27. Another classmate was Arvind Mafatlal, from the well-known business family (Kamath 1983: 59).
28. I.e. from Kochi (Cochin).
29. Quoted from the LIC's centenary volume *Saga of Security*, by Kamath (1983: 162).
30. M.V. Kamath later refers to Padmanabh as Vittal Kamath's 'brother-in-law' so we may assume that the latter's wife was in fact Padmanabh's father's brother's daughter.
31. Today, most middle-class GSB stay in separate family houses, even when the family firm is run on a joint family basis.
32. Dr. Baliga felt that Prema should 'undergo psychiatric analysis'. She did for a while, then stopped.
33. For an excellent study of this kind of power politics in Indian marriages, see Jacobson, 1978.

34. Fifty to sixty people, says Menefee.
35. This is what Kamath says but note that the depression years saw considerable expansion in India.
36. An important industry in South Kanara, originally started by the Basel missionaries in Mangalore.
37. Rao is not a typical GSB name, but it was common with families in British employment.

5

Udupi and its GSB Families, 1947-1980

When Independence finally came in 1947, it was hailed with enthusiasm in Udupi as elsewhere. Most GSB had supported the Independence movement, both in its moderate (Congress) and more militant (RSS) forms. Yet with the promises of the new situation, there were also new problems, not all of them realized or expected at the time. It may be too simple, as Saki[1] does (1998), to caracterize the GSB in South Kanara as a 'comprador bourgeoisie', but the colonial situation had offered many opportunities for this business-minded community, and they had profited from them.

The Nehruvian 'socialism' that followed Independence was not necessarily to the advantage of small-town merchants like the GSB in Udupi. The state needed the collaboration of a 'national bourgeoisie' and several of India's large business families profited from state policy. At the local level, however, much profitable business was curbed. Others expanded within the narrow limits set for business under the new regime, at the cost of families such as the Gundu Nayaks who had supplied a colonial bourgeoisie with imported goods. Yet others, like the Tonse Pais, were able to accommodate to the state in sectors like banking, health, and education, where they supplemented insufficient state efforts. As a caste, the GSB managed to hold their own and expand into new areas, but the different fate of families had much to do with the changing order. Import restrictions introduced during the war were ceaselessly changing from 1944 into the early 1950s, strict controls alternating with liberalization, in an effort to deal with inflation and balance of payment problems (Tomlinson, 1993: 163-6). The constant changes were difficult to deal with for those who dealt in imported goods, and Ramakrishna Gundu Nayak's shop was among those that suffered the most. There must have been other shops all over India that encountered similar problems in this period.

The emphasis on heavy industry in the first two five-year plans did not, of course, imply an absence of consumer goods. As Rothermund notes, such goods was left to the private sector which enjoyed protective tariffs or even complete prohibition of many imports. This, he says, 'tempted many industrialists to go in for shoddy products which could nevertheless be sold at fancy prices and thus yielded enormous results' (ibid.: 131). Older Indians and India-watchers well remember this period, which lasted largely till the beginnings of liberalization under Rajiv Gandhi in the 1980s. This was a period when anthropologists brought Western-produced flashlights or pocket-knives for fieldwork, since the local products were of dubious quality. For the Indian middle-class consumer, then, times were not good, but for dealers in consumer goods, as for producers, profits were practically assured since the lack of competition meant that any goods procured could easily be sold. Thus shops that catered to a not very discriminating market probably did quite well. In those days, the discriminating customer would try to obtain foreign goods from contacts and relatives abroad, or through the lively black market – quite visible in Mumbai or Delhi then – fed by smuggling.

The Airodys were among those who continued their expansion, diversifying into new fields. In 1945, they started 'the silver section, the *puja* items, decorative *prabhavali* (the 'halos' behind the idols) and silver crowns (*kavadoha*) for idols – all made from silver. For this work they brought in artisans from Mysore, and under the Pais' supervision they also made *puja* items pertaining to the Madhava tradition. The Airody products became famous outside Udupi, too.' The centennial brochure, which I quote here, goes on to stress the family's political involvement and engagement with religious and other institutions:

> When we refer to the further development of the firm we must mention the exceptional personality and enormous achievement (of the brothers) . . . (the younger brothers too . . .) were patriotic and social workers and ardent activists of the RSS. In 1948, the RSS was blamed for the killing of Gandhi. When the RSS was banned, the brothers suffered imprisonment. . . .

We may wonder that the family should advertise so bluntly its participation in an organization that was officially banned. But the RSS had a lot of sympathy among the GSB, as it probably had among the small-town bourgeoisie in many parts of India. In a view that has strong echoes today, it was Nehru's left-wing politics that constituted an aberration, and not the RSS. To be active in the RSS, in this view, implied service to the nation, as against the aberrations of national politics.

The brochure then makes a leap forward in time, continuing the stress on serving the nation.

In 1971, at the time of the liberation war of Bangladesh, they (the brothers) donated 1 per cent of their turnover to the defence fund. They donated through the late T.M.A. Pai,[2] and the government thanked them for this donation. Radhakrishna Pai's wife Smt. Anasuya Pai died from cancer, and during her illness Ramakrishna established a primary cancer testing centre in her name. The friendship with Dr. T.M.A. Pai who is the creator of Manipal, became intensified.[3] Being a founder member of the Ayurvedic college of Udupi, he (Radhakrishna) strove for its survival. Radhakrishna Pai was also involved in rendering service to the Gurus,[4] and he was a trustee of the Shri Lakshmivenkatarama temple. He had immense respect for the community pontiffs of Gokarna, Kashi and Kaivalya Maths. Similarly, he was very intimate with the eight pontiffs of the Ashtamath,[5] as well as rendering service to Lord Krishna, Mukhyaprana and Ananteshwara.[6] He was also an ardent worshipper of these deities, and Radhakrishna Pai had a very intensive relationship to the temples.

We may note that they stress the wide range of religious institutions they support: they stand forth here as pillars of Hinduism, not just their own caste establishment. The image that the family presents is one of continuous social activism as Hindus and nationalists, an image quite different from that of the Tonse Pai family. Yet they also stress the association with them, and we should not forget that they claim to descend from the same original family in Goa.

Of all the GSB families in Udupi, it was the Tonse Pais who distinguished themselves by their activities during the first twenty-five years of Independence. They were now entering the most exciting period in the family's history, a series of initiatives that still shapes Udupi life today. By 1950, the Syndicate Bank was one of India's largest and most innovative banks. Some twenty smaller banks were merged with the Syndicate Bank in the early 1960s (Kamath, 1983: 101). The Pais were now able to invest in other ventures. Most important from a business point of view was insurance, but they came to be best known for their work in education. They also entered the political scene.

In 1948, the Government of India embarked on a project of enormous importance for South Kanara. There was no good all-weather port capable of handling big modern ships between Mumbai and Cochin except Goa, which was still Portuguese territory. The government wanted to develop such a port and a committee, headed by Kasturbhai Lalbhai, the Ahmedabad industrialist,[7] was appointed to study possible sites. Representatives of two railways, the Scindia shipping concern, the navy, and the docks manager of Kolkata Port Commissioners were on the committee. Karwar, Bhatkal, Malpe and Mangalore soon emerged as the main candidates for development. The Udupi elite was immensely interested, and it was T.M.A. Pai who took the lead, heading a committee of citizens with Anant as secretary. The Tonse Pais had, by now, definitely joined the leading citizens of Udupi. Kamath, the author of Anant's biography, joined Anant in going to Mumbai to give evidence to the committee. Kamath had also written a couple of well-argued articles in the *Free Press Journal*, as he puts it. 'Development of Malpe meant that the whole hinterland would be developed as well. All banks in Udupi would have benefitted, as most of the people', comments Kamath (ibid.: 151). Malpe was only 5 km away, and the 'twin cities' would, if the port was realized, have grown into an important regional centre, to surpass Mangalore as the main city of South Kanara. The committee was invited by Pai and his associates, and 'the leading citizens of Udupi were there to meet them: a picnic was arranged in St. Mary's Island and even a short film taken of the event' (ibid.). The committee, after detailed study, chose Malpe, stating why each of the other alternatives was found unsuitable. Building a new port here would also imply a new railway, linking the port to its hinterland. This decision was met with enthusiasm in Udupi, but, understandably, not in Mangalore. Business interests there found a powerful spokesman. Srinivas Mallya, a Mangalore man, GSB, the leading Congressman of South Kanara, and at one time secretary of the All India Congress Committee, 'pulled every string he could, used every trick of the politician's trade and finally got his way' (ibid.: 155). Kamath even tells us Mallya went to the *Free Press Journal* and tried to have himself and other advocates of the Malpe cause dismissed. 'To Anant, especially, it was an object lesson in the powers of politics over commonsense', comments Kamath (ibid.). Kamath's view here, is of course that of an Udupi man, and moreover, one who was himself a Malpe activist. He also feels that it was this affair that made Anant enter politics later.

Kalsanka Kamalaksha Pai, who had been to Sydenham College with T.A. Pai, joined the Syndicate Bank as a sub-manager of their Mumbai office. He was then chosen to head their new subsidiary bank, the Southern India Apex Bank Limited, which operated in Kerala and Tamil Nadu. About the same time, says Kamath, he married Anant's sister Saguna. T.A. Pai had started two Apex banks, for Kerala and Maharashtra, to head the bank's expansion in the two states. When the Apex banks were merged with the mother firm in 1953, K.K. joined it – he was later to become its managing director and chairman (ibid.: 92-3).

Around this time, the bank merged with a number of other banks of local importance. From 35 branches in 1950, the bank grew to 218 in 1967. T.A. Pai became managing director of the Syndicate Bank in 1962, and chairman on T.M.A.'s retirement in 1967. One of the first things he did on taking over was to improve basic salaries drastically and overhaul the personnel policy. Free life insurance policies for employees and a Provident Fund were other reforms. He later started the first Indian training school for bankers, and the Syndicate Bank was a founder-member of the Administrative Staff Training College in Hyderabad (Menefee, 1969/1984: 164-5). Relations between T.M.A. and his nephew were not always smooth. Madhava 'did not brook opposition gladly' and from time to time, Anant would threaten to resign. Sometimes he even did so in writing and Madhava would 'promptly accept'. It was Anant's younger brother Ramesh who served as the go-between: 'It happened frequently enough,' Ramesh said later (Kamath, 1983: 77-8).

The bank continued to finance small-scale but productive investment: while 4 per cent of farm credit in India was supplied by banks in 1967, the percentage stood at 17 in South Kanara – not least because of the Syndicate Bank.[8] By 1966 the bank had the largest number of borrowing accounts in the country, with a bias towards small loans (Menefee, 1969/1984: 168). To promote pump irrigation, T.A. set-up a cooperative, the South Kanara Agricultural Development Society. This led to a 'pumpset revolution' in the district, making a lot of dry ridge land cultivable (ibid.: 170). In 1964, a special Agricultural Finance Department was set up. A laboratory for soil tests was set-up at the Kasturba Medical College, then transferred to the MIT.[9] The bank's policy was 'to pump money into agricultural improvements, but in such a way that it could be repaid by the farmers' (Kamath, 1983: 174). Anant 'had a touching faith in the small man'[10] (ibid.: 102). The spirit of openness to the small saver and borrower, and the involvement with rural development continued in his time. He started three cooperative societies (ibid.: 113).

Much of the bank's spirit survived nationalization in 1969, and the Pai family continued to be involved, notably through their brother-in-law, K.K. Pai. The GSB community continued to furnish a large part of the bank's leaders. Still, the loss of the bank meant that the family must find new fields of activity.

Stockholders of the Syndicate Bank received Rs. 36 million in government bonds.[11] T.M.A. and Anant's brother Ramesh proposed to transfer the money to an investment fund and try to achieve a yield close to the 20 per cent that the stock had yielded.[12] More than 96 per cent of the stock was transferred, and Ramesh became chairman of the Industrial Credit and Development Syndicate. The Syndicate name was chosen, he said, 'because it carried a tremendous amount of goodwill'. Ramesh had been in business on his own before taking on the fund, and proved a shrewd investor and a good manager. 'Ramesh is a dynamo, a man of ideas and action,' said T.M.A. of him (Menefee, 1969/1984: 223). Yet it was the crash of their investment fund, much later but still under Ramesh's leadership, that was to symbolize the end of the eminent position the Tonse Pais had occupied in Udupi.

Though the position of the family in finance has now largely gone, the educational empire they built in the first quarter-century of Independence is still going strong. T.M.A. had first launched the idea of a college in 1940, building local support for the idea. To create such a college in what was then considered a peripheral area, and as a private venture, was to prove a hard task. Getting affiliation to Madras University proved the hardest of all, since a large deposit was needed, but through an intensive fund drive and by mortgaging T.M.A.'s property the money was raised and affiliation obtained (ibid.: 67-9). But the university would not accept girls, and the college had 10 girl students. T.M.A. believed in education for girls, and managed to secure the place of the girls already admitted. New admissions were only permitted from 1952, after one would-be student, Shanta Shenoy, had gone to court and written both to Nehru and Indira Gandhi. The letter to Nehru was sent on to the education ministry with no result, but Indira took her letter to her father, who asked the Governor of Madras to settle in Shanta's favour. The university had to oblige (ibid.: 69-71). Madras State donated the site of the college, on the Manipal road just outside Udupi, and by a combination of state grants and fund-raising schemes the campus was built, one building after another. The campus was opened by June 1951, and by 1953 the intermediate college became a full-fledged one. It grew fast[13] (ibid.: 74). Good results have earned a name for the college.

One anecdote explains some of the Pai myth. There was too little money for the main building, so 'one Sunday morning early in 1951, Dr. Pai and his brothers and nephews came to the site where building was going on and started to work, moving gravel and dirt. This was unprecedented: in India men of high position simply do not work with their hands. A small crowd gathered to watch, and boys ran home to tell their parents about the strange happening. Then some of the local people moved in to help (ibid.: 73). It was the beginning of regular work parties, and employees of the Syndicate Bank were soon volunteering to help. 'Sometimes,' says one of them, 'there were so many people that it was hard for the Academy's engineer to find enough work for them to do' (ibid.). The engineer was U.A. Kamath, whom we shall meet later.

One month after the MGM opened its campus, T.M.A. presented the Academy with his plans for Kasturba Medical College. According to Menefee, T.M.A. was motivated to plan for a medical college by his reactions to the policy of reserving quotas for admission to higher education for Scheduled Castes – untouchables – and Scheduled Tribes. The opposition to such reservation policies has remained strong among the GSB, as among Brahmins and other high castes all over India. T.M.A. Pai had recruited a young science graduate as a teacher for his college, but the young man insisted that if he got a place in the medical college at Vellore, he would go. 'It is hard for a Brahmin like me to get a seat there,' he said, 'children of Backward Classes must have preference.' In the end he was turned down because his father was a doctor: 'those with less educated backgrounds must have preference,' it was said. 'I felt strongly about this,' T.M.A. said. 'I wanted to see all opportunities open to people of all castes. I was extremely unhappy at what appeared to be a rise in caste tension after independence.[14] I thought, what will be the fate of our children? We must do something about it' (ibid.: 78-7). He had 13 acres of land in Manipal, Canara Land Investments 107, and then, when the government had offered, in 1934, up to 6,000 acres in Manipal for public projects, T.M.A. asked to have 600 acres reserved for educational institutions, a reservation that would lapse if nothing was done in 25 years. Ultimately, he used 200 acres for his medical college and another 200 for Manipal Engineering College, the latter in 1958, one year before the reservation lapsed.

The financial plan was again audacious. The Academy would charge Rs. 3,000 to reserve a seat, promising that it would be available once the college was built. He donated Rs. 10,000 and his land in Manipal.[15] But when he asked to have the 200 acres he had reserved to build a private medical college, the state finance minister, C. Subramaniam, thought he was mad: no private, unsubsidized medical college could possibly succeed in such an out-of-the-way place. Even T.A. Pai was against the plan, as was Dr. Baliga in Bombay (Kamath, 1983: 176). For almost two years the land grant was tied up in red tape (Menefee, 1969/1984: 78-84). Meanwhile, the affiliation problem cropped up again. To avoid Madras, T.M.A. sought affiliation with Karnatak University. They put down very strict conditions: thus, an anatomy block or facility had to be completed within six months. With the help of volunteers including family members and children from the schools, the building was ready in early 1953. Clinical facilities were arranged for at the district hospitals in Mangalore.[16] Affiliation was accepted in early 1953, but still depended on the approval of the Bombay government, implying a 'hair-raising rush of negotiations' if the college was to open on schedule in June 1953. 'Fortunately,' says Menefee, 'Dr. Pai had the use of the Syndicate Bank facilities and personnel, and the branch managers became his ambassadors in complicated dealings with the governments of two states[17] (ibid.: 80-6). In Mumbai, the finance minister was opposed to the plan though the education minister supported it. K.L.V. Nayak,[18] manager of the Syndicate Bank's branch in Bombay, told T.M.A. the government would probably agree if the Indian Medical Council approved the plan. On the way to see its president, T.M.A. stopped at Karnatak University and was asked what he would do if the Bombay government refused affiliation. 'I will ask,' T.M.A. is reported to have said, 'my people to make my tomb in the building I have erected there and put up a marble slab saying: Here lies a man who tried to build a private medical college. The Madras government was willing to help. Karnatak University agreed to affiliation. But the Bombay government rejected permission to affiliate with Karnatak University' (ibid.: 87). T.M.A. succeeded in convincing the Council's president, and the Bombay government granted affiliation – on trial – for eighteen months. Still, the Central Health Minister R.K. Kaur, opposed to private colleges, said he would 'see that it is closed down'. But the report he asked for before the end of the trial period was highly favourable, and finally the college even received state grants, on a matching basis.

More than a third of the first year students (36 per cent) were Christians, showing the strong investment made by Mangalorean[19] Catholics in education and the professions; 22 per cent were Brahmins, so the percentage of GSB students must have been lower. The college received full recognition in 1958, just in time for the first batch of graduates to have an accredited degree (ibid.: 89-92). It went on to become one of the most prestigious medical colleges in India, attracting foreign students, even Americans at one time. It also hosts a medical museum. The percentage of Brahmins rose to 30 per cent by 1965, while that of Christians dropped to 17 per cent. The first percentage probably included many GSB by then, since businessmen accounted for 33 per cent of the students' parents, and 'probably about the same in 1976'. There were then 886 students (ibid.: 97-8). The growth has continued.

A 12-bed maternity and child care centre was opened in 1953, but T.M.A. wanted a real hospital, and the foundation stone was laid in 1954. The ground floor of the first wing was completed in 1957, but had to be used for the engineering college. In 1961 the Kasturba General Hospital with 150 beds was started. A blood bank was founded 1960, helped by the Rotary and Lion's Clubs. A Medical Relief Society had been started in 1957: with T.A. Pai as secretary it was 'a sort of medical insurance plan' intended to 'render medical service to the rural areas'. It merged with the Kasturba Medical College Trust in 1961. The resulting Medical Relief Trust developed a network of Rural Maternity Centres.[20] Family Planning is part of the service (ibid.: 101-3). In 1973 the hospital and the Syndicate Bank together developed a 'Medicare Plan'. Courses for nurses and laboratory technicians are associated with hospital, which by 1976 had 650 beds and a staff of 400. It has grown since. The dental college was added in 1970, the A.V. Baliga Institute of Surgery in 1973, a hearing clinic in 1974 and a cancer treatment unit – which has since become a separate hospital – in 1975 (ibid.: 108). In 1967, the Valley View International Health Club, a hotel and medical centre, was opened, catering to people coming for a medical check-up, patients' and students' relatives, and tourists. It is also used as a meeting and conference centre, notably by the Syndicate Bank. A school of hotel management is attached to the hotel.

The engineering college proved much easier to realize. Yet here, too, there were problems with the government. The central government sent a delegate to Manipal to consider whether the college could be included in the government's grant-in-aid system. He reported favourably, and the government referred the matter to the southern regional committee on engineering colleges. But its head was A.L. Mudaliar, the vice-chancellor of Madras University who had made so much difficulty about the MGM some years earlier. He would include only one college in then Mysore State in the scheme, and Hassan was chosen over Manipal. The central government was still willing to aid, but then the college must become a Polytechnic

Institute, granting diplomas rather than degrees. This was not acceptable to T.M.A. (ibid.: 115-16). He therefore used the same system as for the medical college but the price of a seat was only half that asked for medicine. The college was opened in May 1957. By 1961 there were full four-year courses in civil, mechanical and electrical engineering. Here, as in the medical college, T.M.A. secured good staff by recruiting those who did not want to stop teaching at 55, the retirement age in public service (ibid.: 113-15). According to the then principal of the college, B.V. Krishna Murthy, the government discriminated against the college in several ways: allocation of building materials, foreign exchange for imported equipment, and scholarships for needy students. But the college grew. New degrees followed and in 1975 the college became the Manipal Institute of Technology (MIT). Research was encouraged.

The MIT has been active in community development; there is a park of small industries at Manipal, and the engineering staff has developed and administerd the planning of the town. One of the first professors, V. Chandrashekar, formerly a public health engineer, 'was appalled at the many mosquitos in Manipal', so he designed and built a complete sanitary system for the budding town. The college provided most of the funds to build a Krishna temple on the hill and a landscaped garden around it. It paid for the town's sports ground. There are six large student hostels (ibid.: 116-19).

In 1969-70 there was student unrest in Manipal: the students demanded an independent students' union. This was dealt with summarily: 'the Academy simply closed down the two colleges and sent the boys home for three weeks. Their parents soon saw to it that they were "straightened out" and they returned' (ibid.: 119). Clearly, there were limits to the Pai family's democratic engagements.[21] The MIT has a good reputation and examination results. Like the medical college, it also has a number of foreign students. Its graduates are found all over India, as also in Europe, America and in the Third World.

Other colleges followed: the Law College in 1957, and a post-graduate college by the early 1980s; arts and science colleges in Kundapur, Mulki, Mudabidri and Sringeri. Karkala's Shri Bhuvanendra College, however, did not originate with the Manipal group but was started as a Sanskrit college by leaders of the local Venkatarama temple. As we saw in Chapter 2, this is quite a tradition in Karkala. Here, more than elsewhere, the temple committee – purely a GSB institution – stands out as the most active cultural institution in town. In 1960, the Academy helped develop the college into an arts and science college. There is the Manipal College of Education, opened in 1965, and colleges of dental surgery and pharmacy, both opened 1967. By 1974-5, South Kanara had the largest number of college students in any district served by Mysore University (ibid.: 135). In addition to the colleges, the Academy at Manipal ran thirteen schools by 1976. Finally, there was the School of Music and Fine Arts, started at Manipal and Udupi in 1958, which has local branches elsewhere. The Yakshagana Kendra[22] was opened in 1971, and the Govinda Pai Research Centre[23] in 1976, with a small archaeological museum attached. In all, thirty-five institutions were managed by the Academy by 1976.

Though the Pai empire is known for its colleges and hospitals, the Syndicate Bank and Manipal, the family also has more conventional businesses, organized through a holding company, Manipal Industries Limited.[24] The Manipal Power Press, a printing press, is separate: it was started by Mohandas – the eldest son of T.M.A. – and Satish, the younger brother of T.A. and Ramesh Pai. The press publishes the *Udayavani*, which has become the most popular Kannada daily in South Kanara, the *Taranga*, a weekly, and *Roopatara*, a film monthly. Mohandas in 1976 also managed Canara Land Investments, the company responsible for land acquisitions and sales at Manipal, which owns the tile factory in Manipal itself. T.M.A.'s youngest son, Ashok, was managing partner of Manipal Bottling Company, producing soft drinks, which is now closed. There are several industries on the hill, owned and run by others but often sponsored or encouraged by the Pai family. Then there are the milk cooperatives and dairy organized by Ramdas Pai, T.M.A.'s second son. They worked with external aid agencies to build a system of milk production in the district (ibid.: 231-7). This cooperative has not attained the position of some other milk cooperatives in India, but South Kanara is hardly a favoured area for stockbreeding.

GSB families continued to converge on Udupi from the countryside and the small country boroughs. Mathab is a small village between Shirva and Mudabidri, very much in the interior and well to the south of Udupi. It was from here that M. Nagesh Kini's grandfather came to Kapu, where he started as a general merchant. His father moved to Udupi, entering the wholesale commodity business, with his stores at the upper end of Old Post Office Road, near the Kalpana movie theatre. This brought him into close contact with the transport business, so he shifted to trucking, and was operating in this line when Gandhi's murder led to his arrest, along with his two brothers, since they were all RSS activists. The local GSB were almost all in the RSS at that time, says Nagesh Kini, and the retaliation hit the community hard. The nationalist sentiment dominated the community. 'We were very nationalist then: Pakistan should never have been created. It was a machination by the British,' he says. He made some rather disparaging remarks about Muslims at this point. His father's business floundered when he was in jail, since the transport business needs a constant presence. Nagesh's father, looking for a new venture, decided to start a printing business which Nagesh inherited and is still running. The printing press seems to attract a steady flow of customers, so Nagesh is doing quite well. He is married to a girl from a Belthangadi family.

It was nationalism that attracted so many people from the GSB community to the RSS, says Nagesh Kini. The critical point here was the Second World War. The situation became very different from the one which, before the war, had 'created' Gandhi. More recently, it was the J.P. movement that represented the real 'turnaround' in Indian politics, he says. This broke the hold that the Congress had on people's minds, and opened the way for a real opposition: the Janata Party and then the BJP. His own family, then, were RSS activists, but many of his caste-fellows were affected by the crackdown on that organization, the Airody brothers among them. He himself, by the way, also went to jail for his RSS activities: this was during the Emergency when Indira Gandhi banned right-wing organizations. Again, he says, this affected a good part of the local GSB community and many went to jail, though the main figures among the Tonse Pais – Upendra, T.M.A. and of course T.A. – were Congressmen. T.M.A. was a very fine gentleman, remarks Nagesh Kini, and stresses the importance of T.A.'s connections for business and banking in Udupi. He does not mention T.A.'s support of Indira, and of the Emergency, but recalls how he fought for Malpe as the main port of south-west India, rather than Mangalore. He, too, remembers that it was U.S. Mallya who was instrumental in defeating T.A. here, and so the port went to Mangalore.

'Whatever made T.A. turn to politics?' asks Kamath, and cites K.K. Pai to the effect that the outcome of the port affair had an important effect on him (Kamath, 1983: 150). 'Till then the Pais had eschewed politics like the devil. Nationalists they were. Their patriotic credentials were there for all to see. For all the charges that they were out to build and feather their own nests, they had been constructive activists. But none of the Pais had gone into elective politics in a big way. But suddenly it must have dawned on them that politics was unavoidable in post-Independence India' (ibid.: 156). In 1952 T.A. was asked by the Congress to stand as their Member of Legislative Assembly (MLA) candidate for South Kanara. He accepted, and won the election. Among many matters he dealt with was that of getting the traditional lot system of Malpe fishermen accepted as a cooperative practice: formerly the whole catch was taxed as the seine captain's income (ibid.: 151). He founded a fishing cooperative at Malpe, visited Norway and Denmark to learn about fishing and cooperatives, and acquired, for Malpe, the first fisheries high-school in the region.[25]

In 1957, T.A. wanted to run again, but his father's last wish – Upendra died in 1956 – was that he should concentrate on Manipal. Instead, he became president of the District Congress Committee and was a member of the All India Congress Committee for many years (Menefee, 1969/1984: 152). Then he was chosen as the first chairman of the Food Corporation of India. 'It was a disillusioning experience,' says Menefee. 'He quickly saw what needed to be done,' but when it came to implementation, he 'ran up against a stone wall. At the end of his one-year term he was glad to quit and return to Manipal where he could get things done' (ibid.: 152). In 1967, Anant wanted to stand as Congress candidate to the Lok Sabha, but 'because of the very power that he had accumulated and the popularity that he had amassed, he had set about a counter current in district Congress circles' and the party chose another man. The election was won by a

Mangalorean Catholic, Lobo Prabhu,[26] from the Swatantra Party. Yet Anant knew the left-wing leaders of the Congress through Dr. Baliga, who later became Nehru's medical consultant. He also knew Indira Gandhi, who had visited Manipal. 'Somewhere in the recesses of her mind,' says Kamath, 'she must have marked Anant out as a useful technocrat whose services could be availed of when they became necessary.' Anant admired Indira (Kamath, 1983: 161).

In 1969, when the Syndicate Bank was nationalized along with thirteen largest banks in India, Indira, then prime minister, asked T.A. to take care of the Life Insurance Corporation of India (LIC). T.A. accepted, though the company was in a bad way and the employees were on strike. He negotiated a fair settlement, then set about consultations with the staff to develop new objectives for the organization, which was transformed.[27] Indira then asked T.A. to stand for election to the Rajya Sabha, the upper house of the Indian Parliament. He was elected, and in July 1972 he became the minister of railways.

Anant had obtained divorce in 1972 and married again that very year. Vasanthi Manjeshwar was from a family hailing from the temple town of Manjeshwar but lived in Bangalore, as she 'wanted to stay away from her co-community people'. When they met by chance, in 1960, she asked whether the Syndicate Bank would manage her family property, but nothing came of it. In 1962, Anant sought her out to pursue the matter and, said she, 'again put him off'. Then in 1966, she was in Mumbai and Anant invited her to come and see the Baligas. They met from time to time, and Anant invited her to stay with him – but he was not yet divorced. T.M.A. was not amused. The divorce came through just as Anant was becoming a minister. He arrived in Delhi with Vasanthi, which raised questions of propriety. The couple flew to Tirupati,[28] and were married there, more or less secretly. This time the marriage, in spite of its unconventional character, was a success. Some have accused Vasanthi of being 'bossy and overbearing', says Kamath, but 'she was certainly Anant's right hand and gave him all her love and strength' (1983: 169). This marriage certainly marks a break with traditional joint family usage, and may stand, symbolically, for a new mentality. Yet even today, it stands out as a singular deviation from the norm among Udupi's GSB families.

Now, T.A. Pai was to taste 'real power'. He was a success as railway minister, reversing the priorities of his predecessor and putting freight before passenger development. The ministry's efficiency and work atmosphere was improved. He also tried to push what – much later – was to become the Konkan Railway, from Mumbai to Mangalore along the coast. After about seven months, he became minister of heavy industry, and shortly after of steel and mines. Next year, the latter ministry was transferred, but Pai became minister of science and technology, then minister for industry and civil supplies in 1975 (Kamath, 1983: 177-86). One of his main challenges as minister of heavy industry was to render the public enterprises more efficient: he succeeded brilliantly.[29]

When Indira Gandhi declared a state of Emergency in June 1975, Anant supported the measure.[30] This is not the place to discuss the Emergency: one good but critical appraisal is by Jaffrelot (2005: 152-9). Kamath is critical. But everybody in Udupi and South Kanara cannot have been so, for in the 1977 elections, which the Janata Party won and Indira lost, Anant was re-elected 'with a convincing – and, considering the rout of the Congress in the North, stunning majority' (Kamath, 1983: 212).

We do not know how the GSB voted then. Many who were close to the RSS probably voted for Janata. Others were Congress followers, but few can have belonged, like Indira and Anant, to its left wing. Yet it is possible that Indira's action-oriented programme and undoubted charisma appealed to the nationalism of many GSB, as a way of getting the nation to move again. Anant was popular in Udupi, and people, as we have seen, still remember his role in the fight for Malpe port. His efficiency in economic affairs may have appealed to businessmen. He had fought for regionally important issues, such as the Konkan Railway. In South Kanara, the lower castes, such as the Billavas and the Moghaveras, have generally supported the Congress, and Indira wanted the Emergency to be a period of social reform benefiting the lower castes.[31] Many low-caste people believed in her programme. In general, it was in the Hindi belt that Indira lost heavily: she fared much better in the south (Jaffrelot, 2005: 341-51; Kamath, 1983: 212).

Anant, like Indira herself, was now in the Opposition. According to Kamath, he 'felt a sense of relief'. The Shah Commission, inquiring into the excesses of the Emergency, commended Anant for his 'refreshing moral courage and resistance to Mrs. Gandhi's overbearing authority', when he gave evidence before it. In May 1977, he addressed the All India Congress Committee in very critical terms:

> Caste politics and group politics became the Congress and those in power were considered more important than Congress workers. . . . The emergency did not affect Congressmen. Did we realize that freedom is indivisible and in the process of standing in the way of legitimate thought and action, we also lost our freedom along with it? Discipline that we were preaching to others was sadly lacking among ourselves. . . . The uncalled for raids and blackmail struck terror in the midst of the people. The family planning program clearly exhibited the trait of sadism. . . . Even the Intelligence Department failed to report the truth because nobody wanted the truth. . . .
> (Kamath, 1983: 214-16)

Still, he continued as a member of the Congress, taking a special interest in economic policy and trade.

But, says Kamath, he neglected his constituency. Some of his friends felt he had become 'too important to interest himself in the nuts and bolts of district and taluk affairs' (1983: 219). Kamath himself feels he was simply getting worn out, tired of politics: 'he was first and foremost a banker' (ibid.). But then, in January 1978, the Congress party split. Indira formed the Congress(I) and was expelled from the party. Anant stayed: he had clearly come to the conclusion that the Emergency had been a mistake.

When Morarji Desai's government fell in July 1979, with several candidates trying to form a new government, Charan Singh became prime minister. The Congress wanted him to join the government[32] and he did so, becoming minister of petroleum. He shifted to the railway ministry a week later. Charan Singh resigned in August as he could not win the support of the Congress (I) group, and the 1980 elections spelt the end of Anant's political career. Standing for Congress, he lost his deposit, beaten soundly by the Congress (I) candidate Oscar Fernandes. As a Catholic the latter too had a strong local base, and his father, Roque Fernandes, had been a popular headmaster of Udupi's Catholic school. The elder Fernandes had been healed by T.M.A. Pai when seriously ill, while Oscar had been Anant's campaign manager in earlier elections.

The Catholic community had asked the government – through Anant – to exonerate their new church bell from import duty, but Anant failed to influence Charan Singh. This episode hardly explains the election result, however. Kamath explains Anant's fall by his change of allegiance. 'How could a man, who only two years ago, was praising Mrs. Gandhi' now condemn her? 'To them it just did not sound right. If he had stood down, they would have understood him and respected him. He was offering himself for re-election and they would not forgive him for that' (ibid.: 230).

To Sadhana Kini, whom we shall meet later, Fernandes' election was partly a rejection of the Tonse Pais. People were starting to oppose their monopoly on important institutions in the district. Oscar Fernandes was elected as a complete outsider to the Pai empire. His being a Christian was of minor importance: what counted was his independence from the local power centres, not only the Pais but also the *maths*. This may be part of the story, but Kini also had another explanation of why the GSB left the Congress. They supported it, she said, till quotas for the Other Backward Castes (OBC) became an issue. We have seen that T.M.A. Pai was against any form of positive discrimination. To accept it for tribes and untouchables was one thing, but with quotas for OBC, as proposed by the Mandal Commission, the openings for Brahmins and other high castes in education and government posts would be seriously reduced. This would also hold for the Catholics, who, like the GSB, were strongly present in government and the professions.

The Mandal Commission submitted its report in 1980, not to Charan Singh's government but to Indira Gandhi's, which followed it. But quotas for the OBC were on the programme of the Lok Dal, Charan Singh's party (Jaffrelot, 2005: 360) and the question was very much in the air. The GSB, in general, had no sympathy for the Lok Dal, which basically represented the peasants. Congress(I), at this time, still seemed to be opposed to quotas, and when the Mandal Commission Report was discussed in 1982, with Indira as prime minister, its recommendations were not acted upon. It is quite likely, then, that GSB voters of South Kanara identified positive discrimination for the OBC with the government of which Anant was part, and voted both against the government and against him. As for low-caste voters, Oscar Fernandes was known as a socialist and a left-winger, and here Anant had lost his credibility by breaking with Indira. Thus he may have lost his GSB supporters on the positive discrimination issue and his low-caste vote by his break with Indira Gandhi. Not much was left. In 1990, the government of V.P. Singh finally adopted the recommendations of the Mandal Commission. But by then, the Congress had lost its credibility with the GSB as an anti-Mandal party: they were quite naturally drawn to the BJP.

By the 1950s Udupi had come of age, and the GSB position among its elite was firmly established. Still, new families came up during this period to become examples of entrepreneurship cited by others. Among them were the Gujjadi Nayaks, a branch of the family from which the Kadpet Nayaks came. Gujjadi Narasimha Nayak is much respected in Udupi, nonetheless so since he is, in effect, a 'self-made' man. Narasimha made his career in the gold business, a field which no GSB in Udupi had entered till then. The GSBs are never goldsmiths, says one informant,[33] though some goldsmiths are Konkani. Narasimha came from a rather poor GSB family, and started his business without a shop, around 1957, said my friend Ananth of the Airodys. Narasimha took commissions for jewellery from particulars at his house, then contracted to have the items made by Viswakarma goldsmiths, taking a small commission for his service. The business grew, and he erected a small shed to receive his customers. 'Only after several years – he had been doing very good business – did he move into his present place,' says Ananth. Now, his 'Swarna' gold shop is probably the most prestigious in its line in Udupi, housed in an elegant shop[34] close to the Sanskrit College – the only Udupi shop to have a watchman in uniform posted outside. Narasimha is often cited to show that the GSB have a real flair for business, and that their position is not just a question of inherited money and position. His story, too, shows that the era of 'rags-to-riches' stories among the GSB is not over. Entrepreneurship is still possible, and it pays.

The Diana ice-cream parlour and restaurant is beloved of the Udupi middle class. On Sundays, it is always full, with families enjoying a day out. It does, in fact, serve ice-cream of remarkable quality, but its vegetarian meals – at a very moderate cost – are also excellent. It is run by two GSB brothers; it was their father who founded the firm in 1961. His idea was to offer north Indian snacks, a first for Udupi and still a main part of the menu. It was hard at first, but gradually the new fare caught on and people started to come. Since then, they have founded a general store nearby, both under the heading of Diana enterprises. Why Diana? 'My father wanted a foreign-sounding name, something that would sound different,' said one of the brothers: so he chose Diana, as the name of a foreign goddess. Business expanded strongly in the 1960s. Diana is known to all in Udupi, but there is currently no expansion of the business.[35] Like the Gujjadi Nayaks, the Diana enterprises stand as an example of the post-Independence arrivals to the GSB community in Udupi, and of their entrepreneurial role.

While new families came up, others lost their pre-eminent positions. In 1975, Ammunje Trivikram Nayak, head of the most prestigious of the traditional business houses in Udupi, died. Trivikram had five sons. The eldest inherited the original shop: he died in January 2005, but the shop is still there. The original shop now seems to be of moderate size and importance. The second son, with whom I spoke, inherited some land and buildings just opposite the original shop, on the north-western corner of Car Street. This was the land that his father bought from the Kalsanka Pais some time before 1937, when that family moved to the temple square. In 1937, the Ammunje Nayaks started their own shop in these buildings, but it was no longer active when the present owner took over. He had not planned to enter business at all: he had trained as a chemical engineer at MIT where he was the only local student. Everybody else in his class was from Gujarat. At his father's death he found himself with the unused property on his hands and decided to enter business as a grain merchant, to revive the oldest line of the family firm. As he put it, it is not easy to make money in this business today. It was profitable in the days when South Kanara was the rice bowl of Goa and much of southern Arabia: today, when rice is imported, it is far less remunerative. And, says he, the times are past when a merchant could sit in his shop and wait for the customers to come to him. Today, it is he who must seek them out. 'It is a buyers' market now,' he says. 'Everything is, these days.'

The third brother inherited the businesses and land opposite, on the north-eastern corner of Car Street. There are two businesses now, run by two brothers. Prabhakar Oil Mills at the Kalsanka end of Car Street is one of them. The other, a retail shop, is called Ammunje Ramanand Madhav Nayak. His and the grain dealers' shop flank the Kalsanka entry to Car Street. Another member of the family, an accountant and financial consultant, has his office just inside the street. Not far away there is a big petrol station, and an even bigger tyre agency, owned by the descendants of the fourth brother. This branch, which was started in 1976, is clearly doing very well these days, and people hint at some family jealousy on that account. The fifth brother is the doctor, Arvind Nayak Ammunje, who has a scanning clinic nearby, also at Kalsanka, a few doors down the street towards Manipal. In fact, much of Kalsanka is still in the hands of the Ammunje Nayaks.

But one member of the family – Ammunje Lakshminarayana Nayak – has established his shop on the 'island' in the middle of the temple square, opposite the ancestral shop of the Kalsanka Pais and close to their plywood agency. He is a cousin of the others: their grandfathers were brothers. This shop was started in 1949. Others in the family seemed to include or exclude this shop, according to the circumstances: the owner, after all, is just a cousin of the five brothers. The same seems to be true of the shop beside it, A. Kodandarama Nayak, a hardware shop which does not specify Ammunje in the firm's name, but which at least one informant referred to as being 'of the family'. It was started around 1980. Another shop, A.V.T. Nayak, acknowledged by the grain dealer as that of a 'cousin', is at Kunjibettu, the suburb where the Pais' MGM College is situated.

Yet another Ammunje Nayak shop, 'Modern Stores' near the bus station, is owned by the descendants of another cousin of the five brothers. Yet, when I asked them whether they were related to the tyre shop and other Ammunje Nayak enterprises, they said 'no relationship'. These latter examples show that once the unity of the joint family is broken, the question of who – and whose shop – is seen as 'part of the family' is highly relative. It would seem to become less a question of genealogy than of actual social relations, rather as Schneider (1968) has shown for American kinship. Thus 'they' are 'relatives' or they are not: they are not really the 'family', unless the division of the joint family is recent enough still to be present in people's minds.

The role of the GSB in Udupi's history, then, is structured by the rise and fall of the main GSB families, and much of our story has been told with direct reference to them. This is also the way in which Udupi GSB tend to see their own history. Historicity here takes on a character different from when the migration from the Saraswati valley to Goa, the Goan experience, and the migration further south, is considered. The first largely concerns the links to the Saraswat cluster of Brahmin castes; the second, the formation of the GSB community. With the history of Udupi, we enter a new stage of segmentation in the objects to which historicity is applied: we descend to the level of families within the caste, seen separately or occasionally as a localized community group. The three stages of segmentation are different in nature. From the Saraswati River to Goa, a smaller community unit is seen to branch off from a larger one; with the migration to South Kanara and the split from the Chitrapur Saraswats, the genesis of the GSB community is complete. The Udupi GSB do not, in the same way, form a branch of the caste. They constitute only an agglomeration of family groups, most of them having branches in other places: their common residence in Udupi is, so to speak, coincidental – an accident of history. At this level, the families have become the unit of reckoning.

NOTES

1. Saki is the synonym used by a left-wing activist reputed to have been killed by the police in one of the first encounters between Naxalites and the police in South Kanara. His history of the region is strongly inspired by Maoist ideas.
2. See under the Tonse Pais.
3. It is interesting to note how this friendship cuts across political affiliations: T.M.A. was far removed from the RSS supported by the Airody brothers.
4. Here is meant the gurus of the GSB *maths*.
5. I.e. the heads of the eight Madhava *maths* of Udupi.
6. The latter two are the deities of two of the oldest temples of Udupi (Chapter 4).
7. For a history of the Lalbhais and their enterprises, see Tripathi and Mehta, 1990: 88-104.

8. These figures are from the *Economic Times*, cited by Menefee, 1969/1984: 168.
9. Manipal Institute of Technology, of which more later.
10. He would cite the failure of the Travancore National Quilon Bank in 1930, when 'all loans up to a thousand rupees had been paid in full and had been recovered by the liquidator' (Kamath, 1983: 102).
11. These could be sold, but tax must be paid on the considerable gains. If kept, they would yield a very low interest compared to the 20 per cent their holders had received for years.
12. To pay dividend quickly, the Syndicate invested in 'bridge' loans to finish hotels and picture houses whose finance had run out, for example (Menefee, 1969/1984: 220-1). They then invested in small and big industries in Karnataka, with considerable success for many years.
13. In 1958 a science block was begun, later the college got its own hostel, and by 1967 work began on housing for faculty (Menefee, 1969/1984: 74).
14. The link between reservation policies and caste tension is not just T.M.A.'s opinion: it is seriously discussed by scholars. Shani (2007), for example, holds that conflict related to the reservation policy has been at the roots of the frightening communal riots in Gujarat since 1985.
15. Then worth some Rs. 1,30,000.
16. The Madras government, through Health Minister A.B. Shetty, issued a notification that all unclaimed bodies in the region should go to the college for dissection. Shetty was a Bunt and thus a local man.
17. K.P. Shenoy, manager of the bank's branch in Dharwar, had assisted in the negotiations with Karnatak University. K.L.V. Nayak of the Mumbai branch took care of contacts with the state government there, and P.P. Shenai, head of the Chennai branch, kept in touch with the Madras health and education ministers to get the Madras government's permission to affiliate with Karnataka. N.K. Kamath of the Bangalore branch was also helpful when Manipal became a part of Mysore State (Menefee, 1969/1984: 86).
18. A GSB, of course.
19. The Catholics of South Kanara are commonly known as 'Mangaloreans'.
20. By 1976 there were such centres at Alevoor, Kapu, Kadekar, Katpadi, Udyavara, Padubidri and Malpe (Menefee 1969/1984: 104).
21. In 1973, two students were expelled for raping a nurse when hospitalized, and there was a violent demonstration to reinstate one of them. 'The students threw stones at the window of Dr. Pai's house, and when he came out on the balcony to see what was happening, he collapsed.

Dr. Shantaram, then student warden, cried to the students: 'Is this the gratitude you show for all that Dr. Pai has done for you?' 'At that the students parted,' says Menefee, 'and the crowd, ashamed, began to break up' (1969/1984: 120).

22. Yakshagana is a traditional dance theatre particular to the Kanara coast. The Kendra has its own troupe and trains young dancers.
23. This research institution has done enormous work on the folklore and rituals of South Kanara. It holds an impressive collection of videos documenting the rich ritual life of the region. It was originally aided by the Ford Foundation, but currently it is in a difficult situation due to lack of funds.
24. There are two large tile works, at Hangarkatta and at Honavara (North Kanara) and a smaller one at Madi, near Manipal. There is the General Construction Company, which 'supplies architectural and supervisory services' for buildings. Then there is Western Roadways, a trucking firm; Manipal Finance Company, dealing in small deposits and loans; Manipal Industries Marketing Division, who are agents for Escort/Yamaha motorcycles and tractors; and the Agricultural Division, dealing in pesticides and fertilizers (Menefee, 1969/1984: 223-4).
25. These schools were first established in Kerala under the Indo-Norwegian project.
26. A close relative of Michael Lobo, whose work on the Catholic community has been so useful to me.
27. In two years the underwritten policies increased from Rs. 8 million to 20 million (Menefee, 1969/1984: 206-8; Kamath, 1983: 142-5).
28. Tirupati is the main centre for the cult of Venkatesha or Venkatarama, and so a favoured pilgrimage place among the GSB. To go there for the marriage avoided the homes of their respective families, while Tirupati's religious importance may have lent some status or legitimacy to the ceremony.
29. Menefee notes that the public sector of heavy industry increased the value of its produce from Rs. 2.8 billion to 8 billion in the Pai years, while losses of Rs. 220 million in 1972-3 had turned to profits of Rs. 700 million by 1975-6 (1969/1984: 209-10). Fourteen public sector companies producing for Rs. 260 crore with losses of Rs. 19 crore in 1972, produced for Rs. 830 crore with a profit of Rs. 65 crore in 1976-7 (Kamath, 1983: 190).
30. In an overseas TV appearance, he said the Emergency 'would go down in history of India as one of the most productive periods not because it brought about a sense of direction and discipline which we have been

losing steadily for some time, but because it dynamised the entire nation to a new sense of dedication and commitment, and, most importantly, to a new articulation of renewed faith in the future of India. . . . ' (Kamath, 1983: 209).

31. Though the Rudolphs deemed that the architects of the Emergency had chosen to speak as leftists and act as men of the right (Rudolph and Rudolph, 1978: 390).
32. Kamath tells how Anant was courted by one group after another, including Morarji Desai and Indira Gandhi.
33. Goldsmiths are generally Acharivalis or Sonarvalis. The latter are the Sonargaras mentioned by Brouwer (1988). Vaishnavas and followers of Madhavacharya, they claim to be Brahmins, and are vegetarians, though like the GSB they eat fish. Most live in the coastal regions of Karnataka. Their main *math* is the Shree Vadirajatirtha *math* at Udupi. They differ from the Viswakarma goldsmiths in that they do founding work as well as the usual goldsmith's work. They were also moneylenders and pawnbrokers, while Viswakarma goldsmiths only engage in such activities 'when there is no local Sonargara Shroff' (Brouwer, 1988: 34-5).
34. The shop is also airconditioned, a rare luxury in Udupi shops.
35. My data on this family is scanty, as the brothers are not very talkative, and also very busy. Thus I know little of their origins and of what they did before founding the present concern.

6

Since 1980: The Present and the Future

By 1980, Udupi had become a diversified marketing centre and with Manipal, a centre of health care and education. The presence of foreign students even lent a certain cosmopolitan character to life in the town. It was the administrative centre of one of India's leading banks, and it remained an important centre of pilgrimage. Udupi had outgrown all the surrounding towns except Mangalore. And yet, even today, it remains a small town in many ways. The GSB families we have met still form the core of its bourgeoisie, which remains a small world where most people know each other. Thus Borkar, for example, knows or knows about most of the Konkani families I met. As a Rajapur Saraswat Brahmin (RSB),[1] his knowledge of the Konkanis probably surpasses that of members of the other castes. But low-caste people also seem to know a good deal about the main GSB families. Certainly, hierarchy is at work here: people know more about their equals and their superiors than of those who are lower in rank.

One feels strongly this small-town ambiance, where power of several kinds – economic, ritual, political – is shared by large family and caste groups, each organizing itself to keep its 'legitimate' share. 'Udupi people are clannish and petty-minded,' said one informant, a Shivalli Brahmin who had been in Kolkata for years. 'People are better in Kolkata.' When he returned to Udupi, he wanted to settle in the old family house near Kalsanka. His brother had taken over the house but did not use it, as he had built his own house elsewhere. Yet he had locked the house, and would not let his returning brother have it. In the end the latter asked the police to accompany him and bear witness as he broke the lock: this cost him Rs. 5,000 in bribes but he said, 'The courts would not only have taken a lot of time, they would also have been much more expensive.' Like most old Udupi families then, his brother had kept the old house. Owning a house in the old quarter of town marks the family status,[2] and established families have a central place in the social life of the town. This also means that members of such families are, to some extent, 'public figures' in town, known to everybody and conscious of the fact. They know they are being observed and commented upon by the public, and feel they should act, in both the theatrical and the instrumental sense, according to the expectations others have of them. This also means that I shall report here a discourse on various families that include criticism as well as praise, asking the reader to keep in mind that the judgements implied are not mine. Small talk of this kind simply forms part of the webs of communication that form the local community. In this sense, Udupi is much like small towns anywhere, and the important GSB families form the central part of the small town elite. Though the Tonse Pais are emblematic of the 'civic spirit' of the town, the reactions to their decline do not contradict the characterization of the town as 'clannish'.

And yet, as U.P. Kamath, the engineer responsible for most of Manipal, put it: 'The community here in Udupi is not traditional. And the problem is that in most of the places – they are all by the sea, except for Karkala – the community is gone, so you cannot study it. To find a traditional GSB community, you must go to Kochi.' It is certainly true that Udupi is a very modern place compared to neighbouring places such as Karkala or Mudabidri. And as the main architects of this modernity, the GSB in Udupi are hardly 'traditional'. But modernity in terms of business and practical matters does not necessarily imply a break with tradition. Rather, a tradition of leadership in creating modernity implies a vocation of continuous innovation. This continuity, while turned towards the future, is only strengthened by evocation of the past. Many of the older GSB shops effectively advertise their age, as if to stress this continuity. Even more present in everybody's mind is the history of each of the leading families. Perhaps the very presence of this living memory makes the exhibition of the past, through inanimate objects, superfluous.[3]

As in small towns all over the world, these leading families tend to stand, metonymically, for the whole community: they are 'the town'.

This is of course basically an upper-class or upper-caste view: every town has a different look to it whether we see it 'from above' or 'from below'. But since I am dealing here with the GSB who dominate Udupi's commerce and, more than any other group, represent the small town's bourgeoisie, it is mainly through their perspective that I present the place.[4]

There was a wind of change with the liberalization of the Indian economy under Prime Minister Rajiv Gandhi, which of course has only continued and accelerated since. A host of new products became available in the consumer market, and the difference is vast between what shops stocked in the early 1980s and what can be bought today. Naturally, those businessmen who were quick to take advantage of the new opportunities expanded, while others were left behind. There is today quite a few shops in Udupi that have closed down or are running at a very low level of activity, and, we may assume, profitability. Thus while some of the cloth shops have expanded, others have shut down or are more or less in the process of doing so.

In the following pages, we shall take stock of the contemporary situation of the various families we already know. Certainly, other castes have established important and viable businesses in Udupi: Catholics, Muslims and Bunts, but also members of the lower castes. The formerly untouchable Billavas and Protestant converts from that caste are present, and for many years the best modern hotel in Udupi has been the Khediyoor, owned by a Moghavera (fisherman caste).[5] Even so, the GSB still dominate Udupi's commerce.

THE GUNDU NAYAKS

After Independence, the business in imported goods that had been Ramakrishna Gundu Nayak's specialty vanished as import restrictions were draconian, and, moreover, constantly changing. Ramakrishna's shop had to be liquidated and his sons had to start all over again. The building at the corner of temple square and V.T. Street, which had been registered in the name of the Ramakrishna Gundu Nayak Memorial Trust, remained in family hands, so they could still use it. Still, the family firm went through a difficult period, and in spite of numerous initiatives, they have never managed to regain their former position. This has not been for lack of trying. At one time the family had several small enterprises in Dubai, when one of the brothers was still working there. When he went to the US, it became difficult to continue: in Dubai, as in most of the Gulf countries (Longva, 1997) you must have a local partner or sponsor, and, says Shailesh, the nephew of Gundu Nayak who heads the Udupi branch of the family, they tend to arrange the accounts and pocket the profits unless you are able to supervise the business continuously. One might think that the family's presence in the US would have been used to ameliorate the position of their Udupi enterprises, but this has not happened. It is Harish, the uncle once active in Dubai, who controls the trust that owns the family property in Udupi.[6] As a public trust, it has the right to take loans from the public, but the trust property cannot be sold, and whoever controls the trust also controls the credit made available to it. Those who are in America, however, take no interest in the Udupi businesses. It is difficult, says Shailesh, to launch any new initiative as long as the present situation of ownership and management continues. The Udupi brothers have no substantial property which can be used as security to finance investment. Thus they cannot do anything with the building, and this hampers the family enterprises in Udupi. Above the three ground floor shops, the upper story is now used as a storeroom for 'Ashirvad', Gundu's pottery and wooden handicrafts shop. The situation for the other two shops, says Shailesh – such as that of his father Ganesh – is more or less as if they were in rented accommodation.

The American branch also has interests in Mumbai, where it owns the Kamath printing works in Thane, and at Vapi in south Gujarat, where there's a factory making cardboard boxes. Mallarama, the elder daughter of Ramakrishna, sometimes comes to Mumbai to look after her business interests there, but she never visits Udupi. The Mumbai and Gujarat businesses originally belonged to her husband, and her son Prakash – Harish's brother-in-law and maternal cousin – is also involved in these firms. They also have a burger joint in America, and they used to run a similar restaurant near the Eros cinema in Mumbai, though the latter is now closed. This was a very profitable business, however, much more so than the cardboard factory, which is run by a manager. Mallarama got a good dowry when she married. Part of it was a flat Ramakrishna had in Mumbai, where he used to go to buy his imported goods. But this flat was sold in the 1970s. It was somewhere in the Tardeo area, where many GSB live.[7] The story of the Gundu Nayak family, therefore, is not really one of a family having 'come down in the world'.[8] The branch based in America is doing very well, but the Udupi branch has been left behind. Though the trust has prevented a final division, the story is one of a family split.

If Gundu had been head of the trust, says his nephew Shailesh, there would have been much better opportunities for credit and investment in the Udupi properties. But Gundu never believed in that kind of finance. He preferred to spend from his own profits. He always played safe, refusing to gamble, says his nephew. Ganesh, Shailesh's father, is much more interested in art and music than in making money. But today, says his son, money is everything, for influence, jobs and all. Even schools, he says, clearly referring to the situation in South Kanara, are purely commercial interests. Formerly they were more community-centred, that is, they were promoted for the good of the caste. The development of the Pai educational empire must be held partly responsible for this trend.

Shailesh himself used to run a welding workshop where he made steel shelves. But one day, while he himself was in Mumbai, the welding gas-bottle exploded. Water must be mixed with the gas, but his workman had let the water tank get empty. The entire workshop was destroyed and has since not been rebuilt. He also had an iron-working shop near the national highway but this too is no longer active. It is not lack of effort, but more than a fair share of bad luck which has kept the Gundu Nayaks from regaining some of their lost position.

THE AIRODY PAIS

We have told how the Airody Pai family has grown from their itinerant trading background to become, today, one of the most important business concerns in Udupi. Today, they advertise not only the quality of their products, but also their contribution to the ritual sector and to the common good of the community. Upstarts at first, they now rival with the best of Udupi's GSB families in ritual benevolence. Their centenary brochure shows their pride in these achievements.

The two main doors, with their sixty kgs of silver, of the Mahamaya temple at Ankola, and the four feet high silver altar of the Satyanarayana temple at Mumbai, were designed under his (Radhakrisna's) supervision. And during the Madhava Samalyara under the supervision of the pontiff of the Pejavar Math, on the pontiff's request, he organized an exhibition stall at Dharma-prakasha showing the *puja* items pertaining to Madhava tradition. Afterwards, there was a special request from Madras regarding these items. Recently, the late Shri D.P. Narayana Bhat, a famous sculptor (*shilpi*), who also received the national award, became Radhakrishna's close friend. Through him, Pai arranged to have fine artistic items made by D.P. Narayana Bhat.

This contribution to arts and religion is matched by social work, indicates the brochure:

They have not forgotten their place of origin, Airody. In memory of the late Airody Subbanna Pai, they donated the library of the Chetana High School at Hangarkatta. In 1968, in memory of the firm's silver jubilee, the Krishna Krupa building at Badagupete (Car Street) was constructed and there they established the Subbanna Pai Memorial Museum of antiquities showing the items that Subbanna Pai had collected out of his own interest.

There follows, in a personalized idiom, the story of what cynics might call a company takeover:

In the business of puja items the late Kalmanje Vyas Acharya was a pioneer and, though they were engaged in a similar business, Airody Subbanna Pai was very intimate with him. After Vyas' demise, his son-in-law K.L.N. Upadhyaya continued the business along with A. Radhakrishna Pai. After the death of K.L.N., his son, Dr. K.V.R. Upadhyaya, continued the business for some time, and in 1986, when he wanted to stop trading due to ill-health, they transferred the property to the Airody Pai group so that the business could continue. This is the finest example of the intimacy between the two firms.[9]

The next part of the brochure, 'Inseparable lives',[10] deals with the relationship of the two brothers, Radhakrishna and Ramnath:

Radhakrishna Pai and Ramnath Pai lived like two bodies and one soul. . . . Ramnath, the younger brother, was very pious, friendly and truthful. Supporting his brother, he became very popular among all. For the progress of the firm, he strived hard. Like Ganeshraya, Ramnath had no issue. One should learn the principles of managing a business from these two (brothers). On 23rd of November 1985, Ramnath died, and Radhakrishna suffered a heavy blow. He told his children to follow the directions and guidance given by Ramnath. Within eight months of the younger brother's death, on 13th July 1986, he (Radhakrishna) too left this world.

The brochure describes the progress of the firm up to 1996, the centenary year. Under the heading 'Continuation of the Tradition', we shift to the third generation:

Radhakrishna Pai had six sons; Ganeshyama, Vaikuntha, Giridara, Subbarna, Sridhara and Ramesha. The elder sons, Ganeshyama, Vaikuntha and Giridara are continuing the ancestral business of selling puja items and household utensils. Similarly, as a part of the diversification of the family business group, in 1983, the pioneering business of household electrical gadgets and television was started by A. Subbarna Pai, and the fifth son, Sridhara, assisted his elder brother. As another phase of diversification, in 1988 the Samparna department store, a supermarket with self-service facility, was started and its management was taken up by Ramesh, the youngest son. The tradition of the late Radhakrishna and Ramnath Pai is continuing without break.

So is the tradition of donating impressive ritual objects to the temples.

For the Mahalasa temple in Goa, a huge bronze lampstand, 50 feet high and of 1500 kg weight, made from panchaloha,[11] was contributed by the firm in 1978. This (lampstand) is a very rare achievement in the whole country. Recently, in 1994, a similarly fashioned bronze flagpole, 42 feet high and of 1000 kg weight, was constructed.[12]

Charity is often aimed at the temples in India, but in South Kanara there is also a strong tradition of investment in education and other public concerns – and every business enterprise of importance has its own charitable trust. The Airodys are no exception:

After the demise of Ramnath Pai, and on the inspiration of Radhakrishna Pai, the Radhakrishna Pai Ramanatha Pai Memorial Trust was established. Programmes in the public interest were taken up and the recognition of talent in the Udupi taluka is notable among them. Such recognition of talent is essential. Every year on Republic Day, those who gain the first, second and third place in the SSLC examination will receive a cash award, and the student who secures the first place from his school will be given a consolation price. And at the Chetana school at Airody one student annually is given a scholarship by the trust. In 1993, the Centenary of the firm was celebrated very simply and for the sweet memory of the event, the A.R.P. Sadhana, a multistorey building, was constructed and there the group's administrative offices were established.

One member of the family, A. Vaikunta Pai, is a trustee of an orphanage run by the *maths*. The president is the *swami* of Pejawur *math*, but among other trustees there is at least one Billava (Mr. Santi, the tailor specializing in school uniforms) and one Sri Nagendra K., possibly a *madhiwala* (washerman). The Airody family's choice of social involvement does, it seems, tend towards supporting what in Udupi would be seen as orthodox, Hindu, institutions.

Next, a separate chapter of the brochure is dedicated to the firm's 'stepping into the gold business', something which cannot be seen simply as a business venture. Dealing in gold, the purest of metals, is a prestigious matter, and the goldsmith remains the uppermost among craftsmen. The Airodys' brochure clearly shows their pride in taking this step: 'As a part of the diversification programme and the most famous phase (of it) the group entered the golden ornament business. Late Radhakrishna Pai had already had the ambition of opening a jewellery shop with new designs and first-class workmanship. In order to realize the father's dream, all the brothers studied this business. Due to the efforts of the Airody Pai brothers, 'Airody Jewellers Pvt. Ltd. was started and is ready to render service to the public. In quality control and design, exemplary service should be rendered with the intention, also, of manufacturing ornaments. According to the ideals of Radhakrishna and Ramnath Pai, we solicit the affection and support of the public in the jewellery business also, along with God's Grace.' I can certainly testify that the shop offers a choice of designs which stand out as among the best in Udupi. We found some traditional patterns, but primarily recent designs from Mumbai, so local ladies may adorn themselves in metropolitan style.

Finally, the brochure announces as 'Future Plan: Extension of the museum':

> Airody R&R Memorial Trust is planning in the future to extend the antiquity museum. The Museum, registered in 1943, is at present situated in the Krishna Krupa building in Badagupete (Car Street), a building constructed as a memorial of the 75 years' jubilee of the firm. For lack of space we have not been able to make it attractive, so we shall shortly transfer it to a spacious building with the aim of giving a better museum to Udupi.

The museum, or rather the collection occupies the first floor above the electrical appliances shop in Car Sreet. It is an interesting and impressive collection, including several pieces that are two or three hundred years old. Once arranged, it should give an idea of the development of the artefacts of the *bhuta* cults, for example. Thus the old *bhuta* masks were quite simple, clearly appropriate to what must then have been very much a 'folk' cult, well before modern and Gulf money produced an inflation in prestigious cult objects made of silver. Other cult items would also demonstrate interesting historical trends. According to Ghanshyam, the present head of the family, the collection should be housed in a new building, closer to the present centre of Udupi, planned for completion in 2006. When I discussed the plans with him in 2004, he had a particular site in mind. By that time they hoped to have found somebody able to catalogue and label the various objects for exhibition.

The Udupi Kamaths comment on the museum: 'The Airodys are buyers of brass and metals, so naturally they come across old things. These things they don't put in the museum: either they are resold or melted down to make new items.' In other words, the Airody concern is seen as vertically integrated: buyers of metal, smelters, re-founders and sellers of images. The museum here becomes a natural by-product of their business activity, reassembling objects too old or rare to be smelted down. This implicit criticism, however, does not alter the fact that the museum objects would be gone today had the Airodys not saved them.

I have quoted their brochure extensively to give an idea of the image a highly successful GSB family wants to present to the world. We see that besides the quality of the business and its goods, much of the store is set on tradition, on maintaining a good name. The brochure returns several times to the ethical qualities and religious devotion of family members. There are echoes, here, of the concept of *abru* or honour known from the literature on Indian merchants. But there are also elements of the benefactor image, as the gifts to temples and the Memorial Trust show. Then there is the ubiquitous image of the 'social worker' – the firm did not just use traditional craftsmen, it 'assisted the home industry'. This implies engagement with social and political issues, and so the family's support of the

RSS is shown as a courageous and self-sacrificing effort, apparently without fear that political opponents would prefer to deal with other firms. These points are, I think, significant.

The Airodys' *kuladevata* is Mahalasa Narayani, whose main temple is at Mardol in Goa. We have seen how they have given a major object – the lampstand – to that temple. Their *ishtadevata* is Venkatarama. It has been a long time, says Anant, Giridash's son, who often replaces his father in the gold shop, since we visited Mardol. Certainly, he himself has not been there for a long time. It struck me as interesting that this remark should come from a member of a family that openly declares its Hindu orthodoxy, and I wondered whether the Airodys have not, to some extent, replaced their family and caste cult with an adherence to a more wide-ranging, generalized form of Hinduism.

I had many a good talk with Anant, an intelligent youth who is now taking daily care of the family's gold shop. He is a Bachelor of Commerce from MGM College, and his is the first generation in the family to have a formal business education. I asked him if he found the education useful for his work. He reflected on the question. 'Yes', he said,

> there are useful things, like accountancy, company law, and so on. But they also teach you a lot of useless bullshit. And anyway, once I got down here (in the shop), everything was completely different. There are so many things to do that I did not know. But it is quite exciting, I am learning all the time. Every day brings something new. Business is a matter of getting to know people, understand people. It is always a question of human relations.[13]

We also talked about the gold shop. I asked whether there had been resistance among the traditional goldsmiths (the Viswakarma Sonagaras) to the opening of such shops. Anant looked puzzled. 'No, nothing of the sort,' he said. 'This is not a new thing. There were already many such shops. Swarna,[14] for example, started around 1957.' Though there are still goldsmiths producing to order and dealing directly with the customer, the trend seems to be for sales and production to be separated. This is clearly related to the demand for new and fashionable designs. What they do at the gold shop is to look continuously for good designs, and then place an order with whoever offers to make it well. They keep a 'catalogue' of standard designs, which customers will consult to pick what they want: 'often, they will ask for some modification, so we have it made for them'. They also, of course, keep a stock for ready sale in their shop. Such shops stock a different range of goods from that of the traditional goldsmiths. The latter generally keep to the old designs, within a regional tradition of jewellery: quite different, for example, from what you will see in Gujarat, in Rajasthan, or even in Tamil Nadu. Swarna and the Airody shop try to follow the latest fashion trends from Mumbai and the catalogue shown to the Airodys' customers comes from a Mumbai firm. The jewellery they stock is thus mainly of modern designs – very attractive, in fact – and aimed at middle-class customers conscious of the latest trends. In effect they do not impinge on the traditional goldsmiths' market but supplement it, since the average goldsmith is too busy practising his craft to act as a designer and follow the fashion at the same time. 'There is no problem,' says Ananth, 'in finding craftsmen to do the work: some work from their home, others in their shop. They don't mind making objects which will be sold by others. It is a commission, that's all. But to make it work, you have to have the contacts. . . .' By taking orders from firms such as Swarna and the Airodys, the goldsmiths can concentrate on what they do best and secure a steady stream of orders, probably welcome since the large number of traditional goldsmith shops in Udupi are not, generally speaking, full of customers all day.[15] What the 'gold shops' of the GSB do, then, is to secure additional work for the best goldsmiths.

Anant asked me what was the situation of 'small shops like this' in the West. Answering as best I could, I said it depended on the business: bakers in France do very well, since their bread is preferred to what you can find in a supermarket. 'What about hardware?' he asked: I felt this was a line where small shops tended to give way to big chains, able to offer more choice and lower prices. 'From thereon,' said Anant perceptively, 'it must be a question of niche.' I asked him, whether his education had not prepared him to think in terms of such concepts as 'market niches'. He smiled and said emphatically: 'No! A good businessman has always had to think like that, even if he may not have been using that word. Being a businessman is not something you learn in theory. You must have a "nose" for it.'

In terms of Sampath's book on family businesses (2001), the

Airodys have now reached the stage of "B. Com.". The young are educated to take over, and so they become 'commerce professionals'. Ghanshyam seems to be leading the enterprises in a rather autocratic manner. But Anant does not seem to feel choked by the family atmosphere. As he put it: 'There is so much to learn.' Talking to him, one feels that stepping into an old – but dynamic – family firm is something which gives him all the scope he could want. He clearly would not want to be anywhere else. That he runs the daily business of their most prestigious shop shows the esteem in which he is held by his elders. If, as I suspect, he will take over leadership of the business one day, he will be well prepared, and will certainly try to develop the enterprise further. It remains to be seen, of course, whether the family unity of the Airodys will last into the next generation. It very well might.

Yet even in this apparently monolithic family there have been splits in the past. The Airodikar branch was founded by a son of Ramdas, the third son of Subbarna Pai, the freedom fighter who used to make *Panchaloha* icons. This branch is commercially active in Udupi, quite independently of the Airody concern. A.S. Pai, the owner of the shop, is a younger son of Ramdas, and to distinguish it from the Airody concern, his name is given as Airodikar on the shop sign. On the wall of his shop, we find the portrait not of his father but his older brother, of whom A.S. seems to have been very fond. There is also a photo of those assembled at a family function to remember his brother. It seems to me there are no members of the larger Airody family in that picture. There was then a split in the family at some point.[16] Though A.S. stressed that his shop is an entirely independent concern, he also gave me a book on the Airody family, and explained the genealogical links with the others. He, however, never told me the reason for the split.

A.S. is the founder of a merchants' organization, the Udupi Zilla Varthakara Sangha. This is not a small organization: according to the founder it has some 3,500 members.[17] All are merchants, though they deal in every kind of goods; no other kind of business is accepted for Sangha membership. They range from big businesses to very small ones. There is no fixed fee for membership, but the organization advertises in all the local newspapers when contributions are needed.

The organization is doing 'social work', which A.S. Pai cites as his main interest beside business: the main aim is to help in providing education to those without means, but they also assist widows or people with disability. A.S. criticizes the Chamber of Commerce in Udupi: it is not independent, just a branch of the Mangalore Chamber. He sees it as a clique of some six to eight families who stick together and try to control everything.[18] 'They do no useful work, they just enjoy – no social work, just having a good time,' he says. They are all big businessmen and take no interest in the problems of ordinary merchants. So the latter needed their own organization, which A.S. duly provided. 'Social work – *seva* – is the main thing for a businessman,' he says 'Business should not only be about money.' To my remark that GSB dominance of Udupi commerce – say, from around 1900 – must now be threatened by competition from other castes, A.S. stresses that almost 90 per cent of Udupi commerce is still controlled by his caste-fellows.[19] Revisiting him one year later, I asked about his organization. As far as I understand, it is very much an ad hoc affair; he issues a call for contributions to some humanitarian project, receives them, and organizes the activity under the name of the 'Take Care Foundation'. 'Membership' of the association is a rather approximate and informal affair.

Yet A.S. does seem to have a considerable network of contacts. They meet in his shop and discuss freely. Here I met Gopal Shetty, a locally known writer and left-winger who is a Bunt;[20] but there's also one Mr. Nayak, a builder, and another who is the proprietor of 'Modern Electrical Constructions'. The latter are both GSB. One reporter from a local newspaper also looked in. A.S. himself has little time to take part in these discussions: the shop is very busy and he has to serve the customers. In short, A.S. runs a viable shop and has many friends and, yet the Airodikar branch in no way enjoys the power or prestige of the original family.

UDUPI KAMATHS

U.A. Kamath, the engineer who built most of Manipal for the Tonse Pais and was the first principal of the MIT, was the first of his family to use 'U' (for Udupi) before his name. U.A.'s father, however, used K for Kallianpur, so his links to the Tonse Pais go back to the days when the families knew each other in Kallianpur. Their family home is just opposite to the house of the Kallianpur Baligas – the family from which Dr. Baliga of Bombay, as also T.M.A. Pai's mother came – and next to the Venkatarama temple.[21] U.A. was responsible for the rebuilding of that temple as also that of the Mahalasa temple in Basrur. In all, he has built or rebuilt about thirty temples in the region. They include the central Krishna temple of Manipal, and he is quite proud of the dome of that temple. In fact, he says, his name should be Siribettu, which is the part of Udupi where he lives – the old quarter of the Chitrapur Saraswats. His father did in fact buy the house from a member of that community. It is an old, typically Konkani house and he is very fond of it. Like K.K. Pai, he is concerned about the schemes to widen the road, which would mean that the house would have to be demolished, and he is very sad at the idea. U.A. is the brother-in-law and close friend of the historian, K.R. Kuduva, while his son, U.P. Kamath is a classmate of the fourth Airody brother, Subbarna, who 'sits' in the appliance shop; U.P. knows him well. We see how the GSB networks in Udupi imply that almost everybody knows or knows about everybody else. U.P., whose ideas of the GSB community in Cochin we have encountered earlier, continues the engineering tradition. The *kuladevata* of the Udupi Kamaths is Ganapati-Mahamaya – 'we are told', says U.P. Kamath, referring to what the Goan pandits say. He feels however that their real lineage deity must be Mahamaya.[22] Their *gotra* is Vaccha.

THE KALSANKA PAI

The Kalsanka Pai family is still well represented in business, though their best-known member, K.K. Pai, reckoned as the head of the family today, is administering the empire of his in-laws, the Tonse Pais. Yet two shops in the temple square are part of the Kalsanka Pai family concern. One is Anil Prabhakar Pai K., a dealer in plywood whose shop is located right in the middle of the temple square, facing the temple end of the Car Street. The shop is run by a nephew of K.K. Pai, the son of his younger brother. This nephew was quick to point out that the shop or family had no connection with the Gundu Nayaks (which, in view of that family's history, is not without significance). The shop's location is surprising in terms of urban geography, for one certainly does not expect to find a plywood trader among the goldsmiths and religious souvenir shops that dominate the block. There was, in fact, a grocery store here, but the site was taken over by the Kalsanka Pai family some twenty years ago (about 1983-4) and they subsequently started the present shop. I have no information on the shop which preceded it and its family, but it is highly probable that this firm too had belonged to a GSB family. I do not know, either, whether the shop went bankrupt, was closed for family reasons, or simply moved elsewhere.

We had the occasion to visit the oldest shop of the Kalsanka Pais on Diwali and found the whole family gathered there, for the *puja* which includes the annual consecration of the account books. Clearly, this gathering was one of the occasions where the family manifested itself ritually as a unit. We met K.K. Pai, and were offered *prasad* from the ritual. 'This is where it all started, back in 1898,' he said. He was on a 'round', having been to quite a number of Diwali *pujas*. From there, the members of the family – some 25-30 persons – went to the plywood shop, no doubt to repeat the ritual in a simpler form.

The Pais' ancestral house is on the eastern side of Kalsanka, towards Kadiyali. It is owned by K.K. Pai, who also used to have his office near the Kalsanka corner of the Gundibail road. This house, says one informant, is one main reason why the municipality has not been able to widen the road, which takes all the traffic from Udupi towards Manipal and is extremely congested.[23] K.K. Pai is a very influential man in Udupi and was president of the municipality in the 1980s. As director of the Syndicate Bank, he was an expansive banker who kept up with the times by frequent visits to banks abroad. The Syndicate Bank continued to flourish in his time, and as director of the bank he gradually became the effective head of his in-law's family, especially after the crash of Ramesh's investment corporation.

Still, one informant held that K.K. is more of a figurehead than a real leader – 'He will turn up at all kinds of functions and talk for hours about nothing.' She clearly implied that people are not really taking him seriously: though they may defer to him apparently, they will go on to do what they want. I met K.K. on his way to distribute the 2004 awards to eminent Konkanis – it was very much a 'ballroom' occasion, held at the Pai's Valley View Hotel. It is typical of K.K.

Pai's position in Udupi's GSB community that he should be chosen to distribute such awards. Figurehead or not, he was certainly the single most eminent personality of the GSB community in Udupi at that time.

The empire of the Tonse Pais, of which K.K. was then the effective head, stands out as the single most outstanding achievement of the GSB community in South Kanara. We have dealt with the growth of that empire – the Syndicate Bank, the colleges, the hospitals, the town of Manipal – in the last chapter. How was all that possible?

'South Kanara,' says Menefee, trying to explain the success of the Tonse Pais,

> was a place of many languages and religions – much more of a melting pot than the interior of India. Here there was gentleness and tolerance, and new ideas were not resisted as much as in the more rigid Hindu societies of the interior or in the north where communal tension between Hindus and Muslims poisoned the atmosphere. South Kanara was a good place to grow up. The time was right, too. India was beginning to ferment in the first third of the century . . . with Independence, pride in India became a new impetus to political and economic advancement. (1969/1984: 256)

I must agree with this characterization: South Kanara was, and remains, a strangely cosmopolitan place.

'And then there were the social and personal factors,' continues Menefee. 'The Pai brothers had the good fortune to be born into the Gowda Saraswat community of Brahmins who had a strong tradition of education and service. It was the custom in this group for a family to educate at least one son for business or professions such as law or medicine' (ibid.). This custom, we may remember, was not very old: T.M.A. Pai's generation was perhaps the second to receive such education – as was the case in his own family. But the GSB would seem to have sided with 'modernity' and 'progress' from the early colonial period on.

'The Pais had their roots in the village life of India, which gave them contact with and confidence in the common man,' says Menefee. 'This they kept all their lives, and it was an essential ingredient of their business success. They were born of the right parents, too. From their father they got early training in strict moral principles, and from their mother a strong family loyalty, a faith in education and a feeling of responsibility to help others. The four brothers all had a strong puritanical streak and an idealism which found its expression in "social work"' (ibid.: 256-7). I will add only that the moral qualities we are talking about here were indeed a feature of the bourgeoisie in its period of greatness: there are parallels between the morality of the Pais in their heyday and some of the great families of the Victorian period in Britain. Common to both were the modernist belief in progress, which in India did not suffer the setback that weakened it in Europe after the First World War.

'They also got from both the Pai and Baliga families a "joint family" tradition of sharing each other's responsibilities, which made them a close-knit group', says Menefee (ibid.: 257). Others have stressed this importance of the joint family in the Indian entrepreneurial tradition (Tripathi and Mehta, 1990; Lachaier, 1999), and probably our own, Western, folklore of entrepreneurship as individual endeavour is seriously faulted by examples that may be exceptional, such as Henry Ford.[24] Family dynasties were important in the founding years of Western capitalism, and many stayed united for several generations. Much Japanese entrepreneurship shows a similar, family-based, tradition (Tripathi, 1997).

Much of what Menefee says is true, then, and certainly the Pai empire was built on relations of trust. It is important to realize that the money for the hospitals and colleges did not come from the Pai family's own pockets. It was not a case of 'charity' as when, for example, a temple finances some cultural institution or some rich financier or firm simply siphons off tax-free money to improve its image and, by the way, provide something socially useful. Menefee suggests that the total direct contribution from the Pai family amounts to about Rs. 2,00,000. Thus it was the will and initiative to create, rather than the financial investment, which was outstanding. 'It was T.M.A.'s ability to elicit cooperation from townspeople and parents, and his talent for organizing the Academy's finances, that did the job,' says Menefee (1969/1984: 122). Kamath, however, remarks that 'the motives of the Pai brothers were frequently questioned and sometimes suspected. The Pais would do nothing if they did not see profit in it, it was whispered.' Indeed, the Pais did make money from most of their undertakings, but, says Kamath, they did not live differently from the rest of Udupi's middle class, and 'did not flaunt their wealth as many of the newly-rich in Mumbai, for example, did. They retained their middle class values' (Kamath, 1983: 84). By the time Menefee wrote, the Tonse Pai family was still well united. U.A. Pai had four sons and T.M.A. four: all were in leading positions somewhere in the family enterprises.

In many ways, the values Kamath refers to remain typical of Udupi's middle class even today. Sure, the rich have new cars and large villas, but there is no Pai mansion nor anything worth that name among any of the other prominent GSB families. Udupi remains, in this sense, a small town where the leading families remain inside the circle of the approachable. To put it in simple sociological terms, most people depend too much on their local networks to try to stand out and apart. There is no mansion in Udupi comparable to the one B. Manjunatha Pai built himself in Karkala,[25] and no family there has tried to imitate landed aristocracy in its way of life, such as happened to many of the biggest entrepreneur families in the West.[26]

Much of the Pai empire's success, then, has to do with a certain solidarity of the middle class, of which the GSB families were the node. This middle-class solidarity which as we have seen did not necessarily manifest itself in the political sphere, was also cemented by clubs, and here the Tonse Pais played a central role. Among T.M.A. Pai's many activities was the founding of Udupi's Rotary Club, in 1957. Under his guidance, new clubs were sponsored in Karkala and Kundapur. One of the first activities of the Udupi Club was to organize a 'blood bank' for the Kasturba Hospital. T.A. Pai, in his turn, founded the Lion's Club in Udupi.

T.A. remained a member of the family: he was very close to his younger brother Ramesh, and they 'worked *in tandem*' on a number of projects. 'But if the brothers disagreed, this was a matter within the family. It was only in his last years that Anant was to feel a sense of isolation, brought about, in part, by his defeat in the general elections and by the distance he had kept between him and others. . . . What he had apparently not realised,' says Kamath with considerable sociological shrewdness, 'was that times had changed. When *he* was growing up, the fortunes of the Pais were still on the ascendant; an inner cohesion sustained them. By the time he was a middle-aged man, those fortunes peaked out and reached a plateau. The clan spirit was giving way to individual enterprise' (ibid.: 84-5).

This seems to be a shrewd observation, and so the reasons for the decline of the Tonse Pais' once-eminent position may be related to the split of the joint family – as has been the case for the Ammunje Nayaks and, we have seen, the Gundu Nayaks, but in a different way.

M. Nagesh Kini, the printer, has his own comments on the decline of the Pai empire. Even before the demise of their mutual fund, says Nagesh Kini, there was a split between the 'Ramesh group' – centered around T.A.'s younger brother whose strategies were ultimately foiled by the bankruptcy of the mutual fund – and the 'K.K. group', headed by K.K. Pai, who was then the chairman of the Syndicate Bank. As Nagesh Kini sees it, the split was not just personal but also concerned financial strategy: Ramesh was very expansive and apt to take risks, while K.K. was more prudent – a typical banker – and followed a more conservative strategy. Ramesh's demise through the failure of his investment fund reduced the role of the Tonse Pais further in the empire they had created. The Manipal institutions are still there, but the role the family plays in them has declined.

'T.M.A. thought only about Manipal,' said one informant.

> He was working all the time to develop Manipal; he did not bother about India or anything else outside, about the larger society. But his successors put their money outside Manipal, they invested elsewhere, and so Manipal has been coming down. They still have heaps of money, but it is invested elsewhere. Manipal is now going down the drain. . . .

Part of the hospital has now been sold to the Premji family, says one informant. Formerly, the Manipal Drug House furnished medecines for the hospital patients. Now the Premji family has made it a rule that no outside medicine can be used. So the Drug House – owned by a member of the Tonse Pai family, a brother of Ranga Pai, has lost a lot of business.

It is no wonder that the Tonse Pais are the family most talked about in Udupi and Manipal. Two books (Menefee, 1969/1984; Kamath, 1983) deal with the exploits of the family, both written in an enthusiastic vein. Many individuals in Udupi are ready to share this general enthusiasm, but there are also critics. One of the latter had a handicapped son and the family actually moved to Manipal to avail themselves of the possibilities of treatment at the hospital. The treatment worked, but the illness had produced a mental handicap. At that time, the T.M.A. Pai Foundation ran a school for mentally retarded children in Manipal, the fees were reasonable and included pick-up by the school van. But at the end of the boy's first year at school the institution was closed, without prior consultation or notice: the Pais simply said they could not afford to continue with the school.

The informant says she tells this story to illustrate how 'charity' works in South Kanara. 'The Pais had crores and crores of rupees,' she says, 'yet they could not find money for this school, even though it was a very small institution having only 18 pupils. Later, she adds: 'All the later Pais had very ambitious wives who liked to spend money on themselves.' T.A.'s second wife is renowned for her charity work, but this critic was caustic:

> She (T.A.'s wife) used to receive government money – 4,00,000 to 5,00,000 rupees a year – for her work with 'handicapped children'. But I never saw any of that work. I had a handicapped child, so I should know: instead of doing this work, they closed the school. Yet T.A.'s widow continued to receive the money – just before her death, she received a grant of 8,00,000 rupees for such work. Where that money went, nobody knows.[27]

She went on to tell the story of how the school driver and the parents managed to get the school running again, but this time the Kalkuda Foundation – run by the *maths* – managed to take most of the credit for the work. 'Everybody wants to put up their name and advertise themselves through "charity", yet when it comes to actual contributions, they give very little. In fact, even the funds of the original Pai-run school was not put up by them, but by the Lion's Club.' This is true of most of the Manipal institutions, she says: the funds really came from elsewhere – outside donations, state grants and contributions, etc. The Pais put up very little themselves. 'So what is called "social work" is sometimes mainly show.' We may note a slight contradiction here: if the funds came from elsewhere – which seems largely to be true – is it really true that the Pais had 'crores and crores' of rupees?

Or, as another contact said after the demise of the Pai's mutual fund, in which many people in Udupi lost their savings: 'Nobody believes them now. They have lost all respect. So many people trusted them with their savings: they would give 15 per cent rather than 7 per cent interest. So naturally people were interested. Then one day they were told that all their savings were gone.'

Jayashankar Kuthpadi, a Billava teacher, social worker and Congress party politician, stresses that the Tonse Pais have done 'an enormous amount of good work for the people' in the Udupi area, in banking, insurance and education. 'They really are respected for these things,' he says, 'but their empire is no longer what it was.' There were 'some financial problems,' and also the old generation is dying out and there is a problem in taking over and furthering the activities through the new generation. He contrasts the 'Pai empire' to that of Dharmasthala . . . which is currently flourishing.

U.A. Kamath, for years one of the closest associates of T.M.A. Pai, spoke very warmly of the founder of the 'Manipal empire'. He also stressed, however, that the Manipal complex was 'no longer family' and that 'things were not the same'. But working for Manipal was special, he said. At one time he was fully engaged in teaching, was principal of the technical college, and also – in his 'spare time' – built all the main buildings at Manipal, from 1957 to 2001. The latter was well after his official retirement. As he put it, 'you cannot just leave' and let the others get on with the problems. And yet, 'you must know when to step aside, so other people can come up'.

Others reiterate rumours of corruption. 'The black money is going to the Pais – K.K. and his friends,' says one informant. Another informant is making a bitter comment on the Manipal hospitals. His elder sister's husband, from Delhi, got viral fever while studying there. He was offered airlift to Delhi or a doctor sent to him down here, but instead special medicine was airlifted from America, since the Manipal hospital insisted they could manage. But they botched the whole thing, maladministering the drug, and his brother-in-law died. 'That is Manipal,' he says. 'No human dimension, only money. That's why I don't like them.' This happened in 1989.

One 'rowdy' in Udupi had a speciality of 'helping' people, says one informant. 'Say, you want your daughter to study at Manipal, and they demand Rs. 8 lakh under the table. So, this man would ask one lakh, then go to Manipal: "you take this girl on, or your own daughter will die." From the girl's father he will ask another lakh, thus reducing the cost of admission from Rs. 8 to Rs. 2 lakh.' It was not clear, here, whether the one lakh actually went to Manipal, or whether the 'rowdy' took it all. Whatever the truth of such stories, Manipal has definitely lost some of its former aura of 'social work', and explanations run from those blaming the Tonse Pais to others implying that things go wrong because they are no longer in control. At one level, of course, these two explanations are contradictory. As manifestations of social change of a family cult that cannot be sustained at its former level, they are not.

Ranga Pai is a younger member of the Tonse Pai family whose main interest is in cultural activities. He is the son of late Ramakrishna Pai by the latter's second wife.[28] Ranga is the deputy registrar of – Manipal Academy of Higher Education (MAHE) where K.K. Pai is the registrar. According to some bad tongues, Ranga was first put in charge of the family hospitals, but proved inefficient, and so he was given this secondary role in the education trust. Ranga, however, is very active in organizing cultural events. Typically, he organized a recital of classical Hindustani music at Manipal, held in the Golden Jubilee Hall of the Syndicate Bank. In spite of this obvious link to a family concern, we did not see any of the other prominent Pais at the concert. Still, the concert was an important affair and several dignitaries were invited, among them the District Commissioner and the Police Commissioner, who both garlanded the performers. It was a concert of high quality. Present too was Mr. Murali, president of the Car Street Friends Club, the dynamo behind numerous cultural activities, notably poetry and music. He often works with Ranga Pai to organize such events.[29]

Ranga Pai was also opening an exposition of paintings at the Ranga Kala Academy downtown a little later. This is the art school housed in the former Virashaiva *math*. It was striking how he arrived, quite simply driving and parking his Zen himself – a contrast to the rather ceremonious arrival of the senior members of the family on such occasions. Describing himself as an 'art and music lover', he struck an individualist note in his speech: 'For the first twenty years of our life, we are under the tuition and guidance of our parents; then, in our married life, the man is tutored by his wife and the wife by her husband. But I feel that we also have to stop and ask ourselves: Who am I? Who am I becoming? And in that part of life, art has a great part to play.'

'Ranga Pai is different from the others,' said one informant. 'Unlike the other Pais he is quite genuine in his efforts on the cultural front.' But, she adds, 'he may not have much of a say in the running of things at Manipal.'

The painter was a young woman from Jamnagar in Gujarat, Hebal Sampat, who had come to Manipal for medical treatment six months earlier. She joined the Manipal Junior Arts School and in four months had produced enough to hold her own exhibition. Her husband is with L&T,[30] and both he and the girl's parents had come down from Mumbai for the occasion. The pictures were mainly landscapes, several of them clearly Western; some of the best being snowscapes. Other dignitaries present were P.N. Acharya, a senior painter of Udupi; A.S. Vishwanath, principal of the Ranga Kala Academy where the exhibition was held, Dr. Mrs. H.J. Gowra, the principal of the Junior Arts School at Manipal, a paediatrician; and K. Damodar Aithal, the president of the Udupi District Working Journalists' Association.

With Ranga Pai we seem to see a conversion from money to culture, a classical theme in literature on the old bourgeoisie. Brought up to appreciate the best in culture, the younger generation no longer fits the merciless world of business and moneymaking. From Boston Brahmins to the old merchant families of Bergen, my home town, the pattern seems to repeat itself. Am I not, as professor of anthropology, the logical product of decline of a family that once exported timber and owned ships? As I will be the first to maintain, the term decline is, in this context, entirely dependent on the perspective chosen.

The great GSB families continue to be important in Udupi, not only in cultural but still, and above all, in commercial activities. As this chapter has shown, they are not just important for what they do: they are also the objects of local myths, of criticism, even of slander. In a very real sense, they are the 'society' of the town – or what in current parlance may be termed the 'people'. More strictly speaking, the 'people' is precisely what they are not. Democracy has evolved, in Udupi as elsewhere in India, and civil society is no longer restricted to a few upper caste groups, as was the case in Karkala around 1900. Even among the bourgeoisie, the GSB have important rivals today: the Catholics and the Bunts are the most important groups, but important individuals have emerged from communities that were once outside the pale, such as the Billavas and the Moghaveras.

Yet the GSB community is still central to developments in Udupi. In 2006, a new complex had come up close to the bus station, housing the kind of elegant shops one associates with big towns like Mangalore or even Bangalore itself. Typically, perhaps, the manager of the very smart clothes shop is an RSB returnee, who grew up in Mumbai – in fact, a nephew of Mohandas Borkar, the estate agent who found us a house in Udupi and who remained one of my best informants and helpers, as well as a friend. But the promoters and owners of the new complex are a consortium formed from two of the oldest GSB families: the Ammunje Nayaks and the Kalsanka Pais. Clearly, the old GSB families continue to be in control, even when the project in question may be too big for the capital a single family firm can raise.

NOTES

1. The RSB have common origins with the Saraswats and the GSB, but have long been separate. Rajapur is a small town north of Goa which was then a port. It is therefore quite likely that they settled in Rajapur to pursue trade. For some time at least, Rajapur was under the Bijapur sultanate, and their living under Muslim rule may have affected their status relative to those Saraswats who went south. But my informants have no recollection of why or when the group settled there, or why they left. At present, the RSB are a caste seen as somewhat lower than the GSB. Apparently, most were farmers until recently and they do not have the same business traditions as the GSB. Mr. Borkar's knowledge of the GSB families is considerable, but the latter generally have little knowledge about the RSB.
2. The reason why he would not allow his brother from Kolkata to live there is more obscure. His moving in would hardly reduce the family standing, unless the returnee was somehow seen as unworthy of the family. Or could it be that housing the brother in the ancestral house would hurt the remaining brother's position as head – in his brother's absence – of the local family group? This would make the returned emigrant's use of the term 'clannishness' more comprehensible.

3. At Manipal, Vijana Shenoy has assembled a number of old Konkani houses and objects in the 'heritage village'. It has not become a public, open-air museum, however: the demand may not yet be there. One might speculate here on the genesis of local history museums which are such a common feature of many small American towns. Is it the rapid social change, engendering fear of the loss of memory, which incites citizens to found such museums?
4. To describe a place like Udupi from the point of view of each constituent community would of course be a lifetime's work, or alternatively that of a large group of researchers. It has not been attempted here. My wife, Marine Carrin, did however work on the Billava community, a formerly untouchable group, while I was doing the GSB, and her forthcoming work may serve as a counterpoint to what I say here. See also Chapter 11, where some critical voices will be heard.
5. It is perhaps significant that this hotel is missing from the main Udupi website, run by a group of GSB.
6. Though he was the youngest of the brothers, he was chosen by Ramakrishna as his successor to administer the Ramakrishna Gundu Nayak Memorial Trust. Mallarama, the elder sister, is still the legal head of the trust, seconded in practice by Harish. 'It is very difficult,' says Shailesh of the relationship to Harish and his sister, Shailesh's aunt Mallarama, indicating that his aunt is, above all, interested in money.
7. Much of old Mumbai is divided into quarters dominated by a single community. There is a Parsi concentration around Kalbadevi Road and the inner part of Colaba Causeway; Goan concentrations further south in Colaba and around Metro Cinema and GSB in Tardeo, for example.
8. They have good marriage connections. Shailesh's *mama* (mother's brother), who is also his father's brother's wife's brother, is Venkatesh Nayak Honavara. (As we have noted, Udupi families put their village of origin as the first part of their name. But the practice varies locally, as we see here: Venkatesh Nayak puts his place of origin, Honavara, at the end. Generally all GSB include the place of origin somewhere in their name, however.) He has an Ayurvedic shop bearing his own name in Sirsi. This Honavara family used to be very rich – 'just as we were,' says Shailesh – and they still own four large houses in Sirsi. Three are rented out and one is empty. Venkatesh also owns an important firm, Nayak Wood Industry, in Sirsi.
9. One informant told a rather different version of this story. 'Airodys had their eyes on that shop for a long time since the rent was very low but here (in the brochure) they want to appear in such a good light. . . .' It is

obvious that rumours and slander are ripe in a small town such as Udupi, and I certainly have no reason to take sides here. But we see how the reputation of each family is constantly scrutinized by members of the public, and the massive assertions of respectability are often countered by underhand allusions to all sorts of vice.

10. Or: inseparable souls.
11. Often described as bronze, *panchaloha* is actually a slightly different mixture of five metals. It is the traditional material for cast statues and other ritual items in this, as in other, parts of India.
12. Probably for the same temple.
13. I learnt about that by overhearing a telephone conversation. His interlocutor talked about what a third person had said about Anant, who answered: 'Don't listen to him.' Then he told his interlocutor what the third person had said about him: 'He said you were a shifty fellow, not dependable. . . . I told him you were my friend. I told him I know you better than he did, so please shut up.' This may not have been business: it clearly was human relations, and may be an example of what Anant meant by managing them. He had just said: 'It is very important to know people, to know their character, to be able to judge it.'
14. The shop of the Gujjadi Nayaks, see last chapter.
15. Yet the traditional market certainly exists or the large number of such shops would not be able to subsist.
16. I wondered whether the split might be related to the RSS activity of the main branch, since A.S. is not of that persuasion. 'Is the trouble with caste important in France?,' he asked me. Yet, when I talked to U. Nagesh Kini, the printer, he said a political reason for the split was unlikely. 'We were all RSS in those days,' he said. This is confirmed by the Udupi Kamaths: there was no split in the Airody family when the brothers were jailed as RSS activists. There was a split, but it came later and had other reasons which they did not know precisely.
17. It will be seen later that A.S. is probably using the term 'member' in a somewhat high-handed manner.
18. He gave no list of these families, but it is, I think, legitimate to think that they are all, or at least mainly, GSB.
19. This remark should not be taken as precise. A.S. did not specify whether he thought in terms of turnover, invested capital, or whatever. I simply conclude that A.S. confirms the GSB domination of Udupi business.
20. He is the uncle of Shambhu Shetty, whom we met at the Budnar *bhutakolla*.
21. We have seen that Dr. Baliga was an important person in T.A. Pai's life.
22. His remark here is interesting. How does this kind of ambiguity come

about? Certainly, migration and the destruction of many Goan temples may have wrought confusion as to the link between a family and its lineage deity. But since most GSB seem sure of the link, what happened to the U. Kamaths? Was there a period when the link to the lineage deity was less important – and less well remembered – than now?

23. The same informant says K.K. has asked several others to give land for the road, but 'he himself will not give'. There have been many plans to widen this road, but all have come to naught.
24. And even if Henry Ford may be something like the prototype of the individual entrepreneur, he certainly founded a family dynasty.
25. Indeed this is the only real GSB 'mansion' I have seen. See Chapter 3.
26. There are many examples: one which comes to mind is the Schneiders in France.
27. Later, but in connection with this, she says 'All the later Pais had very ambitious wives, who liked to spend money on themselves.'
28. Rumours have it that she has now become a mental patient.
29. Information from our young friend and part-time translator Rohit.
30. Larsen and Toubro, one of the most respected engineering firms in India. Though the founders were Danes, the company as such is entirely Indian.

7

Lions and Foxes: Jointness and Splits

In a small-town merchant milieu, there seem always to be families which are rising as well as those who fall or have fallen. Those who are rising tend, of course, to be considered as social upstarts, 'nouveau-riche', even if they have become both rich and powerful. There are also those whose past is well remembered, but whose present is simply 'no longer the same'. Yet, and this is as clear in Udupi as it was in Yankee City (Warner, 1942), such families may retain a flavour of 'old bourgeoisie', even if their financial and social resources are no longer what they once were. The merchant world, indeed, is a world of 'lions' and 'foxes' in Pareto's terms. In his theory of the circulation of elites, there are those who have arrived – the 'lions' – and the 'foxes' who challenge their position. The latter have acquired, or are acquiring, the qualities necessary to grasp and hold leadership. 'Lions', however, tend gradually to lose these qualities as they grow too confident in their position. The Airodys are, in this sense, definitely still foxes: they are maintaining a spirit of challenge and entrepreneurship. The most obvious example in Udupi of a family of 'lions' is probably the Ammunje Nayaks and more recently the Tonse Pais. Ramakrishna Gundu Nayak was certainly a fox in the 1920s, but must have been quite a lion before the war and its aftermath broke his business.

Ammunje Trivikram Nayak's grandfather was one of the first from the GSB community to establish himself in Udupi and he came from a family that had been important in the region for centuries. He soon became the main dealer in rice and grains in the town. The family, as we have seen, owned most of the land at Kalsanka. They stayed united – and powerful – till the death of Trivikram Nayak in 1975. Since then, though there are a number of Ammunje Nayak firms in town, they no longer form part of a single concern and only one of them can be described as really important.[1] Thus the family may serve as a typical example of the fate of the Indian business family: as long as the family is joint, the synergy of its various activities makes for an important business concern; once the family divides, the fortunes of each member may vary greatly, and though some may meet with success, others will see their business decline. The fall from lion status then seems often to pass by the division of the joint family: the rise of foxes, on the other hand, often depends on their unity.

The Ammunje Nayak concern flourished under Trivikram Nayak, but when he died in 1975, the business was, as we have seen, divided. The division of the joint family was of importance not just to the family but to the whole local GSB community and 'everybody' among the Udupi GSB seems to remember the division of the Ammunje Nayak family and concern as an important event. It meant, effectively, the fall of the most important business dynasty in town[2] and changed the game for everybody else. At the same time, such division is seen as a failure of family solidarity, so it reflects not only on business matters but also on the family's reputation. There is no mistaking the pride of the Airody Pais in their unitedness. Yet, as the grain dealer from the Ammunje family told me, 'my greatest capital is the Ammunje name. Over the centuries, people have come to have confidence and trust in us. Even today, the Ammunje name sells.'

While one brother's petrol pump and tyre concern is almost aggressive in its modernity, the other four branches of Trivikram's original firm have a traditional aspect. Yet tradition can also be re-invented in highly contemporary terms. The owner of the oil mills is proud of producing only pure coconut and *til* oil, by traditional methods, and with no kind of additive whatsoever. This is now becoming a sales argument. The mills were started in 1956 by his father, and occupy two sides of the street; the filling machines on the left, and the actual mills and the shop on the right, if one looks towards Kalsanka from the temple square. The coconuts are delivered at the shop by small-scale local growers, mostly Billavas, who dry the coconut flesh themselves. In the 2003-4 season, the copra price rose sharply – from Rs. 30 a kilo to Rs. 42. This was problematic for the small firm that could only with difficulty recuperate the cost from its own sales.

The residue from pressing the oil is sold as fodder for the cows, and is held to ameliorate their milk production.

The *kuladevata* of the Ammunje Nayaks is Damodar, at Jamboli near Margao in Goa. Mahalasanarayani, whom the oil mill owner mentions along with Damodar as his *kuladevata*, is 'called the queen of god – Saibini'. Damodar is called Saib. 'The Jamboli temple is in the forest,' says the owner of the oil mill, 'and close to the river. You have to bathe in the river (Fanta) before worshipping at the temple.' There are about fifty to sixty *kuladevata* temples in Goa, he says, and the biggest and the most important of them is the one dedicated to Mahalasanarayani. He goes once or twice a year to Jamboli: sometimes, however, he has been only once in two years.

He himself now lives in Kadiyali, a suburb of Udupi, close to its Mahishamardini temple. He has chosen this goddess as his *ishtadevata* 'because we live close by' – an unusual choice among GSB and apparently an individual one. To him, the Venkatarama temple is above all a caste temple. An elder brother who is a medical doctor lives close by, at Kunjibettu, and the grain dealer lives in the same general area, near MGM college. None of the Ammunje Nayaks live at Kalsanka now, and they all have separate houses. As the grain dealer puts it – 'Life is different now'.

The secretary at the oil mill is also a GSB, whose Kamath family came from Bailoor, south-east of Udupi. His sister is at Karkala. This family has Urtaya Mahamaya as its *kuladevata*, whose temple is not far from the Damodar temple. 'We came from Goa a hundred or two hundred years ago. One hundred years ago we were at Bailoor. My father came here to Udupi seventy years ago,[3] and we have been here ever since. I was born here,' says the secretary. This again, then, seems to be a family which does not have its own shop.

The split in the Ammunje Nayak firm has not produced a lasting conflict. The members of the family I met stress that they are still one family: they worship together and meet socially. The split has hurt their position as the first business family among the Udupi GSB. Still, however, the name is prestigious, and they are still counted among the first families in town.

Among Udupi families, the Airody Pais are, as we have seen, remarkable for their unity, making them today the strongest single family firm in town. They are also among the oldest family concerns still active in the temple square area, but even so, their name does not carry the prestige of the Ammunje Nayaks. They have a number of shops in central Udupi, covering a large variety of merchandise, and all carry the 'Airody' logo, making the corporate nature of the family enterprise more visible than is the case for most other family firms in town. Before the family came to Udupi, they were living at Airody, just north of Kallianpur. We have followed the growth of their firm in Udupi and it will be clear that more than most GSB families, they have incarnated, for many generations, the capitalist spirit that Weber identifies with Protestantism. This implies, if not 'worldly asceticism' – a term with which I have some difficulty – at least a certain degree of austerity, in the sense that consumption is restrained in order to privilege saving and investment. They certainly do not differ in their way of life from other and less successful families of Udupi's middle class, and what is more, they have a reputation of being tight with their money. In calling their supermarket 'Little Pai' the family is perhaps marking precisely this spirit, that of the entrepreneur who refuses to show off in conspicuous consumption as the 'great families' are supposed to do. It is this spirit that I identify with the 'foxes' of Pareto's model of elite circulation, when transposed to the commercial sphere. It is as if the Airodys have decided to remain foxes in Pareto's term, avoiding the changes that lead to loss of the necessary competitive spirit. Working silently but determinedly, they are in fact undermining the position of 'older' and more flamboyant families such as the Ammunje Nayaks or, indeed today, the Tonse Pais.

This spirit relates to consumption as well as business deals: the Airodys are certainly not stingy in their ritual expenditure, as we have seen. Such expenditure should not be seen as consumption, however, but as investment, since it establishes a reputation for the family.[4] In Western terms, the spending on temples may be compared to sponsorship or other forms of publicity. Yet in spite of their magnificent gifts to temples, the Airodys are still seen by those who do not like them rather as 'misers'.

The history of the Tonse Pais may illustrate the transition from foxes to lions. In the 1920s, when they had but a single shop and were just starting the Syndicate that was to grow into a bank, the

Tonse Pais were foxes too. When the first cars appeared in Udupi, T.M.A. stuck to his bicycle. The transition may be symbolized by the villas they built at Manipal. Then, by T.A. Pai's first marriage, they were taking a step identifying them with Udupi's elite, gradually becoming lions. Today, they are very much, as we have seen, in a position where their preeminence is contested. They are losing control of their empire and the family does not seem to be as united as it once was. The failure of their investment fund, led by and identified with T.A.'s younger brother Ramesh, was a major blow to their name and social prestige in Udupi. So many had trusted in their capacity to deal with financial adversity: when these people lost their savings – at a time, it is true, when a large number of similar investment funds all over India, went bust[5] – that trust was irremediably broken, and almost overnight the Tonse Pais became 'speculators' who had dealt with other people's money in a high-handed manner. Ramesh, who died a couple of years ago, seems to have been broken by the fall: he moved to Bangalore and leadership of the family's interests in Udupi passed to K.K. Pai, his brother-in-law.[6] Of the next generation, Ranga Pai is the most in view, but as we have seen, he is identified with cultural activities rather than business. The family's career then is in a way typical of those lions in the bourgeoisie who, having had their day in business and finance, continue to represent culture and refinement.

The picture of small-town life painted through opposing the Airody Pais to the Ammunje Nayaks implies a cyclical image of the bourgeoisie, where nouveaux riches rise and old families fall. This is an image we recognize both in literature – where it was one of the main sources of the novelists' plot and sense of drama for perhaps a hundred years – and in classical sociology, where Weber and Pareto are the most obvious references. It may be useful to us to see exactly what the two experts were saying about this cycle.

Weber, as we know, was particularly interested in the way the Protestant ethic coincided with or led to a spirit of capitalism. With the early Puritans and Calvinists, the ethic imperatives of their religion led them to value work and its fruits in a new way, leading to continuous investment rather than accumulation. Weber clearly opposed this spirit to that of the traditional merchant, and implied that as he wrote (1904/1930) the early spirit of capitalism was no longer predominant, at least among the big capitalists in Germany. They were becoming rentiers as Pareto would have called them, adopting an aristocratic lifestyle. Similarly, Veblen distinguished his 'leisure class' from the entrepreneurs (1899).[7] The grand bourgeoisie of the turn of the century, then, appears to Weber rather like Veblen's image of it, as the protagonists of conspicuous consumption. This has not really happened to the Udupi bourgeoisie – at least not yet. Even the lions retain a middle-class style of life, even if they have elegant villas and new cars.

Pareto (1966) analyses the change from foxes to lions in terms of 'residues'.[8] By this term, which never gained currency in the social sciences, Pareto implied a social-psychological process: the psychological make-up as well as the norms followed by the individual or group changed along with experiences and social position. Thus, apart from the analytical gloss, Pareto's model parallels the plot of novelists such as Thomas Mann, the three-generation 'model' of builders, consolidators and spenders.

Pareto stresses how

> people have confused, and the confusion continues, in the single term 'capitalists', two different categories: (a) property-owners and owners of savings; and (b) entrepreneurs. This greatly militates against a proper understanding of the economic phenomenon, and even more the social phenomenon. In reality, these two categories of 'capitalists' often have different interests; sometimes their interests are opposed and create an even greater conflict than those dividing 'capitalists' and 'proletarians'. The entrepreneurial class embraces individuals in whom combination interests – indispensable for success in commerce and industry – are well developed, whereas among the class of people who are simply savers individuals in whom residues of aggregate-persistence predominate are strongly represented. As a general rule, therefore, entrepreneurs are adventuresome and always on the look for novelty as much in the social as in the economic domain; they are prone to accept change, indeed they hope to profit from it. Mere owners of savings, however, are often quiet, timorous people, like rabbits ever ready to take alarm; they hope little and fear much from change for bitter experience has taught them that it is they who will have to pay for it. (Pareto, 1966: 263-4)

Subsequently calling the two categories *S* and *R*, 'speculators' and 'rentiers', he proposes that the former induce change and progress, the latter stability, but there are 'evolutions, innovations and revolutions' which the rentiers will support . . . a revolution may be made against the speculators' (ibid.: 264-5). Thus there is not an implicit cycle, as there is for foxes and lions: otherwise, very much the same logic is present.

The two types have certainly existed and co-existed in the Udupi community, but opposition or conflict between rentiers and speculators – perceptible, for example, in the opposition between the Ramesh and K.K. Pai factions of the Tonse Pai empire – do not seem to have played a major role. It has often been remarked that the Indian business communities tend to be cautious rather than daring, thus closer to Pareto's rentiers than to his speculators. This would seem to be generally true of the GSB, but, as for Indian capital as a whole, cautiousness does not mean lack of initiative. Evidently, the corporate nature of the joint family is important here. If the young are adventurous, the elders may still be conservative, and so the corporate family strategy tends to be a compromise between the two trends.

In Udupi, however, the cycles over time, as Pareto describes them for elites, are more explicit. Indeed, the GSB families are not just businessmen, and their rise and fall is not restricted to pecuniary activity: honour (*abru*) and prestige, as well as power, is involved. Thus they are, indeed, elites in a wider sense, and the opposition between rentier and entrepreneur is secondary since both may influence family strategies. Yet the history of the community does show some traits of cyclical development, where entrepreneurship dominates one phase, consolidation another.

The 1890s were clearly a gründer phase, as the town was practically new as a centre of business, and so everyone among the GSB who founded a business in Udupi at the time was something of an entrepreneur. Some of them were young men when they made the move, some were middle-aged, but we can hardly talk about a generational shift until First World War or the early 1920s. But as we have seen, the shift then was towards growth and diversification.

A special case here is the Syndicate Bank. But as we have seen, commentators have somewhat overstated the daring nature of this initiative. In fact, it was one among a large number of small banks to appear in the region during the 1920s. Moreover, expansion in the handloom industry provided a background for its growth. This, of course, does not reduce the entrepreneurial character of the initiative, as the Syndicate Bank was at the time a highly original type of financial institution. But the entrepreneurship lies more in its special character than in the simple fact of starting another bank.

This dynamism accelerated through the 1930s, in spite of the 1929 crisis which, as we have seen, often brought forth new initiatives in peripheral countries. The growth continued, accelerating around 1945-7, when many new immigrants came to Udupi from the countryside. The 1950s seem to have seen a steady, continued growth, in spite of the austerity imposed on the middle classes by Nehruvian socialism. The growth, then, was not really broken until it started to accelerate in recent years with the general expansion in the Indian economy, but especially, from around 2000, with the effects of the boom in Mangalore.[9]

Throughout its history, then, the Udupi GSB community has shown a gradual growth where new initiatives of an entrepreneurial character are taken from a base of traditional and continuing business. The typical speculator has been rare, the rentier type common, but progress has come from an intermediate type, the cautious but deliberate entrepreneur.

But if this long period of growth has benefited the GSB, it has also brought competitors. The Catholics had been present from early on, but their role in business in Udupi has expanded considerably in recent years. The Bunts have started businesses too, especially since the 1970s, a timing probably related directly to the effects of land reform, as many families must have used their compensation money to invest in business. The Bunts have been particularly important in such growth sectors as hotels, which otherwise might have been a fertile field for GSB investment. Apart from the Ammunje Nayak concern mentioned, the GSB also seem rather weakly represented in the motor trade, which is currently experiencing a strong boom. Thus at least since the 1970s, the field for GSB business has been limited by the presence of competing castes, which are strong in some of the more lucrative trades.

In Udupi, it is clear that some families maintain an entrepreneurial spirit, like the Airody Pais, while in other families this spirit is lost – or, which is different, the spirit may be evident in some branches of the old family but not in others. The latter seems to be the case with the Ammunje Nayaks, where some of the branches – notably the one centreing on the large tyre shop – have got rich, while others, like the wholesale grain store, seem to have declined to a point where it is highly probable that the business will not survive into the next generation. This is why I find Pareto's simile of foxes and lions more apt than his rentier-speculator axis. As noted above, one decisive factor in these different fates is the continued unity or the split in the joint family. It is important, therefore, to ask which factors are determinant for its maintenance. While some of these are personal or specific, there are also more structural factors, common to the joint family in business.

Sampath has dealt with the problem of generational change in Indian family business (2001). He sees the family business as going through five stages, of which the third is decisive for the fourth and fifth. The first stage is the entrepreneurial phase (A). It is followed by the phase of growth and multiple management (B). C is the phase of confrontation, where splits and/or resolution of conflicts take place. This tends to be a static period in terms of growth. In phase D, the enterprises suffering from a split enter a phase of disintegration, while those which have resolved their conflicts enter a new phase of growth. This may be further strengthened in phase E, the stage of professional management, while such management of an already disintegrating business tends to end with its dissolution (Sampath, 2001: 189).[10]

In the first phase, 'it is essential that the progenitor makes his succession plans about who will take over the reins of the organization after him. This raises the most fundamental question: will it be his son, brother or a professional?'. The simplest solution is, of course, to have a son capable and willing to take the work further; but if there are more sons than one, 'it is always better to make it clear in advance what will belong to whom after the death of the progenitor' (ibid.: 189-90). Though Sampath does not say so, the matter is clearly easier when the hierarchy of sons is clear, and among the GSB the relative seniority of brothers predisposes for a division of authority with the eldest son as the head. This does not always work in practice, however, since there is no intrinsic reason why the elder brother should be the better businessman.[11] Sampath stresses that 'the progenitor should make as many entities as there are contenders and clarify everyone's future roles' (ibid.: 190). What he does not say, but which is obvious from my experience both in Udupi and during earlier fieldwork in Saurashtra and in London, is that such division of roles is much easier when the business has indeed expanded into several distinct entities: this may be why many Indian businessmen seem to prefer opening a new branch whenever a son is mature to run it, rather than expanding the original one. The father will then keep the original business to himself and leave it, usually to the eldest son, on his death.

Phase B – the phase of multiple management – is when these plans will be put to a test. Here, everything we have said about maintaining the unity of the joint family seems to hold good: 'Neither leaving the son or daughter alone nor overcontrolling him or her solves these problems.' There are many different ways of solving them, but they remain much the same whether the elder brother is in charge or not. In the Airody family, the leader seems to have opted for control and discipline, but he has also seen to it that each of the active partners has his own business to run. There are indications in my data that precisely this was not the case when the Ammunje 'empire' split. The father may have retained control of the whole business for too long.

Phase C is evidently the most difficult phase: it arises when the stress and conflict implied in phase B comes to a head. There are, as Sampath puts it, 'ego clashes that push the parties away from each other,' and so an outsider's help – a business counsellor or simply a family friend – is necessary here, in his view, if a lasting resolution of conflict is to be achieved. Such intervention, however, depends on a minimum of consensus to limit conflict and maintain unity (2001:191).

Disintegration or growth may mean either or both, according to which of the split branches of the family business we choose to follow. The result will, of course, depend on both the qualities of that particular family member and on the nature of his branch of the business. There is no doubt, for example, that a tyre shop, whoever runs it, will have lived with a booming demand for a generation now, while anybody staying in the wholesale grain business – in Udupi at least – will have gone through hard times. In such cases, being senior may not be an advantage: if the elder inherits the traditional business that founded the empire, he may find his opportunities limited, while younger brothers who inherit more progressive offshots will prosper.

Among Udupi businesses, only the various enterprises of the Tonse Pai empire may be seen as getting into the last of Sampath's phases, that of professional management, in the sense that 'the successors move into advisory and policy roles and let professionals run the company'.[12] K.K. Pai may be seen here as somebody who is both a kinsman and a professional. What is happening, however, as with the youngest generation of the Airody family, is that those scheduled for succession are professionally trained in commerce. Most GSB businesses in Udupi, then, are confined to the first four stages. But here, the problems of succession indicated by Sampath seem highly relevant. The problems are similar, after all, whether we are talking of the large all-India conglomerates or the small-town family firms.

It will be clear, I think, that we find in the Udupi GSB community both very traditional commercial practices and initiatives that go beyond them, such as entry into new lines of business. The latter is not a recent change: the 1920s were full of such initiatives, such as the Tonse Pais' entry into banking, the Kadpati Shenoys' photographic studio, or indeed, Ramakrishna Gundu Nayak's dealing in imported goods. There are many other examples of new initiatives, before and after. In other words, traditional business practice does not exclude, but rather coexists with entrepreneurship.

Most discussions on the concept of entrepreneurship in the social sciences regard Schumpeter's work as the point of departure.[13] Schumpeter stresses the importance of innovation, of 'a new production function'. Innovativeness then stems largely from the individual and thus tends to lead us towards explanations of entrepreneurship in terms of personality. As Tripathi and Mehta point out, the American environment which Schumpeter observed from his professorship at Harvard did little to modify this individualist perspective (ibid.: 5). In joint family bussinesses, the idea of entrepreneurship may stem from a single individual, but he must convince the group and especially the family head to put it into practice. Our various remarks on the importance of the joint family in Indian business imply, of course, a criticism of this individualist stance.

In Schumpeter's post-war collaboration with Cole, however, his theory of entrepreneurship took a more precise form, which also opened up for group initiatives. Cole talks of 'purposeful activity or integrated sequence of decisions of an individual or a group of individuals undertaken to initiate, organize, or aggrandize a profit-oriented business unit . . .' (Cole, 1959: 7n). Schumpeter himself now equated 'innovation' with a 'creative response' to business conditions (1947: 150). The problem which then appears, of course, is to distinguish the entrepreneur from any other capable businessman: it is hardly possible to be successful in business without a minimum of 'creative response' to market conditions. Is a businessman an entrepreneur, then, every time he launches a new venture?

Later contributors to the debate, such as McClelland (1965) tended to concentrate on the 'achievement motivation' of individuals. Hagen (1962) in his turn developed a whole theory to explain why some individuals develop this kind of motivation and especially why some of them should choose to apply it to business activity. Here again, we return to the concentration on the individual, and we must again distinguish between the birth of an idea – which may well be understood as an individual contribution – and its implementation, which must depend equally on the individual's environment in the decision-making process. Tripathi and Mehta, in their turn, stress that for the individual 'the perception of gainful opportunities and the choice of strategy to exploit them are essentially responses to the world around him as *he* sees it'. Thus 'the individual and environment must be regarded as the two crucial elements in an integrated theory'. In other words, the entrepreneur is an integral part of a wider social process, a 'constellation of forces', as Tripathi and Mehta put it (1990: 8-9). In other words, ideas are not born of individuals in isolation, but result from their interaction with the environment, and the important phase of forging the idea into a business strategy may well be the result of discussion and debate within a decision-making unit, such as the joint family. For the anthropologist, turning to the individual's environment necessarily implies a consideration of culture.

Seen in this context, a mercantile community such as the GSB also serves as a vehicle to transfer categorizations, values and recognized strategies of business from one generation to the next.

A more analytical model which situates entrepreneurial activity as a creative response in the context of exchange patterns and value discrepancies had in fact been formulated in 1962, but has not been as widely used as, I think, it deserves. This may well be because Fredrik Barth and his colleagues (1962) used it initially to analyse social change in northern Norway, a region which tends to escape the attention of development economists. Barth takes as his point of departure, not an indifferentiated 'market', but the actual circulation of goods and services and the values attributed to them. This model, then, sees the market as always 'imperfect', in the sense that similar goods and services may be obtained in different ways and at different prices. In a different context, Barth develops the model in relation to the cost of labour in Darfur, western Sudan.[14] Here, 'work parties' were a traditional institution, and if they were used to produce marketable goods (tomatoes being his example here), then the actual cost of labour is far inferior to even the lowest daily wage. As long as the 'entrepreneur' was able to exploit this differential cost in labour, he could obtain profits far in excess of what was possible in a region – such as in central Sudan at the time of his writing – where labour was a marketable resource.

To Barth, entrepreneurship should be defined by the exploitation of such differential costs or prices: the individual's innovativeness consists in discovering the potential of this discrepancy in values, and to exploit it through opening up new 'channels of conversion'. The possibility of 'entrepreneurship' would persist for as long as the differential is there to be exploited.[15] In the Darfur example, the differential would disappear when and if labour in the region had to be paid a wage only slightly inferior to what was paid in central Sudan, that is, when the difference would be offset by the transportation costs.

The model may be applied to a number of situations. Thus the first tradesman to offer a certain type of goods for sale in a particular location benefits locally from the additional costs, seen from the customers' point of view, of travelling to obtain the same goods elsewhere. The tradesman, in such cases, will be able to maintain a higher profit margin. Or, as a classical example of business history, when Ford introduced the assembly line and produced cars at unheard-of, low prices, he benefitted from a value discrepancy for many years since his dominance of the low-price market, once assured, made entry costs prohibitive for his competitors.

Such a value discrepancy may be exploited in many ways. One, I think, is present in our discussion of the Airodys' gold business: by offering the customer a choice of the latest Mumbai designs, and then contracting to make the jewellery, the customer is spared a whole lot of time and work in finding the design and then explaining it to the goldsmith, or, alternatively, going to Mumbai. To the goldsmith, it saves time in dealing with individual customers, time which can more profitably be spent in producing the goods. And to the Airodys, I think, the premium of advanced design combines with the advantageous pricing that a goldsmith may accord to an important customer in producing a comfortable margin of profit.

Or, take the early years of the Syndicate Bank. The Tonse Pais were buyers and marketers of handloom goods. They also financed the weavers. Such individual moneylending was certainly more profitable, in terms of interest rates, than what the bank could charge. But by creating a bank they were certainly able to finance more weavers. Thus the profits of the bank ended by far exceeding anything possible from individual moneylending.

In both cases, the entrepreneur interposes himself as a new link in the chain of exchanges, and this constitutes the innovative aspect of his entrepreneurship. To do so profitably, however, the entrepreneur must analyse his commercial environment to locate the new niche. The Airodys – and Gujjadi Narasimha Nayak before them – must have perceived a demand for more fashionable jewellery among Udupi's ladies, and also perceived a bottleneck in the traditional goldsmiths' marketing arrangements. The Tonse Pais must have seen the handloom industry expanding and felt the demand for capital beyond what individual firms could provide. Just as Ramakrishna Gundu Nayak must have felt that the Udupi buying public was ready for imported goods they otherwise had to go to Bombay to buy. It was clearly cheaper to bring the goods to Udupi than to ferry the buyers to Bombay, and a profit margin on the sale of the goods could be found within this difference.

The criteria of value discrepancy offers a possibility to pinpoint precisely the 'innovation' of the entrepreneur, which may stem from location, new production techniques or organization of production, or in fact any other way to secure a market niche where profitability is superior to the going rate of whatever business one is in. Such entrepreneurship may be temporary, such as when a tradesmen succeeds in acquiring a certain quantity of stock at a low price, or lasting, as when a policy of innovation allows a company to offer products 'in a class by themselves', thus encashing a profit bonus. A particular image of quality, too, may maintain a price differential relative to comparable products and thus ensure superior profit – provided that the image is not bought at too high costs in production or marketing. The advantage of this analytical model is that it is capable of treating with enterprise in a traditional bazaar economy, or sophisticated 'merchandizing' in the contemporary market, on equal terms. I think, too, that the model translates easily into the way any good businessman – such as Airody Anant Pai, for example, would think and plan his business activity.

Looking at entrepreneurship in this way, we see that it is and has been present for long in GSB history. The decision taken by many families in or around the sixteenth century to settle in South Kanara and exploit the growing market for rice in Goa would itself have been a case of entrepreneurship – at least until there were so many competing exporters of rice in the area that profit margins would tend to narrow. Settling at Kalsanka in the 1890s to exploit the location near the bridge and the pilgrimage centre would have been another case. Since then, our account of the growth of Udupi offers a number of examples: the Airodys entering one business after another but always building on their existing networks in Udupi would be a case of continuous, but relatively cautious, entrepreneurship. The manifold initiatives of the Tonse Pais from the 1920s to the 1960s were more novel: entering education was a daring venture, and the efforts of the Syndicate Bank, in its early years, to mop up the potential in small savings accounts was certainly a novel and 'entrepreneurial' approach for a banker.

What I would like to stress, however, is the coexistence of very traditional, bazaar-oriented ways of doing business with entrepreneurial capacity and initiatives, often within the same family. It is here, I feel, that many Western accounts of the Indian economy tend to err in posing an opposition between these two 'sectors'. In Udupi, the bazaar remains very much the foundation of the modern economy, and the strategy of business houses such as the Airodys may rather be compared with those of portfolio investors – a parallel we owe to C.A. Baily (1989) – who prefer to mix daring, potentially very profitable titles with those regarded as sure, offering moderate but stable interest. They, of course, combine the rentiers and speculators of Pareto's interpretation. Yet at the same time, the attachment to old shops and old lines of business is clearly more than a strategy: it has an important emotional dimension since the 'family firm' is so closely related to group and individual identity.

The preceding discussion adds another dimension to this ubiquitous presence of the 'family firm'. What does it take for a family firm to retain its entrepreneurial capacity? To do so, it must be capable of generating new ideas, but equally important, the internal organization must be such that these ideas are heard and, if promising, thoroughly discussed. Menefee certainly implies that this was the case in the Tonse Pai family during its ascendance. We may note that the family included members who had studied and travelled widely: T.M.A. when studying medicine in Madras, Upendra during his various bursts of schooling in different places. One classical way of generating ideas then is to expose members of the family to new impulses by study, travel, or other means. This, I feel, is why the Airodys and other families now invest in proper business education for the younger generation. In Udupi, there is no need for such education to maintain a going concern[16] but it may prove useful for discerning new opportunities. Running the joint family as a going concern, then, must involve a certain openness to new ideas – typically coming from the younger generation – as well as maintaining a social climate where such ideas can be discussed, weighed against the experience of the older members, and wrought into a coherent strategy under the leadership of the family's head. Participant observation of such processes are of course not often possible.[17] But we may I think suppose that the most efficient business families over time are those where this difficult blend of openness, discussion and authority is achieved. Splits in the family are, I suppose, often the result of a breakdown in this process.

It should be clear from the above how closely most of the Udupi GSB families are attached to the 'family firm', i.e. to their original shop in Udupi and to whatever cluster of businesses may have grown around it. Establishment in Udupi marks the most recent and the best remembered stage in family history, and many families, such as the Kalsanka Pais, have taken as their first family name the quarter of Udupi where they first settled. Others, like the Tonse Pais, identify themselves by the name of the village from which they came to Udupi. As a tendency, the latter category are more recent arrivals, but there seems to be no hard and fast rule as to when – in terms of generations – a change from one to the other takes place. In view of the importance of the Manipal enterprises, one might well have expected the Tonse Pais of Manipal to become Manipal Pais, but this has not (yet?) happened. The Manipal Pais is a term that is, in fact, used for this family, but rather by outsiders to Udupi, people who know about the Manipal complex but who may have no idea where Tonse is.

The identification with the family firm points to a central theme in caste identity: the GSB are merchants. Yet we must not forget that some generations ago landowning was a very important occupation in the caste, and here again, the Tonse Pais may be seen as an example. Few families would today characterize themselves as mainly a landholding family: the land reforms, of which the last took effect in 1973,[18] have certainly had an effect here. But the change from landholding to business has been gradual, ranging over centuries rather than generations, and the timing of this change varies with place as well as with individual family histories. The identification with the firm also entails a holistic view of the family, and as we have seen, especially from the way the two large Pai families – the Tonse Pais and the Airodys – present their own story, the ideology of family solidarity is very strong. Brothers should pull together, and in this context it is immaterial whether the family, juridically speaking, has one or several legally registered firms, just as the question of whether brothers actually live together may be quite immaterial to the ideological unity of the family.[19]

Pierre Lachaier (1999) has described nicely the attachment of families to their firms. Among the Kutchi Lohana of Pune and Mumbai, as among the GSB of Udupi, the portrait of the firm's founder is ever-present behind the desk. Usually, says Lachaier, the founder of the main branch of the family firm is some three generations distant from the present, junior partners. In the publicity of these Kutchi Lohana firms, as found in the various publications of the caste organizations, the three generations often figure as a hierarchy of 'firms'. Thus the main firm, in large script, thrones at the top of the advertisement, taking perhaps half the space. Below this, there may be one or two second-generation 'firms', identified with sons of the founder. At the bottom of the page we find the third-generation 'firms', some of which may in fact be named after babies. As Lachaier stresses, these advertisements, which he finds in the annual repertories of the caste organizations, cannot be directed at customers, since the overwhelming majority of the Kutchi Lohana community in Mumbai or Pune are in the same business, that of jute bags. Instead, suggests Lachaier, a main point of the advertisment is to assert family continuity as a measure of stability and credit-worthiness: naming junior firms after babies is precisely a way of asserting continuity towards the future.

As Lachaier underlines, the Kutchi Lohana community he studied is special, in that the whole local caste group is concentrated in a single business. Yet for this very reason, his example may be posed as an ideal type of the 'family firm', or 'merchant lineage firm' (FLM) as he prefers to call it. Two points stand out as particularly important here. One is the double nature of the 'firm': its organization is that of the local lineage segment, and its head (*karta*) is usually the head of the family. Authority relations within the 'firm' are essentially those of the lineage or joint family: it is possible analytically, but difficult in terms of social practice, to detach the 'business' dimension from kinship. The other point, related to the first, is that relations between 'firms' are fluid. It is indeed difficult to describe the grandson's 'firm' as an entity distinct from those of his father and grandfather: often, there is considerable vertical integration. The junior firms collect used jute bags directly from grocers and other users, repair and store them: the senior firm is the main selling agency and also the one which may buy sacks in quantity. To satisfy the requirement of a particular customer, then, the head of the family – and the 'main' firm – will draw on the stocks of bags held with his junior kin. There will be separate account books: but transactions within the family can hardly be seen as market transactions, even if the prices of transfer within the group of family 'firms' are often fixed at market value. In other words, asks Lachaier, are we talking of one firm or a group of firms? At the exterior of the family, however, the frontiers between 'firms' may be fuzzy too, as one may share a contract with in-laws or other associates, and divide the spoils by friendly agreement. At one point then we may see the whole local Kutchi Lohana group of Pune, for example, as an entity operating in a market economy, and in that case as an 'enterprise' holding a local monopoly in the trade of jute bags – not forgetting that there are kinship links and business arrangements linking this group to other local Kutchi Lohana communities, in Nasik, Mumbai, or elsewhere.

If we envisage a period when all GSB merchants in the Udupi area were basically dealers in rice, we may hypothesize that they functioned in a way rather similar to the Kutchi Lohana jute dealers described by Lachaier. At least from their establishment in Udupi, however, there began a process of functional diversification, which has continued since. Today, different families are in many kinds of business; some have themselves diversified while remaining united like the Airodys, while some, like the Kalsanka and Kalsankar Pais have divided according to business specialization. It is clear that the fluid situation Lachaier describes does not really apply to Udupi. And yet there is certainly a measure of collaboration as well as competition between the 'family firms'. Within each family, or functionally specialized branch of a family, however, the relationship between the 'sub-firms' certainly remains deeply entangled in family and kinship relations.

Lachaier also describes family empires in the mechanical industry of Pune, and here he shows a pattern markedly different from that of the Lohana jute dealers. Typically, says Lachaier, the founders of firms in the mechanical sector were cadets, and so broke with family tradition. Sometimes, they have managed to attract their elders to the firm: sometimes, the new firm effectively founds a new branch of the lineage. We then enter into dynamics which correspond closely to what Sampath (2001) describes: the problems of keeping the family firm – or rather here, groups of firms – together, and to retain family control.

Lachaier, however, shows clearly how the differences in organization between the 'industrial lineage firms' of the mechanical sector and the 'lineage merchant firms' of the jute trade are related to technology and its organizational constraints. In the jute business, expertise is acquired through experience and learning within the family, and is largely common to the different levels of the business, so any lineage member may, in functional terms, fill any slot in the system. There is no need to acquire expertise from outside.

This is not the case in the mechanical industry, or, if so, only at the level of sub-contractors concentrating on relatively simple procedures. For a firm like Kirloskar, the pride of Pune's industry, it certainly helps control and diversification that the founder's family has invested greatly in engineering education for most of its male members. Even so, at the level of such a concern, no engineer – family or not – can possibly monopolize all the necessary expertise, even for a branch factory. A level of non-family technicians and managers becomes necessary and rather than the fluid boundaries between 'sub-firms' that we find among the Kutchi Lohana, large modern groups like Kirloskar find it necessary to exploit company law precisely in order to delimit and define separate domains, not least so as to secure strategic nodal positions for family members. It is obvious – and Lachaier agrees – that in the modern sector the degree of family influence – as well as family unity – varies greatly. We need not follow up this line, for none of the GSB family concerns in Udupi are comparable to company groups like Kirloskar. Yet they may share important traits with these modern conglemorates. They may well be composed of several lines of business, calling for a degree of independent decision-making and, incidentally, making vertical integration difficult or impossible. In such cases, they cannot retain the segmentary structure of the Kutchi Lohana jute firms. On the other hand, few are large enough to need managers or experts from outside the family, at least not to the point where such groups threaten the family's hold over the business. Rather, the relationship between lineage and joint family structure on the one hand, and the structure of business relations between the branches of the firm, may vary according to each case, within and between families. Lack of 'fit' between seniority in family terms and profitability or importance of the various branches of business may well lead to stresses and strains in the family firm. It would seem that this is the most obvious and probably most common factor that leads to division of the family and its firm, and to keep the family united in spite of this calls for considerable authority and managerial skill. The problem here is basically the same as Bailey identified (1961) when analysing the breakup of the joint family among peasants in Orissa.[20]

A well-established merchant family has, of course, benefits from staying together that do not apply to poor peasants,[21] though such benefits may apply to peasant families who have both land and a name. Staying together, then, is not simply a question of pooled resources, for the name – as a marker of collective identity – is important. Among merchants such as the GSB, the name, as identified with the family and the firm, is like a trademark, and when the name is good, every family business will benefit from its reputation. If a split spoils this reputation, the results may be disastrous. Nevertheless, the negative effects of splitting off – and perhaps having to adopt a non-family name – will be proportional to the link between the markets and market images of the new and the old trade. The Airodys have been explicit in adopting the same logo for everything the family does: should they take up a motorcycle dealership, for example, this strategy would produce something like Airody Motors. A younger son of an established family branching off and severing most links to the family firm might, alternatively, operate without the family reference, as, say, Nava Bharat Motors. If the junior wants to stress his caste affiliation, we might have Venkatesha Motors, for example.

There is now a vast literature on Indian merchants and businessmen, covering a long historical period, many castes and regions, and a large number of trades. We have indeed come a long way since Weber (1961) wrote of the businessman as something of an 'outsider' to the caste system, and his observations on Indian business certainly no longer hold as such. Commerce has been an integrated and sometimes an integrative part of Indian society for a very long time, and no sociological account of a regional caste configuration can reasonably leave the businessman out.[22] Yet, as we have seen in the introduction, this is precisely what indigenous constructions of 'traditional society' tend to do – at least this is true both for Saurashtra and for South Kanara. We have seen, too, that a similar perspective – no doubt borrowed from their South German background – underlies the Basel missionaries' characterization of the GSB as similar to 'Jews'. This perhaps indicates that the tendency to push merchants away from the ideological construction of society is more than a regional curiosity. We might hypothesize that it is a typical trait of 'peasant' or possibly 'feudal' ideologies. Among writers who have dealt with this problem, David Hardiman's contribution stands out (1996). He stresses the conflictual but complementary relationship that obtains between the two groups whose central values tend to differ considerably.

Numerous writers have tried to analyse more closely the specific traits of the Indian commercial tradition, usually concentrating on two aspects: the importance of family and caste, and the 'conservative' strategies of Indian businessmen. Among these contributions, Baily's work on north Indian towns in the eighteenth and nineteenth century (1989) stands out as particularly broad in scope and rich in detail. Here, I shall concentrate on Baily's analysis of business strategies.

Baily continuously stresses the dimension of risk as fundamental to understand the strategies of Indian businessmen in this period. Like others, he speaks of the 'portfolio' nature of investment, notably in the larger firms. We have seen that this applies also to contemporary GSB firms in Udupi. 'From early youth', he says, 'children in merchant families were taught that good business involved the constant division of capital into small, manageable portfolios. One such formula was built around the letters of the Hindi alphabet: K = *kam*, work; KH = *khana*, food; G = *garna*, to hoard (jewellery, etc.); GH = *ghar*, house and so on. This was taken to mean that work produced food; then a merchant should purchase jewellery which could stand as security in time of need and a dowry for daughters, followed by a house in which to carry on business. Other rhymes and jingles taught that capital should be divided into at least four portions. One portion should be hoarded as coin; one used to buy jewellery; one lent out at interest, and only one quarter invested in trade' (1989/92: 396).

This hedging attitude shows in Udupi's business climate. A typical example here is the Airodys' investment in new lines of business over many years, while simultaneously keeping up their old lines. It would seem indeed that many business families prefer, when possible, to 'gamble' one part of their capital on potentially profitable but relatively insecure investments while keeping other parts engaged in sure but low-profit lines. This is no doubt a wise strategy, but it contrasts sharply with the tendency of many large firms today to sell off those branches of the business which give little profit, in order to concentrate investment where profit is high. The latter strategy is, of course, related to a situation where the manager is, in the last instance, but a paid servant to the shareholders, and moreover, where the latter are but the representatives of investors in their turn. Here, the manager's brief is to maximize profit at all costs. In such a situation, capital is fluid, moving easily from one business to another.

The small-town Indian businessman is in a very different situation. His capital consists not just of buildings and stock, but equally the family's *abru* – its good name and creditworthiness – in his small-town world. *Abru,* in this sense, probably suffers from the closing of any well-known family concern, profitable or not, and this may be why many families maintain shops which are no longer really profitable. Even when a shop has been closed for some years, the premises often stand unused rather than being converted or sold, as if to convey the message that the closure is only temporary.

Business is, of course, largely a matter of credit. Again, in a small-town world such as Udupi, credit is very much a matter of trust, and trust is, to an extent, predictability. Keeping old businesses going is thus a way to maintain existing credit ties as well as providing (formally or informally) security for riskier investments. In these days of more formal credit such as bank loans, it is important to keep family businesses divided into separate concerns, so that losses and debts in one concern do not affect the others directly. But at the same time, the existence of these sister concerns, especially if they are seen as sure payers, bolsters a demand, say, for deferred payments in a business which did not come up to expectations.

Though individual branches of a family may be more or less successful, and thus more or less worthy of credit, the family name and its image remain a reference for trust. Lions will struggle hard to maintain their image of creditworthiness, and foxes will try hard to acquire one. Gifts to the temples or bids at temple auctions – discussed later – are important elements in the continuous claims for financial respectability, and may be compared to the way a stock market is influenced by various news from different firms. As in a stock market, nobody can know exactly the creditworthiness of any player in this game. In Udupi, conspicuous consumption is mostly restricted to the religious sphere: buying an unnecessarily expensive car, for example, is not seen as a strategic move since it breaks with the image of prudent spending that is associated with successful business families. Much thought seems to be given to spending in such a way that this image is maintained. While lions have to be careful not to show their diminishing returns, and keep up en image of 'business as usual', foxes generally maintain prudency implying that they are accumulating, rather than spending.

Only a few examples, such as the manor of B. Manjunath Pai in Karkala, point to a different strategy. We may surmise that such lavish spending is associated with quite exceptional success stories.

NOTES

1. The most visible part of this firm is its large garage and tyre agency, not far from Kalsanka.
2. The Tonse Pais' various activities are not similarly seen as 'business'.
3. They would have arrived in Udupi, then, in the early 1920s.
4. Here I share the position of Douglas and Isherwood, 1979.
5. It was related to the 'dotcom crash'. The rules for investment funds changed redically in its wake. I want to stress this point, and there are many people in Udupi who feel that Ramesh was far more unlucky than incautious when his leadership of the fund led to bankruptcy.
6. As the former – and successful – director of the Syndicate Bank, as well as an in-law, K.K. may have seemed a natural choice. But many people seem to feel that his leadership shows the lack of first-class business acumen in the direct line. K.K., after all, is not a Tonse Pai.
7. I am not using Veblen here, since conspicuous consumption is not blatant in the Udupi bourgeoisie. Such conspicuousness passes, as we have seen, through the ritual sphere.
8. Residues correspond to non-logical action, says Pareto. They are the expres-

sion of certain sentiments (Paragraph 798 in the *Trattato de Sociologia Generale*: Pareto, 1994: 186). These sentiments change according to the position of a group in society. Thus, the qualities that make social ascension possible are weakened during a period of social supremacy, so that the incumbent elite gradually has to give way to a new one who possess the residues that lead to success.

9. There was expansion of Mangalore new port and new petrochemical factories were established. New building complexes have sprung up, partly transforming the 'garden city' into a much denser cityscape.
10. This, I may add, would seem to be because the professional managers lack the emotional attachment to keep a business going even when profits become dangerously low. This attachment is precisely what characterizes continuous family ownerships.
11. As for the Airodys, we may note that the present head is the second brother – yet there has been no split.
12. The banks, however, have used professionals for quite some time now.
13. But there were antecedents. See, for example, Tripathi and Mehta's discussion in their introduction (1990: 1-4) for some of the early French contributions.
14. This was, of course, long before the present troubles in the area.
15. Implicit here is the absence of monopoly: as others start to exploit the same conversion channels, competition would tend to reduce the differential. The value discrepancy would, in effect, disappear.
16. This seems equally to be true for the jute-sack business of the Lohanas, as described by Lachaier (1999), where business education still seems to be rare.
17. The authors dealing with the Tonse Pais, cited in chapter five, have, however, tried to describe this type of process.
18. There were several stages in the land reforms of the late 1960s and early 1970s, which I do not propose to detail here. In the Udupi area, these reforms have been quite effective. Farther inland, this is not always the case, and it is possible that some of the Karkala GSB families, for example, still have considerable landholdings. We may also note that plantations are exempted from these reforms. But here again, plantations are found farther inland, and so this exemption hardly concerns the Udupi area.
19. Among those who underline this point, distinguishing between family ideology and actual co-residence is A.M. Shah (1973). I also came to the same conclusion in my study of the London Patidars (1980: 92-124).
20. Bailey's point was that equity between brothers was possible when all were active on the farm, but became very difficult to maintain when

some had a salaried job elsewhere. The contributions to the common fund would become more and more difficult to compare, and often, the salaried person would feel exploited by the cash demands of his brothers.

21. Benefits of staying together are obviously related to a unit being big enough to use the work contributions of all members and to provide them all with reasonable means of livelihood.
22. For a comparative analysis of the merchants' role in the caste system on the west coast of India, see Tambs-Lyche, 2007.

8

Kinship and Alliance in a Small-town Bourgeoisie

In Udupi, as in most small towns, we have seen how family is a reference which recalls stories of success or failure, unity or schism, and stereotypes of the family's character or 'ethos'. Families may incarnate what anthropologists call a 'kinship system', but the rules and structures of kinship, here as elsewhere, are culturally implicit.[1] Familiar with matrilineal as well as patrilineal kinship, people in South Kanara are more conscious than most of their implications.[2] But conceptually, the 'family' is something else.[3] The qualities of each family are argued in terms of history and anecdote: the first concerns the family's rise or fall, typically over several generations: the latter metonymically incarnates the essence of family traits, independent of time and place. Some family members take on a mythical persona, such as T.M.A. Pai, the founder of Manipal. When anecdotes are told to show family traits, the individual becomes a 'typical' member of his family.[4] To escape this identity is possible only by leaving permanently and becoming independent of caste networks.[5] This is unusual, for with their history of migration the GSB have a strong tradition of keeping links to their 'home place'. Kinship is important here, and so are the lineage temples, even when annual visits become impossible, as when a migrant is settled in the UK or in the US. It is still seen as important to follow news about the temple, now often through Internet, and send contributions, directly or through kin, on important occasions. The lineage temple then serves as a node around which kinship identity is ordered, not least in the relative absence of kinsmen. And, wherever a number of GSB is settled, they tend to keep up community links.

Being a GSB then implies membership in a named family group recognized by other GSB, and others in South Kanara, as an integral part of each individual's identity. The 'we' referred to as family is the *wangad*: in practice, these are the Kalsanka Pais, the Kadpet Nayaks, and so on.[6] The family name is like a trademark, from which the individual's qualities are inferred. It also identifies the family firm, concomitant in the stereotypic image with the family itself. A person may or may not take an active part in the firm, but will still use terms like 'we' and 'us' when referring to it, as if the shop represents the senior family members, and the independent lawyer, doctor or otherwise who speaks, were junior, irrespective of age.[7] There is always a note of regret when speaking of a business that had to be given up.[8] In this small-town world, then, nobody escapes ascription[9] to a family, even those who have broken with relatives. Ascription to a new 'family' can only happen over time, when the breakaway has become the founder of a new branch.[10] This often happens on migration: after a couple of generations the new branch is seen as a 'family' in itself. A schism also produces new branches.[11] Division of the joint family and the firm does not always lead people to think and speak in terms of separate families, however. Families may divide or remain joint, but in both cases people may treat them as a single family if they still stand as a unit in ritual terms,[12] as when gathering for Diwali at the ancestral shop. To keep separate at such times is to insist on a split.

This identification tends to favour the undivided joint family, seen as an ideal. But no GSB – indeed, no middle-class Indian – is stranger to the strains and stresses that family unity imposes on the individual. Thus while admired, unity is also criticized, and the harmony the leader claims is often doubted by others. Among the GSB, such debate is clearly linked to the idea of the family firm. Unity makes one strong, in business perhaps more than elsewhere, and efforts to maintain family unity are easily interpreted in terms of commercial strategy. In positive narratives, unity results from interpersonal harmony, in negative accounts, from the iron leadership of a strong family head at the expense of his juniors. Since leadership is both familial and commercial, the obvious accusation about strong family firms is that they put money above everything else. Conversely, the leader will claim he can give each member a role where his capabilities are free to develop. Both versions may contain part of the truth, variously represented in different families and at different times.[13] Among the Udupi GSB, as among many middle-class groups in India, the struggle for family unity and its conflict with individual affirmation is intimately linked to survival and success in social life. Family unity and conflict are the main dramatic arenas of everyday life, ever-present in life-stories and anecdotic accounts of social life.

We have referred to the division of the Ammunje Nayak joint family which broke the pre-eminent status it once had in Udupi. Yet the Udupi Kamaths referred to them as one family; while, as they said, 'there are two Airody families'.[14] Clearly they felt the split in the latter family was of a different nature. The Ammunje Nayaks – in spite of rumours of jealousy between the branches – stress that they are still on friendly terms: as the grain dealer said, 'we all go to all the functions in the different branches of the family'. When A.S. Airodikar held a function in memory of his elder brother, however, the 'big' Airody family was not represented. Thus the family firm and the family itself are not congruent entities. While the Airodys are both a family and a family firm, the Ammunje Nayaks remain a family though there is no united firm any more. The question of who comes to family functions is the most obvious sign of family solidarity, or the lack of it. Such solidarity may survive a split, but no firm could survive the breakdown of these signs of family solidarity.

The *wangad* is patrilineal and exogamous, but the reference for marriage or incest regulations is the *gotra*, which indicates descent from a particular *rishi* or holy man, one of the founders of Brahmanic learning and ritual. It is seen as a clan, since the exact descent from the *rishi* in question may not be known.[15] The *gotra* is exogamous, as is also the case, in principle, for the *pravara*.[16] Each *gotra* has three to five *pravaras*, which bear the name of a *rishi* or saint whose teachings are transmitted by descent. The *rishi* that stands for a *pravara* is seen as the *shishya* (student) of the one who stands for the *gotra* to which a *pravara* belongs. Yet, the same *pravara* may be found in different *gotras*, as if a student could have several teachers, and some *pravaras* retain the name of the teacher. Thus, the Naidhruva and the Kashyapa *gotras* should not intermarry, since both have the same three *pravaras*. In principle, this should also apply to the Bharadwaja and Gautama *gotras*, since both have the *pravara* Angiras in common. In practice, however, as for Brahmins all over India, the ban on marriage within the *pravara* seems to be less strict than that on marriage within the *gotra*.

The first sixty-six families that came to Goa 'belonged only to ten *gotras*, the Kanyakubja Sharmas belonged to three of these *gotras* and the later batch of families[17] belonged to eight more *gotras*' (V.N. Kuduva, n.d.: 11). P.R. Kuduva gave a complete list (Fig. 6) of these eighteen *gotras*, with their respective *pravaras*. To structure it, he gave the 'genealogy' of the eight original *rishis* (Fig. 7). He also listed the *kuladevatas* of most GSB *gotras* (Fig. 8), and the *gotras* of the Smarta families of the Kavale *math* (Fig. 9).[18]

Gotra	*Pravaras*
1. Vatsa	Bhargava, Chyavana, Apnavan, Aurava, Jamadagnya
2. Kaundinya	Vasishtha, Maitravaruna, Kaundinya
3. Kaushka (or Kaushika)	Vaishwamitra, Aghamarshan, Kaushika
4. Bharadwaja	Angiras, Barhaspatya, Bharadwaja
5. Vasishta	Vasishtha, Indrapramod, Abharaswat
6. Jamadagnya	Bhargava, Chyavana, Apnavan, Aurava, Jamadagnya
7. Mudgal	Angiras, Bharmyashwa, Maudgal
8. Atri	Atreya, Archananas, Shavashwa
9. Shankha Pingal Kaunshya	Angiras, Ambarish, Yauvanashwa
10. Gautama	Angiras, Ayasya, Gautama
11. Angira	Kevilangiras, Barhaspatya, Bharadwaja
12. Naidhruva	Kashyapa, Avatsara, Naidhruva
13. Kashyapa	Kashyapa, Avatsara, Naidhruva
14. Vishwamitra	Vishwamitra, Devarata, Audala
15. Shandilya	Shandilya, Asita, Devala
16. Dhananjaya	Vaishwamitra, Madhuchchandasa, Dhananjaya
17. Sankhyavana	Goma, Vasishtha, Sankhyayana
18. Gargya	Angiras, Barhaspatya, Bharadwaja, Gargya

Fig. 6: The eighteen *gotras* of the GSB.

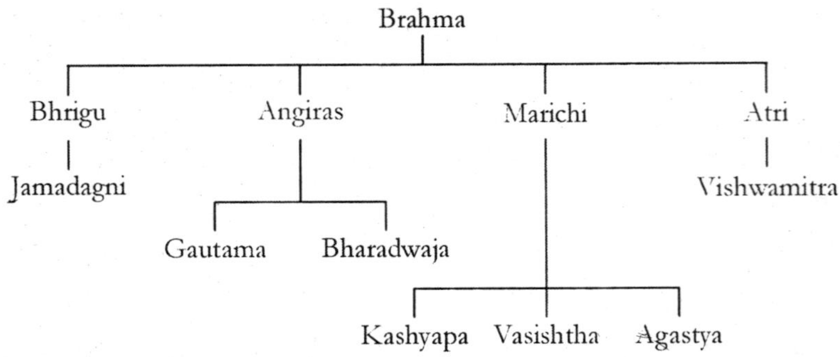

Fig. 7: The spiritual genealogy of the sage-ancestors of the main GSB *gotras*.

Gotra	*Kuladevata*
1. Kaushika	Mahalasa, Shanta Durga, Santeri, Kamakshi, Nagesh, Damodar, Maha Ganapati, Lakshminarayana
2. Gargya	Mahalasa
3. Bharadwaja	Mahalasa, Shanta Durga, Santeri, Damodar, Mahamaya, Devaki Krishna, Maha Ganapati
4. Atri	Mahalasa, Kamakshi, Damodar, Gajanan
5. Jamadagnyavatsa	Mangesh, Devaki Krishna
6. Kaundinya	Mangesh, Ramanath, Gajanan
7. Vatsa	Shanta Durga, Santeri, Nagesh, Ramanath, Maha Ganapati, Lakshminarayana
8. Kashyapa	Ravalnath, Mahamaya, Gajanan, Maha Ganapati
9. Gautama	Mahamaya, Maha Ganapati
10. Vasishtha	Mahamaya

Fig. 8: Incomplete list of *kuladevatas*, as attached to GSB *gotras*.

All Kuduvas belong to the Kaushika *gotra* and have the same *kuladevatas*, since these relate to *gotras*, not surnames. Thus no Kuduva can marry a Kuduva. But Pais, Shenoys, and others belong to several *gotras*, and here people of the same surname may marry each other. Each *kuladevata* is 'incarnated' in the lineage temples, giving a concrete point of reference. Though incomplete, these lists (Figs. 8-9) give an idea of how family name and *gotra* intersect, and the combination of lineage temple and family name form a 'grid' which usefully maps the community. This is not a genealogical chart, as used by the Rajputs,

Surname	*Gotra*	*Kuladevata*	*Mainly settled in*
Kini	Vatsa	Mangesh	Udupi
Shenai	Vatsa	Mangesh	Parkala
Shanbhog	Kaundinya	Mangesh	Haldipur, N.K.
Shenai/Gaithonde	Kaushika	Shanta Durga	Karkala
Family of Shri Bantwal Mangesh			
Rao/Mazumdar	Kaundinya	Mangesh	(?)
Family of Shri D. Ganpata			
Rao/Nayak	Kaushika	Nagesh	Kozhikode
Mudkate			
Shenais	Vatsa	Mangesh	Kundapur taluka
Ananta Shenai	Vatsa	Mahamayi	(?)

Fig. 9: *Gotras* of the Smarta (Shaivite) families of the Kavale *math.*

for example. Since *gotras* are clans rather than lineages, the genealogical links are implicit, and since family names cut the 'genealogical' lineages into minimal units defined by their 'place of origin', historical continuity over an extended time scale is given by adherence to the lineage temples rather than by descendance. This seems to be a Brahmin specificity, relating possibly to the intimate connection between ritual and kinship among the Brahmins.[19]

The spiritual heritage of the Brahmins is further concretized through the *shakhas* – sometimes referred to as the *sampradaya* – which may be translated as a particular tradition of interpreting the scriptures. Similarly, Brahmins follow different *sutras*, or ritual prescriptions, and each sub-group is attached to one of the four Vedas.[20] In this way, each *gotra* is attached to a particular Veda and should perform their rituals according to particular *sutras*. Individuals are conscious of these attachments, and they seem to be strictly observed. As M.M. Prabhu, of Kaushika *gotra* and a follower of Ashnaya Sutra, puts it: 'If I have a marriage performed according to a *sutra* to which I do not belong, then that marriage will be null and void – legally.'[21] These rules have nothing to do with priesthood. It is as Brahmins, not as priests, that families are attached to a particular Veda, *sutra*, and *shakha*. It is in this sense, rather than in terms of their knowledge of the texts, that Brahmins are 'followers of the Vedas'. To be a Brahmin, it is not necessary to know how to perform a ritual, but one must know the tradition of ritual practice to be followed. This knowledge, however, is enough to identify with the great Brahmin tradition in a way that makes a Brahmin a different kind of Hindu from anybody else. In terms of kinship, all this is inherited cultural capital,[22] as well as, since ritual transforms the qualities of the worshipper,[23] an inherent part of Brahmin personality.

As an example of a family and its current branches, we may use the genealogy of the Tonse Kinis, a larger lineage unit which includes the Alevoor Kinis of Ideal Studios in Udupi. The family came from Tonse, but from there they went to Alevoor. Other branches went to Bailoor and Perdoor. The Kinis came to Tonse from the Shiroda area close to Margao in Goa, where their lineage temple dedicated to Kamakshi,[24] is situated, around 1700. On important ritual occasions, such as Shivaratri or Navaratri, members of the family will go to Shiroda. Several branches of the family are still at Tonse, where they were farmers at first, then became merchants. Some members of the Alevoor branch are still in agriculture. Their family temple[25] is the Venkatarama temple at Kallianpur, next to Tonse. The Alevoor Kini branch now has some 500 members, in India, Germany, the United States, England, and other countries. If we count all descendants of the Tonse Kinis, we arrive at 2,000 to 2,500 people.

The genealogical work of U.J. Kini (n.d.) lists five branches of the Tonse Kinis still based at Tonse. Other branches are identified with Kalsanka, Kallianpur, Bailoor, Perdoor and Alevoor – ten branches, or minimal lineages, in all. Two members of the senior Tonse branch live in Udupi: one of them is a lawyer. Of the second Tonse branch, one is at Udupi, the other at Manipal. The third Tonse branch has a heavy concentration in the vegetable and flower businesses in Udupi and Malpe.[26] Nothing is said about the whereabouts of the fourth and fifth Tonse branches – may be they are still at Tonse. The Kalsanka branch stems from Narayan, born 1865, who may have settled there around the turn of the century as part of the GSB influx during that period. One member of the branch is still in Udupi, a retired employee of the Syndicate Bank. No members of the Kallianpur branch are in Udupi, and for the Bailoor branch there is no data. The Perdoor branch has half a dozen members in Udupi or Manipal, working in various concerns. Apparently, they have no business of their own in Udupi.

The Alevoor branch is apparently the strongest in Udupi.[27] Of thirty male members of the last two generations, thirteen are in business or are hoteliers (43.3 per cent), seven are students (23.2 per cent), two are working in banks and one of them retired (6.7 per cent), there is one doctor, one accountant, and one press reporter. One is a factory worker, while four are unspecified as to profession (Kini, n.d.). Excluding students, well over half of the working members are in business. This may not be typical, but indicates the importance of business in this branch, especially as banking and accountancy are also related to business.

Their general merchants shop was started around 1950, and the gold shop in 1980. The elder brother, Suresh, born 1942, runs the gold shop. His father Vaman, born around 1910, had ten children, of which six were sons. Vaman was the sixth of eight brothers: he had one sister. The father of Vaman, an only son, must have been born around 1880: it is not clear whether he or his father, first settled at Alevoor. The father must have been born around 1855. Suresh is the fourth son of Vaman, who must have been the founder of the first of the Udupi shops.[28] Suresh was thirty-eight when the gold shop was established and seems to have taken care of it from the start. The general merchants' shop seems to be run by one of Suresh's nephews. Close to the shops is the office of Alevoor Premaraj Kini, advocate.[29] Some members of these generations are in Mumbai. The businesses are still run in common, but the various families dwell separately. The Alevoor Kinis are still seen as a single family in Udupi, in spite of their diversified occupations: no split has taken place.

My informant studied at Manipal, and his children went to the Sharada School and studied at MGM College, both belonging to the educational trust of the Tonse Pai family.[30] The links to the Pai empire is clear (Kini, n.d.). Nine members of the family were employed in the Syndicate Bank. Through their connection to the Tonse Pais, the Tonse Kinis are found all over India: Mumbai, Bengaluru, Udupi, Hubli, Hyderabad, Shimoga, Manipal and Mangalore. The families must have known each other from Tonse, and there may have been marriage connections, though I have no information on this. The matron of the Sharada Residential School, is the widow of a Tonse, but not an Alevoor Kini.[31] Her husband had been a chemical engineer, and they had lived in Lucknow, where her husband had died. She then returned to Udupi, where her family has stayed for at least three generations.[32] There may be others who are linked to the Manipal complex in some way. Apparently, this link between the families is one reason why Mrs. Kini avoided the drudgery of widowhood by holding a responsible post.

Kinship organization in the GSB community generally resembles that of other Hindu communities of north India, being patrilineal and patrilocal.[33] But there is a tendency, as elsewhere in western India,[34] to honour lasting alliance with affinal lines through cross-cousin marriages.[35] Thus the scriptural interdiction – often cited for north Indian Brahmins – of marrying cousins up to the seventh degree is ignored or disregarded among the GSB.[36] K.R. Kuduva affirmed that 'Saraswats have never bothered with this rule. It is common to marry in the mothers' line. That will make for a tightly knit family,' as he puts it. 'Yes,' says U.A. Kamath, the engineer, 'Saraswats may well marry into the same family several times. But there is no rule. The bond between in-laws is very important: brothers-in-law are often friends.' His family has married Kallianpur Shenoys, just as the Tonse Pais tended to marry Kallianpur Baligas. Kamath is the brother-in-law of P.R. Kuduva, and they are close friends.

With matrilateral cross-cousin marriage, the alliances are asymmetric, and wife-givers do not take wives from wife-takers. The latter point is a general pattern in western as well as in northern India and relates to rank: wife-takers outrank wife-givers.[37] The exchange is aptly characterized by Lévi-Strauss as 'generalized', as cousin marriages become part of a lasting relationship of reciprocity and business collaboration. But informants say that patrilateral cross-cousin marriage with the father's sister's daughter is equally possible among the GSB, and both types of marriage occur in my data. 'Marriage with mother's brother's daughter as well as father's sister's daughter is very common,' says P.R. Kuduva. 'They will belong to different *gotras*.'[38] Patrilateral cross-cousin marriage implies that the father's sister is seen as having taken the *gotra* of her husband. At marriage, the wife changes her *gotra*, her *kuladevata*, and her first name. In the husband's household she will be known by her wife name, in her natal family by her girl name.[39] Thus the woman is seen as transferred, on marriage, from one *gotra* – and thus from one family – to another. Here, the GSB follow a more strictly patrilineal way of thinking than the Rajputs of Saurashtra (Tambs-Lyche, 1997), which contrasts with many other castes of western India where the transfer is symbolically stated at marriage but never seen as absolute (Jacobson, 1978). Yet we have seen – T.A. Pai's first wife is one case – that women of Udupi, like those of central India, may use the return to the natal family as a sanction against the husband. The affinal tie is strong and the ritual transfer of women on marriage does not imply a cutting off of their ties to the natal family.

At the corner of VT Street and Old Post Office Road a general store is run by Mr. Kamath, some forty years old, from Salagrama near Kundapur. His father-in-law ran the shop before him, but died some five years ago. 'It was lying idle, so I decided to take it over,' said Kamath. I asked him if his father-in-law was also his *mama* (mother's brother). 'Yes', he said, surprised that I should have guessed. Here, then, the son-in-law, who was also the nephew, inherited the shop.

Marriage with both cross-cousins implies that the relationship between in-laws, as opposed to north and western India, should be symmetric, with no status difference between wife-givers and wife-takers. While some informants maintain that the difference between the sister's husband and the wife's brother is the same as in north India – the former outranking the latter – others say they are more or less equal.[40] K.R. Kuduva says they are designated by the same term, *bavaji*. The relationship, he says, is called *meono*. But some say there are two different terms. Indeed, the son-in-law – daughter's husband – is sometimes in an inferior situation with the GSB: when working in his father-in-law's firm, he seems to be treated more as a client than as a partner.[41] We shall return to these terms later.

Dowry is the woman's property and divorce implies compensation and a break in reciprocal relations. Marriages are cemented and secured by these alliances, and they are in turn strengthened by marriage. Still patrilineal descent, not alliance, remains the primary reference of the system, and cousin marriage remains an option, not a norm. It is seen as a way of perpetuating the bond between families – not least in terms of business strategy – and offering the girl the support of her natal family; her family's views will be respected since the marriage is only one aspect of the relationship. But the businesses will be kept separate, since they are related to the family name, and the dowry is not used for the groom's business.[42]

GSB dowries are never as high as among the Bunts or the Gujarat Banias. The marriage does not constitute a business alliance, and business considerations are not important for the choice of a groom, says P.R. Kuduva. It is rather a question of finding somebody of good standing with a good profession or business. The maintenance of a marriage link, he says, is more due to affection and such considerations than business liens. The woman will feel more comfortable in a family that she already knows. Others maintain that business considerations may, indeed, play a role in the choice of partners.

We shall now look at marriages in one family over a couple of generations. This is an example and not a sample: the Gundu Nayaks are not a typical family. Still, their recent marriages illustrate some of the themes discussed here. They are of the Kaundinya *gotra*. Their original *nag* shrine is near Barakuru, from where the family came to Udupi.[43] Though using Kadpet in their name, the Gundu Nayaks are not related to the Kadpet Nayaks, which is why they are known as Gundu Nayaks. Ramakrishna Gundu Nayak, an important figure in Udupi, married a girl from the rich and prestigious Rama Rao family of Mangalore,[44] a link which certainly helped in establishing his business. This link has not been repeated, however, and this may partly be due to the problems of Ramakrishna's business in early independence days. They had eleven children:

Herur Mallarama Kamath, the eldest daughter, married a Herur Kamath, who emigrated to the USA. Her husband's father, Herur Vitthal Kamath, manufactured fireworks in Udupi, with a shop next to the Diana ice-cream parlour. Mallarama is now a widow, living in the USA. She returns to Mumbai every now and then, where she has interests, but 'never comes down here'.

Kadpet Gundu Nayak, the elder son, called Gundu after his grandfather,[45] runs a shop in the family complex, dealing in wooden handicrafts. He married a girl from another Nayak family and is the head of the branch of the Gundu Nayak family in Udupi.

Kadpet Venkatesh Nayak, the second son, is now in Bengaluru.

Herur Prema Nayak, the second daughter, married the paternal cousin of her sister's husband, so the link to the Herur Kamaths was strengthened by this marriage (Fig. 10).

Kadpet Ramesh Nayak is in the USA, a doctor in the National Health Service and a follower of Sai Baba. His wife runs two schools in Maryland. Apparently she was not a relative nor related to the spouses of the other siblings.

Kadpet Ganesh Nayak runs another shop in the Udupi family complex. He married the sister of his brother Gundu's wife. There was no particular relation between the families before this alliance (Fig. 11), but marriage between two sisters and two brothers reinforced the affinal link.

On Kadpet Umesh Nayak I have no further information.

Kadpet Jagadish Nayak died young.

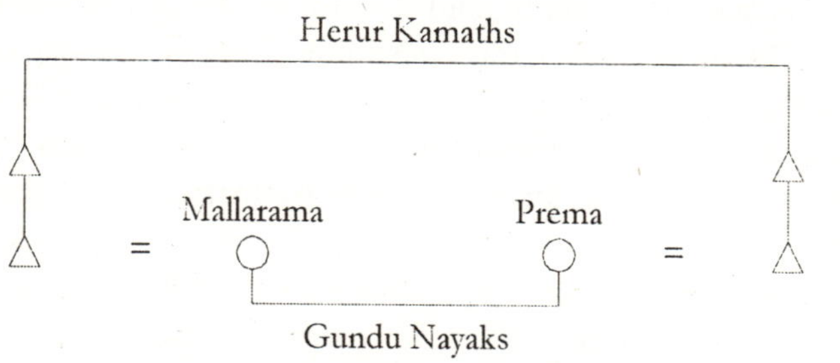

Fig. 10: Mallarama and Prema: Two sisters marrying two patrilineal cousins.

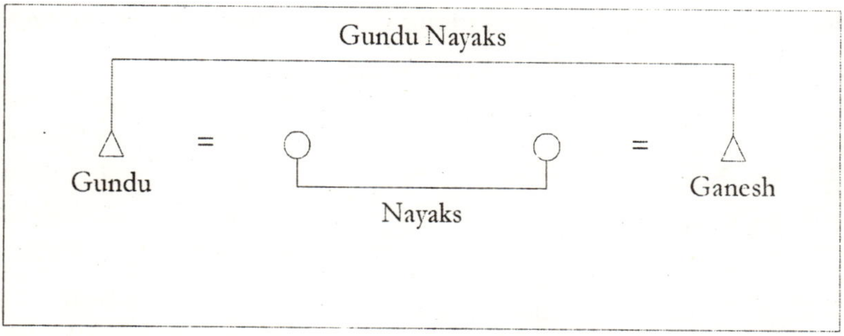

Fig. 11: Gundu and Ganesh: Two sisters marrying two brothers.

Vasanthi Kumbala married an officer of the Canara Bank: I have no information on her husband's family, but they do not seem to have other affinal links with the Gundu Nayaks. She is now a widow.

Jayasethi Prabhu married N.D. Prabhu from Nileshwar in Kerala. He was in the navy and spent some time in the UK. Now he 'sits' in the general store in the family complex. The family says he is not 'in the business', just 'sits there and helps now and then'. Still, he seemed to be taking care of the shop. His position in the family, then, is not entirely clear.

Harish Nayak is also in the USA, as a supervisor in American Airlines. He is in practice heading the family trust which owns the family complex in Udupi. This situation, which means that the Udupi branch can do little to improve their property, is a source of conflict. Harish married his niece, Mallarama's daughter, in the USA (Fig. 12). It was a real 'love marriage,' says Gundu with a wry smile. Shailesh, Ganesh's son, rather implied that Mallarama had engineered the marriage, which would cement her authority as the elder sibling in the US branch of the family, and also implied that no dowry had to be paid. On another level, this constitutes the third marriage link in one sibling group to a single family of affinals, the Herur Kamaths. The marriage reverses the direction of Mallarama's and Prema's marriages. It is true that this unconventional marriage[46] took place in the USA.

It will be seen that among Ramakrishna's children, two sisters married men who were patrilineal cousins, and two of the brothers married sisters. Then, Harish married his niece, his sister's daughter, who belonged to the family to which the Gundu Nayaks had given two sisters in the last generation. This marriage implies a direct

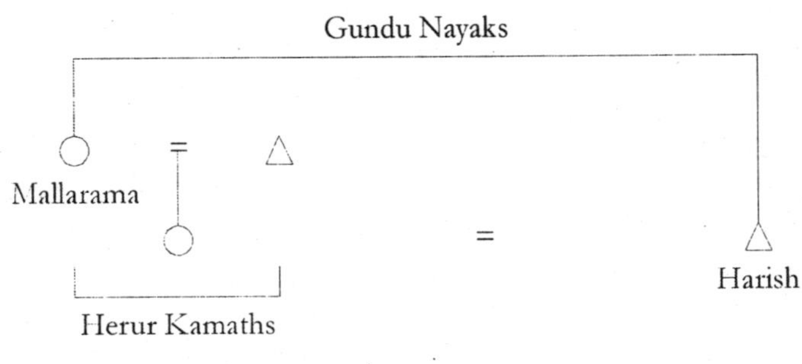

Fig. 12: Harish Nayak marrying his sister's daughter.

exchange in Lévi-Strauss' terms, and a break with asymmetrical, hypergamous, alliances. Harish must respect his elder sister, but would also be a wife-taker, superior to the Kamaths. In the present generation, not only did Shailesh's cousin marry her maternal uncle, but Shailesh's second sister married a cousin. The latter was, I understood, a matrilateral cross-cousin marriage, so the groom came from the Nayak family of Shailesh's mother, which is the family of his aunt, Gundu's wife. This, too, was a third marriage to cement an existing alliance, but again in the inverse direction: wife-takers became wife-givers.

These examples show that the hypergamous implications of asymmetric alliances is not unduly stressed among the GSB. In fact, there are cases where the wife's family was clearly more prestigious than that of the husband, as when Ramakrishna Gundu Nayak married a girl from the Rama Rao family. The mother of T.M.A. Pai and his brothers came from a Baliga family superior in status and wealth to the Tonse Pais, and T.A. Pai's first wife came from an 'established' family in Udupi at a time when the Pais were still seen as upstarts. We have seen, too, that in spite of his being a 'wife-taker' N.D. Prabhu is not accorded a place equal to the brothers in the family firm. Clearly, uxorilocality has a negative influence on the brother-in-law's relation to his wife's brothers.

Shailesh, Ganesh's son, was preoccupied with his marriage plans in the autumn of 2005. He had his eyes on a Pai girl from Kumta, but her *gotra* was Kaundinya, like his own. Normally, this would render marriage impossible, but he had seen some knowledgeable people, including the managing trustee of the Venkatarama temple in Mangalore, who felt it might be done if the families were distant enough. I was curious about this exception to *gotra* exogamy, but neither Shailesh nor I knew enough to discern the fine points of the question. Later, Shailesh seemed to give up the project: there may have been too many complications.

What emerges from the various marriages of the Gundu Nayaks is not so much a set of normative rules as a practice where marriages are made in a context of establishing and maintaining reciprocal relations with a limited number of families – as opposed, both to the narrow and enduring, normatively supported, alliance of Dravidian kinship, and to the wide-ranging networks typical of African and north Indian kinship.[47] The GSB pattern clearly reflects interest in a mercantile community: alliances are useful, but there is no point in dispersing relations too widely. This is very similar to what we find in the north European bourgeoisie in the late nineteenth or early twentieth century.[48]

I had not the chance to attend a GSB wedding in Udupi, but we went to an RSB wedding.[49] The groom was a cousin of the Borkar brothers, on the father's side. A pharmacist, he lived in Mumbai, was some thirty-five years old, so it was a late marriage. The bride's family was from near Karkala, but lived in London, with her two sisters. They were all nurses, living with the husband of the elder sister. He belonged to the groom's patriline, so there was a repeated marriage alliance. The bride was thirty-two years old. Sunil Borkar stressed that among the RSB, practically the whole ceremony is held by the bride's family: no important ritual would have taken place in Mumbai. There were some three hundred guests, a moderate gathering for a high caste, but it was a late marriage and the partners were not of particularly high socio-economic status.

In the middle of the stage there was a double *mandala*, one each for the groom and bride. The seats for the couple were at the rear of the stage, and the various implements of each Brahmin – one for each family – were kept on either side of the stage. Off-stage were the bride's and the groom's 'chambers', the bride's to the left facing the audience, the groom's to the right. The *mandala* in the middle was divided by a white screen hung across the stage: the groom stood facing the screen, looking away from the audience, and the bride behind the screen, facing the audience, but hidden from view. Thus there is a studied symmetry in the arrangement of the stage, indicating that the marriage is taking place between two 'parties' – the families – that are more or less equal.

The screen was held by the two elder Borkar brothers.[50] On both sides of the screen, men (in front of the screen) and women (behind the screen) from both families threw rice at the groom and bride respectively, while repeating *mantras* spoken by the priests. After numerous *mantras* and generous throwing of rice, the screen is lowered, and the couple see each other 'for the first time'. In fact, they had met once before, but living in Mumbai and London, they did not know each other beforehand. At the moment of lowering the screen, there are more *mantras* accompanied, once again, by throwing of rice. For the next stage of the ritual, the couple change places: the bride is now in front. They exchange symbolic 'foods', including *Ganga Jala* – water from the Ganges. The groom's mother decorates the head of the bride with flowers. Then, the groom's parents, led by the priest from the bride's side, repeat a number of *mantras* spoken by the latter while making a series of offerings to the bride, notably of Ganges water. The sequence is then repeated, in what looks like exact symmetry, by the bride's parents for the groom, and led by the priest from the groom's side.

Then comes the *kanyadan*, the 'gift of a virgin', where the parents of the bride, led by the two priests acting together, 'give away' their daughter. This sequence corresponds to what we know about other Brahmin marriages, as described by Stevenson (1920).[51] The bride's mother offers a plate full of various substances to the groom. The groom seems to recite the usual verses – 'I am the best young man of my age' – cited by Stevenson, accepting the bride. But as Sunil remarked, 'These *mantras* are in Sanskrit, so one does not understand them.' The gift of the virgin is followed by that of a gold chain for the groom, given by the bride's mother, but tied on by the Brahmin. Then the marriage necklace of the bride is brought, carried by the groom's mother on a plate filled with rice, and put around the bride's neck. This necklace, too, is of gold, but the ritually important part is the black stone pendant called a 'kamala'.[52] Putting it on puts the final touch to the *kanyadan* part of the ceremony.

Finally, the couple are seated in the two chairs at the back of the scene, and tied together with a white sari. They are now congratulated by the families, starting with the uncles and aunts of the groom's family. Others follow in descending order of importance, with guests, such as ourselves, towards the end.[53]

The wedding, as is usual in India, finishes with a meal for all guests. Apart from the main family members, people seemed to choose their seats freely, with no 'breaks' in the line. Though many guests were not RSB – friends, colleagues, and so on – most were from high castes.[54] Only the priests ate separately.[55] Sunil Borkar explained: 'This is because though we are Brahmins, we are not really accepted by other Brahmins since we eat meat. That is true of the GSB also. So there is no need to be exclusive, like other Brahmans are.' After the meal, the priests light the *homa* fire in the middle of the stage and the newly-wed couple make offerings to it. Those familiar with Hindu weddings may note that the fire is not lit earlier, so there is no fire during the *kanyadan*, as also the lack of another element – the 'nine steps' where the couple circumambulate the fire. Apparently, these otherwise common elements do not form part of the typical RSB wedding.

This particular marriage was framed by several strategic factors: the opportunity for the groom to migrate to the UK was an obvious attraction which influenced the marriageability of the girl – past the usual marriage age – as well as the demand for dowry. The example underlines the importance of marriage as part of strategic practice, not a field dominated by normative factors. But what I wish to stress here is the symmetry of the marriage arrangements.[56] The ritual seemed to underline the equal status of the bride's and groom's family. This may surprise those used to north Indian marriages. Of course, this was an RSB, not a GSB marriage. But like the marriage, the kinship terms of the GSB indicate a tendency for absence of symmetry, for example, from those of the Gujarat Patidars (Pocock, 1972).

The kinship terms that follow should be read with some caution, since I did not do a systematic study of them. What follows is a mixture of data from informants and the *Konkani Samantara Shabdakosa* (Ubhayakar et al., 2001), which lists terms for the GSB, Saraswats, and Catholics.[57] It shows varying usage with alternative terms for the same relation: including the lack of agreement on brother-in-law terms, as noted.

Ascending generations and cousins: There are several terms for father and mother: father is *ãnu*, *bappu* or *bana*, while mother may be called *ãmma*, *ãyi*, *avayi* or *mãta*.[58] Of the father's siblings, the father's brother is called *mauni*, *mahvali* or *banulyo*, while father's sister is *mauvli* or *akkal*. Mother's brother is sometimes called *mama*, as in north India, but also *mavlo*. Mother's sister is *pacchi*, *mavshi* or *mauli*. Note that *mauvli* (father's sister) is the feminine of *mavlo* (mother's brother), to which two terms *mauni* (father's brother) and *mavshi* (mother's sister) seems closely related. These four terms for aunts and uncles seem to be variants of a single term, indicating a bilateral rather than a patrilineal mode of thought. The distinction between mother's and father's side becomes clearer, however, in cousin terms: paternal cousins are called *akkal putr* (or *putro*) for the father's sister's sons and *akkal dhu* (or *dhua*) for father's sister's daughters. Maternal cousins are similarly called *maulal* (or *maulil*) *putr* and *maulil dhu*. Thus, while several terms are used for uncles or aunts, only the lineally distinctive terms are combined with the words for 'son' and 'daughter' to distinguish their offspring. It is here, of course, that the question of marriage calls for clarity – since mother's brother's daughter is the preferred bride for a man. I have not found any terms distinguishing parallel from cross-cousins, grouping the latter as marriageable: in spite of the lineal distinction, then, the terminology 'fits' the idea that all cousins, except father's brother's children, who belong to ego's own *gotra*, are potential marriage partners. The terms for grandparents are puzzling: while two terms, *appo* and *ashu* are given for grandfather, they do not seem to distinguish between mother's and father's side, while only a single term, *appi*, is given for grandmother. The terminology then has traits of a bifurcate-merging type, since grandchildren too are distinguished only by sex. This fits marriage with the paternal cross-cousin, and differs from north Indian kinship terms while implying some similarity to the Dravidian type (Fig. 13).

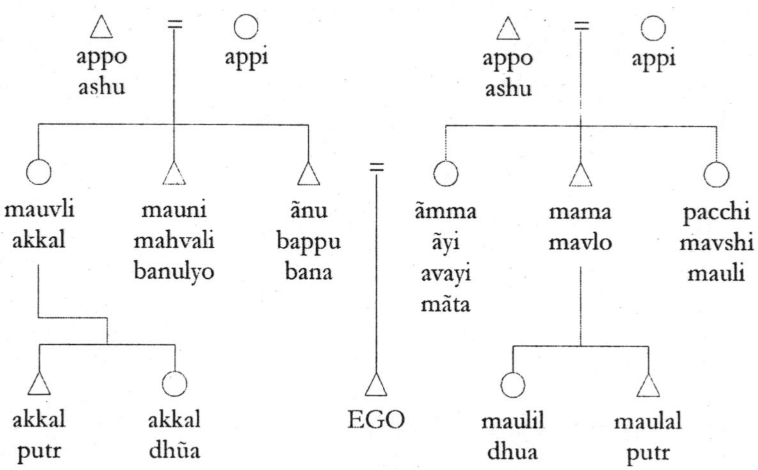

Fig. 13: Terms for Ascending generations and cousins.

Own generation and in-laws: The terms for siblings show a double tendency. Thus the terms *bandhu* and *bhavu* are used for brothers irrespective of relative age, as may the terms *bhanini* and *bhayili* for sisters. Yet the older brother may be specified by the terms *dhadbhar* or *ana,* without any counterpart for younger brothers: the elder sister is *avka,* while the younger sister is called *bhav.* Thus the principle of seniority is present but terms ignoring relative age are also used. This corresponds with a general respect for elder siblings paralleled by a tendency to stress the equivalence of all brothers or sisters: in practice, individual qualities may challenge the status due to differential age (Fig. 14).

In a similar way, both elder and younger brother's wife may be called *bovaj*, but only the younger brother's wife is called *jav*: the latter term is also used for the wife of a female ego's husband's brother. A male ego calls his wife *bayl*, *jaya*, or, in more formal language, *priyatma.* Her brother, to him, is a *bovaji*, the term used for both brothers-in-law, or he may be called *sala,* the north Indian term which stresses the wife-giver's inferiority. For his wife's sister he uses the term *mevali*, not used for his brother's wife. She is, as noted, a *bovaj,* but if married to a younger brother, she may be callad a *jav.* For the male ego's sister's husband there are two terms (Fig. 15): whether married to a younger or an elder sister, he is called either a *bovaji* or a *mevalo.* The same terms are used for the wife's brother, again indicating a symmetrical relation between affines which, as we have seen, alternates with the asymmetrical north Indian pattern. A female ego uses one of these terms, *bovaji,* for the brother of her husband. Her husband's sister is called *naladh* or *nalandh*, clearly variants of the same term. Finally, she

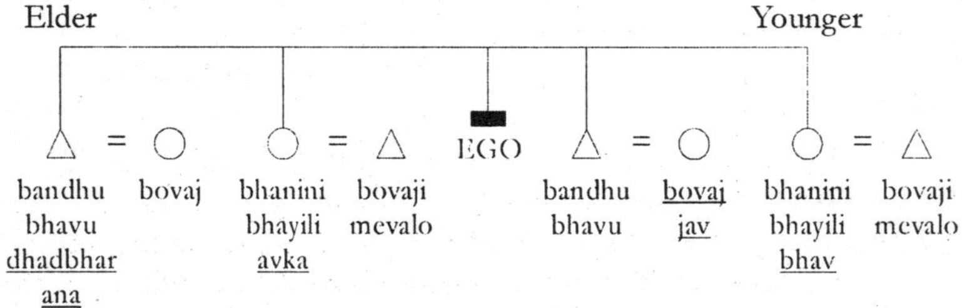

Note: Age-specific terms are underlined.

Fig. 14: Terms for siblings and their spouses.

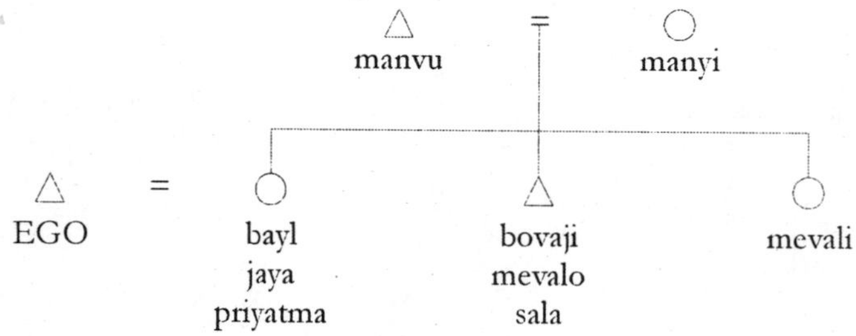

Fig. 15: Terms for in-laws: Male Ego.

has several terms for her husband: *pati, bammalu, bhamo, pralasthya* – the latter being, like *priyatma*, a formal term rarely used (Fig. 16).

Descendants and brothers' children: The terms for son and daughter are, respectively, *putr* and *dhuv*. The son's wife is *sunu* and the daughter's husband *javayi*. The children of both couples are *natu* (boys) and *nati* (girls) without distinction, reminiscent of bifurcate-merging patterns. All brothers' sons, irrespective of their seniority, are called *putalyo*. The brother's daughters may all be called *dhuvaji*, but there is a special term for the elder brother's sister, *putadi*. She may well be the first of the siblings' children to marry, and so the first of her generation to leave the joint household. She may even be close to her younger uncles in age, which may be why she is the only one of the siblings' children to be known by a special term (Fig. 17). A man's sister's children are *bhavvo* (male) and *bhavvi* (female). For a female ego, these terms are used only for the brother's children. These terms show the importance of cross-cousin marriage: for a man, they designate matrilateral cross-cousins of his children, and for a

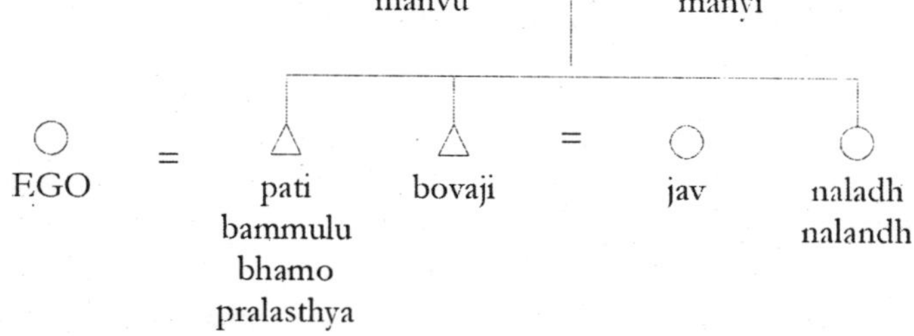

Fig. 16: Terms for in-laws: Female Ego.

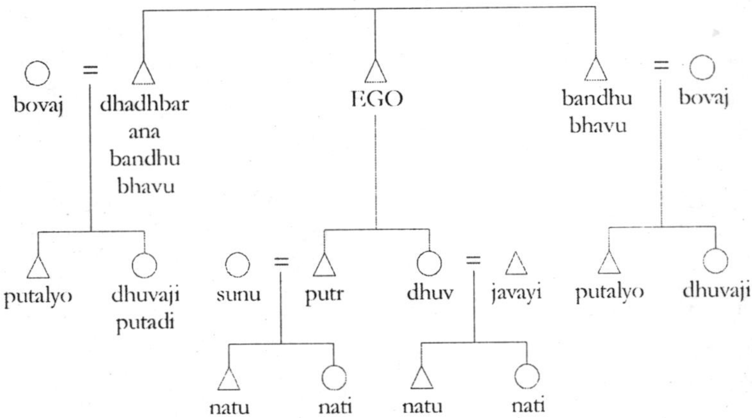

Fig. 17: Terms for descendants and brothers' descendants.

woman, patrilateral ones: the preferred marriage partners of one's offspring (Fig. 18).[59]

Further comments on the terminology: It is clear that symmetric and asymmetric terms coexist. It is often possible to distinguish affinals from agnates, while alternatively, the same terms are used for both. While the former usage corresponds to north Indian kinship, the latter alternative does not fit this pattern.[60] But the distinguishing feature of Dravidian kinship, the distinction between cross and parallel cousins, does not figure at all, except when used by the ascending generation to designate the nephews and nieces which would be the subject of preferential matrilateral cross-cousin marriage.

The material fits Irawati Karve's point (1953) that kinship in western India represents an intermediate form between the south and north Indian pattern. I would be wary of a diffusionist implication here, however. In my view, the logic of kinship among the GSB has nothing to do with the prescribed alliance typical of the south,[61] but is rather

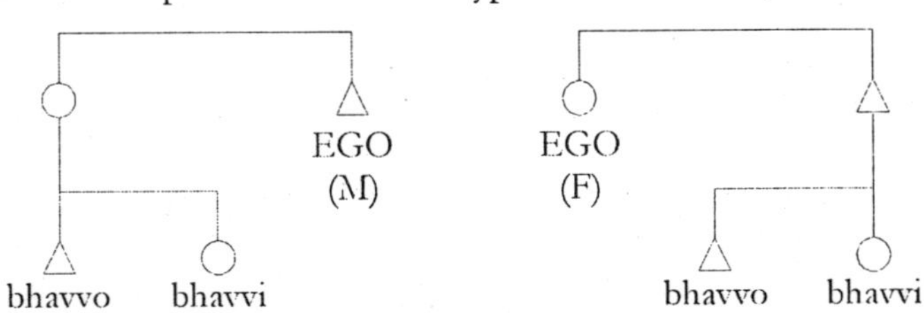

Fig. 18: Terms for the marriageable children of siblings.

a variant of northern, Indo-European kinship modified by a high incidence of cousin marriage. What we need to know is how the alternative terms are used in practice.[62] Are symmetric terms mainly used when cousin marriages have drawn the allied families together, so that the web of relationships resembles Dravidian kinship? Are the asymmetric terms used mainly when a single marriage links two families? The answers would call for an extended study, which I have not been able to do.

Ambiguity as to patrilineal or bilateral categorization of relatives does, indeed, seem rather common among the European bourgeoisie.[63] The similarity as well as the differences between the terminologies, suggests that the commonality of these examples is not inherent in kinship as such, and I suggest that the ambiguity is rather related to a particular type of pragmatism in kin nomenclature cross-culturally common to bourgeois communities. The farm and the firm both influence kinship, but their influence is not the same. The assumption would be that symmetric nomenclature is used in interpersonal relationships, and the asymmetric pattern when it is important to distinguish the patriline from affinals, as when referring to marriage or the family firm. In the latter case, uncles differ: they belong to separate firms. But in interpersonal terms, one kind of uncle may be as close as another[64] – indeed, the mother's brother may be closer since he does not form part of the hierarchy of agnates (Radcliffe-Brown, 1952: 26-30). Thus there are situations when uncles are uncles, and others, when one is part of 'us', the other of 'they'. We may wonder why the paternal grandfather among the GSB, as 'ancestor of the firm', is not singled out by a separate term. But the founder, and other agnates crucial to the firm, are seldom denoted by kinship terms: they are known by proper names or initials. It is as if these commanding personalities are beyond the level reached by kinship terms.[65] Such terms may indeed be used when no confusion is possible: 'yes, it was my grandfather (*appo*) who founded this firm'. In that case, only the paternal grandfather could be meant.

The ambiguity, then, is not due to insufficient fieldwork but to the embeddedness of kinship in other social relations. GSB marriages are, and certainly were, alliances between families usually involved in business and strategic considerations may have been as important as kinship rules.[66] In such a situation, rules would tend to be blurred.

In the material presented, we clearly see the link between kinship and business. The family and the firm have been, and remain, closely associated. This does not mean that they are always contiguous. But the family name remains a central reference in business, as it does for local history. Individual identity is circumscribed by family identity, and so kinship remains a central concern in the community.

The link between business and family belies the assumption that kinship is opposed to modernity. It is precisely as families that the GSB have been agents of modernity in South Kanara, and there is no sign that this link is weakening, at least as yet. Clearly, a transformation of business into limited companies with openly traded shareholdings might reduce the pertinence of kinship for business. But such trends are so far perceptible mainly at the very top of the business hierarchy in India, where, even so, nobody will contest the continuing importance of the large business families. Kinship, so important in developing modernity through business, is likely to remain an important factor in the foreseeable future.

NOTES

1. As elsewhere, many concepts and categories relate to the domain anthropologists call 'kinship'. These are not implicit, but do not necessarily fit together in a logically structured whole since common language privileges a number of meanings and values implicit to each concept. Traditional study of kinship constructed a logical structure from kinship terms, rules and norms to form a 'kinship system'. Whether such structures 'exist' in the minds of informants (emically) or only in the anthropologists' mind (etically) is an epistemological question I do not discuss here. By calling them 'implicit', I wish to say that they can be deduced from explicit language relating to kin, but that such deduction is not usually done by informants themselves.
2. South Kanara contrasts with regions (such as much of Europe before recent Third World immigration) where an image of 'normal' kinship rules and practices prevail. In South Kanara, the presence of highly divergent kinship rules precludes such an image: kinship becomes a matter of 'our norms' *versus* 'theirs'.
3. Anthropologists have long discussed the universality of the 'family'. I imply here that 'family' and 'kinship' are not part of the same semantic field, though they overlap, so 'the family' should be seen as a universal domain of diffuse solidarity, borrowing Schneider's (1968) term, rather

than as a conglomerate of 'primary' kinship relations. I distinguish, then, a moral domain where 'family' is an important concept, from structural constructs of kinship relations. Since cognition and evaluation are linked (Bateson, 1972), this distinction is only relative.

4. Caste is not 'simply' an extension of kinship, but in terms of social relations, the individual's link to his caste passes by the family. While this does not affect the idea that his qualities stem from his ancestors, and thus from his caste, neither does it preclude 'the presence of the individual' (Dumont, 1965, 1966) in other contexts. The reduction of the individual to a 'case' of the family qualities is a semantic inference, and so is highly context dependent.
5. I came across only one example, a medical doctor, son of a PWD engineer who worked in many different parts of India. This apparently estranged his parents from the caste network, replacing it with a professional circle. The doctor was attracted to Aurobindo's ideas, and after studies in Pondicherry he settled there, near Auroville, the 'ideal city' of the Aurobindo movement. Here he is centrally located in a network which seems to have replaced his caste links. As he says, he comes from a Mangalore family but has no particular links to Mangalore now. With Aurobindo, he saw caste as originally based on individual qualities, so that Brahmins were the original intellectuals irrespective of birth (Dutt, 1960). This position makes it possible to negate the importance of caste in social terms, while not necessarily renouncing the intellectual qualities of Brahminhood.
6. I follow here K.R. Kuduva's use of the terms: *dadalo* for an extended lineage, and *wangad* for 'family' or minimal lineage. For the Chitrapur Saraswats, however, Conlon uses *vangad* for the extended lineage and *dayadi* for the minimal one (1977: 33). I did not come across the latter term.
7. Usually, when the business is good, the elder son takes over leadership on his father's death, but the business may go to the youngest son if his brothers have found more lucrative occupations.
8. In their work on education in Huddersfield, England, Jackson and Marsden (1966) use the term 'sunken middle class', working class descendants of middle-class families, some of whom once had their own business. The authors' point is that such families retain middle-class values and practices, making it easier for their children to re-establish middle-class status through education (Jackson and Marsden, 1966: 67-70). There, as in Udupi, the 'cultural capital' (Bourdieu, 1972, 1980) of such families sets them apart from the working class. But the presence of caste in Udupi seems to make culturally explicit a distinction which remains important, though implicit, in Huddersfield.

9. The term 'ascription' is used here consciously, to evoke Parsons' distinction between ascribed and achieved status. Such ascription is seen here as semantic, however, rather than as part of an abstract and implicit structural grid.
10. The break implies double ascription for the ancestor: as descendant of his ancestors, and as ancestor of the new branch. For his descendants, the founder's ancestors are secondary to membership in the branch he founded.
11. The schism again produces double ascription, linked, not by 'and' as for the founder, but rather by 'but': A.S. Airodikar is an Airody, *but* he is part of a branch that split off from them.
12. This is one reason why I would separate the normative and structural aspects of 'kinship' and 'family'.
13. I stress there is no automatic 'normative mechanism' to keep the joint family together. To do so is hard work, and everybody concerned is aware of that. We may rather see each member's adherence to the joint family in transactional terms. The difference from the contemporary West is that the practical advantages of sticking together are more real to the Udupi GSB, as indeed they were in the Western bourgeoisie when the family firm was still central. Though not absent in the West, the role of the family's economic and cultural capital in forging individual destinies remains very important in Udupi. Promotion through education implies going to expensive, private schools, to a much higher degree than in the contemporary West.
14. The others, of course, are the Airodikars.
15. I follow here the old distinction in anthropology between lineage as a patriline with an explicit though not necessarily exact genealogy, and clan, where the genealogical links are implicit or unknown.
16. This is a complicated matter, which G.S. Ghurye discussed thoroughly. In some cases not only the *gotra* and *pravara* are exogamous, but certain *gotras* are seen as patrilineally related and form groups where marriage between the *gotras* of the same group are prohibited. According to Ghurye, this is the case for both Chitpavan and Madhyandina Deshastha Brahmins of Maharashtra. In these groups, the mother's natal *gotra*, *pravara*, and patrilineally related group of *gotras* are also excluded from marriage alliances (Ghurye, 1932/69: 250-5). For Uttar Pradesh Brahmins, *gotras* are grouped in larger exogamous units but *pravara* links are not taken into account (Blunt, 1931: 44; Ghurye, 1932/69: 256). Ghurye further cites a letter from Chapekar, whose work on the Chitpavan he cites, to the effect that Kashmir Brahmins (the Pandits of

Madan's work) 'do not even know the *pravaras*' (op. cit.: 256-7). Ghurye also concludes, from Anantha Krishnan Iyer (*The Castes and Tribes of Mysore*) and Srinivas (1942: 32-7), that among Kannada Brahmins '*pravaras* are either absent or are not paid any heed in marital selection' (Ghurye, 1932/69: 258). Finally, he notes that Gangopadhyay (1964: 42) found very frequent intermarriage between the Shandilya and Kashyapa *gotras* among the Radhi Brahmins in Kolkata, in spite of these two *gotras* belonging to the same 'patrilineal grouping' of *gotras* (Ghurye, 1932/69: 257), which would have been exogamous among the Chitpavans or the Deshasthas. Clearly, then, there is room for considerable variation in Brahmin kinship.

17. 'Family' here is clearly *wangad*.
18. Conlon (1977: 47) gives a complete list of Chitrapur Saraswat *gotras, kuladevatas,* original settlement (North or South Kanara), the number of surnames, and the percentage of each *gotra* in the caste censuses of 1932 and 1956. I do not have comparable data for the GSB.
19. The points most comparable for Rajput lineages to the lineage temples of the GSB would be their fortresses, capitals and *jagirs*.
20. V.N. Kuduva refers to these traditions, and gives some examples: 'In terms of Shakha, there are Shakalas (Saraswats) and Barkalas. The Saraswats are following the rituals – *grihya sutra* – of the Ashwalayana Sutra. The Smartas are of the Bhagavata Sampradaya. The Kaundinya *gotra* follows the Rig Veda; the Kaushika the Yajur Veda; and the Bharadwaja the Sama Veda.' He continues: 'Kaushika *gotra* still perform their *upakarma* on Hasta Nakshatra in the month of Shravan prescribed for the Yajurvedis and Samavedis and also perform it on Shravana Nakshatra . . . (they) were originally, like most of the Northern Saraswats, Yajurvedis . . . (but) From the end of the 13th century they have been Rgvedis only . . .' (1972: 11-12).
21. By legally, here, he refers to the rules practised by the *gurus* of the *maths*, but also the reference to community custom in terms of Hindu family law.
22. In Bourdieu's sense.
23. A point particularly well put by C. Malamoud (1989).
24. Kamakshi is, they say, the same as Kamakhya in Assam. Her temple there is one of the most important Shaktapithas in India, where parts of Sati's body fell when Shiva had been swinging her body in grief and anger after her suicide (she killed herself when her husband Shiva was refused access to a gods' party by her father Prajapati). It was Sati's yoni – her generative organ – which fell at Kamakhya, so that goddess is the

very essence of female powers. To what extent she retains her character when transposed as a lineage goddess of the GSB is less clear: see next chapter.

25. This is the term my informant used here, clearly distinct from Kamakshi as the lineage deity. I take it that Venkatarama at Kallianpur is the *ishta-devata* of the Tonse Kini group of minimal lineages.
26. I have not spoken to members of this branch.
27. Alevoor is only some five kilometres from Udupi.
28. His picture is behind the desk of the shop.
29. Curiously he is not mentioned in Kini's work as an advocate. He may have been classed as a businessman (the two are of course not exclusive), or he may be among the 'unspecified' for reasons not clear to me.
30. Mr. Acharya, its principal, is also a GSB: his family is from Udyavara, south-west of Udupi.
31. He may have been Manjunatha (no. 1-15 in the genealogy) from the senior Tonse branch.
32. She has been several times to the USA, where her son, an architect, is established in Chicago.
33. The patriline is called *Dadalo.* The term for the wife's patriline translates as 'other people', says U.P. Kamath. He felt the GSB in Goa must originally have taken wives from among the local people.
34. This specificity of western Indian kinship, which was pointed out summarily by Irawati Karve (1953), has recently been further explored, for Maharashtra, by Véronique Beneï (2000). It does not necessarily include all castes of Western India, however, notable exceptions being the Chitpavan and Deshastha Brahmins mentioned in note 16 to this chapter.
35. Conlon also refers to this practice among the Chitrapur Saraswats (1977: 48).
36. The contrast is clear to the Pandit Brahmins of Kashmir, who would 'no more derive their own successors (lineal descendants) exclusively from their ancestors (lineal ascendants) than they would give wives to those from whom they have taken them' (Madan, 1987: 233, and Madan, 1965: 105).
37. This is clear from Pocock's study of the Patidars (1972). But even here there are variations. The asymmetry where wife-takers outrank wife-givers characterizes the upper crust of the caste, in Charottar (between Ahmedabad and Cambay), as well as the poorest Kanbi/Patidars of that area, who take wives from Saurashtra whose caste membership may be in doubt. But in north Gujarat, H. Patel (1966a and b) has shown the

existence of 'Anawari' or brother-sister exchange among the Patidars, which annuls the status difference between affines.

38. Krishna Bhatt says that marrying the cousins on both sides is not unusual among Brahmins. Shivallis do it, he says. He may take his clue from Dravida Brahmins who have a variant of Dravidian kinship.
39. Thus P.R. Kuduva's wife was named Chitra by her own family, but as his wife she is known as Manimata.
40. Sunil Borkar, the youngest son of the RSB Borkar family, says the respect due to an elder brother is as important as ever. He also stresses the difference between *sala* and *bhanevi/bhanej*. But in spite of their lower status, the RSB may be closer to northern Brahmin traditions, and they do claim to be more 'traditional' than the GSB. They speak, they say, a 'purer' Konkani, less mixed with Kannada words. Rajapur, from where the caste takes its name, is between Goa and Ratnagiri and was then a port of importance. It is likely that the RSB were merchants then. Rajapur was under Bijapur for some time, and the RSB way well have been more influenced by north Indian ideas than the GSB. Sujeet, Sunil's elder brother, says there is certainly a difference between wife's brother and sister's husband, but he uses the same term for them: he also uses *mama* both for mother's and father's brother, and a single term for the aunts. But he knew no RSB who had married his cousin.
41. This goes against the grain of wife-takers outranking wife-givers: it is difficult to say, however, whether his junior position is due to economic factors – working for his in-laws – or due to the kinship relation. It is possible that the son-in-law's position in such cases is particularly weak precisely since it goes 'against the grain'.
42. This, I was told during my fieldwork in Gujarat, is common practice among Banias there.
43. This was the only GSB family to refer to their *nag* shrine. Such shrines are general among landowning castes in Tulunadu, and the *nags* (serpents) are the autochthonous spirits of the land. It is likely that other GSB families also have *nag* shrines wherever they held land in Tulunadu. Unlike the lineage deities, *nags* would not set the GSB apart from others or underline their Brahmin status. This may be why no other GSB mentioned them.
44. This was one of the most influential GSB families in Mangalore. In 1890, for example, one member stood for a seat in the municipal council and lost very narrowly to Nayampalli Shivarao, a Saraswat (Conlon, 1977: 96).
45. The names Gundu and Ramakrishna have alternated through generations, another parallel to many Western bourgeois families.

46. Such a marriage would have been quite conventional in the context of Dravidian kinship, such as among the Bunts. But the strong consciousness in the region of the differences between Dravidian and northern ideas of kinship, makes any influence of Dravidian practice on Harish and Mallarama's choice unlikely.
47. The practice of cementing alliance by marriage leads to several ways of promoting such unions. A girl student at Manipal was staying with the Borkar family, while her mother, whom they know well, worked in Dubai. She was 'left in charge' of the Borkars, but also seemed to be a 'prospective bride' of Sunit, the elder brother.
48. Thus Max Weber fell in love with one cousin but married another. Among well-known Norwegians, the composer Grieg married a cousin. In my own family, my grandfather and his brother married two sisters.
49. They rented the marriage hall of the Gurunarayana temple, belonging to the Billavas. The RSB have no hall of their own in Udupi, and nobody seemed to mind having the function in a hall associated with a lower caste.
50. Thus from the groom's side.
51. There was, however, no *madhuparka*, the giving of five sacred substances of which the central one is honey.
52. This is said to be the object most clearly symbolizing the marriage.
53. Unlike at Gujarati Patidar weddings, gifts are not given at this stage, and there is no public announcement of the gifts and their value. At this RSB wedding, the gifts were just put on the side for opening later.
54. There were two servings of food, however, to serve everybody; the families and the high-status invitees generally ate first – though this did not seem a very strict distinction either.
55. At another temple meal at the Mahalingeshwara temple, the vegetarian Brahmins (mostly Shivalli) ate separately from the RSB, who were the *jajmans* of the ritual.
56. There was no 'royal' procession of the groom come to fetch his bride, as in north India or in Gujarat.
57. I have used the terms for Gauda Saraswats. Different terms are given for the Chitrapur Saraswats and the Catholics – though all three descend from a single community. This may add to the number of alternative terms.
58. In my work on Gujarat and its goddesses, I accepted Pocock's statement that the term 'Mata' (goddess, but also various nameless spirits) for mother is unknown in that language. We here find it in Konkani, a closely related language, which casts some doubt on Pocock's supposition that the term may have nothing to do with 'mother'.

59. These terms are also used by the Christian Konkanis, mostly of GSB origin. Marriage with matrilateral cross-cousins seems quite common among Catholics too, as seen from many examples in Lobo's work (2000).
60. At least for the high castes, though 'bilateral' tendencies are known to exist among low castes.
61. There was no hint of prescriptive alliance. Nor did I come across any case of 'failed cousin marriage', quite common with the Bunts: when the expected marriage does not occur, partners may show symptoms of loss – love and desire having been channelled toward the cousin since early age.
62. A larger sample would give a better idea, say, of the statistical incidence of cousin marriage. But this would not modify the argument here, as I question the appropriateness of each alternative term to a given relationship.
63. Thus in Norwegian families of the old bourgeoisie – normally descended from Danish, Dutch, British or German immigrants – the terms 'uncle' and 'aunt' are used indiscriminately, but the terms for great-uncle and great-aunt, which are not used by other families in Norway, are restricted to the paternal line. Thus they are father's father's brother and father's father's sister and, in some cases, father's mother's father and father's mother's sister but never mother's father's brother or mother's father's sister. On the mother's side, these are simply uncles and aunts. Specific terms for mother's brother, father's brother, mother's sister and father's sister are never used by these families, though they are used among other categories in Norwegian society, notably in older variants of Neo-Norwegian usage, which related to a peasant society where the various uncles and aunts would 'belong' to different farms. Swedish also has four different terms: Sweden, unlike Norway, has never been a colony.
64. In Udupi, at least, maternal uncles may well live in the same town or even on the same street.
65. Schneider's argument (1968) that kinship terms do not constitute a closed system but always stand as alternatives to other ways of identifying persons is relevant here.
66. I am here taking the view that kinship is above all a practice, following Barth (1955) and Bourdieu (1972).

9

Religion and Ritual

The GSB may be businessmen, but they are very conscious of being Brahmins. They know other Brahmins see them as unorthodox, since they eat fish, practice cousin marriage, and generally do not conform to the modern image of Sanskritized Brahmins. But, they say, Saraswat Brahmins are referred to in the early texts and are among the oldest documented Brahmin groups. Their 'unorthodox' traditions are very ancient, they feel, and tend to take them as authentic. To them, modern claims to orthodoxy come from upstarts eager to gain ascendancy over established groups like themselves. The GSB need not invent tradition, while others, like GSB emigrants, are 'the most traditional – but they do not know the tradition'.[1]

This consciousness of belonging to an old and established community is important to GSB identity. Caste is positively valued, since the GSB are proud of their community and value their Brahminhood highly. But, as befitting an old elite, they tend not to stress caste too much: high status is taken for granted.[2] 'When I invite my friends to some function, they will not be asked because of their caste,' U.A. Kamath, the 'builder of Manipal', said. 'Most will, of course, be GSB, but others will be included.' Thus he invites relative equals, but such social equality may extend to members of other castes. He feels too much fuss is made about caste. 'Being a Brahmin does not mean you keep apart from other people. But you should keep yourself pure. You must have your bath four times a day.' One Brahmin friend of his would drink from anybody's cup – but take care to purify himself afterwards. 'You must keep the *rajas* and *tamas* out of your body, keeping only the *sattvic*.[3] This is the point: the blood must be kept pure. Everything you eat enters into your blood.' This is, of course, a common view in India, regulating diet but also other kinds of behaviour.

It is important to realize that purity here is relative to the necessities of life: this is a religion of the *grahastha,* the householder (Madan, 1982 and 1987), not of the *sannyasi* or renouncer, free to order his life in isolation from the impurities of ordinary life. The GSB have great respect for their renouncers and support their *maths* both economically and morally. But in ordinary life, impurity is ever present. This is the background to the vigilance of householders with regard to purity. U.A. Kamath was among those who took a spade and started to work manually when the medical college at Manipal had to be built, leading the work in the midst of people from all castes: as an engineer, he is not afraid of such un-Brahminical work. But precisely because of this, constant vigilance is necessary to restore purity by ablutions and purifying rites.

Every Brahmin family has a *salagram*, a polished stone which is the central object of worship.[4] U.A. Kamath holds the family *salagram* now, though it really 'belongs' to his elder brother, who is in the US.[5] The *salagram* ritual, he says, is not difficult once you memorize the *mantra*: 'you take it out, you purify the water ritually, then you wash the *salagram* with it and finally you wipe it thoroughly. But the ritual is very demanding in terms of purification: of all rituals it is the one where you must be in the purest state. So it is a real responsibility.' He who takes care of the *salagram* must take greater care than other family members to respect food rules and other aspects of behaviour where purity is at stake. The *salagram* rites contribute to unite the family, since they are done on behalf of all its members. The one who performs them is, in effect, the head of the family.

Other Brahmins, like the Shivallis, look askance at the GSB for eating fish, and the GSB are aware of this criticism.[6] But there is no hesitation to accept the fish-eating tradition: it was the sage Saraswat, after all, who urged the caste to eat fish when the Saraswati River dried up and vegetables became scarce. And though quite a few women desist from eating fish, the tradition carries no stigma in the community.

We tend to think of Brahmins as vegetarians. But Brahmin vegetarianism is historically problematic, since the Vedas refer to animal sacrifice (Alsdorf, 1962). 'It is shown to be there in the Veda,' affirms U.A. Kamath, like most Western orientalists, and in contrast to many modern Hindu critics.[7] He believes in the efficacy of such sacrifices. When still a boy, everytime he was sick, his mother would say, 'We must sacrific a fowl.' They would get some low caste person to buy one, for sacrifice at the Kapu Mariamman temple, 'which belongs to the community'.[8] I asked him if it worked: 'Oh yes,' he said, smiling. He says cow sacrifice was the reason for the more generalized ban on animal sacrifice. 'People were abhorred, so they banned it.'[9] 'That is pure theory,' retorts his son. But U.A. Kamath continues: 'All this non-violence is the work of the Vaishnavas. It came from them.'[10] He belongs to the minority of GSB who are Shaivite, and implies that we must not confound these non-violent ideas with 'Hinduism'.[11] Yet, as noted, he stresses the necessity of keeping away from everything that is of *tamasic* or *rajasic* nature.

We are reminded here of Pocock's ideas of a development 'from a state of symbiosis between pure and impure castes to a more univocal dependence upon Brahmanic values only' (1973: 41). In his view, the stress on purity has evolved from an older state, where different kinds of sacrifice were distinguished by purpose rather than degrees of purity.

'Hinduism' as such is a modern term, dating from the time of the Bengali renaissance. The older term used in English was 'Brahmanism' (Frykenberg, 1989). Certainly we must distinguish between modern ideas of Hinduism as one 'religion' and the multiple religious ideas found among 'Hindus'. In his excellent introduction to Hinduism, Jacobsen says: 'Hinduism is not a homogeneous religious tradition, but a term under which we group a family of religious tendencies without any common core' (Jacobsen, 2003: 13; my translation). Klostermaier is more restrictive: 'The question "What are the essentials of Hinduism?" will receive as many different answers as people one asks,' he admits, but maintains that Hindu orthodoxy may be distinguished from hereticism. The opinions he presents, he says, 'may not be acceptable to all. But they represent authoritative opinions and should convince the reader that, contrary to some popular assumptions. . . . Hinduism is not simply the sum total of all other religions and the doctrinal tolerance of Hinduism has definite limits'

(Klostermaier, 1994: 13). The difference between Klostermaier's position, and Jacobsen's which I share, is largely explained by the weight given to the scriptures by Klostermaier, and to folk traditions by Jacobsen and myself.

As Pocock says (1973: xiv), the differences between popular religion and the purified philosophies in Hinduism are paradoxical only if we insist on looking for a unified Hindu system of thought. The problem here is similar to that of the 'caste system': it is our notion of 'system', not the observed phenomena, which creates a paradox.[12] For U.A. Kamath, there is no conflict between his need to keep 'pure', to mark his distance from the *rajasic* and *tamasic* elements of the universe, and his acceptance of these forces as real. To deal with them, one has to use means that correspond with their nature.[13]

In Goa, Smartas (Shaivites) are in a majority among the GSB, but in North and South Kanara and in Kerala, most are Madhava Vaishnavites. Smarta and Madhava GSB are conscious of their differences, but there is no conflict: they intermarry and dine together. Most Udupi GSB are Madhavas, but some are Smarta, including the Udupi Kamaths and the Kadpet Shenoys.[14] You can tell from the surname, says P.R. Kuduva, whether somebody is a Madhava or a Smarta. Each groups has two main *maths*, the Smartas have the Gaudapada Acharya *math* at Ponda, Goa, and the Chitrapur *math* at Shirali, near Bhatkal. The Madhavas have the Gokarna *math*, near Gokarna, and the Kashi *math* at Varanasi. In North Kanara, most follow the Gokarna *math*, but some are followers of Raghavendra Swami, also a Madhava.[15]

It was the Kashi *math* that introduced Madhava's ideas to the GSB, adopting this philosophy in 1540, when its Swami initiated its first Madhava *sannyasi* (P.R. Kuduva, 1997). The oldest GSB *math*, the Gaudapada Acharya *math*[16] keeps to the Advaita doctrine. Founded some 1,200 years ago, it is said to be the oldest *math* in India. It was certainly the first Advaita *math*, established by Gaudapada Acharya, the preceptor of Shankara. 'Before that time,' says P.R. Kuduva, 'there were no *maths*, only *gurukulas*.'[17] Expert on *math* history, he says the Advaitas of the Acharya *math* 'don't make any difference between Vishnu and Shiva.' This seems logical: the Brahman of the Advaitas, the supreme Godhead that is one with the spirit of the universe, has no form. Thus it is neither Shiva nor Vishnu. Conventionally, however, it is usually identified with Shiva.

The GSB religion, in fact, shows a mixture of Shaivite and Vaishnavite elements. Typically, many deities are 'Vaishnavized' by adding Narayana or Narayani to the name, such as Shankaranarayana, Lakshminarayani or Mahalasanarayani. The Shankaranarayana temple in Udupi belongs to the Chitrapur Saraswats, who are Smarta, and is much older than the Venkatarama temple.[18] Thus the combination of *rajasic* and *sattvic*, Shaiva and Vaishnava elements, predates the schism between Chitrapur and Gauda Saraswats around 1700 (Conlon, 1977). The Shankaranarayana image at Manjeshwar was installed by the Konkanis several hundred years earlier, according to M.M. Prabhu, long before the Chitrapur Saraswats split from the larger caste, and this god is typical, though not exclusive to the two castes. In other cases, there is a prefix or suffix indicating the peaceful nature of the deity, such as Shanta Durga, the peaceful Durga. 'Shanti' indicates *sattvic* rather than *rajasic* qualities: Durga is otherwise seen as a fighting goddess. It is as if these names were intended to stress 'Sanskritization' or 'purification' in relation to an earlier, less peaceful or pure state.

Kamakshi is one deity to which no such prefix or suffix is added but in her temple she is paired with another goddess, Shanteri, who seems to represent her peaceful double.[19] Kamakhya or Kamakshi is intimately bound to the Shaktist orientation, far from the peaceful character of Lakshmi, for example. Pairing her with Shanteri may have tackled this problem, without weakening her Shaktist qualities.

The Vaishnavite element in GSB religion also implies *bhakti*, devotion, and the cult of Venkatarama is typically a *bhakti* cult. The wave of *bhakti* cults in south India, starting in the late sixth century, preceded the great Vaishnava philosophers, Ramanuja and Madhava. The movement reached the west coast in the ninth century (Narayanan and Veluthat, 2002: 388).

Madhava's Dvaita philosophy insists on the separate existence of deity and devotee, The first of his two 'cardinal doctrines' were, according to Shanbhag (1990): (i) in all respects Lord Vishnu alone is supreme and the highest; (ii) this entire universe is truly and ultimately real. It is the absolute distinction between the two that separate the Madhavas from other Vaishnavas, who generally subscribe to

Ramanuja's Vishishtadvaita. This is described as an opposition to Sankhya philosophy as well as to Shankara. 'Against Shankara, he affirms the reality of souls and of the material world; against Sankhya, he proclaims the dependence in which the created world finds itself in relation to the Divine One. For him there are three entities: God, the individual souls, and the material world.' (Esnoul, n.d.: 115; my translation).[20] Thus both doctrines legitimated, by formal exegesis, devotion to a personal deity. Such devotion was, in principle, excluded from Shankara's monism, since the separate existence of the devotee was seen as an illusion. The transition from Shaivite to Vaishnavite religion, among the GSB, must have implied more than a change of divine allegiance.

In spite of the division between Smarta and Vaishnava GSB, the Venkatarama temples stand as social markers for the community as a whole. Their role is not just religious: they constitute networks of communication and organization, as well as symbols of the caste. But who is Venkatarama, and how did he come to be associated with the GSB? He is not specific to them: the cult caters to many castes, from all over India. Venkatarama or Venkateshwara, often called Balaji, is seen by his followers as the Kaliyuga *avatara* of Vishnu.[21] His main and original temple is at Tirupati in Andhra Pradesh, which may have been one of the places where the *bhakti* movement originated (Narayanan and Veluthat, 2002: 387-8).[22] The Tirumala-Tirupati complex is probably India's most frequented pilgrimage, and commonly seen as the wealthiest. The sacred mountain, Tirumala, is known by numerous names[23] in which all strands of Vaishnavism merge.

When Varaha – Vishnu's boar incarnation – had re-established the Earth, he 'decided to live there and asked Garuda, his man-eagle vehicle, to bring the divine hill Kridachala from Vaikuntha, his heavenly abode, to establish his new home on earth' (Krishna, 2000: 3). Here he occupied a temple on the western side of the Swami Pushkarni sacred pool. But Varaha's appearance 'was so frightening that Brahma, the Gods, the Saptarishis (seven sages) and other celestials prayed to Vishnu, requesting him to assume a more peaceful form and live on the hill to protect his people'. Thus Vishnu settled there, 'lotus-eyed', 'holding the *shankha* (conch), *chakra* (discus), and *gada* (mace)', with

Bhudevi (Mother Earth) and Lakshmi by his side (ibid.).[24] Venkatesha or Venkateshwara is known as the destroyer of sins and the giver of prosperity (Krishna, 2000: 4).[25] Vishnu[26] left Tirumala for Vaikuntha at the beginning of the Kali age. But Brahma felt that people remained pious only as long as Vishnu remained on earth. The sage Narada was told to bring Vishnu back, and after many difficulties he did so.[27]

The Cholas ruled the Venkatachala region, and grazed their cattle on the hill. Lakshmi knew about Vishnu's new abode, and appeared as a milkmaid, Brahma and Shiva following her, as a cow and a calf. Lakshmi sold both to the Chola queen. Grazing at Tirumala, the cow found the anthill where Vishnu lived, and let her milk flow over it. The cowherd, furious, 'threw his stick at the cow, but Vishnu took the blow and saved the cow'. Amazed, the cowherd fell dead (ibid.). The Chola king came to investigate, and Vishnu cursed him for his servant's sin, then relented: the king would be reborn as Akasha Raja[28] and 'gain merit when his daughter Padmavati married Venkatesha'.[29] Vishnu, looking for herbs to cure the cow's wound, now meets Varaha. The boar offers Vishnu land to stay on the hill, if he will pay the price. But since Lakshmi, the goddess of wealth, has left him, Vishnu has no money; so he offers Varaha the first prayer and offering of food from his devotees (ibid.: 9). The land was given, and Varaha provided the services of Vakulamalika, who gave Vishnu medicine and fed him with milk and honey. Vakulamalika in fact, is Yashoda, Krishna's mother.

Akasha Raja, the Chola king, rules the land but is childless, until he offers a great sacrifice. As the land is ploughed for the sacrifice, a thousand-petalled lotus appears, containing a baby girl. Called Padmavati from her lotus (*padma*) birth, she is an incarnation of Lakshmi. As she grows into a ravishing young girl, the sage Narada appears, predicting she will be married to Vishnu. That day, Vishnu, as Venkateshwara, is hunting in the forest. He pursues an elephant into the royal gardens where he meets Padmavati, who falls in love with him. Vishnu returns to Vakulamalika, tells her of his past birth as Rama and of Lakshmi (thus Padmavati) as Sita: in the Kaliyuga they will be reunited as Srinivasa[30] and Padmavati.

Different strands of Vaishnavite tradition unite in the story: with

Vakulimalika we approach Krishna, we have a reference to Rama, while Vishnu himself appears both sleeping on the *shesha* (snake) and as the boar. Padmavati is a Jain goddess[31] as well as Venkatesha's wife. Thus the Tirupati myths unite a maximum of sacred figures, privileging Vaishnavite tradition.

Vakulimalika leaves for Akasha's capital to arrange the marriage. Vishnu takes the form of a female astrologer, precedes her to the city, and tells the queen that Padmavati has fallen in love with 'Srinivasa, the Lord of Venkatachala'. They must be married within three days, or she will die. An old woman will soon arrive to arrange the marriage. The sages Brihaspati and Suhka fix the auspicious time of the marriage, and all the gods and sages come to the wedding.[32] Vishwakarma builds a beautiful city for the couple and Indra constructs the wedding pavilion.[33] But Venkatesha[34] still has no money. He takes a loan from Kubera, the god of wealth, promising to repay 'within a thousand years'. 'To help him repay his dues, pilgrims still shower him with money. By helping their Lord, the devotees believe that their Lord will help them in return' (Krishna, 2000: 11).

The wedding is celebrated in grand style, and Lakshmi rejoins her husband on the hill. 'The Lord tells her of his debt to Kubera. To help him, she should enrich his devotees who would give him money and wealth. Lakshmi agrees, and returns to live in his heart, whence his name Srinivasa, or the dwelling place of Sri or Lakshmi (ibid.: 12-13).

At his wedding, Srinivasa promises Brahma that he will redeem the sins of all who come to Tirumala.[35] As the Kaliyuga progresses, evil and chaos increase in the world. Venkateshwara says he will withdraw into a stone idol, and communicate only with his devotees (ibid.: 21). This, then, is the *murti* still standing at Tirumala. The Chola king Thondaimaan comes to see the Lord, and Srinivasa suggests he build a temple on the hill, which he does (ibid.: 13). Thondaimaan and Vishwakarma make all the arrangements and objects for the temple festivals. Thondaimaan becomes a renouncer, attaining liberation (*moksha*) on the hill.

The myth establishes Venkatarama as an incarnation of Vishnu, and his GSB followers see themselves as Vaishnavites. But, as Krishna (2000) points out, the iconographical marks of the god are not so clear. Vishnu is said to have come to the mountain with his '*shankha* (conch), *chakra* (discus), and *gada* (mace)', all marks of Vishnu, but the original image lacked these symbols. The conch and discus he presents today are later additions. The original figure has a crescent mark on his forehead, matted hair (*jata*) like Shiva, snake-shaped ornaments, and a 'cobra slung over his right arm'. While Skanda is the main Tamil male god associated with hills – and related to Subramaniam, god of snakes – cobras are often shown with Shiva. Then, the drapery of Venkatesha resembles a sari, and the *murti* is bathed on fridays, the day for the ritual bath of goddesses or women. Sandal paste and turmeric, female adornments, are used, and on the *vimana* (spire) of the temple we find the lion, symbol of the goddess. Still, the identification with Vishnu is found in the *Silappadikaaram*, written about the eigth century AD, and as a Jain, its author should have no reason to prefer Vishnu over Shiva.

The early Vaishnava poet-saints saw both Shiva and Vishnu in the figure of Venkatesha.[36] Shrivaishnava hagiography[37] tells us that the image was originally Hariharan, half Vishnu, half Shiva – and Shaivites, too, claimed a part in it. This led to dispute, and the local ruler called Ramanuja, the Vaishnava philosopher,[38] as a mediator. He proposed to place before the image a trident and a drum, Shaivite objects, as well as the discus and conch, symbolizing Vishnu. In the morning when the sanctuary was opened, the image had taken hold of the discus and the conch, and the matter was closed (Davis, 1997: 261; Esnoul, 1964: 95-6). Another version says Ramanuja won a debate organized by a Yadava king[39] to decide whether the image was Shiva or Vishnu, and so it became a Vaishnava cult (Krishna, 2000: 50-3). It was certainly seen as such when it reached the GSB some centuries later. Krishna feels the god may be of folk or tribal origin.[40] The image may well have belonged to a forgotten cult, neither of Shiva, Vishnu or any other current god. This ambiguity makes Venkatarama fit well into a caste with a Vaishnava majority, a Shaiva minority, and a large number of lineage deities who combine Shaiva, Shakta and Vaishnava elements. But whether Venkatarama's ambiguity stands as a model for the lesser deities, or whether all are influenced by a common tendency of syncreticism, is a question I cannot answer here.

Riches and debt are central to the Venkatarama cult. The merchant's wealth is invested in merit, helping the god pay his debt; the story is steeped in the imagery of money. Lakshmi's engagement to enrich the followers endears the cult to merchants. There is a divine circulation of funds: from Lakshmi to the followers, to Venkatarama, and back from Lakshmi, while the money for Venkatarama pays the internal debts of the celestial community.[41]

The temple on the hill seems to be mentioned by the grammarian Tholkaappiar, around 200 BC.[42] Then, in the second century AD, the poet Maamoolanar mentions the hill. The *Ahanaanooru* and the Shaivite saints Nakkirar and Kanakkayanaar refer to the place, which must have been known more or less continuously from the first reference. None of these writers refer to the cult of Venkatesha, however. The name Vengadam or Venkatadri may refer to the removal of sins, but equally to the burnt forest slope. Though Krishna feels it 'very likely that the God was known by 200 BC' (2000: 55), this remains conjecture.

Thondaimaan who discovered the statue was a Chola. The imperial Cholas ruled the area from about AD 800, but Thondaimaan may have been a lesser Chola prince. Krishna states he 'probably lived around AD 550, the pre-Pallava period to which the style of the main stone statue corresponds'.[43] He is said to have established the kingdom of Thondaimandalam, still used as a name for the district. Eleven inscriptions at the site date from Pallava times: thirty-one are assigned to the Cholas (Jha, 1978: 203).

The *Silappadikaaram*, a Jain epic of the eigth century AD describes the image as a Vishnu: by then its conch and discus were added.[44] But the author says sun and moon shone on the image, so it must have been in the open, and the temple cannot yet have been built. Yet Venkateshwara's and Padmavati's temples have been dated to 'some time earlier than the eighth century' (Sharma, 1978: 181). The statue is in pre-Pallava or early Pallava style, considerably older than the temple. Krishna says it belongs to about the sixth century.[45] From the eighth century the existence of the sacred hill and its cult is well documented. Several donations are recorded from between AD 830 and 850 up to the time of the Yadavas, but it was under their rule (AD 1184-1355)[46] that the temple expanded towards its present importance, and Ramanuja decided that its god was an *avatar* of Vishnu.[47]

According to Narayanan and Veluthat (1978/2000: 397-8), the temple became prominent at the time of the Alvars (sixth to ninth century AD), a period when such temples became a central feature of south Indian religion. The temple with its numerous out-buildings recall the royal palace, and the processions and the services offered to the deity resemble those of a king, a parallel underlined by Narayanan and Veluthat, who see these temple cults as rising in parallel with the medieval kingdoms of south India (2002: 402).

The area then came under the Vijayanagara empire[48] until its fall. During their rule the temple entered 'a phase of unprecedented glory'. Deva Raya II, the greatest of the Vijayanagara rulers, is known to have worshipped Venkateshwara,[49] though some traditions claim he was a Virashaiva (Jackson, 2007: 188). The stone steps from the city of Tirupati to the temple at the top of the hill were constructed in the fifteenth century[50] (ibid.: 174-6). From around 1650 Tirupati was under the Sultans of Golconda, then the Nawabs of the Carnatic. After a threat by Muhammad Kamal to plunder the temple, the British took over its revenues until they were ceded to the government of the Madras Presidency in 1933. Management was then handed to a board of trustees, an arrangement which continues – under the government of Andhra Pradesh – to this day.

The main festival lasts ten days, beginning on the first day of the new moon of Bhadrapada. It is called the Brahmotsavam, the festival of Brahma. The Swami Pushkarini, the main tank of the temple, is where the devotee starts his ritual by bathing. The bath is said to remove all sins, grant all desires, cure all deformities of the body and 'ensure the avoidance of all types of hell' (Krishna, 2000: 21-2). The ritual day starts at about 3 a.m., with the awakening of the lord.[51] The *suprabhatam* – awakening prayer – is sung.[52] The image is decorated with flowers,[53] and water is brought from the Ganga.[54] Then, in the Kolovu or Darbar, the previous day's accounts and the current and next day's almanac is read before the Kolovy Srinivasa, an auxiliary *murti*,[55] and the 1,008 names of Venkatesha are recited. Then there is the wedding of Venkatesha and his two consorts, Sridevi and Bhudevi.[56] The image is fed cooked food,[57] first presented to Varaha, behind closed doors. All pilgrims are entitled to free food as *prasad.* The songs of the Alvars[58] follow, and the 108 names of Venkatesha[59] are recited, before cooked food is offered again. The images of Venkatesha and his two consorts are swung.[60] Now it is nightfall, and the thousand oil lamps outside the temple are lit,[61] the night prayers[62] recited, and sweets offered to Venkatesha. Finally, a velvet bed is spread on the swing before the image is put to sleep[63] (Krishna, 2000: 94-7). The ritual day, then, consists in a full day of service to the Lord, reminiscent of what is done, for example, for Krishna by the Vallabhacharyas of Gujarat.

Such ritual is typical of *bhakti* cults, in treating the deity as a person whose multiple needs can be satisfied by his followers, and offers ample opportunity to show their devotion in a concrete manner. Such devotion does not necessarily imply money, but the form of worship offers considerable scope for the donor to contribute in beautifying the ritual, and, incidentally, advertise his own economic credentials.[64] The singing of the *bhajans* of the Alvars does not exclude new compositions, and the god of Tirupati continues to inspire a large number of poets, including many GSB. Tirupati functions as a sacred centre in GSB culture, in spite of its location far from their homes. As Jackson points out, such centres provides a unifying factor in the otherwise decentralized network of Vaishnava *bhakti* cults, and the tradition of composing and singing *bhajans* provides another (2007: 186-7).

Each weekday has its particular ritual, and there are annual festivals of which the Brahmotsavam is the most important. There is considerable ritual activity, then, at the temple, offering numerous occasions for the GSB to travel to Tirupati throughout the year. While all of my informants do not go to Tirupati reguarly, most do so once in a while.

According to Vasantha Madhava, the cult of Venkatarama[65] in South Kanara spread from Karkala. GSB informants, however, say the Mulki and Karkala temples are about the same age.[66] The Udupi temple was built in 1896, and to Vitthala in the south, the cult arrived only in the 1920s. You will find Venkatarama temples wherever there are GSB, says P.R. Kuduva, though only Vaishnavas worship him.[67] The worship began during Vijayanagara times. Today, the cult is emblematic of the GSB community in north Kerala and on the Kanara coast. The Venkatarama temples are centres of community activities: we have seen how the GSB banks drew their branch managers from the temple committees in the early days.

People come and go all day at Udupi's Venkatarama temple. Typically, men 'drop in' during working hours. There are, of course, devotees for the morning and evening *pujas*, but in Udupi, they do not form a crowd, except on Sundays.[68] Rather, the temple is a place for occasional spiritual refreshment, visited frequently by the GSB, but at their convenience rather than at fixed times. But there are many special events taking place in the temple.[69] One example may be the Bhajan Mahotsava held at Kallianpur in November/December 2003. This was a full week's programme of *bhajans*, religious songs in the *bhakti* tradition. There were Konkani songs, such as those composed by the GSB P.N. Nayak, but also all-Indian classics by Ramdas or Tukaram. A vendor of cassettes was doing a nice trade. Such events draw people to the temple in Kallianpur. This may well be an economic necessity, for many GSB have migrated to Udupi and other towns, and the congregation is now quite small for what was once an important temple. Such initiatives are important, then, to draw the crowds.

K.R. Kuduva wrote three articles for the jubilee memoir of the Venkatarama temple at Udupi (1997), and another for the souvenir of the *diksha* of the present *swami* of the Kalvaljapura *math* (1999). The memoir publications clearly serve to muster the local community, most of the local GSB businesses contributing by advertisements. As sponsorship, they establish the relative importance of each business family within the community. One imagines, indeed, each family head inquiring about the advertisement space bought by his counterparts, to make sure his own firm occupies space commensurate with the importance it wants to assert.

Most Venkatarama temples are frequented only by the GSB, but there are exceptions, such as the *utsava* organized by a non-GSB businessman, Mr. Banana, in Karkala. It was well attended, and made into a festival of lights: thousands of small oil lamps were niched in the walls of the inner building, with beautiful effect. The large five-armed torch stand was placed in front of the door to the inner temple, and this too was lighted, as was the *dipastambha* (a great pillar lighted with oil lamps). A local group, with some very good singers, were singing *bhajans*. As usual, the women were ringing the *puja* bells to the left side of the entrance, men those to the right.[70] The overwhelming majority of the public – some two to three hundred – were GSB, some arriving in buses from surrounding villages. The atmosphere was festive, and people clearly used the occasion to meet family and friends. The *utsavamurti* (procession deity) was taken out in procession in the golden palanquin, and the procession, too, was lighted by torches. It made the tour of the GSB quarter, going down Car Street to the bus station, then turning back to Car Street and following it up to the last GSB house, beyond Manjunath Pai's mansion. Outside every house, and at the mouths of the side-streets, members or representatives of effectively every GSB family in town were waiting, making offerings to the *utsavamurti* and receiving Venkatarama's blessing. Thus Mr. Banana's *puja* was turned into a community affair, marking GSB territory. At the same time, the central position of the temple and of the GSB community in Karkala was asserted, and if anything enhanced by the fact that Banana was not a GSB himself.

Other important events take place in the lineage temples, like the Maha Vishnu Yaga at the Mahalasanarayana temple, in December 2003.[71] For South Kanara devotees, this temple at Basrur, an old town[72] north of Udupi, is much closer than Goa.[73] There is no administrative link between this temple and Mahalasa's temple at Margao. It is the lineage temple of the Tonse Pais, who donated greatly for its reconstruction in 2001, led by U.A. Kamath, the builder of Manipal. Mahalasa is not among the well-known goddesses of the Hindu pantheon. But the Maharashtrian god Khandoba's wife is called Mahalasa, and Sontheimer identifies her with Parvati. She is a demon-slayer, however, and in some ways closer to Durga.[74]

The *yagya* lasted several days. It was done to increase the power (*shakti*) of the *murti* of Mahalasa. The main function was in the morning; in the evening Mahalasa was taken out in procession. Four oracular mediums were possessed, and this was repeated once a week or once a month.[75] Sixteen *vaidiks*[76] came from Goa, and a lot of expensive stuff was bought for the sacrifice. These *vaidiks* must be highly learned, but it does not matter where they come from; they need not be attached to the Mahalasa temple in Goa. They were seated in a circle around the sacred fire, for which there was a special *mandapa* (dais) in the courtyard, south-east of the main building (Fig. 19). They recited *mantras* continuously, except for a brief pause for a meal. While the *yagya* was still going on outside, a number of the *vaidiks* entered the main shrine to read their *mantras* silently – their 'books' open before them – while others keep chanting outside. In the front yard, to the right of the entrance, a group of women wore flower garlands, which seem to be a kind of 'devotional service' (*seva*).

Though it is private and caters to the GSB community, I was told that 'any community, any Hindu is welcome' at the temple. Many devotees came in their 'Brahmin dress' – loincloth and scarf – so the sacred thread was clearly visible. They were dressed for ritual, not as casual visitors, and you had to look twice to distinguish priests from the public: the former wear red loincloths while devotees wear saffron-coloured cloth. Most of those so dressed came early: latecomers among the men were in 'Western-style' pants and shirts.[77] The crowd was not particularly large, perhaps a hundred to a hundred and fifty

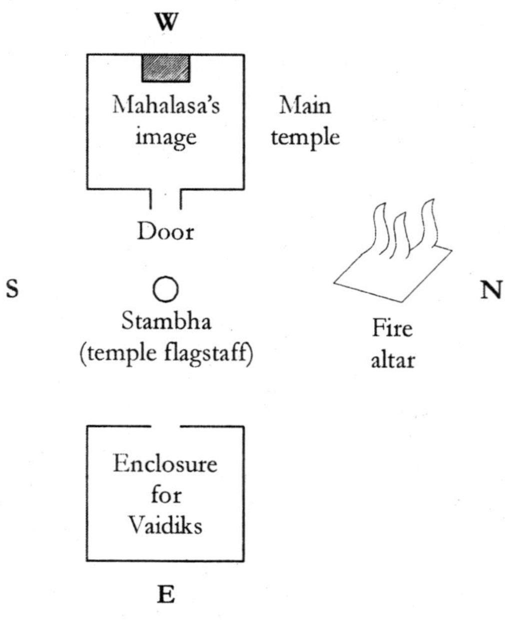

Fig. 19: Situation sketch of the *yagya*.

in all. But all were evidently devotees of the temple, many of them *kulavis*, or members of lineages having Mahalasa as their *kuladevata*.

My presence seemed to cause consternation, mainly among the priests from Goa. The lay people were less sceptical, and the cassette-seller remembered me, since we had met at the Bhajan Mahotsava at Kallianpur. Mr. Pande is from Shimoga and he is not a GSB. His friendliness influenced the others. The reaction of the priests was comprehensible: in Goa, Europeans are mostly tourists who have a very mixed reputation. Such a tourist might not be an auspicious presence. I met a student of the Manipal Polytechnic who is a *kulavi* – his *gotra* is Ahamkara. I talked to the man who sells the *puja* tickets, an Uppinagudru Pai from the island Uppinagudru close to Kundapur. He is a marine engineer who has travelled widely. His brother, who was with him, is a medical doctor in Kundapur. He studied in Bombay, and lived there from 1965 to 1975, but wanted to serve his native place. 'You will find that is typical of Indians everywhere in the world. They always remember their native place and stay in touch – that is also one reason for their success.'[78] Mr. Pai's remark underlines the lien, for the GSB, between a tradition of migration and fidelity to the point fixed as the 'native place' – as if the latter was reinforced by the former.

I met H. Prabhakara Nayak, a *bhajan* singer who performed at Kallianpur. He is a merchant from Harikhadige.[79] Music is his 'hobby' – he is not a professional. He is from the Atri *gotra*, and Mahalasa is his *kuladevata*. Then I talked to a lady from Shimoga, Shakuntala V. Shenoy. She is not a *kulavi*, 'only a *bhakta*', she said. She is of the Kaundinya *gotra*, and her own *kuladevatas* are Maha Ganapati and Devaki Krishna. Here, she came for the '*bhakti* and for the beauty'. Retired, she used to work for the Karnataka State Electricity Board. She is a widow, but wears a green sari, not the traditional widow's dress. This kind of *yagya*, she says – a forty Rama Nama *yagya* – will next be performed in 2008, in Mumbai. Another was held in 1997. Until the Mumbai *yagya* she had vowed to fill 1,000 notebooks with the lines '*Shri Ram, Jaya Ram, Jaya Jaya Ram*'. One book has 1,280 lines; she shall write the sacred line 12,80,000 times. This is clearly a personal, devotional project: I do not know to what extent it is influenced by her being a widow.

Mr. Nayak and Mrs. Shenoy discuss *bhajans*. 'In this area, only the GSB are really active in developing the *bhajan* tradition,' Mr. Nayak tells me. 'Other communities are not so active. There are some individuals, but they are few'.[80] To an untrained ear, the GSB *bhajans* seem particularly melodious.[81] His sons are also doing music; one is playing *tabla*, another sings classical music and plays the harmonium. His sons are passing the Gandharva Vidya Mahamandal exams to get a government certificate in music. One, in fact, is up for his exams this very day. He feels the current fashion for classical music will benefit the *bhajan* tradition. In Shimoga, too, says Mrs. Shenoy, there is an active milieu for *bhajan* singing. Every Saturday, in almost every place where there are GSB, there will be *bhajan* sessions.

The discussion underlines the wide range of reference for GSB religion. To discuss *bhajans* – emblematic of the medieval *bhakti* tradition – at a Vedic sacrifice, close to the fire altar, does not seem inconsistent to the GSB. Nor does the practice of possession[82] at a Vedic rite. Syncretism is not an apt term here, for elements mingle but do not merge, save for the identity of gods such as Shankaranarayana. Nor is polytropy (Carrithers, 2000), though it may fit the religion of GSB individuals. The wide range, taking in strains of Hinduism that seem contradictory, is a feature of collective worship, not individual choice. The eclecticism of GSB religion contrasts sharply with the caste-specific practices of Saurashtra, or even of the GSB's Tulu neighbours. It is as if the GSB have no need to mark their identity by specificity in religion, it being taken care of in other ways.

At the end of the day, there is an auction of the goddess' saris, donated by the devotees earlier. The number auctioned was considerable, and everybody followed the proceedings with great interest. The simplest saris, worth a couple of hundred rupees, are offered first and tend to be sold quickly, at slightly more than market price. As more and more expensive saris come under the hammer, excitement mounts: there are more bidders, and the differential between the original price and the bids increase, from Rs. 400 or 500 to Rs. 3,000 or 4,000. Then, at the end, come the finest silk sari. I do not know its original value, but it was sold at Rs. 30,000. Two bidders – an unidentified lady and a merchant from the Kalsankar Pai family, held out till the end, and as both were equally determined, the audience held its breath. At last the Kalsankar Pai got the sari, to the applause of the audience. As he mounted the stall, his pleasure and pride were evident. It was clear that I had witnessed an important competition for status and prestige, which would benefit the coffers of the temple. This kind of implicit donation to the temple certainly will be remembered and will reflect for some time on the standing of a family.

Several points about the GSB community emerge here. First, it is striking how worship at the *kuladevata* temple has a socially integrative effect: for the *kulajis*, who live in different places, it is an occasion to experience a sense of common belonging. This Durkheimian effect is almost visible. The ritual is also an affirmation of Brahmin status, not just since all are GSB, but explicitly, in the display of traditional Brahmin dress, which most never wear publicly. Then, the relaxed atmosphere of the public contrasts with the respectful attitude often seen in temples: here, the GSB feel at home. This must be strengthened by what P.R. Kuduva said, that every GSB male may, in principle, go before the altar and perform his own ritual. Here, the attitude to Mahalasa's altar and priests differed from the behaviour towards the *vaidiks* and their fire altar. It was striking how, most of the time, people paid little attention to the prestigious fire sacrifice. It was as if, having paid their respects – and their money, for such a sacrifice is expensive – they were happy to let the specialists get on with their job. There was a change in attitude, however, when the time came for possession, and one of the *vaidiks* would incarnate the Goddess. Now all thronged around to see. The possession was hardly spectacular: the rather corpulent priest simply swayed to and fro in a vaguely feminine manner.[83] But the Goddess had come, and to the audience, this was clearly far more important than the Vedic ritual.

Oracles are, in fact, a key element of the GSB religion. Kalabhairava oracles – *darshan* – used to exist in many of the GSB temples, but only one, at Mulki, is still active in South Kanara.[84] P.R. Kuduva stresses that, ever since the GSB left the banks of the Saraswati, they have been under Bhairava's special protection. This link between community and god then predates the identification with Venkatarama.

Bhairava seems, indeed, mainly to figure in this protective role in his various forms.[85] Sontheimer notes that in the Deccan, Bhairava is the *kshetrapal*, 'the protector of the field and the settled village' (1997: 27-8), and he sees the rider-hero god Khandoba of Maharashtra as related to Bhairava[86] (1997: 47-51). The Bhairava worshipped by the GSB does not seem to have a horse, however. Where Bhairava is found, Shiva is usually present, and sometimes Kali. Often, Bhairava is perceived as male consort of the Goddess in her fierce form.[87] We may assume, then, that the GSB cult of Bhairava dates from a period when they were closer to Shaktism than now, as also indicated by the presence of Kamakshi (Kamakhya) among the *kuladevatas*, a transition noted by M.G. Pai (1997). Briggs shows Bhairava as the main deity of the Kanphata Yogis, who sometimes serve as his priests (ibid.: 139).[88] These Yogis were well versed in magic and alchemy,[89] and the temple myths of Chidambaram in Tamil Nadu tell an interesting story in this regard.[90]

> The Nataraja shrine belongs only to the Thillai Brahmin Dikshitars. In olden days, Dikshitars during their tenure of *puja* used to place a copper sheet at the holy feet of Swarna Kala Bairavar every day when closing the shrine and when they opened the doors the next morning, the copper sheet would have been changed to golden sheet by the grace of Bairavar. And with the proceeds of the golden sheet, the Dikshitar would run his family. Hence they had no desire for any extra income. (Meyyappan, 1998: 44)

'It is not known,' adds the author, 'why and when the alchemy of copper turning into gold ceased.' Perhaps unusually for a great temple in Tamil Nadu, the Nataraja temple of Chidambaram 'owns no lands', he notes, apparently to explain why such extraordinary divine measures were appropriate.

The protective role Bhairava plays in GSB religion, has apparently not been affacted by the transition to Bhakti Vaishnavism. There are two Bhairavas, says P. R. Kuduva: Kalabhairava (the black Bhairava)[91] and Agnibhairava (the fire Bhairava, from *agni* or fire).[92] Kalabhairava drives away evil spirits by speaking mildly, but Agnibhairava chases them by fire, taking burning cowdung in his hands.[93] The oracles at Kallianpur[94] and Ullal were Agnibhairavas; at Mulki and Karkala, they were Kalabhairavas. Though only Mulki is now active, K.R. Kuduva speaks of all in the present tense, as if the god is still there, a dual structure, implicitly present even if no Agnibhairava is impersonated.

The oracle at Mulki is active at least since 1750-60 and has remained with the same family, the GSB Parimar Nayaks, ever since. Transfer of the oracular function in one patriline seems to have been the rule in GSB temples. I asked the trustees if there would be a problem in recruiting new mediums if the line dies out or young people refuse to take on this 'calling'. They stressed that it is a demanding task, since the medium is under severe restrictions: he must never eat outside his own house, for example. But, they said, in this family they know that if they fail to perpetuate the oracle, some serious calamity will come over them, and they are keen to continue. The present medium was editor of the Kannada journal *Vasanthikatta* in Mangalore, and has been a sports journalist of the *Udayavani*. Still he responded to the call for mediumship when the place was left open by his father's death.

The seances are held every Sunday. Before the session, the chief trustee showed me the treasures of the temple, the kitchen and the court for mass feeding, and gave me their *Hariguruknipa*, the souvenir of their Kumbhabhisheka of 4 January 1997.

The chief *patri*[95] and other priests arrive as the *arti* is performed to the main image of Venkatarama. The music is loud and intense. Before the possession starts, an accountant receives offerings and writes receipts for them. After a while, the medium begins to shake: he is not facing Venkatarama but the wall facing north, and I assume Kalabhairava's image is on that wall.[96] Then the fire is taken out for blessing the devotees, and the medium comes out. He is clad in a red *lungi* and carries the arms of Kalabhairava: *patta*[97] and *mudra*.[98] He dances slightly, the *patta* in his right, the *mudra* in his left hand.[99] After a brief dance, the main *patri* and *trustees*, in the inner court, acknowledge the offerings received from Tirupati and Dharmasthala. They are presented to the medium, who accepts them.

Now, everybody goes outside, to the position 'on the doorstep' or first *mantapa* to the outer court. Here, the main *patri* is placed. The medium strikes his back with both weapons, then 'blesses' the *patri* by briefly posing his weapons on the *patri*'s head. This sequence is repeated throughout the session, before each new question is posed. One *patri* poses several groups of questions; then another takes over. This day, four *patris* were thus active, all priests at the temple.[100] During the session, a young assistant kept the register of 'clients' and informed the *patri* so he could call the relevant group. The way each interpellation was made was striking. The *patri* would present the 'case', calling for a short remark from the medium. This remark would be answered by the devotees, and sometimes commented upon by the *patri.* Then followed a 'conversation' between the medium and devotees, often individually with each of them, and some exchanges lasted as much as ten minutes. In one case, the husband first had a series of questions answered by the medium, then his wife followed. She asked supplementary questions – or asked for clarification. It was rather like a consultation with a doctor or a psychologist – very different from the brief and somewhat elliptic answers I have seen other mediums give. The medium must not move during the session. At the end of each consultation, he throws *kumkum* on the clients, saying *santosh* or similar soothing words. I have never seen a medium looking so concerned with his devotees during an oracular session, and people have faith in his good sense. Personal and health problems are main themes of the questions, as at other oracles in the region, but one businessman wanted advice on computerizing his business. All the time, people were very serious. I was told that not only GSB, but people from 'all castes and communities' come. Thus I met one Bunt who had come for consultation.[101]

At Gurupur, just north of Mangalore, there is another oracle consulted by many GSB. The oracle is of Satyadevata, who is really Kallurti,[102] the sister of the stone-mason *bhuta* Kalkuda. Satyadevata seems to be a term 'Sanskritizing' this female *bhuta*, who is very popular in South Kanara. Some say the Gurupur oracle gives *darshan*[103] only to the GSB, others say the medium is available to others. This oracle, then, caters to a caste usually deemed not to believe in *bhutas*. A typical, middle-class GSB visitor commented:

> Our common belief is that *bhutas* protect, but if they get angry, they punish. That is why we call them *daivas*, not *devas*; *devas* protect, but they do not punish. Normally, we do not believe in these *daivas*, it does not mean we don't believe, but we do not go in for . . . very few (among us) are followers of the *bhutas*. There may be animal sacrifice, the *patri* may be taking liquor, there may be a crude feeling, decorations may be crude, etc.[104] So the best class of people do not go to such events.

But the Gurupur oracle is different. 'To this place, doctors, engineers, the best class of people are coming. The particular thing about the Gurupur oracle, is that vegetarian people serve the oracle.[105] The worship, the decoration, everything is different from that of the ordinary *bhuta* cults. It is 'more like a temple'. The Kallurti manifesting here is different: she is 'Shanti Kallurti', the peaceful Kallurti, also called Satyadevata, the deity of truth. Again we see the tendency to prefix a *sattvic* quality to a *rajasic* or *tamasic* deity. These remarks may be taken as typical of the GSB attitude to the *bhuta* cults. The visitor goes on to comment on the cult of the *nag*, the autochthonous snake spirits, marking a distance to them, like he does to the *bhuta* cults.

The Venkatarama temple at Gurupur does not differ from other temples dedicated to this God in South Kanara. Venkatarama is flanked, on the main altar centrally placed in the temple yard, by secondary deities. These vary from one temple to another: here they are Srinivasa and Vadediraja, underlining the Vaishnavite character of the cult. Around the court, as in other Venkatarama temples, there are four deities, one in each corner. Going around clockwise, they are Hanuman, Ganapati, Maleshini Mata, and Garuda. Only Maleshini Mata is particular to this temple: more usually, Lakshmi occupies the third corner.[106]

In front of the entrance to the temple is Kallurti's stone, said to be put here some 600 years ago, long before the temple was built.[107] She is flanked by a Mahaganapati. The temple is said to belong to thirty-seven GSB families, and seven of them have their lineage gods represented in or around the temple. They are Kallurti, or Satyadevata, Kalabhairava, Brahmara, 'Mute' Brahmara, Shakti, Mukhyaprana (a name for Hanuman), and Kshetrapala. All are said to manifest themselves through oracular mediums, who are GSB priests, like those of the Venkatarama cult. The Brahmara stone is worshipped by the local Prabhu family, while the 'mute' Brahmara cult serves the Hanumanta Prabhu family. Shakti is worshipped by the Krishna Kamath family, and Kalabhairava by several Bhatt families.[108] Kallurti is worshipped by the Yeltimar Shenoy family, of whom more later.

Kallurti, the female *bhuta* who has no obvious link to the GSB religious tradition, is found here among seven very heterogeneous deities. They belong neither to the named deities of the GSB pantheon, nor to the pan-Indian gods. None correspond to the lineage deities at Goa, to which all GSB families are linked. The Gurupur group seems to represent an additional level of local family rather than lineage deities, not found elsewhere in the GSB religious landscape. Brahmara may be identical to Brahmaru, a lower-level spirit found in connection with Digambar Jain holy places in the Kanaras, who again may correspond to Bermeru, lord of the forest, connected to the *bhuta* cults. Brahmara would seem to be a GSB adaptation of this figure, etymologically linked to Brahma, though the links to the Brahma of the Trimurti are not clear. Kshetrapala is the guardian spirit of all Jain and many Hindu temples of the region. Shakti is of course present through the many goddesses in the GSB pantheon, but as a separate figure, I have come across her only at Gurupur.

Kshetrapala and the two forms of Brahmara represent a substratum of minor deities which link the various local *bhutas* to the 'higher' cults. Through the double nature given to her at Gurupur, Kallurti/ Satyadevata has been given a similar position. Shakti's place here recalls the position that Masti – local contraction for Mahasati – occupies in relation to the *bhuta* cults of North Canara.[109] It is as if the GSB devotees of the Gurupur temple have found, in various adaptations of local cults, models for a level of deities below their lineage gods but separate from the *ishtadevatas* and on a level superior to the personal favourites.

The Yeltimar Shenoy family came to Yeltimar near Puttur in South Kanara some three hundred years ago. They ran a hardware shop in Puttur, lived in a beautiful old house outside the town, and seem to have had a safe standing within the bourgeoisie of that little town. But around 1990, the widowed father died, while business was declining. His son and daughter, just reaching adulthood, were left to fend for themselves. She had reached marriagable age, while he had, as yet, little experience in running the firm. To this problem was added that of raising a dowry for the marriage, and to find a groom, for which they had limited connections.

The inauspicious event of the father's death was followed by others, and they realized that they had neglected the cult of Kallurti, who had a sanctuary[110] on the family lands and was seen as their protectress.[111] They decided to renew the cult and adopt her as their *kuladevata*, while doing their best to keep the family business going.[112] In this difficult situation the brother went to see the Gurupur oracle. The medium immediately recognized him. 'I see you belong to the family that has faith in Kallurti,' he said, and then: 'I see you were eager to get recognized (as such).' When the brother put the problem of his sister's marriage, Kallurti promised she would be married within a year. A partner was found, but their horoscopes did not tally.[113] Kallurti took it upon herself to ward off the evil influences indicated by the horoscope. She said the engagement would take place on a specific day, and so it happened. But the wedding over, another problem surfaced. The sister had 'special problems with fertility', or as her brother put it: 'It seems that the problem of the horoscope has been displaced (from marriage) to issue': till 1993 his sister had no child.

This example is unique: no other GSB family I know have a *bhuta* as their *ishtadevata*. The link to the land is important here, as are the difficulties of the siblings, making them look for new sources of divine support. Even so, this story and the Gurupur complex show the possibility of partial integration of GSB religion with the *bhuta* cults. No such examples are found at Udupi, however.

The *ishtadevata* is the 'chosen deity': the choice may be made at the family level or by an individual. Venkatarama is by far the most common *ishtadevata* among my informants, but two have chosen Ganesha. So did T.A. Pai, who, at the time of his death, had over six hundred Ganesha figures in his home (Kamath, 1983: 172). The choice is interesting, since the Ganesha cult is done at home, making the person independent of the temple community. Is this a reason for choosing an *ishtadevata* different from Venkatarama? One Ammunje Nayak informant had chosen Mahishamardini as his *ishtadevata* 'because we live nearby', as he put it. Since this temple is dominated by other communities, this, too, would produce relative independence in relation to the community and the committee of the Venkatarama temple.

But such personal religious beliefs may manifest itself in other ways. T.A. Pai was a follower of Sai Baba, 'and did nothing of major importance without consulting him, or at least getting his *darshan*' (Kamath, 1983: 172-3). He often called on the gurus of the GSB *maths* and was given the *devi stotra* by the Shankaracharya of Sringeri. The *kuladevata* of the Tonse Pais is Mahalasanarayani, and they are closely linked to her temple in Basrur. But they also sponsor a religious institution which, on the face of it, is very far from GSB religious practice: the Babusthana at Manipal. Babu is a *bhuta* of the low castes, whose capacity for healing, including mental illnesses, is famous (Carrin, *in press*). At present, Ashok Pai is the main trustee.[114] In Kemmanna – near Kallianpur – the *gutu* family[115] of Bunts are *jajmans* of the Babusthana. Sponsoring a low caste *bhuta* then is no news among powerful families. Yet the Tonse Pais are Brahmins, and supposed to stand apart from low-caste cults, much more so than Bunts. Nevertheless, these cases of sponsorship and attachment to gurus show the importance of choice in the religious field.

Whatever the reason for these choices, *ishtadevatas* may define a ritual space independent of the community, open to the expression of personal religious feelings. In a community such as the GSB, where much of religion has a marked communitarian character, this independent space is important.[116]

We have seen that oracles are important with the GSB. While they are ubiquitous among most castes in South Canara, the GSB traditions seem to predate their migration to the area, as the case of Bhairava shows. But modern oracles are found among the GSB as among the Tulu-speaking castes. One particularly interesting oracle in Udupi is Sadhana Kini.[117]

We got to know about her from Mrs. Borkar. She had never heard of the Gurupura oracle, reputed among the GSB, but, she said there was a medium in Manipal, Sadhana Kini, popular among local Konkanis. She had been there herself. Kini's possession is not violent, Mrs. Borkar said, like that of most popular mediums: she gives *darshan* sitting in her armchair, eyes closed. She is possessed by the sister of Kalkuda, Varte.[118] Mr. Borkar said, 'It is not really *darshan*: she is just concentrating.' He did not mention Varte. Students often go to Kini to see if they will succeed in their exams, and many Konkani intellectuals go there. She has no temple, but receives her clients at home, arranging the consultation by phone. It is her lodger, a Sindhi motorcycle mechanic, who does the *puja* for her session.[119]

I had a long discussion with Sadhana Kini, who showed me an image of Devi symbolized by a *kailasha* over which is placed a kind of mask and red colour. Sadhana Kini is from a Bantwal family, but born and bred in Hubli, where she learned Hindi and English at school, using Konkani at home. She went to the Catholic College at Bantwal, studying in English but talking Konkani with classmates and family. Bantwal was a dense GSB community, and 'the temple was the centre of everything'.[120] Venkatarama 'is our *gramadeva* – our *sthanadeva*,' she says, 'he is our god of each place. That is why there is always one Venkatarama temple in . . . all the towns and large villages of this area.' Coming from outside, going to a Catholic school, she felt like an outsider to 'all that'. That is, she says, perhaps why she chose, later in life, to keep away from temples and gods. She feels Christian influence has been strong, with its ideal of charity. The temples, she says, only look after their own, and do not care for the poor. The Christians are different.

Ever since her first menstruation, she used to fall in trance – 'talk a lot about important things' – at full moon and new moon days. She does not know whether a deity is involved – she does not care about deities. When she was young, her parents thought her trances were due to some illness. 'They were very modern, enlightened, and all that.' They took her to a neurologist who prescribed medicine but the trances continued. For her, this did not seem very special; yet she used to predict things – at school, for example, she might say: 'we will get leave this afternoon' – and at lunch they would be told that some leader had died and get the day off. 'There were lots of things like that. . . .

Sadhana Kini does not want to comment on the problems people put during her seances: she is in trance and cannot remember the questions or the answers. But she says people return to tell how the case is developing: she sees her activity as 'social work', not as mystical or religious. She criticizes other oracles, like those in the temples, as 'done for the money'; she does not do it that way. She does not want to criticize anyone else's religion, 'it is simply part of culture' – but she has not been to a temple for many years, nor does she want to go.

She married a man from an Ullal Kini family, who was in the Corporation Bank. Their older son was in the hotel management school at Manipal, where he knew Suneet Borkar, and so she came to know that family.[121] Their younger son had haemophilia, and in 1992 her husband got a transfer to Manipal so their son could be treated there. The treatment worked, but the illness produced brain damage, so he is mentally handicapped. When her son's troubles became evident, her husband took her to a lot of oracles, but she would get possessed herself, so she had to stop. This was when friends told her she should make use of her gift. It was in February 1997 that she began to do so.

We have not exhausted the field of GSB religion in this chapter. I have not dealt with death rituals, which are elaborate and extremely important for Brahmins. Gradually transforming ghosts into manes or ancestors, they are fundamental to the continuity of the lineage. Here, I have stressed the importance of the lineage deity and temple, which also contribute to this continuity. In worshipping together at the lineage temple, the *wangad* also constructs history, at the level where the local branch split from its lineage of origin. These origins are effectively re-enacted on visits to the lineage temple, since its location in Goa represents the village of origin, even if the temples had to be rebuilt outside the original area. At the lineage temple, a larger community is also enacted, as *kulavis* from different local lines meet there repeatedly. In a similar way, the Venkatarama temples unite the community of the present locality, and so recall the history of that settlement. But since these temples unite *kulavis* of different lineage deities, and since they are emblematic of the caste, this is where unity of the GSB community as a whole can be experienced. They may also meet, of course, on pilgrimage to Tirupati. This, in terms of historicity, refers to the community that once lived together on the banks of the Saraswati. And then, there is yet another level, where individual or family needs are taken care of as they arise. It is here that Kalabhairava, the protector, comes in, and deals with such problems in his oracular sessions. And while these traditional oracles seem to be disappearing, others are coming up outside the caste in South Kanara but also inside it, as we see in the example of Sadhana Kini.

Temples, like oracles, continue to attract considerable investment – emotionally and financially – in South Kanara. Certainly, any process of 'secularization' is far from evident. Rather, religion continues as a main focus of social and emotional involvement, and my impression is that its importance is increasing. This does not, as we have seen, exclude change, and one feels that the role of expatriates among the GSB, in funding new temples and modernizing old ones, is increasing. This trend may well lead to further change, since the expatriates are 'the most traditional – but they do not know the tradition'. But it is not likely to diminish the importance of religion as a field for social competition and creditworthiness.

NOTES

1. This trait seems typical of old elites, as for the UU (Upper Upper) class in Yankee City, who look at the richer but recently established LU (Lower Upper) as upstarts (Warner, 1945, 1963: 174). It is also a trait among 'Lions' when challenged by 'Foxes' (Pareto, 1966). Henry James, in the *Ambassadors* describes the flats of Miss Gostrey and Madame de Vionnet. Stretcher, the hero, recognizes the latter's as 'founded much more on old accumulations that had possibly from time to time shrunken than on any contemporary method of acquisition or form of curiosity' as opposed to Miss Gostrey's 'museum of bargains' (Douglas and Isherwood, 1979/1996: ix-xi).
2. This relaxed attitude contrasts with the Patidars in London, and in Saurashtra. They stressed the particular qualities of Patidars, explaining as well as legitimizing their upward mobility. They were clearly 'foxes' in Pareto's terms (1966), contrasting their own entrepreneurial qualities with the 'traditional' – and relaxed – outlook of Banias, the established merchant castes.
3. The GSB, as Brahmins, refer more than members of lower castes to the three *gunas* and their attendant qualities. For an analysis of the place of the *gunas* in the Hindu life-world, see Marriott, 1989.
4. Esnoul says that only Vaishnavites revere the *salagram* (1964: 93). U.A. Kamath, a Shaivite, implies that all GSB families have one. Madan (1982), writing of Shaivite Brahmins, seems to take the *salagram* for granted, and Stevenson (1920: 165) notes that the Shaivite Nagar Brahmins use the *salagram* in their funerary ritual. Madan relates the *salagram* to fecundity. Though the Pandit Brahmins of Kashmir believe that all elements of the child are contained in the seed, 'the mother's menstrual blood provides the "oil" or "bed" for the seed to grow. . . . It is because of this fact, some informants said, that Hindus worship the black stone *saligrama*, the symbol of Vishnu, the preserver, which resembles the womb in shape' (1982: 230).
5. The responsibility of looking after the *salagram* lies with the joint family head. The qualificative 'really' implies that the elder brother's absence does

not imply a split in the joint family, though the *salagram* should stay in the family's 'home place' and be looked after by the senior member residing there.

6. Indeed, when reference is made in the literature to this custom, the term 'water vegetable' is sometimes used.
7. One such critic was Swami Narayana of Gujarat. He held that the word 'ajā' in the Vedas, usually translated as 'goat', actually meant vegetables and other vegetarian offerings. See Dave, 1967/1974: 95.
8. There are three Mariamman temples in Kapu today. The one belonging to the GSB has banned animal sacrifice. In another, controlled by Bunts, fowl are sacrificed but only outside the temple walls. In the third temple, controlled by the Moghaveeras, such sacrifices are fully accepted. This division is recent: 'formerly' there was only one temple, which accepted animal sacrifice. Apparently, the GSB controlled it. Kapu, like Mulki, once had a strong GSB community. U.A. Kamath seems either to refer to the original temple, which *should* have belonged to the GSB still, or to the new GSB temple which, implicitly, *should* have accepted animal sacrifice.
9. There is a long history of debate about the 'sacred cow complex'. A classic contribution is Alsdorf, 1962. Said one Indian friend in France: 'The cow is really like our mother or sister – that is why we cannot imagine eating beef.' The cow as a mother-image is of course very widespread in India.
10. I am inclined to think it is right, but the matter is too complicated to be discussed here.
11. See note 1 above. This self-assurance with regard to 'true' Hinduism is typical of the GSB.
12. The term 'world religions' assimilates 'Hinduism' to notions of religion more proper to Christianity or Islam, where a single sacred text produces a certain degree of unity.
13. Some Christians, of course, believe in the real existence of the Devil. A few years ago, a heated debate in the Norwegian State Church concerned the permissibility, or even necessity, of exorcism by State Church priests.
14. They are followers of the Gaudapada *math* at Goa. Two other important Smarta families in Udupi are the Parkala Shenoys and the Tonse Shenoys.
15. The *Bhasti Punali Kashanaya: Marathi matha Konkani bhashgalla tulanath makka, dimeshi matha Saraswati Brahmana prachina itihasa* is the main work on Saraswat history and on their *maths*, says K.R. Kuduva. I have not been able to consult this book.
16. The *math* is just behind the Shanta Durga temple at Ponda; the Kashi *math* also has a branch there.

17. Narayanan and Veluthat relate the formation of *maths* to a return to orthodoxy, following the wave of *bhakti* reform in south India (1978/ 2000: 407). The GSB, then, did not convert to Vaishnavism until this 'return to orthodoxy' got underway, but they must have been among the first groups to adopt the new trend.
18. Some four hundred years, people say.
19. Kamakshi is identified with Kamakhya in Assam, one of the main *shaktapithas* of India. Here, the yoni – the sexual organ – of Sati fell when Shiva swung her body in rage after her suicide. She had killed herself when her father refused Shiva access to his feast – in protest against her secret marriage to Shiva, the wild god distrusted by the father-in-law. Kamakshi is also the main goddess of Kanchi. She was 'fierce', but her nature is said to have been changed by Shankaracharya, who 'converted her to *bhakti* forms (Stein, 1994: 342, who cites Raman 1959: 13). This would have happened in the eighth century. No mention is made here of Kamakshi's peaceful pendant Shanteri, however. The two instances of 'taming' the goddess may therefore well be entirely separate.
20. Writing of the Vaishnava poet Annamacharya, Chandrasekhara affirms: 'the world is real, and prakriti is also eternal and unconscious, made of the three *guna*s, and therefore subject to change – it is 'a teleological order periodically created, sustained and withdrawn by God' (Jackson, 2007: 205-6, citing Chandrasekhara, 1990: 46-7).
21. He has nothing to do with Rama, though he too was a king, and came from Ayodhya, like Rama. The GSB claim that Venkatarama is the elder of the two.
22. The authors feel that this 'northernmost point of Tamilakam was also the point of contact between the Aryan and Tamil ways of life' and go on to propose 'that the *bhakti* movement was a byproduct of the Aryanizing or Sanskritizing influence' (Narayanan and Veluthat, 2002: 388).
23. It is called Vaikunthadri, since it was brought from Vaikuntha, Vishnu's heaven. Simhachala refers to Vishnu's lion-man form Narasimha: here Vishnu, taking this form, killed the demon Hiranyakashipu. Varahadri is the home of Varaha. Srisaila is the mountain of the goddess Sri, or Lakshmi. Anandadri or Kridadri means the site of Vishnu's divine happiness, play or sport. Pushkaradri is the place where the red lotus grows in plenty. Gnanadri means the place of knowledge. Chintamani is the one who grants desire, while Teerthadri is the place of *tirthas* or sacred watering-places. Dharmadri, the place of Dharma, is derived from Dharmadeva, the god of righteousness, who did penance on the hill. Kanakadri means the place where gold and precious stones were found.

Narayanadri, the place of Narayana, is named from a Brahmin who performed austerities here and had the hill named after him. Narayana is also a name of Vishnu. Nilagiri, the blue mountain, is said to derive from Nila, a chief of the Vanaras who once lived here. Srinivasagiri, the mountain of Srinivasa, relates to the story of the god's marriage; and Garudadri to the mountain being brought from heaven by Garuda (Krishna, 2000: 20). It is also called Seshadri since 'its shape resembled Sesha, Lord Narayana's thousand-hood snake' (Krishna, 2000: 3).

24. Here, Krishna refers to the Venkatachala Mahatmya of the *Varaha Purana*, said to be written by the sage Suta.
25. He is also known as Balaji – Vishnu as a newborn child but also said by Krishna to mean 'Universal Mother'; as Narayana, Perumal (The Great Lord), Malaiyappa (Lord of the Hill), and Govinda, the shepherd Krishna.
26. Krishna refers to the *Bhavishyottara Purana.*
27. The sage raised a tamarind tree on Venkatadri and below it he formed an anthill. Then he went near the Ganges to discuss the problem with the sages gathered there. They could not agree on how to bring Vishnu back, so the sage Bhrigu went to Satyaloka, met Brahma, behaved rudely, and was ignored. He continued to Kailasa, where Shiva was sporting with Parvati. 'Disapproving, Bhrigu left for Vaikuntha, where he saw Vishnu reclining on the serpent with Lakshmi by his side. Bhrigu kicked Vishnu on the right side of the chest, the abode of Lakshmi. Vishnu got up, bowed, washed the rishi's hands and feet and pressed them. He apologized for his inactivity and gratified Bhrigu, so Bhrigu returned to the banks of the Ganga and told the other rishis they should pray to Vishnu for salvation (Krishna, 2000: 7-8). There is a contest here between the gods. Brahma reacts to Bhrigu's bad manners by ignoring him, and Shiva shocks the sage with his sexual mores. Only Vishnu replies to the sage's rudeness with respect: thus, we are told, only Vishnu forgives sins and gives redemption. But Lakshmi was angry that Vishnu had 'apologized to the rishi who had kicked her abode' so she left for Karaveera Kshetram (Kolhapur in Maharashtra). 'The unhappy Vishnu then left Vaikuntha to return to Venkatadri, where he lived incognito in the anthill' (Krishna, 2000: 8).
28. King of heaven, or heavenly king.
29. A man gains merit by marrying his daughter to a superior, an important implicit in the rite of *kanyadan.*
30. Another name for Vishnu/Venkatesha.
31. Jainism was strong in south India by the time of the Alvars and Nayanars (sixth to ninth century), but declined partly due to their efforts.

32. The wedding procession passes the sage Sukha's hermitage. Venkatesha accepts the sage's offering of fruits, but asks how Sukha will feed the rest of the procession. 'The sage replies that if he could satisfy the Lord, everyone else would automatically be satisfied' and all 'had a strange feeling of having had a good feast, without having eaten' (Krishna, 2000: 12).
33. Brahma also lit two lamps to burn eternally at the temple, and made Venkatesha promise ever to reside there (Krishna, 2000: 14).
34. The most common gloss of the name Venkatesha is 'remover of sins',[34] found in Puranic literature from around the tenth century AD. But in the *Vayu Purana*, *vem* is derived from *amrita*, 'nectar', and *kata* from *aishwarya* or affluence. As Krishna notes, this gloss may be seen to account for the qualities of the God, rather than an etymology (200: 49). But the term *venkatam* or *venkadam* appears much earlier, in the Tamil grammar *Tolkaapiyam*, dated to about 200 BC. Here, it is constructed from *ven* (burning) and *kadan* (debts), which would indeed reflect on the meaning of the present cult.
35. Sin here is not *pap* but *vem,* while *kata* is glossed as immunity (Krishna, 2000: 14).
36. Pey Alvar sings: 'In him, my father on Tirumalai, the two forms have gracefully blended into one' (Krishna, 2000: 52-3).
37. *Arayirappatikuruparamparaprapavam.*
38. He lived between AD 1017 and 1137.
39. The king was himself a Vaishnavite.
40. This would fit Narayanan and Veluthat's idea that the cult was a result of Aryanizing influence. A 'tribal' or local god would have been assimilated into the Indian pantheon, much as the Pallavas, who 'seem to be closely associated' with the cult, was 'one of the early Dravidian dynasties which were thoroughly Aryanized', and 'seem to have used a Sanskritized tribal name as their dynastic title' (2002: 388). Thondaimaan, the Chola king – the Cholas were feudatories of the Pallavas at the time (Sastri, 1976: 174-5) – is said to have discovered the image half-buried under a tree, its feet in an anthill (Krishna, 2000: 52) – clearly either a reference, or the origin of, the myth of Vishnu's abode when he resided 'incognito' on the hill.
41. The imagery of money here is clearly that of a gift economy in Mauss' sense (1966), rather than the modern imagery of the market.
42. Here, the hill stands as the northern limit of the Tamil land, with Kanyakumari at the southern end.
43. Thondaimaan is believed to have been an illegitimate son of Kulottunga Chola of Thanjavur. He may have been related to the Pallavas (Krishna,

2000: 57). The period (AD 550) would have been just before, or at the very beginning of, the *bhakti* movement.

44. The reference seems to show that these objects cannot have been added by Ramanuja (2000: 55).
45. Krishna feels the tradition of worship is older: many wooden or terracotta figures were replaced when stone sculpture became common in the south (2000: 56).
46. As feudatories of the Cholas.
47. We may note that Ramanuja was dead when the Yadavas gained power; the slip in dates is slight, however, and need not concern us here.
48. It is said to have been their *ishtadevata.*
49. Dirks says the Tirupati temple 'was established largely under the patronage of Vijayanagara' (1987/89: 89).
50. This was done at the behest of Shathakopa, a Vaishnava sage of the time of the poet Annamacharya (1408-1503). Shathakopa is also said to have rehabilitated the Vaishnava monuments on the hill.
51. The *murti*, which 'sleeps' in the Shayana Mandapa, an auxiliary building, is now brought to the *garbhagriha.* Here, *arti* is performed with milk, butter and sugar, which is offered as *prasad* to the devotees, with sacred water, *tirtha*, believed to have been worshipped by the *devas* during the night.
52. Followed by *bhajans* sung by a descendant of Talapakkam Annamacharya, the first writer of such poetry.
53. The *thomala seva.*
54. By a descendant of the sage Tirumala Nambi, one of the first sages of the mountain.
55. Kept in the Tirumamani Mandapa.
56. It starts with *puja* to the five principal gods, then the wedding is held 'according to Vedic rites', the three images exchanging garlands. The donor financing the rite receives 'a gift of cloth and a coin'.
57. *Naivedyam.*
58. The Vaishnava poet-saints, central to old Tamil literature.
59. *Madhyayana puja.*
60. *Dolotsavam.* This takes place in yet another hall, the Aina Mahal.
61. The *sahasra dipalankara.*
62. *Ratri puja.*
63. *Ekanta seva.*
64. We may compare, here, with Thoothi's discussion of similar monetary investment in the Krishna cult of the Gujarat Vallabhacharyas (1935) and its importance for the arts.
65. Krishna Bhatt says Venkatarama is also known as Thimmappa, and worshipped by lower castes of this area.

66. Some include the Kallianpur temple in this group.
67. We should note some ambiguity here. Though most Indian languages do not distinguish between respect and worship, there is a distinction here. Thus no harm will come to a Shaiva who shows 'respect' to Venkatarama, even if he is not a 'worshipper'.
68. These *pujas* draw more people, it seems, in Mangalore. Still, the use of the temple does not resemble that of sectarian communities like the Swaminarayana temples in Gujarat, which are always full for *satsang*, communal worship on Sundays.
69. In September 1993, the Udupi temple had a visit from ISKCON. This should not be seen as a sign of alliance with the Hare Krishna movement: I never met any GSB who belonged to it. But ISKCON has a 'village ashram' in South Kanara, it is financially powerful, and acting as its host may prove useful in the larger field of Hindu politics. I never saw, however, any overtly political manifestation at the Venkatarama temple, as when the Pejawar *math*, one of the *ashtamaths*, received a whole delegation from the BJP.
70. The *bhajan* groups are on the women's side of the entrance, while the *hundi* for contributions is on the right.
71. It was Krishna Bhatt who told me of this event.
72. Basrur was once an important town, and a port. Now it has effectively become a village.
73. There is another Mahalasa temple at Harikhadige, near Hiriadka. This is closer to Udupi, but I met no Udupi GSB who regard themselves as *kulavis* of that temple.
74. Khandoba has a second wife, Banai, from the Kurava tribe who, for Sontheimer, 'essentially reflects the fertility and eroticism of the early Tamil Valli'. Mahalasa, who kills the demon with a lance (and thus recalls Durga), 'is from the higher community, but of a slightly jealous nature, even cantankerous, and too domestic. She sits high on her horse, her nose turned towards the sky, whereas poor Banai is standing on the ground holding a sheep in her arm and reaching up to hand Khandoba some fruit or other food' (Sontheimer, 1997: 53-6). Mahalasa here is the daughter of a Lingayat merchant (1997: 26). We cannot assume that this Mahalasa and her GSB namesake are the same deity, even if Sontheimer identifies Khandoba with Bhairava (1997: 27).
75. Information from Krishna Bhatt. The mediums are called *darshanpatris*.
76. *Vaidika* means 'of the Vedas' and signifies Brahmins who keep to Vedic rituals – as opposed to Vaishnava, Shakta or other traditions. This is how the term is used in Maharashtra (Saraswati, 1977: 61). Among the GSB,

it denotes temple priests who know Vedic ritual. They need not be GSB: what is important is their learning.

77. The women were, of course, in saris.
78. This pride in Indian success overseas is typical of many Indian communities, not least in South Kanara, with its tradition of overseas migration.
79. Where, as I have noted, there is another Mahalasa temple.
80. There are many *bhajanmandalas* (*bhajan* halls) in the coastal area, catering mainly to Moghaveeras and Billavas. I have no idea of their musical creativity: Prabhakara Nayak spoke of composing new *bhajans* rather than singing them, and there is a constant production of new *bhajans* from the GSB community.
81. I wondered if their style might be due to a degree of Portuguese influence.
82. Possession and oracles are often seen as elements of 'folk religion'.
83. I was not sure the possession was a success. The medium seemed unsatisfied, but his superior reassured him.
84. The Chitrapur Saraswat also had an oracular tradition. But Pandurangashrama Swami of the Shirali *math*, whose candidature as guru had been confirmed by the oracle at Vitthala, put an end to this tradition in the last quarter of the nineteenth century (Conlon, 1977: 142).
85. Bhairava is a somewhat evasive figure in the Hindu pantheon, and is represented in several iconographic forms. He 'has from eight to twelve forms, but he is best known as Kal Bhairom' (Briggs, 1938/1969: 159-60). Tridents are seen by Briggs as the weapons of Bhairava: they are also symbols both of Shiva and the Goddess. When associated with Bhairava, they are usually painted red. Briggs notes that in Punjab, Bhairava 'wards off disease and death and protects both men and cattle' 1938/1969: 160-1). In the shrine of Gorakhnath at Gorakhpur (UP), Bhairava is the guardian deity (ibid.: 87). He is also seen as the *kotwal* or guardian of Varanasi (Briggs; Sontheimer, 1997: 20). He presides over death at Varanasi, giving or denying permission to die there – which implies the destruction of all negative *karma* and the attainment of *moksha*. Thus the worship of Bhairava should precede any other ritual act at Varanasi. Devotees who do not succeed in dying at Varanasi will say they were not granted permission by Bhairava (Knut A. Jacobsen, *personal information*). I am not here trying to know how Bhairava entered the GSB tradition, but Abhinavagupta refers to him in relation to Kunkunamba, 'the Mother of Konkana' (White, 2003: 113), and we may wonder whether he was particularly important in the Konkan when Abhinavagupta wrote, in the eleventh century (White, 2003: 15). Most of the GSB *gotras* are supposed to have been in Goa then.

86. Either as a form of Bhairava, or as a member of a family of gods deriving from the same prototype.
87. Babb (1975) sees Bhairava as a male consort of the fierce goddess, who as the agent of *purusha* (the male principle of order or structure) contributes to appease her when she is dominant. When married to Shiva, she takes a peaceful form dominated by him. White underlines the role of Bhairava as the male counterpart and master of the *yoginis* in the Tantric tradition (2003).
88. In Kanphata religion, Shiva is the central deity. Kalabhairava is worshipped on the dark eighth day of *kartik*, held to be his birthday: he is then seen as a manifestation of Shiva (Briggs, 1938/1969: 144). Briggs sees Bhairava as representing Shiva's 'terrible' aspect (ibid.: 152, 159), which he identifies with the Vedic Rudra (ibid.: 158). He also held, however, that Bhairava and his consort Bhairavi were 'Tantric gods' who entered popular Buddhism in Bengal under Mahipala before AD 1020 (ibid.: 245). Sanderson (1985), in describing the Hindu schools of thought of medieval Kashmir, associates Bhairava with Shaktist or even tantric tendencies, and White (2003) provides ample documentation of this connection. Bhairava is associated with snakes and black dogs (Briggs, 1938/1969: 134-5: Sontheimer, 1997: 51-3; White, 1991). But Bhairava is also called 'Lord of the fishes' (White, 2003: 103), a point which was not mentioned by my fish-eating informants. Crooke notes that left-hand Shaktas use an image of Bhairava (or Durga) to kill an enemy: the image is placed so that the deity's weapon pierces a doll representing the victim (1896, I: 137).
89. They are sometimes said to have invented gunpowder.
90. The Kalabhairava image at Chidambaram shows the deity with his dog. In his right hand, he holds what looks like a flattened stick which resembles the *patta* of the Mulki oracle. It is no longer possible to see what he holds in his left hand.
91. Briggs mentions a temple to "Kal Bhairab" at Kathmandu (1938/1969: 79) and another at Varanasi (ibid.: 83). At the latter, both the black and the white bhairava as found, as a pair (ibid.: 84-5). Both forms are also found at the Kanphata monastery Dhinodhar in Kacch (ibid.: 113).
92. As the name suggests, the latter is associated with Agni. I have no further explanation.
93. I came across the same technique of exorcism in Rajasthan (1997: 134-7). The spirits are 'burnt' away.
94. It was sought out by my Moghaveera friend Karunakaran after his sister's disappearance in 1996. The oracle told him to accept her disappearance and forget about it, he says. It has not been active 'for some 5-6 years', he

said in 2003: the old medium died, and they have found no successor. Krishna Bhatt says that the Gurupur darshan of Kalabhairava is still active.

95. In South Kanara, the mediators between the oracle and his public are called *patris*.
96. It cannot be seen from where I, and the public, stand.
97. A long flat stick rather like a cricket bat. It must be made from the skin of a black bat.
98. A round stick, rather like a walking cane.
99. Both the medium and the chief *patri* have designs in white on their bodies. I got no explanation for these designs.
100. I did not get any particular explanation for this change of mediators.
101. I had met this man at the Savantar's Kambala a week earlier. He owns a house facing the Kambala field.
102. I first got this information from Krishna Bhatt, but it was confirmed by others at Gurupur.
103. Manifesting through possession, as the word *darshan* is used in south Kanara.
104. He continues: 'Areca flowers are *tamasic* exclusively meant for *bhutas*. . . . And liquor (toddy) will be offered openly – because it is the right of that dancer. The places will be wild forests, in the interior, that kind of thing.'
105. Normally, it is the SC or low caste people who serve as mediums.
106. It is not clear who Maleshini Mata is, but she may be Mahalasa, closer to Durga than Lakshmi in character.
107. No sources or informants mention the Gurupur temple as particularly old. They may, of course, be wrong.
108. Some belonging to the Bhatt priests, some to another Bhatt family of the GSB; it was also implied that he is worshipped here by non-GSB Bhatt families. The Shivalli Brahmins also use this name.
109. The *bhuta* cults in North Canara seem to have a more archaic character than in the south. See Carrin, 2002a.
110. The sanctuaries to *bhutas* in the region are called *bhutasthanas*.
111. As they put it: Kallurti came to Yeltimar, where the Shenoy family settled some three hundred years ago. Whether they settled on her land, or she came to their land, was not clear. A *bhuta* is not an autochthonous spirit, but relates to the land as owned, or to the family as owners. It may be taken over if another family gets hold of the land. Here, the question of whether the Shenoys were the first owners of the land is, perhaps explicitly, not answered.

112. I was told later, however, that the business had folded, in spite of Kallurti's protection.
113. Mangala was in the eighth house, he told me.
114. Krishna Bhatt commented drily on this question: 'Because you need somebody of some economic substance.'
115. That is, the 'family of the manor'.
116. We may think of the 'polytropy' of Carrithers (2000). But I am inclined to stress the disjunction between individual choice, and the socially determined cults to family and caste deities, not necessarily linked.
117. One GSB bank employee is also an oracle, having his consultations at his home on Sundays, like Sadhana Kini's.
118. This, they say, would mean that there must be a shrine to Kalkuda nearby. But there is no such shrine in Sadhana Kini's house. My wife was told by Mrs. Borkar that the two deities to which Sadhana Kini's possession is attributed are Varte and Devi. Mrs. Kini herself showed me a Devi, but no Varte.
119. He is an expert at customizing Enfields. His family came to Mumbai after Partition; his brother has another garage in Goa. He left the 'hustle and bustle' of Mumbai – and found Manipal ideal for the work he likes to do. Kini has two sons, but they do not assist her oracular activities. The Borkars say it is her husband who does the *puja*, but this is incorrect, as Mr. Kini is deceased.
120. This, of course, was the Venkatarama temple.
121. Her son was among the first to pass, so he got a job immediately and is now working in a hotel in Bengaluru.

10

Class, Caste and Ethnicity in the Age of Hindutva

The sense of identity among the GSB is strong, but to what social entity does it refer? Is it based on caste, as one might expect from literature on India? Or should we look to the historical role of the GSB as the core of a regional bourgeoisie – an identity based on class? Do they see themselves as an ethnic minority, Konkani speakers among Tulus? I shall argue that caste, class and ethnicity elements all have their place in GSB identity, while none of these serves as a base of identification in itself. Rather, GSB identity, based on their consciousness of themselves as a historically distinct group, forms a whole which the GSB do not decompose. Moreover, I argue that collective identities in general do not follow the theoretical distinctions social scientists make between class, caste and ethnicity.

I shall use the term community for the entity to which GSB identity refers. This is the term most English-speaking GSB use, and so avoids part of the translation problem: in India, moreover, everybody is seen as belonging to a community. But this common usage does not save us from the perils of imprecision, for, as Carrithers and Humphrey note, 'sociologists . . . are entitled to ask more of a term than that it be in common usage' (1991: 6). They propose five criteria to identify community more precisely,[1] but I shall not use them here, as they seem to me to imply a danger of reification.[2] I would hold, rather, that community, like many other social phenomena, is above all a constructed entity, which implies that constructs may differ.

The GSB agree that their community is a *jati*, the term Westerners usually translate as caste. But this common translation is inaccurate. The word *jati* is derived from a verb that means 'to be born', and so may be translated as 'those who have a common birth or origin'. Species of animals or plants are *jati*, as are cars from the same producer. Local communities, where members have various origins, are not. To say one belongs to a particular *jati* then may be translated as being of the same breed. The GSB are proud of their breed.

Yet my informants feel they are not particularly caste-conscious. The GSB do not act as a caste, says U.A. Kamath. 'People will solidarize first and foremost with their family. The caste is there, of course, but it does not have the same importance as for some people.' There is some truth in this.[3] The GSB talk about their families, their business, and their *kuladevatas*, but little of the community as a whole, whose position largely seems to be taken for granted.

Other castes, in fact, have stronger caste organizations on the collective level.[4] Much of the GSB strength is not collectively based in this sense. The banks, for example, may be GSB institutions in that members of the caste founded and still dominate them, but they are not 'caste banks', such as the Billavas, the Catholics, the Moghaveera fishermen, or to some extent the Bunts have. Initiatives seem to have come from one or a few allied families.[5] Yet taken together, these banks dominate banking in the region, and the 'caste banks' were started in opposition to the GSB banks. Thus it is the challengers who act collectively: the dominant defend their position along other lines (Tambs-Lyche, *forthcoming*). A similar point may be made for education: when the GSB started the Canara High School in Mangalore – a caste institution – they were challenging the educational monopoly of the Christians and the Chitrapur Saraswats.[6] And yet, when the Manipal complex was instituted, it was run by a GSB family with no connection to the Canara school and college, and no attempt was made to merge or in other ways assimilate the two institutions. By then, the Christian monopoly was broken, and unity was not necessary to assert the GSB position.

It is perhaps significant that the RSB have a website designed to give a unified image of the caste: many sites deal with the history and culture of the GSB, but there is no such central site. As the RSB site puts it, for them it has been a struggle to arrive at a better position in society. No such struggle is evident when one looks at the GSB today. There may have been a phase, perhaps just after their exodus from Goa, when they were highly cohesive and organized, by V.N. Kuduva's indications (1972), mainly around their temples. Another phase, around the turn of the century, took off with the foundation of Canara High School and the Bank of Canara. This phase is now over, though these enterprises are still dominated by the caste.[7] In a sense, then, Kamath is right: the GSB do not act as a caste. But this in no way diminishes the caste consciousness of families and individuals.

For the GSB are highly conscious of their difference from other elite communities of South Kanara. There are several other Brahmin communities. Chitpavans, as immigrants, have a relatively low status in South Kanara, says Dr. Nandavara, a Tulu writer and at one time president of the Tulu Academy. Sthanika and Shivalli Brahmins have much higher status here. Haviks too, have high status – they are Kannada-speaking, while the Shivallis are Tulu Brahmins. Makala Brahmins are of much lower status, though they too are Tulu speakers. Dr. Nandavara, very much a Tulu intellectual, continues: 'Jains are not from here. They came from the North and settled here, marrying Bunt ladies. They were really merchants. . . . At Karkala, Belthangadi and Mudabidri, you will find a rich Jaina community.'[8]

For P.R. Kuduva, as for U.A. Kamath, Brahminhood is clearly more important than Konkani identity. To identify with the Brahmin *varna* is certainly a form of caste consciousness, but there is no Brahmin community, or rather, such community must be imagined at a more distant and abstract level than the *jati*, since the latter is concretized through ritual and marriage relations and may incarnate through a caste association. Brahminhood is above all a point of reference, implying a particular set of values. Strong identification with these values is typical of the more 'Brahmanized' GSB. But this identification is but one element in GSB identity, and is complemented by a view of the caste as agents of progress and modernity. If we compare the discourse of strongly 'Brahmanized' individuals with, for example, the views of K.K. Pai and Mr. Prabhu, the brother-in-law of the Gundu Nayaks, we see the variability of GSB views. One pole stresses their Brahmanical, Sanskritic identity and their descent from the people of the Saraswati valley, another stresses the 'secular' character of the community ('I am not very religious,' said Mr. Prabhu). In Puttur, we met Mr. Shenoy, a typist, and his wife. Inviting us for tea, Shenoy proceeded to read to us the description of his community from the old South Kanara Gazetteer, which stresses the enlightened and progressive character of the GSB. He clearly wanted to show that his own view of the community was supported by competent authorities. This identification with progress and enlightenment was clearly central for T.M.A. Pai, and I have identified it with the historical role of the bourgeoisie, a class-based identity. Yet it is not class in itself, but the qualities associated with a particular class position, that emerges from GSB discourse.

A.S. Airodikar's remarks on business show the consciousness prevalent among GSB of being *the* merchant community of the area, to the extent of, perhaps, exaggerating the dominant position of the community in business. For A.S., this almost goes without saying, so it is no problem that his association is 'open to merchants of all castes and creeds'.

We see that different oppositions are used to construct the idea of a GSB community. There is caste: with the exception of those who have been excluded and not readmitted – and 'nobody' is excluded nowadays – the boundary of the caste is clear. A question of whether one is a GSB will receive a clear yes or no answer. This is different, for example, from the moving divide between Kanbis and Patidars that Pocock (1972) describes from Gujarat. But if the Udupi GSB identify themselves with the local business 'community' or the town's bourgeouisie, they do not exclude the presence of non-GSB members of these two categories, just as there are other Brahmins and other Konkani-speaking groups. The caste therefore remains the reference for community identification, even if it never acts as a single group, and the network of any individual never reaches the whole caste. In this sense, the GSB caste is an imagined community. At the local level, as in Udupi, most GSB know or know about other members, so the 'Udupi GSB' consists of a limited and known number of individuals. But the local group is not a community, for each member will feel as close to kinsmen or affinals residing elsewhere, as to many of his townsmen. What produces the feeling of community in everyday life is, I would hold, precisely 'that they are groups of kin and caste mates known to each other in village, neighbourhood, or marriage circle'. This, say Carrithers and Humphrey, 'is not an interesting use of the term 'community' (Carrithers and Humphrey, 1991: 11). Yet this interpersonal dimension is the very essence of how community manifests itself in real life: beyond these networks community can only be imagined. An essential part of that imagination, I would hold, is the idea that these networks overlap, that my affines in their village have their own affines elsewhere, until we reach the boundary of the community. Thus the GSB participate in 'community' through the specific reciprocities of their networks, and assume, by imagining '*the* community', that all GSB do so.

Being a GSB implies ways of acting and thinking conceived of as typically GSB. An anecdote may illustrate the business ethos of the GSB. I was with A.S. when a Manipal student and his mother from Delhi entered the shop. They bought household goods amounting to some Rs. 500. A.S. calculated on a slip of paper, and stated the result. 'You should give some concession,' said the mother. A.S. did not follow up this remark. The son took out his calculator, and arrived at Rs. 539.50, Rs. 20 less than Airodikar. The mother immediately proposed to pay Rs. 540. Airodikar recalculated, confirming his first result. The student offered his calculator, which Airodikar handed to his wife. Not used to such hi-tech equipment, she bungled the calculations, arriving at about Rs. 10,000. 'It does not work properly, she said. The student offered to show her how to use the calculator, but the mother handed Airodikar a Rs. 500 and a Rs. 100 note, saying: 'take Rs. 540'. The student re-calculated: this time, he arrived at Rs. 549.50. A.S. offered to recalculate again, but the mother said, 'We haven't got much time.' Airodikar returned Rs. 70 change, so actually, Rs. 530 was paid. I suggested that the student might have calculated wrongly on purpose, but he made no comment. Who was fooling whom? The 'bargaining' here constituted a complex chunk of interaction, but I think Airodikar knew what change he would give, and felt the Delhi couple was wasting time.

Important here is the opposition between the old lady, who haggles, the son, who wants precise calculation, and the merchant. A.S. is quite willing to give a discount, but as a professional he does not haggle;[9] he calculates in his head – probably with regard to the profit margins of the various items – what his price will be, and will not be moved by interference. He simply ignores other propositions and calculations, and states his price. It is as if he says, implicitly 'Why didn't you trust me?' Thus he maintains the dignity of the professional trader, while offering a discount which ought to satisfy his customers, here, his discount was greater than what the haggling old lady demanded.

It seems the GSB were the leading traders – or at least prominent among them – in Mumbai in the eighteenth century but lost out to Parsis and other Gujarati communities in the nineteenth century. Yet they were still present in the nascent colonial bourgeoisie. Thus, among students at Elphinstone College in 1870, there were 34 per cent Parsis, the community with which colonial Mumbai is identified; 34 per cent Brahmins, and 9 per cent 'Prabhus' or GSB (Ellsworth, 1991: 50). Kuduva's study (1972) suggests a similar development for Cochin.

As members of the bourgeoisie, we may compare Christian Konkanis with the GSB. Both Father Alexander d'Souza and Michael Lobo feel that Christians are less commercially-minded than the GSB, and also less family-minded. The GSB seem always to have their 'family shop' somewhere: this is not so of Christians. John Fernandes, the Ayurvedic medicine producer at Kallianpur, holds that while the GSB have always been traders, few important industries have been started by them. Christians were less important as merchants, but may have as many industrial entrepreneurs as the GSB. The history of the Mangalore tile industry seems to confirm his view. Started by the Basel missionaries, it was taken over and soon dominated by Catholics. The GSB entered the field later. It seems true in South Kanara, that the GSB have been slow to take the step from traders to industrialists. Why? Probably, since trade remained profitable and was well known, only a minority of the GSB were ready for the risks of industrial investment.

For criticism of GSB dominance I turn to S.M. Kunder, a former bank functionary and union man, who now runs a stationery shop on P.P.C. College Road.[10] He is a Moghaveera (fisherman), but left the traditional occupation through education. This was before current developments in fishing, which have made it quite an attractive career. Kunder is the son of a *sahukar* (moneylender) at Mulki, who used to arrange loans for the fishermen with the local GSB in the slack season.

He would be responsible for some seventy fisherman's families. Then the family took up government land at Manipal, below the present Valley View hotel. They also used their country boat to ferry people across the river there, for a 3-*anna* fare. There were four Patils[11] in that village who were RSB: they would take Rs. 500 from the tenants and pay Rs. 100 to the government, says Kunder. There were many RSB in such intermediary positions around Udupi, he says – sometimes they were the rent intermediaries of the *maths*. He implies that their corrupt practices were typical of Konkanis, GSB as well as RSB.

S.M. Kunder went to a village school beyond Manipal, then to the Christian High School in Udupi.[12] There, the Christian boys would kneel for prayer. He, like the other Hindu boys, would just stand behind and mumble the prayer after them. Then he went to school at Manipal, where Ramesh Pai was two years ahead of him. Later, he worked as a clerk at T.M.A. Pai's house to keep the register of college students. He got a very low wage: that was the system of the Pais, he says. They paid lower wages than others, and lower than government rates, even to college lecturers. After about three years of service – he had fifteen days left – S.M. Kunder asked for a pay increase, but Ramesh, who had become his boss by then, said: 'If you are to get an increase, then you are the sister of Krishna.' Kunder got angry, and left, in 1961. He then went to T.M.A. and applied for work with the Syndicate Bank. He was told he could have a job the next day, but he would have to go to a rural area for three years before he could come back to Udupi.[13]

He describes T.M.A. as a gentleman. 'Very different from Ramesh,' he says, adding: 'I am not saying that Ramesh is not a good man, but he was like that. . . .'[14] 'The Pais,' he says, 'Madhava especially, and then T.A. Pai, did a lot of good work. They became *so* popular and *so* well off, but then the next generation took over, and now they are going down. . . .

In the end Kunder applied, instead, for a job with the Bank of Canara, and got it. Later, he worked for them at Bangalore.[15] There, he had a problem with a supervising officer. For three weeks, he and his friend came to work in dhoti and shirt, letting their beards grow. At one meeting, he talked about the problem to some 3,000 bank personnel, saying, 'Let them sack 1,500 employees!' The next day, his adversary excused himself, but soon Kunder was fired. After some time he was taken back, then fired again. He was very active in the Union of Bank Employees, he says, 'and in those days I was very callous: I did not care about anything'. He became quite well known as a labour activist and retired with a good pension, also receiving a pay-off which helped him buy his present house.

At first he leased his house – and shop – from the Shoriyar *math*. Then he bought it, and now its value has increased comfortably, he says. The shop is now mainly a pastime – he writes poems and reads a lot. 'People should not expect to write well before they have reached a certain age and experience,' he says. 'Young people may relate one experience or another, but they do not have the full understanding of it.' He sees himself as a communist and agnostic: 'Krishna, Jesus, all these people, they are like Koti-Chennaya or Kalkuda, they are just men. Look at Mother Teresa, she did some great work; now she has become a saint. Gandhi, too, was just a man, but ten generations from now, people will talk of him as a God. God is something else, he is formless, nameless – we do not know him.'

Of his experience in the Bank of Canara, Kundu says: 'I was not a Konkani, not a GSB. So, the GSB would stick together, they would have the hook, as we say – a Moghaveera expression: they would stick together and only promote their own kind.' So Kundu often encountered problems, and opposed the GSB as a labour activist. But he is against reservation as a means to secure jobs for the lower castes: 'The conditions for all should be equal, then the need for reservation will disappear,' he says, His views are strongly anti-caste, and he feels all barriers of caste or religion should be made to fall.

Tulu speakers often use the ethnic term, 'Konkani' to describe the GSB. But they themselves are no more eager to be defined in terms of ethnicity than they are to stand forth as a caste. K.R. Kuduva stresses that the term 'Konkani' is a misnomer. 'There is a Konkani language: there is no Konkani community. You might at most speak of a Konkanastha community. But . . . there are many other Konkani communities: in Goa, there is everything, from top to bottom. There, the Saraswats are not known as such: they are simply known as *bamno*

(Brahmins) just like here, in Tulunadu. "Brahmin" generally refers to a Shivalli.' Indeed, in South Kanara, there are Catholic Christians, mostly Konkanis converted from the GSB community.[16] There are Chitrapur Saraswats who branched off from the GSB around 1700 (Conlon, 1977). The Rajapur Saraswat Brahmins – RSB – are also closely related.[17] The Vaishabs are *vanis* or merchants. The Sonargaras or goldsmiths are also known as Daivarajya Brahmins. The Kudala Deshastha Brahmins are supposed to have links to the Deshastha Brahmins of Maharashtra. The Marathi Naiks are Konkani speakers in spite of their name. The Mahalias are farmers, while the Ulupis are manual labourers. Among Muslims, the Navayats of this area – particularly concentrated in Bhatkal – speak their own, Islamized brand of Konkani.[18]

The Konkani language is an element of GSB identity, but as a marker it is ambiguous. It is commonly seen by the GSB as an 'unwritten' language. Due to the Catholic missionaries in Goa, Konkani may claim to be the first Indian language to appear in print, in the sixteenth century, but this fact is seldom cited by the GSB, who prefer to point to the first printed medical treaties from Cochin. Their authors were Saraswats,[19] and used the Devanagari alphabet – an 'Indian' script – while early Goan texts used the Roman alphabet.[20] Even the books published by the Konkani Academy in Mangalore, in Kannada script, are easily identified as written either in 'Christian' or 'GSB' dialect.[21] The RSB, too, have their own dialect, and are proud of their Konkani which they see as 'purer' than that of the GSB.[22] Christian and GSB Konkanis combine only in the field of language, and even here only the existence of the Konkani Academy produces a certain amount of collaboration. Thus the language incarnates the history of the various communities, and its variants stand witness to the 'Konkani diaspora', migration of Konkani speakers like the GSB, as well as conversion to Christianity and Islam. It is not Konkani that is used as an identity marker by the GSB then, but rather their own dialect and elements of literary tradition.

It is striking how the literature stresses writers, journalists and playwrights writing in Konkani. Yet Konkani remains a language for insiders. It is typical, says one visitor to A.S. Pai's shop, of GSB culture that community members are able to adapt wherever they go, in India or in foreign countries. But the talk soon turns to language: 'Our language, too, is perverted,' says Mr. Nayak, another visitor. 'We have picked up so many Kannada words. The Christian Konkanis speak much purer Konkani than we do. They have kept so many Sanskrit words.[23] There follows a discussion on the language itself. 'It is closer to Marathi,' says one; 'It has so many Bengali words,' says another; which makes Gopal Shetty, a Bunt and a Tulu writer, remark 'there are so many common words in the Northern languages, you cannot easily say which word comes from where.' He is probably right. But as soon as he leaves, all criticize the Tulu language, saying it is just a mixture of Tamil and Malayalam, not as old or classical as either, and 'also, it has no script'. Somebody remembers that Konkani has no script either. . . . All feel I should have made greater strides in Konkani: 'it is such an easy language'. The whole discussion is a fine example of how discussions of Konkani culture immediately turn to language, a question which seems to fascinate most Konkanis. But this very fascination shows the language as problematic, rather than as the sure marker that prestigious national – or regional – languages are.

The Venkatarama temples and other institutions of GSB culture also seem to be active only inside the community. The committees of Venkatarama temples serve as a focus for the local organization of GSB communities (Kudva, 1972). But there is also a long history of 'private' temples, built or endowed by a single family. Thus there is likely to have been – and still to be – a tension between the 'collective' spirit as in the Venkatarama temple committees, and a more 'familistic' spirit where competition for status and influence is predominant.

It is as if Konkani culture was a private matter, while GSB economic, social and political activity was quite visible.[24] Is there a parallel to Jews here? One has almost the impression that there is a reluctance to stress GSB specificity in public, while, at the same time, GSB identity in terms of networks and ethnic awareness is strong. In other words, there seems to be a case here of ethnicity without ethnic activism.

Some GSB feel that the caste is losing its cultural specificity. Mr. Nayak, the visitor to A.S. Pai's shop, wonders if I find anything worth writing about in their culture. It has been so much destroyed, he says; fifty years ago there would have been much more to report. 'The culture is fast going down,' he says. Thus *Kabi* art is an old specialty of the GSB caste.[25] This traditional art is now extinct in South Kanara, but it is still seen in North Kanara and in Goa.

South Kanara, in fact, is where modernization and development has gone the farthest. 'To find traditional Konkanis you must go to Kochi, especially Kadangulu. Konkanis down there are twenty or thirty years behind.' It is in Kerala, in Kochi and Ernakulam, that GSB customs are seen in the purest form, confirms P.R. Kuduva. The first printed book in Konkani and in India, was printed in Kochi in the sixteenth century, he says. It dealt with Ayurvedic medicine, written by a Konkani pandit from Cochin.[26]

'This area is getting so "modern", Udupi, especially. Other places (around) are emptied of Konkanis. Mulki has a beautiful settlement near its Venkatarama temple, but it is almost empty now. The people have gone elsewhere. This is true also of Kallianpur, and other places. . . .' He is referring then to the urbanization of the caste. But there is also overseas migration. The GSB are now spreading out all over the world, says U.A. Kamath. And those who go abroad often become more 'traditional', in the sense of claiming to be traditional. That is very much the case in the GSB community, says U.A. Though the migrants claim to be traditional, however, they are in fact losing their traditions.

Another element in GSB identity is the Goan origins of the community. We have seen the position Goa occupies in GSB historicity: yet perhaps the most salient aspect, and most frequently cited, is the resistance implied by leaving Goa under Christian pressure. K.R. Kuduva, however, puts little stress on Goa but underlines the early presence of Konkanis all along the coast. The import of this view is that their presence as traders predates 'traditional society' so the view of Konkanis as 'immigrants' is false. 'Here, we are in Tulunadu,' says P.R. Kuduva. 'Yet it is wrong to speak of the Tulu, since Tulu is just a language; one should speak of Tuluvas, people from the Tulu country.' This mirrors his unwillingness to use the term Konkani for the GSB. In stressing territory rather than language, he is implicitly reacting against the exclusion of Konkani speakers from the 'people of Tulunadu'.

He links the GSB directly to the Indus Civilization, thus stressing their place at the very roots of Indian culture. The Saraswat community, he says, is the only one found all over India, speaking almost all the regional languages.[27] Here, the GSB are linked to mainstream Brahmanical culture, coming from the north. The views of Bannanje Babu Amin, a Billava author and activist, link Tulu culture to pre-Hindu, Dravidian roots. These views have very different inferences, for example, in relation to Hindutva.

Babu Amin comments on the force of the new, integrative Hinduism. Billavas, he says, are becoming well off, so they are forgeting their traditional culture and adopting 'this' Hinduism. 'Moghaveeras too, they even send their boys to the *maths* now, to become monks.' Mohan Kothiari, a Billava turned tailor, whose 'Ideal tailors' has the monopoly of school uniforms for the Pai schools, is 'very much a Hindu, and has been quite active in the VHP. So many of our people[28] are turning to these people. Actually, they are just inciting the people.'

'Formerly,' says Babu Amin, 'Yakshagana[29] was played by illiterate people, and Brahmins looked down upon it. Now they have captured it, using Sanskrit words we cannot even understand. Now they are talking about Bharata Natyam, Natyashastra.'[30] Babu Amin has his own publishing house, started in 2001,[31] a year before he came back from Mumbai where he spent some years publishing a Kannada newspaper. Of the Brahmins, he says bitterly: 'They have got tongue. They have got power . . . . I am begging for money to publish my books.'[32] The *maths* will sponsor books by Brahmins, but in my community they will not even understand the value of these things.' Then he adds: 'Now even the idea of folklore is being taken over by these people.' Wherever Brahmins are in charge, 'there will be this Brahmanical rhetoric and *Sanskritization*'. But, he says, referring to the *bhuta*-heroes of his own caste, 'Koti-Chennaya was for Billavas only, and they fought injustice.' While the shrines called *bhutasthana* were outside and open to everybody, a *daivasthana*, says Babu Amin, was always placed inside somebody's residence. 'Now these Brahmins have made us build separate *daivasthanas*, to get the benefice of serving at them, by offering *puja*, *brahmakailasha*, and so on. Formerly, the Brahmins would never enter our houses for *puja*.' Thus the *bhuta* cults have been transformed. 'Formerly the shrine was just a plank for the *manju-daiva*[33] and none of the present silver ornaments or masks had been introduced.[34] At that time, people hardly had enough to eat at the beginning of the rainy season. Even a zamindar was a poor man then. So all these things were introduced with the coming of more money and with the Brahmins.'

This Babu Amin sees as a refrain in the history of his community; 'the investment is done by Bunt, Billava – other communities: but the whole investment is appropriated by the Brahmins. Thus, Billavas used to do the puja for the regional snake deity, Nagabrahma: that is why we are called pujaris.'[35] Subramanya, a deity who has an important shrine and pilgrimage centre in the hills of South Kanara, is in his view a 'kind of brahmanized version of Nagabrahma' whose cult has been appropriated by the Brahmins. *Nagamandala* – a very elaborate ritual where snake figures are drawn to an intricate pattern and worshipped with special dances, is, he says, another such example. When he was young,[36] there was a ritual called *ashlesa bari*, offered to Nagadev: it was simpler and much cheaper than *nagamandala*, which was then very rare. 'They (the Brahmins) used to see our pockets first, to see what the client was capable of paying. When some *nagadosa*[37] is there, these Brahmins will decide that *nagamandala* has to be done. We are being looted by these people.' At the oracle of the goddess temple at Ambalpady,[38] the mediums are Billava or Badigara, 'but the Brahmins there try to project themselves as the real representatives of God. Brahmins have insidiously appropriated more and more of our culture – they have spoilt our culture,' he says.

In these contestations, it is mainly the *maths* and the Shivalli Brahmins who are targeted. The GSB have another role, related to economic dominance. Before leaving for Mumbai, Babu Amin worked as a clerk for a GSB company in Car Street. Once his assistant – a GSB, now manager of the company – 'called me for a temple ceremony but I did not go. If I had gone there, I would have to eat separately.[39] I would have to eat in the Pandal area. I told him after eating, you will not allow me to take out the banana leaf, but you will engage a small girl of your community to do that work. I told him I will take whatever I want at my home and be satisfied – I will not come there just to be humiliated, or for other members of my community to be humiliated. My GSB boss was surprised I should be "of that kind". He was a BJP[40] stalwart. So there was some tension.' Babu Amin left the job after two years.

Babu Amin is no kinder to the *maths* or the *sannyasi* orders than he is to the Brahmins. 'When you enter *sannyas,* you should get rid of all (worldly) bonds, you are only allowed to show some respect for your mother. But now, even at the Sringeri *math*, relatives of the Sankaracharya are occupying all the important posts. Some *sannyasis* are even married, but they go back and offer *puja* as if they are in *sannyas.* The Madhava *maths* still have a strong influence in Udupi. They are pretending to be open,' says Babu Amin, 'but in fact they are quite exclusive. Why should we need these people? You can offer *puja* in your own house. If you are a Christian, you can offer *puja* to God yourself. Why should we need these intermediaries?'

Jayashankar Khutpadi, a retired Billava teacher of the Christian High School, stresses the link between Konkanis and corruption. He once had a pupil who wanted to enter the Sharada High School, part of the Pai 'empire'. At that time, Rs. 1 lakh had to be paid as bribe. Jayashankar, an active Congressman, also stresses that many Konkanis are BJP supporters.

There is a saying, says Krishna Bhat, among Shivalli Brahmins:[41] 'If there is dense forest, send the goats.' 'Konkanis are like that, they will clean up everything. They are not straightforward.'[42] 'They are energetic and hard-working,' Bhatt continues, 'but they are not educated. The owner of Diana was like that: *ham gel nao men* – he is our man, is he not?' If you go to the booking agent and you speak Konkani, you will get a ticket: if you don't, you will be told that none is left.' But if other castes tell stories about the Konkanis, the latter return the compliment: There is a proverb, says M.M. Prabhu: 'When a Bunt becomes powerful, he becomes a Ballal: when a watersnake becomes powerful, he becomes a viper.'

My point here is that whenever people in South Kanara hold such views, they come up against the dominant position of the GSB in business and the economy in general. What S.M. Kunder says of the Bank of Canara, others say more generally. The GSB are a privileged group, and they 'stick together' to defend their position. As a dominant group, they are quite naturally criticized and contested by those who try to rise in the hierarchy or change the rules of the game. While others are conscious of being dominated or blocked by GSB solidarity, their opposition reinforces the need for it. Briefly, there is a strong class aspect to the position of the GSB in South Kanara, and this influences both the GSB self-image, their social organization, and the image members of other castes have of them.

Babu Amin stresses that Tulu culture has 'nothing in common' with Brahmanical culture. 'The Tulu culture was the original culture of this land, but it no longer exists in its original form, since it has been influenced by Brahminical culture. We cannot help it,' Amin says. 'It has become a part of ourselves now.' He winks at Mohandas Borkar[43] as he says this, and Borkar winks back, as if both wish to stress that this historical relationship has nothing to do with personal friendship. They were schoolmates and neighbours when they grew up, and are still friends. 'Though,' says Babu Amin, 'I was but a poor cultivator and their family was rich at that time.' Babu Amin stresses that Tulu culture is *aliyasantana* (matrilineal) and that its fundamental beliefs are quite different both from Jain and from mainstream Hindu beliefs. He gave me five books he has written, on various aspects of Tulu culture, including a volume of short stories based on his own experience. Among the many differences he points to between Tulu and Brahmanical culture is the fact that in Tulunadu the dead were buried, not burnt.

I talked to Sadhana Kini about the position of the GSB community in South Kanara. The GSBs and the Tulu activists cannot be compared. She says: 'We have that,' pointing to the sacred cord, 'and they don't, so there can be no direct comparison. The GSB feel they are *the* Brahmins, and so they don't care too much about the others; while the Tuluvas see them as immigrants and outsiders. There is very little contact between the two; they each live in their different worlds,' she says.

I asked the Udupi Kamaths if the Tulu regional movement does not present a problem. U.A. did not see it that way. 'You see, this is a very cosmopolitan area. People are used to dealing with others who are different. N.T. Bhat, former vice-chancellor of MGM and a Shivalli Brahmin, feels the GSB are not really a minority – only in linguistic terms. They are still very strong economically and otherwise. Still, as he put it, 'they like to be under the great Hindu umbrella,' in other words, he agrees that the GSB tend to be among the best supporters of the BJP.

In South Kanara, more than in most regions of India, the autonomy of local cults is strong, and the effort of assimilating them to a pan-Indian, mainstream Hinduism by no means complete.[44] It is arguable that the *bhuta* cults are not Hindu in their origins. They resemble, rather, the spirit cults typical of popular Buddhism, detached from 'proper' Buddhist religion. In South Kanara, the *bhuta* cults may have grown under the aegis of Buddhism or Jainism.[45] Given the importance of these cults, South Kanara is imperfectly or incompletely Hinduized.

To some extent then, what we see reflected in Babu Amin's criticism is the role of Brahmins as Hindu missionaries.[46] They are, as Srinivas might have put it, the emissaries of Sanskritization. What does not emerge from Srinivas' work is the resistance such endeavours meet – and which was as evident to me in Gujarat as it is in South Kanara, even if folk religion there was much closer to what we commonly regard as 'Hinduism'. Rather than taking the 'unity in diversity' of Hinduism for granted, then, we must recognize a continuous and often antagonistic discourse where local elements are, or sometimes are not, taken into the 'Hindu' fold. As one Brahmin remarked of the lower castes in Gujarat: 'I think these people are not Hindus.' To be or not to be a Hindu is not the issue, however, since the category 'Hindu' is a very wide and rather leaky umbrella. The question at the local or regional level is rather: what kind of Hindus are we to be? Quintessential to that question is the position allotted to Brahmins.

In South Kanara, as elsewhere in India, Brahmins control only part of the ritual other castes see as important. As we see from Babu Amin's remarks, to what extent such control is accepted is a matter of debate and quite often of conflict. But this teaches us something fundamental about the Brahmin's position in Hinduism: his claim for spiritual preeminence and ritual expertise is precarious, and needs constantly to be defended. Since Brahmins tend to see themselves as a civilizing influence, however, defense may turn to attack, as Brahmins try to extend their religious influence at the cost of ritual specialists from non-Brahmin castes. This contested expansion is the context of what is today called Hindutva, the identification with a pan-Indian, synthetic 'Hinduism' emblematic, not only for 'Hinduism' as a world religion in opposition to Christianity or Islam, but also for the 'Hindu' nation as an imagined community in Anderson's (1983) sense. The obvious European parallel is the Evangelism of the nineteenth century, which was forceful precisely since it was both an affirmation of the 'converted' and an effort to 'convert' a population not yet seen as properly Christian. The Christian nation was, for nineteenth-century evangelists, a nation in the making they strove to realize: present-day Hindutva and Hindu 'fundamentalism' draw their strength from fighting on a similar, double front, with its visions part of the future, not of the past.[47]

Several communities may be imagined by the same minds. This is paralleled in politics by what emerges from Lobo's work on Konkani Christians. Some were 'freedom fighters' and Gandhians; some supported a specific Christian Independence Party; yet others were elected to seats reserved for the Anglo-Indian community or led Anglo-Indian organizations. Some 'anglicized' their names.[48] This ambiguity also characterizes the role of Konkanis during the colonial period and the independence struggle,[49] with strains and stresses within the community.[50] Is this part of the reason for the 'low-profile' character of Konkani ethnicity? Here, Konkani literature may stand as a politically 'neutral' subject, so interest in language and literature becomes, not just a way to understand the culture of the community, but also the various strategies of asserting ethnicity.

In November and December 2003 there were several processions organized by the BJP or allied groups in Udupi. One procession passed close by while I was talking to K.R. Kuduva in his shop. He did not in any way refer to the demonstration, nor did he leave his shop to observe it. My impression is that many people – not only the GSB – may be voting BJP and supporting the party, but when there is a political demonstration, 'men of substance' – like the GSB merchants – stay away. Perhaps youth or non-working elders from the family are sent to participate, but looking at the manifestations, I do not feel they form an important contribution to them. Most of those taking part give the impression of being from the lower middle class or below, with some youth and a few 'intellectuals' thrown in.

In Karnataka as a whole, the Janata Dal and its several offshots played the leading role in state politics for some time, with various avatars of Congress as their main rivals. In Udupi, however, the main parties in recent times have been the Congress and the BJP. As is usual in India, people tend to associate the parties with caste. The Janata Dal is seen as mainly supported by Bunts, though there are Bunts active in the Congress and in the BJP. The weakness of the Janata Dal in Udupi is relative: it is much stronger in the countryside. Congress has strong support from Billavas, while the BJP is strong among the GSB, though for many years the head of the VHP in South Kanara, often seen as the 'cultural wing' of the Hindu nationalist movement, was Mr. Alva, a Bunt. The Hegde of Dharmasthala – himself a Jain – who may be the most influential individual in the district, is playing a neutral role. 'I make speeches against communalism,' he says. The CPI(M) is weak but has some support in the district, especially among the *bidi* workers.[51] 'They are almost entirely communist' says Dr. Nandavara, former president of the Tulu Academy.

The position of the *maths* in relation to Hindutva varies. 'The Adyar *math's* Swamiji,' says Jayashankar Kuthpadi, 'is purely a religious man, honest and independent; his counterpart at the Pejavur *math*[52] is a strong supporter of the BJP, and has received delegations from the party'.

Dr. Nandavara told us in October 2003 that the RSS was trying to mobilize the Koraga untouchables through the Satyanarayana sect. Other RSS supporters are mainly Brahmins and businessmen,[53] including Konkanis, he says. Nagesh Kini, the printer, said of the early post-Independence period that 'we were all RSS in those days'. Today, many GSB in South Kanara support the BJP.

This support for the Hindu right is of some importance here. The RSS was born from a long line of Hindu conservatives, dating back to the Hindu Mahasabha of the nineteenth century.[54] In 1924 V.D. Savarkar published *Hindutva: Who is a Hindu*, which came to be a fundamental text for Hindu nationalism (Jaffrelot, 1993: 39). Communal riots in Nagpur formed the background to the founding, by Savarkar, of the RSS in 1925. Its leader, Hedgewar, wanted to transcend caste to establish the unity of the Hindu nation. The RSS was conceived as a cadre, trained in a military manner with strict religious norms. The organization is based on the local *shakha*, where members, the *swayamsevak*, practice physical training and, twice a week, follow political classes. From 1927, Hedgewar took the title of *sarsanghachalak,* supreme leader, the saffron flag of Shivaji became the object of a veritable cult, and a corps of officers, *pracharak*, was formed. The *pracharaks* should renounce professional activity and remain unmarried, devoting all their energy to the cause (ibid.: 43-50). Members wear, since 1926, a uniform of khaki shorts, white shirt, and a black cap (ibid.: 63). The movement spread quickly. There were eighteen *shakas* in 1928, more than a hundred in 1932. In 1940, M.S. Golwalkar took over as leader (ibid.: 60-1). Regarded as a guru by his followers, his book *We or Our Nationhood Defined* is the central political text of the movement. Here, the main task is to construct the Hindu nation, while the problematic of the state is left in abeyance. Jaffrelot, in fact, puts us on the guard against an identification of the RSS with European fascism (ibid.: 64-7).

By 1940 the organization claimed 100,000 *swayamsevaks*.[55] Jaffrelot notes that many activists in the Quit India Movement were dissatisfied with the results – British repression but no real progress towards independence. He also notes the attractiveness of the RSS for many Hindus at a time when Muslims were busy mobilizing for a separate state (ibid.: 78).

The disenchantment with the Congress, which grew throughout the 1930s, led to strong support for the RSS among the GSB (Kamath, 1983). The Civil Disobedience Movement that Gandhi started in 1932 declined quickly. From 14,803 in January the number of convictions declined to 2,791 by September, and the movement, by then, had 'ceased to bother the British Government' (ibid.: 51). 'When the Civil Disobedience Movement petered out and was voluntarily withdrawn, Jawaharlal Nehru, among others, felt a sense of "spiritual isolation" and complained to Gandhiji of the toning down of Congress ideals. Gandhiji's answer was that his ideals had not changed and, he said, "I fancy that I have a knack for knowing the need of the time"' (Jaffrelot, 1993: 51-2).

'Did he really?' asks Kamath, pointing to 'simmering discontent' among the rank and file. By October 1934 Gandhi left Congress politics to concentrate on his programme for village development. 'The country resounded to arguments pro and con Gandhiji and his several ideas of rural reconstruction. . . . For each of these questions,

Gandhiji had a clear answer. But his answers only served to raise controversies and even more significantly make people think. What the Mahatma did was to raise the conscience level of the urban elite to higher levels' (Kamath, 1983: 52-3). This may have been the beginning of a process that estranged many GSB from Gandhi and, gradually, from the Congress. Yet in 1937 a Congressman, C.J. Varkey,[56] won the election in South Kanara (ibid.: 53).

'But it was not non-violence alone which was the subject of debate in the four corners of India,' says Kamath. There was the question of what to do in the event of a war. Subhas Chandra Bose felt India must side with the Axis since 'your enemy's enemy is your friend'. Many, says Kamath, especially the young, thought he had a point. Then there was the problem of the Muslim League under Jinnah. When Japan swept through Asia after Pearl Harbour, 'the public was not necessarily out of sympathy with Japan's success; every British reversal was received in many homes with quiet satisfaction. The feeling was that it served the British right. There was also a sneaking respect for the Japanese for being the first Asian power to put the white man in his place' (Kamath, 1983: 54-6).

The main leader of the radical wing was Bose, who had been an important leader of the Congress and its president in 1938-9. On the outbreak of the war he left the Congress to found his own Forward Bloc, feeling that now was 'a golden opportunity to strike a blow at English for the freedom of India' (Vasantha Madhava, 1995: 151). He was arrested, but escaped, and turned up in Berlin in March 1941. Via Japan he went to Singapore, and was welcomed by Rash Behari Bose, president of the Indian Independence League. Rash Behari soon handed over leadership of the INL to Subhas Chandra, and from this base Bose wrought the Indian National Army (INA). He formed a government in exile, which Japan, Germany and Italy recognized, along with Burma, Thailand and Nationalist China. They accompanied the Japanese army to Nagaland, and occupied the Andaman and Nicobar Islands (ibid.: 151-2). In 1943-4, Gandhi's prestige was at a low ebb, and even Nehru thought about breaking with him. At that time 'the heroic deeds of Subhas Bose's Indian National Army were on everybody's lips . . . the arrest of three INA Army commandants . . . had electrified the populace' (Kamath, 1983:

94). Bose's movement collapsed, however, with Japanese withdrawal and defeat, and Bose himself was killed, probably in an air crash, in August 1945.

Bose's adventurous career made him a hero. He 'acquired a halo of martyrdom and apotheosis,' says Vasantha Madhava (1995: 152). The trial of 20,000 INA prisoners at the Red Fort in 1945 led to protests all over India.[57] The trials were followed by a mutiny in the Navy (ibid.: 160-1). Clearly, the radical nationalists had an appeal well beyond a minority of extremists. In his biography of T.A. Pai, Kamath notes that 'many of Anant's friends hailed the emergence of Netaji – as Subhas Bose came to be known – and there was debate whether Netaji's stand in seeking Japanese assistance to win freedom for India was the right one' (1983: 88). Then came the Quit India Movement of 1942. The repression of that period is not our subject here, but as we have seen, this movement too petered away.

As a young boy, Rajni Kothari, the political scientist, was active in the Quit India Movement: he participated in youth rallies, 'held street-corner meetings, picketed school-going boys and girls and even tried my hand in some semi-violent activities such as derailing British goods trains. . . .' 'On my return to Bombay,' he says,

> I found myself not fully satisfied with the way Independence was negotiated,[58] not just because of the traumatic division of the country into two but also because of my being influenced by more radical streams in the student and youth movements that were associated with the immediate post-1942 period. The return of the leaders of the Indian National Army (INA) led by Netaji Subhash Chandra Bose in South-East Asia and the release of highly inspiring individual leaders like Jayaprakash Narayan, Aruna Asaf Ali, Achyut Patwardhan, Ram Manohar Lohia, who had been associated with the 1942 struggle, inspired many of us. I was also to some extent drawn towards the RIN mutiny . . . the British had tried to suppress it through a massive display of violence . . . though young, I found myself enlisted partly as volunteer and partly as a budding radical youth. I had for a while joined Subhash Bose's Forward Bloc, associated myself with the Left wing of the Student's Federation and in small steps started taking part in the trade union movement. To some extent, all this may have happened in fits and starts but, seen together, it was all part of a continuous process of awakening among the youth of the day. (Kothari, 2002: 78-9)

A Westerner may be surprised at the combination of support for Bose – whom we remember as 'the Indian who sided with the Japanese' – and left-wing activism. But a shrewd observer like Kothari should make us see the situation a little differently. The main item on the agenda, in 1942,[59] was to get rid of the British, and impatience or even exasperation with regard to Gandhian methods would seem to have been widespread, especially among the youth. They wanted more radical action, and this made socialist leftism or Bose's military way seem part of the same basic alternative. The feeling of a possible 'sell-out' by acceptation of a separate Pakistan, was another point uniting many who were becoming critical of the Congress.

The harsh measures adopted by the British against the Quit India movement strengthened the radical wing among the nationalists. One of these leaders was Jayaprakash Narayan, who repudiated Gandhi's non-violent views. Escaping from jail, he trained a guerrilla force – the Azad Dasta – in Nepal. Arrested in May 1943, he was liberated by his associates, and left for Kolkata, where he tried to establish contact with the Azad Hind Movement. He was arrested again, however, in December 1943 (Vasantha Madhava, 1995: 149-50). JP, as he came to be known later, would continue to play a role on the Indian political scene: his anti-corruption campaigns were the beginnings of unrest in Bihar and Gujarat in 1973-4, which incited Indira Gandhi to introduce a state of Emergency later. Another 'terrorist', Siaram Singh, was active in Bihar till 1944 (ibid.: 150). Closer to home for the GSB, but probably farther from them in political terms, the Kisan Sabha and the Communists led peasant unrest in Kasaragod district – now in Kerala, but then in South Kanara, and part of the Tulu-speaking area – and four of their leaders were hanged in 1943 (ibid.).

So, when Independence came, many may have felt, like young Kothari, that it was a kind of 'phoney independence' (Kothari, 2002: 97). This does not explain why many GSB in Udupi were becoming RSS supporters, but it provides us with a background and helps redefine our Western stereotypes of what was happening in India at the time. Nagesh Kini is probably right when he says that Gandhian policies, which seemed right in the 1930s, no longer appeared so to many Udupi GSB by the 1940s. The RSS, incarnating Hindu values and opposed to the Partition of India, eschewed the compromises

Congress had negotiated with the British, while as merchants, the GSB had no reason to support socialist ideas.[60]

Still, there was much support for the Congress in Udupi among the GSB as among other castes. The Tonse Pai family seems to have supported Congress, as T.A. Pai did later. But then the issue of reservation which, as we have seen, may have been among the factors that inspired T.M.A. to create his empire of colleges at Manipal, took on a new aspect after the Mandal Commission's report in 1980.[61]

South India had been in advance of the north regarding the establishment of positive discrimination for depressed or backward castes, a policy first instituted in the princely state of Mysore in 1921. In Madras Presidency, the Justice Party had worked for similar reforms since 1920, and non-Brahmin quotas were introduced by the Congress government in 1937. From 1950, such quotas were seen to conflict with the Constitution. Locally, most opposition to the quotas came from Brahmins, and we may assume that the GSB were among them. The state of Karnataka, formed in 1956, thus inherited a long-standing debate, and radical quotas were introduced from 1959. But in the famous Balaji case of 1963, the Supreme Court invalidated the measure. New attempts to introduce quotas followed in 1967 and 1968, but were again judged unconstitutional by the courts. In 1972, Chief Minister Devraj Urs again raised the issue and quotas were established, followed by court cases: the politics of positive discrimination were finally established by 1983. Less than half the posts in government service were now open to applicants on merit (Jaffrelot, 2005: 266-76). These conflicts certainly influenced the GSB electorate, and probably many left the Congress as the party supported the quota system in the 1980s.

When she came to South Kanara, Sadhana Kini had no links to any party and no political experience, though she had long been active in 'social work'.[62] Since she was known for such activity she was asked to stand for election by the Congress I. She was approached by the BJP too, she says. She won the election; and now 'there is no looking back'. But it feels natural to her that she should be in the Congress I; she would not have joined the BJP.

Sadhana Kini was elected to the *taluka* council. On 1 January 2004, she took over responsibility for public finances. I remarked to her how road works seemed to crop up everywhere now, and I asked whether this had anything to do with her new responsibility. 'Yes', she said without hesitation. She clearly saw herself as 'cleaning up' earlier misuse of money, to 'get the work done'.[63]

Her activity in the Mahila Samaj seems important to her. Asked what the Samaj is doing, she says that depends on the president. Some Samaj are simply socializing, some spend their time in discussion meetings, some receive grants from government to do social work, mainly in health care or nutrition programmes for mother and child. The latter is her choice. I asked whether ideas from Western feminism had entered these associations. 'Not at all,' she said, adding that such ideas were of no relevance here.

I mentioned the support for the BJP, and earlier involvement of the GSB with the RSS. 'Yes,' she said, 'most of the GSB are now supporting the BJP. But this is mostly the Congress' own fault. The reservation policies are responsible for it. You must know that there are several classes of reservation: SC, ST, Backward A, Backward B, and the problem is that there is very little left for the "general" category. In fact, here in South Kanara, the only communities that fit into this "general" category are the Shivalli Brahmins (they are almost all BJP) and the GSB. So naturally the GSB oppose these reservations.'[64] Kini spoke out against reservation before accepting to stand for elections, so the party knew her position, but selected her anyway. She continues to speak against the reservation policy. 'Before the reservation policy came into it,' she says, 'the GSB were all Congressmen – so many prominent GSB were active in the Congress.' Mr. Nayak, however, her visitor from Bantwal and a family friend, remarks that the Jan Sangh was, as he puts it, also created by the GSB: he feels the right-wing position of the community is not new. To Kini, however, it was the reservation question that estranged the GSB from the Congress.

Kini may exemplify opposition to the Tonse Pais from within their own community. We may remember the story about the school for mentally handicapped children, which she sees as typical of 'charity' in South Kanara. Even the funds of that school were not put up by the Pais, but by the Lion's Club. 'This is true of most of the Manipal institutions,' she says. 'The funds really came from elsewhere, outside donators, state grants and private contributions, etc. The Pais put up very little themselves. So what is called "social work" is sometimes mainly show."[65]

She did not mention the Emergency and its attendant conflicts, but commented on the election of Oscar Fernandes, who defeated T.A. Pai. To her, this was partly a rejection of the Pais: people were opposing their 'monopoly' on important institutions. Oscar Fernandes was elected as a complete outsider to the Pai empire. To Kini, his being a Christian has very little to do with his popularity and his re-election since. He does, however, appeal to people as an 'outsider' to major local power blocks, such as the *maths* or the Pais. In her analysis at least, it is not caste but rather competition between these power blocks that characterizes Udupi politics.

What, then, does caste, class and ethnicity mean to the GSB? They all make sense to members of the community, but only as aspects of a GSB identity that transcends each one of them. To say that somebody belongs to a caste makes little sense in India: everybody does, and to characterize identity we must know what that caste is like. The three letters 'G, S, B' unite some of the caste's central characteristics: they are Brahmins, they are Saraswats, and they come from the North. All these are important references for identity, but only a particular combination of them makes a GSB. Then, no description of GSB identity is complete without the merchant element: the GSB are business Brahmins. As such, they have not only a long history manifest through *gotra*, *pravara*, *shakha* and *veda*, but another one, as a merchant bourgeoisie contributing in their own way to the history of their part of India. And of course they do not simply have a culture – they see themselves as cultured, and the vehicle of this culturedness is their Konkani language, which links up with the memory of Goa. In this listing of elements, we find caste, class and ethnicity as anthropologists see them, but none of these alone can account for the specific cluster of identity elements that make a GSB.

NOTES

1. These criteria, briefly cited, are as follows: (1) a common culture, belief, and practice, as well as some common interests, (2) significant differences from the surrounding society in these respects, (3) a consciousness of

separate identity and identification with the community, (4) a community must be effective as a collectivity in social, political, and/or economic life and finally, (5) it must be able to reproduce itself (Carrithers and Humphrey, 1991: 6-7).

2. This is particularly true of point (4) above (note 1), where the authors add that 'the community must, as such, be a distinct causal agent' (Carrithers and Humphrey, 1991: 6), but reification is also implied by (1) and (2), since, to paraphrase from Barth's view of ethnicity (1969), it is not 'objective' cultural differences, but the way people stress and use them – or even invent them – that produces boundaries between groups.
3. I said that caste seemed to be more important for the Banias of Gujarat, for example, and he seemed to agree.
4. Conlon's work (1977) on the Chitrapur Saraswats shows precisely how that caste tried to evolve a collective identity through associations. It is not that such associations are absent among the GSB, but that other factors seem equally important. I would stress that their businesses and commercial importance offers the GSB alternative ways of manifesting their presence. The Chitrapur Saraswats, employed mainly in bureaucracy and clerical work, do not have the same facility.
5. Yet, if we believe the testimonies of people like Kundar, the GSB in the banks are very conscious of who is an 'insider' and who is not.
6. Conlon, writing of the Saraswats, says 'there was little question at the time about whom the Konkanis had to overtake' (1977: 97). The Saraswat school had begun classes in 1867. But when they tried to have their college recognized as 'first-class' in 1892, the application was rejected. The Catholic Saint Aloysius college had received this distinction in 1887 (ibid.: 90-2).
7. Perhaps it is a sign of the times that the Dharmasthala combine is now the most dynamic socio-religious force in South Kanara.
8. Thus, he says, 'Pandiraj Ballal – their *bidu* is between Mudabidri and Karkal – owns the big tourist hotel in Mudabidri, one posh hotel on Mount Road, Chennai, and a tourist bus company.'
9. Contrary to a common idea among Westerners, haggling is not a common practice among professional merchants in India, though it is done at particular places, such as vegetable or fish markets. The professional merchant works to fixed prices, from which he may deduce a 'commission' for a good customer.
10. P.P.C. College, founded and owned by the *maths*, lies at the southern end of VT Street. PPC College Road runs from the southern end of VT Street to the fishmarket. It is a residential road with little commerce, so

Mr. Kunder depends for customers on those already familiar with him and his shop.

11. A Patil was a tax collector. Each Patil would have been responsible for the taxes of his part of the village.
12. This was the first high school in Udupi, founded by the Basel Mission. It has brought education to the lower castes, though at one time it served the GSB and other high castes, being the only school of its kind in Udupi.
13. The Syndicate Bank headquarters were then at the corner of the main street and Court Road in Udupi itself, on the old lands of the Mukund Nivas. The headquarters at Manipal had not yet been built.
14. I talked with Mr. Kunder in the autumn of 2003, when Ramesh was still alive. He died in January 2005.
15. Fourth floor, he said, next to 'Kalpana'.
16. There all said to be four castes among them: Bamjano, converted from the Brahmin community; Charos (sometimes identified with kshatriyas), converted from Bunts, Jains and others; Sudhir, who are converted shudras; and finally Gaudi, who are untouchables converted to Christianity. Almost all Catholics in this region are Konkani speakers, while the Protestants generally speak Tulu.
17. Chitrakar Saraswats 'are our brothers, they left because of conflict about a *math* three hundred years ago' (see Conlon, 1977), says P.R. Kuduva, 'They were excommunicated some three hundred years ago. They were known as the Shenapanche – the five *gotras* of Shenoys.' Now there is no conflict with them, he says, so intermarriage is possible. 'Just like there is no bar between Smartas and Madhavas. Now the Chitrakar Saraswats have six *gotras*, while the GSB have eighteen. The sixth *gotra* joined the Chitrakar Saraswats later. All Chitrakars were originally called Shenoy. Now they are known by the village of their ancestors, though unlike the GSB they put it at the end of the name, instead of at front.' The RSB, however, are considered lower than the GSB and marriage with them would be impossible, says P.R. Kuduva.
18. The Navayats do not really enter the discourse on Konkani identity – they do not stress any link with other Konkani-speaking communities except that of language. Rather, they stress their *vilayati* ('foreign' or 'Western') connections, as descendants of Islamic immigrants. For a discussion of the category Navayat, see Kolenda, 1996.
19. I use this term here to denote the ancestors both of the GSB and the Chitrapur Saraswats.
20. Both alphabets are still used for writing Konkani, along with the Kannada

script and the Urdu alphabet, by different communities and in different regions.

21. The president of the Konkani Academy was then Father Alexander d'Souza, who had replaced Basti J. Shenoy. The academy alternates between GSB and Catholic presidents. Shenoy wrote a book on the Indus Valley Civilization, a significant point in view of the claimed origins of the GSB. Father d'Souza, a diocesan priest from a Puttur family, was director of Father Müller's Hospital in Mangalore for many years. On his retirement the Karnataka government appointed him as president of the academy. The academy's publication programme stresses culture, language and literature. Father d'Souza stresses the importance of the Konkani dialects: among the books recently published is the *Konkani Samabtara Shabdakosha*, a comparative dictionary of Konkani dialects. The publications of the academy are all printed in Kannada script, but the GSB writers use their own dialect, while the Catholics use theirs.
22. RSB Konkani is quite different from GSB Konkani, says Sunil Borkar. 'You may say it is closer to Marathi.' It is 'purer' he says, and has less slang-like expressions. Christian and GSB Konkani are mutually intelligible, but they are immediately recognizable by any Konkani speaker.
23. 'For cloth', he says, 'they say "*vastr*" while GSB say "*goellan*"– or else we use the Hindi word "*kapad*".'
24. The *bhattil*, the way of life of the Kashmiri Pandits, 'is constituted of fundamental purposes of life – the *purusartha* or *abhipraya* – largely centered in domestic life,' says Madan (1987: 233-4). There is clearly a parallel here.
25. It is a way of decorating the walls of the house, by whitewashing them, then painting them ochre. Finally the ochre is scratched away to form designs of gods and other objects, which stand out in white against the ochre.
26. Among Konkanis, *pandit* means a learned man. But in Tulunadu and Kerala, it means an Ayurvedic *vaid*, as it does here.
27. He mentions Konkani, Marathi, Gujarati, Rajasthani, Punjabi, Kashmiri, Hindi (up to Bihar and Orissa), and Bengali. The latter is contested by others.
28. Billava and other low castes.
29. A traditional sung theatre form, danced in particular costumes and to a sustained rhythm, which has become part of the established 'folklore' of the region.
30. Bharata Natyam is a form of classical Indian dance. *Natyashastra* is the Sanskrit commentary on dance.

31. The publishing house is called the Kemmalaje Janapada Prakashana.
32. He is a prolific author on subjects of Billava uplift.
33. House spirit.
34. This is clear from the Airodys' collection of old *bhuta* cult objects, much simpler than what is seen today.
35. *Pujari* (those who do *puja*) is used as a synonym for Billava. The latter term, 'archer' alludes to the caste's role as warriors for the landowning Bunts.
36. Thirty or forty years ago.
37. *Nags* (snakes) are autochthonous deities who should be venerated, but it is hard to make sure that they are satisfied. *Nagadosa* are afflictions cast on people by offended *nags*. The cure lies in ritual to satisfy them.
38. A few kilometres south-west of Udupi.
39. The Billavas were formerly seen as untouchables, a status now contested, since thay have improved their position considerably in recent years.
40. Babu Amin used the term BJP, but that party did not exist then. The boss was, he explained later, active in the Jan Sangh, historically one of the parties that was later to unite in the BJP.
41. Krishna Bhat is himself a Shivalli.
42. 'They used to be like that: now it has changed,' he adds.
43. It was Mohandas Borkar who took us to see Babu Amin.
44. We found it difficult to explain to the participants in the Annual Conference of the Kolkata Institute of Historical studies, held in Udupi in 2003, what exactly the *bhutas* were. Participants were ready to accept them as folkloristic spirits; it proved practically impossible to explain that they are the major figures of regional Hinduism. Exempt from this failure to understand the regional pattern were the delegates from Kerala, who recognized in the *bhutas* similar figures known to Kerala Hinduism.
45. Thus the conference delegates show a typical reaction of mainstream Hindus to such phenomena.
46. There is a traditional view that 'Hinduism' is not a missionary religion. This position misses a large part of the dynamics of Indian religious life, today and yesterday, as well as ignoring the very active missionary work of several Hindu sects in the West in recent times.
47. I do not imply some sort of 'evolutionary lag' by comparing nineteenth-century Europe to the India of today. Similar historical forces may be at work at different periods and in different regions: it does not follow that they correspond to some 'stage' in a common process. Still, the process of national integration, which characterized nineteenth-century Europe, is an important element in today's India. Like many nineteenth-century

European elites, the Brahmins in India tend to feel they have a particular role to play in this process.

48. The Lewis family (originally Luis) is a typical example.
49. Oliver Lewis' alluded to his grandfather being a 'policeman for the British' during Second World War. The grandson implies that this was problematic in relations to those who stood for Independence.
50. See below for the RSS involvement of GSB.
51. It is a home industry, and they work on contract – 2-3 days a week – earning perhaps Rs. 1,500 a month.
52. Who took over the responsibility for the Krishna temple from the beginning of the year 2005.
53. They are of course rivals of the Muslim businessmen, who are mostly Congress supporters.
54. Jaffrelot (1993) is brief on these beginnings, but some of the factors involved have been dealt with in Carrin and Tambs-Lyche, 2008.
55. British intelligence estimated the number at 60,000.
56. Professor at St. Aloysius College in Mangalore.
57. One lakh demonstrators took to the streets in Kolkata, demanding release of the prisoners. A second demonstration followed in February 1946.
58. 'Both because the 1942 movement entered a low ebb and because of the news of Gandhi, Nehru, Patel, Azad and other national leaders being released from jail for engaging in negotiations with the British' (Kothari, 2002: 78).
59. 1942 was the year of the Cripps Mission, when the British promised Dominion status to India after the war. Gandhi called this a 'post-dated cheque upon a crashing bank', and the Congress reverted to its non-cooperation stance, launching the Quit India Movement (Vasantha Madhava, 1995: 140).
60. The alliance between Nehruvian socialism and the 'national bourgeoisie' has been discussed profusely in the literature. But small business could not benefit from such an alliance in the same way as the big conglomerates.
61. The Mandal Commission had been appointed in 1978 by Morarji Desai, prime minister of the then Janata government. The commission recommended very extensive quotas for the OBC. Its report was published in 1980, but it was not acted upon by Indira Gandhi's government. Its recommendations were, however, adopted by V.P. Singh's coalition government in 1989.
62. She has no need for a job, she says, so she has time – and since her husband was a bank manager, 'there is plenty of money'.
63. Her comments on politics were given in the last chapter.

64. I understand that she sees a big difference between the SC/ST reservations, which may be defended, and the 'backward' reservations, which cannot, at least to their present extent.
65. Even the ubiquitous bus stop sheds, said to be put up by such and such a donor (Lions Club, Kalkuda Foundation, etc.), are largely paid for by state or taluka funds. Such a shed cost about Rs. 50,000; the donation may be Rs. 20,000, and the public funds pay the rest. So the public contribution goes unheeded. To her, it would be better if everything was paid by public funds, equally paid for and accessible to all.

Conclusion

There are, we have seen, several Konkani-speaking communities in South Kanara. All these groups tend to be seen as 'outsiders' or 'immigrants' by Tulu speakers, and in spite of this diversity, the term 'Konkani' is used in common parlance as a synonym for the GSB community. The significance of the term is clear: to Tulu speakers, Konkanis are immigrants, and remain so in spite of their long-standing presence in South Kanara. As noted, flight or emigration from Goa is central to the GSB image of themselves, yet members of the community were present in coastal Karnataka, and in Kerala, well before the Portuguese came. The earliest references go back to the thirteenth century, and even those who arrived in the eighteenth hardly qualify as recent immigrants: many of us would probably be immigrants in this sense. Why then do Konkanis become outsiders to an area where they have lived so long? Marking them as outsiders can hardly be referred to 'immigration' in any common sense of the word. Rather, the Konkanis are intrinsic others, an otherness more comparable to the identity some Europeans have bestowed on Jews.

The Tulu movement is central to any understanding of the region South Kanara, and Tulu speakers eagerly volunteer numerous details about their 'culture'. The welter of *bhutas* correspond to our stress on myth and historicity, for the word *bhuta* is said to derive from the Sanskrit stem *bhu*, to exist, a translation of *bhuta* being 'the one who has been'. Anthropomorphic *bhutas* are seen as humans deified on or after their death, and in some cases – notably Koti and Chennaya – their life is commonly seen as historically attested.[1] Even when not tied to historic events, *bhutas* are closely linked to the landscape, which abounds in places where a *bhuta* performed some particular feat or passed through on the way to some nodular event in myth. Thus the *bhuta* cult is not easily transposable to other regions; on the other hand it sanctifies Tulunadu as the scene of religiously significant events, underlining the importance of the *bhuta* cult for the regional consciousness and for the Tulu Movement.

This movement then constructs Tulunadu as a proto-nation, a land with its own religion, culture, language and social system. This construction is complete in itself, with its own tradition of social justice manifest when the royal *bhutas* incarnate in oracles and hold court during the *nema*. The order is exclusive, however, for by implication those who reside in Tulunadu but do not share in its culture are outsiders. This affects a number of groups, not just the GSB but also the Konkani-speaking Catholics, the Protestants (who are largely converted Billavas), the Muslims (of whom there are several distinct groups) and the various 'immigrants' from other parts of Karnataka who speak Kannada rather than Tulu. This division of insiders *versus* outsiders largely explains why the GSB, with their long residence in the area, are still spoken of as 'immigrants'.

Tulu society, even in this narrow sense, is not hermetically closed, however. There are a number of links both to larger Hindu society and to specific groups. Thus the Protestant missionaries have been important in the work to make Tulu language known: the dictionary written by Männer (1886) was long the main source on the language, and the earliest printed literature in Tulu – as well as the first printing press in the region – was the work of the Basel missionaries.[2] The existence of Muslims is recognized in the *bhuta* cults: Bobbariya, the seafaring *bhuta*, was the son of a Muslim father and a Jain mother, and representatives of Muslim communities may be present and take the *bhuta's prasad* in many local rituals. Jains indeed have a long history of integrating the *bhuta* cults in their own ritual complex: *bhutas* then commonly become the guardians (*kshetrapalas*) of their own *tirthankaras*, and at least one *rajandaiva* – Ullalti – is said to have been a Jain princess. In fact, the Jains are mostly Tulu speakers[3] and there are Jains active in the Tulu Movement, though they do not share the central position of Bunts and Billavas.

The Konkani Catholics largely remain external, but there are links between the GSB and the *bhuta* cults, as we have seen in the case of the Gurupur temple. Most clearly, when the GSB own land, they generally honour the cult of the *bhuta* attached to the land. Some individuals or families – like the Yeltimar Shenoys of Puttur – even choose a *bhuta* as their *ishtadevata*, though this is unusual. The Airody family has for generations been main suppliers of *bhuta* images in Udupi, and do not seem to discriminate between the production and sale of these figurines and those of the all-Indian gods, which also they sell. They have, we remember, a private museum of cult objects – including those for the *bhuta* cults – which underlines their image as particularly devout Hindus. For the moment, let me simply note the existence of such links, in spite of the 'immigrant' status of the GSB community.

The existence of several groups who are outsiders to the ideological construct of a Tulu society, yet parties to the actual functioning of social organization in the region poses a problem for our analysis. Should we accept that there is one 'caste system' concomitant with the construction of Tulu society which excludes important groups? Or should we take the total division of labour in the region as our point of departure, viewing the assertions of a 'Tulu society' solely as an example of political ethnicity within the 'system'? May we legitimately accept the term 'system' for the cluster of Tulu-speaking castes, where important social functions, notably those of the merchants, are lacking? Clearly, the problems we run into here imply that there is something wrong with our initial presuppositions.

Among such presuppositions is the idea that a region coincides with a bounded social system. The concrete problem here, with regard to India, is that the groups that constitute a regional caste order do not share the same boundaries. The GSB, present along the belt from Goa to southern Kerala, have a distribution that goes well beyond South Kanara, where Bunts are dominant. Though Billavas are found in most of the area, they are heavily concentrated towards the coast: the Moghaveera fishermen even more so. Inland, in fact, considerable labour is done by immigrants from Kerala. The actual mix of castes therefore varies considerably, even within Tulunadu. This exemplifies the general problem: caste territories do not coincide, and what seems a coherent boundary to one group may not be so to another.

Secondly, holist constructions of caste 'systems' – regional or pan-Indian – are themselves part of arguments about the social order, sustained by group interests. This, I argue, is true not only of regional constructions such as that of the Tulu regionalists, but equally so of integrist, Brahmin-centred views of the Hindu nation at the pan-Indian level – a perspective many GSB share. Nor is this point true only for India. When Western sociologists (Davis and Moore, 1945) tried to introduce a functional theory of stratification, seeing society as a system where the rewards of any category corresponded to the functional importance of their contribution, critics soon put their finger on the sore point: who defines that importance? Clearly, those in power tend to do so, and labour or peasant movements contest their judgement. Briefly, in any local context, dominant groups are likely to refer to different holistic constructions as part of their argument while contesting groups stress division or conflict, and so the holistic views cannot be seen as common to the various communities, even on the regional level.

We do better, then, in reserving a place in ideology for assertions about bounded, systemic wholes, while regarding social systems as such as basically open and unbounded. This means that we have to identify the processes that generate systemic regularities from within, rather than deducing functional specificity from a higher level limited by boundaries, as Dumont (1966) and most theorists of caste as a system including Quigley (1993), have done.

More generally for India, there is an identification with the collective 'we',[4] which shows the importance of family and caste as categories of reference, and tends to mask the importance of the individual.[5] The GSB are a community eminently conscious of, and interested in, their own history, and several families have maintained genealogies or commissioned genealogists to write their family history. This historicity is a central element in the construction both of individual and group identities, as also in the construction of the 'imagined community' (Anderson, 1983) of the caste. It lends to group identity a number of particular qualities, which certainly strengthen community feeling but also works to underline the image that other castes in the area has of the GSB as 'immigrants'.

The reference to history in constituting identities is more than mere identification with the past. As Inden notes (1976), patrilineal continuity, coupled with the results of consecutive marriages, produces the 'substance' of the family, of which the individual is a part (Tambs-

Lyche, 1995: 138-9). It is as if the Indian individual – certainly, a large number of the GSB I met – are conscious of the potted history of the habitus that Bourdieu (1984) takes as largely unconscious.[6] In other words, while the Western individual of whom Bourdieu writes is largely an unconscious product of the history that delimits his field of action, the historicity present in GSB culture makes these limitations conscious. It is on this level that I, for one, tend to doubt the 'individualism' of Western culture, unless a lack of historical consciousness is regarded as such.[7]

Historicity, then, is not external to the organization of the GSB community, but an integral part of the consciousness of its members. I have argued elsewhere that grasping this historicity is fundamental to our understanding of Indian society, not least what is known as the caste system (2004: 11-17). It strongly influences what Bourdieu would call the 'habitus' of the society's members (1972, 1980). I am sceptical to that concept, however: in trying to exclude rational choice from action patterned on tried and known practice, Bourdieu seems to me to evade the question of intermediary or limit states, where the actor hardly knows whether he is doing one or the other. It seems to me that much of our deliberation takes the form of choice between forms of action which we perceive as 'rational', but which are strongly conditioned by a common sense which derives as much from habit-inspired schemas felt to 'make sense' as from a rational calculation of consequences. The latter are, I feel, as rare as the unquestioned carrying out of established practice – for the latter, in most cases, presents itself as one of several alternatives. Viewed in this way, the concept of habitus certainly manages to include patterns of deliberation that go beyond what Barth (1966) calls rational choice. But Barth's approach becomes far more inclusive if we substitute 'reasoned' for 'rational', which seems to me a better term on close reading of Barth's essay. Reasoned choice would include both calculating behaviour in choosing a car, and the more whimsical decision to try a new kind of beer because it seems to fit a particular mood.[8] This discussion might seem ephemeral, were it not for the fact that so many of my GSB informants like to do, and often actually do, things in a 'traditional' manner – something which is very evident when looking at their shops. On this point, we are reminded of

Madan's Kashmiri Brahmins, with their constant reference to *bhattil*, the Brahmin way of doing things (Madan, 1987: 30-2). There is, among the GSB a constant reference to tradition – to 'culture maintained' or 'culture lost' – which in its turn is strongly related to historicity. Thus we might infer that the traditional character of so many GSB businesses is due to a preference of tried and tested ways of doing things – until we discover that the same family, in some other shop, has gone in for blatant modernity. We then realize that reasoned choice is at work, as when icons are sold from very traditional locales while groceries are sold by the same people from the town's most modern supermarket. The choice here seems to be founded in ideas about customer preferences, and becomes part of business strategy rather than habitus. And yet, as we have discussed earlier, this strategy of hedging the bets between new but daring and safe but moderately profitable activities, seems typical of Indian merchants to a point where it may, in itself, be seen as part of their habitus in Bourdieu's sense.

Thus, most of the GSB I met seem highly conscious of belonging to a long line of members of a specific, delimited community with whom they share and are seen as sharing certain values and dispositions. As Bourdieu stresses in his exposition of the habitus concept, however, this belonging only determines individual choice in so far as it is the base from which such choices are made, and as such constitutes the point of view from which the individual may survey a landscape of possibilities.[9] Thus habitus, here, implies a restricted view: we are far from the ideal of the economic actor, having access to all relevant information in making a choice. In preferring the notion of reasoned choice, I take into account the restrictions – cognitive as well as circumstantial – acting on the individual when he surveys alternative modes of action.[10]

With these qualifications, I have used here the perspective of the strategic actor as a general methodical tool, an actor involved in a web of relationships interpreted in the transactional mode (Barth, 1966). Such an approach leads directly to the questions posed by Barth with regard to ethnicity, i.e. how the cultural difference between members of a community and outsiders are organized and maintained (Barth, 1969). Many of the questions I ask in this volume, then, are those I tried to answer in an earlier work on the Patidar immigrants from Gujarat in London (Tambs-Lyche, 1980). There, I tried to show that the separateness of the community was in fact useful to the individual Patidar in several ways, rendering possible the evaluation of own conduct in a matrix of values different from that of the encompassing British society. It also opened the way to numerous types of career, built on specific transactional relationships within the community – careers that would not have been possible without the protective barrier constituted by the ethnic boundary.[11] Similar perspectives are, to some extent, applicable to the 'immigrant' community of the GSB in South Kanara. But there are differences, some of which stem from the nature of the encompassing society itself, while others have to do with history. The Patidars had been present in Britain at most twenty years when I lived among them, while the history of the GSB in South Kanara goes back hundreds of years. Still, their exclusion from Tulu Society and their consciousness of their Goan past makes the GSB acutely conscious of their distinction from the surrounding, or as I put it in the earlier work – the encompassing society.

There are indeed important differences between British society and the variant of Indian society we find in South Kanara. There are also significant differences in class position as between the London Patidars around 1970, when I studied them, and the Kanarese GSB. The former still belonged, for the larger part, to the working class, though they exhibited the values and aspirations of the middle class and were consciously engaged in an effort to achieve upward mobility (Tambs-Lyche, 1980: 130-4). The GSB on their part mainly belong to the established bourgeoisie: it may even be held that in South Kanara, the GSB are the bourgeoisie *par excellence,* economically and culturally. They are no longer upwardly mobile: they are comfortably close to the top and have been so at least since colonial times.

Readers used to the description of Indian society in terms of caste may be surprised by this reference to class. Yet by any standards, class – whether seen in Marxian or Weberian terms[12] – is an important dimension of Indian society. The person who, dressed in an impeccable white shirt and neatly creased trousers, steps out of his new car is immediately identified as 'middle-class', while his caste may not be known. Incomes and living standards are as much a part of daily discourse as are questions of caste, and the ever-present fear, among the Indian middle classes, of losing or weakening their economic position is as evident to the observer as considerations of caste.[13]

The specificity of Indian society, however, is precisely the concern with 'status groups' as Weber might have termed the castes, whose members are seen as sharing inherited qualities and a number of common values. In England, generalizations about working-class and middle-class values served my analysis well. In India, such simplification is neither desirable nor possible. It is necessary, therefore, to discuss here the particularities of what we generally refer to as 'the caste system'.[14]

There is ample evidence of the importance of caste, but far less obvious is how we should conceive of the 'system', and to what extent is there a 'system' at all. The efforts Dumont (1966) made to show an inherent logic generating an ordered hierarchy have been amply criticized since (Bailey, 1959; Berreman, 1961; Béteille, 1990). As I see it, Dumont's main problem was his attempt to derive the empirical pattern of social organization from an analysis of ideology, mediated by structures which, as Lévi-Strauss (1952) has underlined, are basically imposed by the anthropologist's interpretation, rather than by the material itself. The empirical constellations of caste are in fact highly variable, and an interpretation in Dumont's terms would lead us to consider a large number of deviations from the 'standard' pattern. On the other hand, if we try to generate these various patterns directly from the sociopolitical conditions of each region, we do indeed miss Dumont's central point: there is something common to caste hierarchies all over India, manifest in the tendency, ever present, to order the various groups hierarchically. It seems to me that the problem can be solved only by separating ideological constructions from sociopolitical conditions. While a certain commonality of caste ideology is present everywhere India, this ideology coexists with very different empirical situations.

With these reservations, we can indeed learn from Dumont, and it is in my view a mistake to throw out his analyses of caste ideology with the bathwater of structural functionalism in which it is submerged. What we should retain, I feel, is his insistence on a hierarchical view of social relations, leading actors to order interaction into sets of superiors and inferiors.[15] We should also accept that many actors tend towards a holistic view of society, in which the ritual division of labour implies a complementarity of tasks inherent in the maintenance of the social order, and in which certain precepts rank these tasks hierarchically. Central to Dumont's analysis is the superiority of the Brahmin, due to the latter's responsibility for the maintenance of the cosmic and social order, viewed as two aspects of a single whole. This is what, in Dumont's view, gives preeminence to religion and priesthood over the exercise of worldly power and authority. I would hold that this is the essence of an ideological position found all over Hindu India, though its importance may vary. What Dumont failed to see and critics like Berreman (1961) pointed out from the start, is that this is an ideology largely held by Brahmins – and rather obviously related to their own interest – rather than a world-view shared by Indians of all castes. For the GSB, however, the preeminence of the Brahmin is a central ideological precept, in no way invalidated by its contestation by various other communities.[16]

What Dumont gave insufficient attention to is that other castes or 'estates' have other points of view, as I have underlined in my work on Saurashtra (1997, 2004). Thus Rajputs and other dominant castes there tend to construct a hierarchical order centred on their own authority, a view closer to Hocart's or Quigley's view of the caste system (Hocart, 1950; Quigley, 1993). Merchant castes (particularly in Gujarat) tend to privilege the ascetic orders; especially those that are sponsored by their own community, to the detriment of the Brahmins. Lower castes often tend to an anti-Brahmin ideology which stresses the importance of their own work and the injustice of their low position. Brahmins seldom serve lower castes as priests, so the latter have their own ritual specialists – from their own caste, or from specialized non-Brahmin communities.

Thus, as a complex society, the Indian social order has room for several and conflicting ideologies. Of these, the Brahmin-centred, holistic view of society as a ritual division of labour is but one, but it might reasonably be argued that it exercises an ideological hegemony in the Indian world. This is what Srinivas' analysis of 'Sanskritization' (1952, 1962, 1967), as well as Saraswati's work on Brahmanic ritual traditions (1977) imply. Srinivas also sees Sanskritization – the gradual adoption of Brahmanic ideas and customs – as a process: India is becoming more and more Brahmanical. This analysis begs historical analysis, and we should note Susan Baily's opinion, that Brahmins and their values gained considerably in importance during the eighteenth century, especially in the domain of the Marathas and other Hindu 'successor states' to the Mughal empire (Baily, 1997; 1999: 64-96). If Baily – and others – are right, then Brahmin hegemony is historically recent and cannot be identified with 'traditional' Indian society. Contesting ideologies have also been growing in importance, at least during the twentieth century. I feel we must take ideological contest and conflict with differing historical and regional outcomes as fundamental to such a complex society as India is, rather than suppose Brahmin values to be at the heart of an ordered system.

It would seem to be a general feature of the ideologies of the dominant that they are inclusive, indeed holistic, projecting a view of society as a whole where they themselves come out on the top. Contesting ideologies do not need to develop holism to the same degree, since their target is deconstruction of hierarchy rather than its construction. But regionally dominant groups do construct social wholes, limited to their own domain, thus opposing a regional hierarchical order to the all-Indian one. The Bunts of South Kanara, as well as Saurashtra's Rajputs, are obvious cases here.

This view of ideology implies that society is seen in a Weberian mode, as the scene of competition between interest groups, rather than as an integrated system. I used this approach in my analysis of caste in Saurashtra (1997, 2004). There, common interest tends to group castes into what I called estates – again following Weber – among which we find such socio-economic constellations as the dominant, landowning castes (*darbar*), merchants (*bania*), peasants (*khedut*), and so on. Yet these groupings are, of course, by no means the only possible ones. Different types of interest may produce a criss-crossing pattern of alliances, as they do in South Kanara, where a regional stress on Tulu language and culture to some extent unites the dominant Bunts with their former Billava tenants.[17] At the same time, there is considerable opposition – along socio-economic lines – between these two groups, while the Moghaveera fishermen, who are equally speakers of Tulu, generally stay away from the regional movement. Thus various groupings propose different social entities as a base for holistic formulas: Hindu society (here, too, Brahmins tend towards this formula), Tulu society (especially Bunts), Class (many Billavas, often in solidarity with Moghaveeras), and so on, and there are political tendencies and organizations corresponding to each of these formulas. Complexity, then, in the Indian context is not simply a matter of many specialized groups sharing a territory as well as a political and a cultural scene, but also of differing conceptions of how this common aspect of the life-world should be represented and understood.

All this means that my approach to Indian society, here, is one which may be common to complex societies. Specifically Indian is the cultural construction of what Weber termed status groups, in other words, the indigenous concept of caste. Let us remember though that the term caste is of Western origin, and only translates approximately such Indian concepts as *jati* and *kaum*. What remains basic, however, is that every Indian is conscious of belonging to a particular, named group in which membership is inherited, and which implies certain inherited qualities. These may be viewed positively by the members themselves, or negatively by outsiders, and the latter characterization is important for the relative rank of the group. In both cases, the groups' characteristics – positive or negative – tend to be stereotyped. Such qualities are intertwined with the history of the community: when a member of a caste wants to explain to others whom he/she is, reference is often made to the past of the caste. 'We were the bowmen and soldiers of the Bunts in the old days,' say the Billavas, implying both their subordinate status and their qualities of courage and valour. It is through such representation of the past that the qualities of caste members are shown, and this seems true whether we talk of high or low castes. Such historicity, then, is not incidental to the caste 'system' but an integral part of it. It is through history that society shows itself as what it is, as Dumont (1957) held, and history seems an endless source of myths used to legitimate or contest the position of the group in the overall order. Myth is argument

(Leach, 1954), then, constantly used to prove or disprove group assertions, and I hold that caste ideology is largely constructed from such myths, providing for contestation rather than harmony.

In an earlier work (2004), I chose to see the crucial process in caste dynamics as that of creating and maintaining rank difference. I tried to show how interaction in public situations is organized on the presumption that such differences are important, so that encounters commonly define situations in terms of relative rank. Central to my analysis here was Marriott's conception of 'ranking transactions' (1976, 1989). This produces rank difference in situations, but leaves open the problem of how to integrate them at a higher level of generalization. My point, then, is that this openness reflects the reality of Indian society, where precisely this level is one of competition and contest.

Complexity is itself a factor here. As Rex points out (1970), in complex societies we depend on a classificatory grid to designate the many kinds of people we meet: we cannot treat them all as individuals with the degree of specificity this implies. I have tried to show (2004) how Indian culture provides such a classificatory grid, where caste is but one – though a pertinent one – among the criteria. While classificatory devices of this kind are common to complex societies, the tendency towards ranking is particularly strong in the Indian context.

The advantage of this approach is that ranking does not need to refer to a single scale of values, such as the pure-impure dimension that Dumont proposes. Ranking may take a number of criteria into account, and I hold that actors in India do in fact refer to several types of criteria in order to establish relative rank.[18] These include caste, but also age, dress, markers of economic status, and other factors: their actual use depends on the context as well as the ranking strategy that each actor follows in a particular situation.

People in South Kanara have no problem in assigning rank to the GSB they meet. Some are obviously well-off; all are Brahmins; many are merchants. In terms of interaction, all this places them in a relatively high position. This does not exclude ambiguity, however. The Shivalli Brahmins see themselves as superior to the GSB, citing such criteria as diet, since the GSB generally eat fish. They also stress their importance as priests, a distinction which is itself ambiguous (Parry, 1980; Quigley, 1993). In their view, the GSB, as merchants, are not 'real Brahmins'. They do not deny the GSB's claim to Brahminhood, but hierarchize Brahmins into the real ones and those who are Brahmins mainly by name. The GSB contest this, but not very energetically, since they have other resources and are conscious of their own economic importance. Their defense of fish-eating is significant: it was a strategy for survival as the waters of the Saraswati were drying out, producing famine. Fish-eating thus becomes proof of their ancient Brahmin status, their northern origins[19] and direct descent from the Indus River civilization. Thus they can take the Shivallis' criticism lightly. Other local castes more or less share the Shivalli view, but still regard the GSB as a high and powerful caste. They are frequently jealous of the economic position of the GSB.

The GSB know they are powerful and do not doubt their prestige. But, conscious that changes in Indian society favour their challengers rather than themselves, they defend their privileges. Thus, nostalgia for a past when such challenges were few strengthens their stress on historicity, since the past was in some ways better than the present. Yet economic growth and overseas migration offers new opportunities to them also. Will they be able to retain or even improve their position? This, I feel, is a question on everybody's mind today in the GSB community. Here, present challenges not only strengthen consciousness of the past, but also identification with the community and its possible futures. In this, the GSB are typical of modern Indian elites, and so this book may be seen as a contribution to explain why caste remains as strong as ever in contemporary India.

We have seen that perspectives from ethnicity, caste and class are all relevant to understand the place that the GSB occupy in Indian society. It may be well to resume, here, the main elements of that position, and analyse it without regard to pre-established categories. Central to GSB consciousness is a sense of what has recently (Appadurai, 1991; Robertson, 1992) been called deterritorialization. In spite of centuries of settlement in South Kanara, the GSB see Goa as their real homeland, while their origins lie in the North, with the Saraswati River as an important reference. This long historical perspective makes them a migrant community in their own appreciation, based on a diasporic schema where time and place converge in a sense of constant movement. Paradoxically, this does not exclude attachment to the places that mark these moves: the present settlement where most of the family (*wangad*) is concentrated, its place of origin as memorized in the family name, and the lineage temple and its village in Goa. The present settlement is no less important for those who have left it, so recent migrants – to Mumbai, to the Gulf, to the West – try to maintain the links. It is as if forward movement – and GSB are proud of their capability to move and do well in new places – engenders a backward-looking mental movement, as if the consciousness of going forward produces, dialectically, a tendency to trace, mark and invest sentimentally the road travelled.

Marine Carrin (2002b) shows how the Santals, another people eminently conscious of their movement, invest their myths with the memory of origins – invented or real. Alex Haley's novel *Roots* (1980) testified to a similar search for origins among American Blacks at a time when such memory was lost. It would seem to be this tendency to look back which produces the particular kind of historicity we are dealing with here. Historicity, as movement, may here be opposed dialectically to Tradition, which is seen as constant. GSB have 'always' been true to the essence of Brahminhood: Kalabhairava has 'always' protected the caste, and so on. Historicity and tradition thus complement each other in showing how the GSB have remained true to their 'essence' through the vagaries of history.

Both historicity and tradition imply collective memory.[20] We have seen how the GSB investment in memory produces a realization of being different from surrounding people. They, no doubt, have their origins, but these are not 'ours'. Here, too, there is a dialectical movement: as a minority in numerical terms, the GSB are ideologically excluded from Tulu society, but the memory of migration makes of this relation one between the static and the dynamic: the locals stay in place, but the GSB came to this region and 'made it what it is'. As agents of the market economy and of modernization, they are like colonizers in their own view rather than immigrants that had to accommodate and adjust. 'We' are the agents, 'they' are the material upon which we act and have acted. The contrast here to the Patidars who had to carve themselves a niche in the encompassing, British society (Tambs-Lyche, 1980) is clear. The role of the GSB as transforming agents in South Kanara is clear not only in terms of their obvious economic role, but, in their view, in terms of culture: as representatives of Brahmanic Hinduism, the GSB have contributed to make Tulunadu a part of Indian civilization, which is thus seen to have spread from North to South. Thus when some informants claim that the GSB were the first Brahmins in the region, before the Shivallis, this may or may not be historically correct, but is of central importance to the civilizing argument. The colonizer's argument is also important for the image of Goa: central Goa was, in this view, transformed by GSB immigration based on community-based exploitation of the rice lands divided into regular plots, into a truly civilized and Brahmanized land, spoilt only by the persecutions and destructions of the Portuguese. The remembered lands then become landscapes not just traversed but created by the migrants: and there is pride as well as a sense of loss implied by their memory. The GSB stand out, in their own historicizing project, as a uniquely creative community, which has also carried, through its peregrinations, a Brahmanical tradition claimed to be older and truer than that of most Brahmins, since it comes from the heartland of the Indus civilization, and thus contributed to the making not just of the lands the GSB themselves transformed, but of all India.

Deterritorialization is perhaps not such a good word, then. Territory, or territories, does in fact play a major part in the construction of GSB identity. But the role played by these territories is very different from that of an autochthonous people. We might be tempted to speak of 'imagined territories', in the sense that they figure above all in the abstract sense, never as the 'native soil' out of which the population has, as it were, grown. The latter idea is, of course, a construction too; what is different is not its constructedness but the mode of construction. One mode identifies an organic and static link to place; another the process of movement and the transformation of places. And this latter construction is clearly not recent: we cannot link it, as the term deterritorialization implicitly does, to the present globalization process. As Manger (n.d.) points out, globalization is not new to the Indian Ocean, since several communities have spanned its shores since times immemorial. In that context, the GSB are not exceptional:

nor so in India where, as I have pointed out (2004: 93-4), so many of the people one meets come from 'elsewhere'. It is better, then, to view GSB identity as one example of a type that has been with us in history for quite a long time.

This type, linking its identity to movement through time and space, constructs identity through a type of historicity different from that of people who identify with a fixed territory. In the latter case, not just the placiality but also the time dimension is differently constructed. As Barth (1975) has shown, place may even replace time as the main dimension in the construction of coming-into-being, so that the time sequence of events only imperfectly orders the events themselves. Or, as seems to be the case when the Billavas of South Kanara identify, in their proximity, the places that figure in the myth of their heroes Koti and Chennaya. These are organized by the sequence of the myth, but the myth itself does not have an evident anchoring in time.[21] The sequentiality of the type of historicity through which the GSB think their past is clearly different. I suggest that what distinguishes different types of historicity, then, is the way events – which often imply reference to place – are organized.

GSB historicity shows one way of organizing such references, characterized by three stages, each of them sequentially providing a foundation myth for differentiation of the community: the Saraswat Brahmins, the Gauda Saraswats of Goa with their lineages, and the 'places of origin' of each family and its family firm. Though this organization approaches that of a historian's narrative, we must be careful to distinguish the two: they merge only in so far as the latter, too, uses sequential time and provides a functioning myth for the delimitation and identification of particular social groups.

An important point here is the relation between individual and group identity. One founding myth, like that of Koti and Chennaya, may invest each member of the group with qualities exemplified by the heroes: the myth 'shows' that Billavas are valourous, true to their lords, and capable of sacrifice – just as the myth 'explains' that they are often badly treated by their masters. The myth dimension of GSB historicity certainly shows the qualities of members of that community: initiative, capability for organization, and fidelity towards Brahmanic tradition being some of them. But the sequential organization of historicity also shows that times change, calling for new solutions to new problems, and this, with the change of place and of local interlocutors, means that tradition cannot be simply a way to act: being a GSB calls continuously for new ways of incarnating the identity, which for that very reason is sublimated to an essence beyond specific actions and ways of life. The very fact of being a GSB therefore implies a dynamic element on the behavioural level matched by an insistence on maintaining tradition on a level of intentions and reflections. So, it becomes important for the GSB, living in a present which may be located in South Kanara or well beyond India, to keep open the links backward to place of origin, to lineage temple, and to the mythical past.

In this context, it seems but natural that most GSB should identify politically with a unit which transcends local society and culture in Tulunadu, that is, with the nation, and specifically with the Hindu nation. Thus the main political alternative to a line which runs through the RSS to the BJP, has been the Congress, the party identified with the nation in a secular sense. It may be that most GSB supported the Congress till the Mandal Commission introduced reservation for the Other Backward Castes. It is obvious that this policy would but strongly against the motivations of a Brahmin community which has been used to seeing itself as at once the secular and economic elite in South Kanara, and as the main representatives of all-India Hinduism in a highly unorthodox region. Their country is not Tulunadu, but India: and as, moreover, a cosmopolitan community strongly involved in migration, the GSB take it as a natural thing that they should be outsiders to, and opposed to, a regionalism that defies the larger Indian perspective.

Today, as is the case for many Indian castes, the GSB have become a transnational community, and so India is now just one point of reference. Yet it is important to distinguish here between the transnational and the international dimension. The GSB diaspora certainly forms one small part of the general process of globalization, but the global spread does not seem to produce any fundamental change in the values and 'habitus' of caste members. Rather, these extend, to a wider field, traits that were already present in the caste. It is indeed possible that the future will see families identified as the

Chicago Nayaks, the Ottawa Pais or the Manchester Kamaths. But the fabric that constitutes the community's social organization is of a resilient nature, and though relationships stretch with migration, they do not often break. Manchester or Chicago GSB will continue for many years yet to make occasional visits to their lineage temple in Goa. Moreover, one family may have business interests spread in many countries and places: USA and Britain, the Gulf, Mumbai and Bengaluru, and the traditional Konkan-Kanara-Malabar area. Marriages will, for some time yet, link families in strategic networks that cross national boundaries and oceans. The resilience in organization here must be seen in relation to the fact that such spread-out links are nothing new. With improved communications, the strain of long-distance relationships today may be no stronger than they were when Mumbai and Mangalore were linked by slow steamers, or when Honavara and Mangalore were several days distant by ox-cart.

As long as the relationships are stretched rather than broken, the imagined community of the GSB remains a central reference for its members, whether in the US, the UK, or in India. Though members of many different Indian communities may associate and collaborate abroad, caste retains its specificity in this situation quite as much as in India. The transnational dimension, in fact, probably strengthens caste as opposed to a generalized national, regional or linguistic identity. This means that Indian identity, at home and abroad, is more closely tied to the own community and less to the nation as a whole, or rather, the imagined community of India becomes constructed around the role that the GSB can or will play in it. As a business community, the GSB tend to see this role as part of a project to develop India by private trade and industry. As Brahmins, they tend to conceive of the Indian nation as a Hindu community of which Brahmins are natural ideological and religious leaders. As a community based in several countries, GSB tend to see India as a symbolic power whose strength and prestige directly affects their own status abroad. It is therefore quite natural that a typical GSB position, politically and ideologically, should be that of a Hindu nationalism built on the interests of private enterprise.

NOTES

1. There is presently a great deal of research, amateur and professional, attempting to pin down the historic realities surrounding the myth of Koti and Chennaya, not least by Billava organizations.
2. The Basel missionaries started the first printing press in South Kanara in 1841 (Scholler, 1935: 66).
3. The main exception are the Jain priests, who are mainly Kannada speakers.
4. 'For two centuries,' says Tandon of his family, 'we had been moving along the banks of the Jhelum river. . .' (1961: 9).
5. I have argued elsewhere that 'these links are partly responsible for what Dumont (1966) sees as an absence of the individual in Indian society' (1995: 139).
6. 'History incorporated, made into nature, and thus forgotten as such, the habitus is the acting presence of all that past from which it has been produced . . . it is at the same time what confers to praxis the relative independence of exterior determinations of the immediate present. This autonomy is that of a past acted upon and acting which, functioning as accumulated capital, produces history from history and assures the continuity of the changes that the individual agent makes. . . .' (Bourdieu, 1980: 94: my translation) For 'continuity,' here, Bourdieu uses the term 'permanence'.
7. It is of course not obvious that Westerners lack historic consciousness. I would maintain, however, that the degree of historicity of GSB identity would be unusual in the West, though I have met a number of Western individuals whose 'memory' of family history goes well beyond my own seventeenth-century limit.
8. The position taken here differs somewhat from my earlier discussion of this theme (2004 : 218-19).
9. The metaphor used here is mine.
10. For constraints on choice, see Brox, 1972; Tambs-Lyche, 1980: 20-3 and Tambs-Lyche, 2004: 165-6.
11. This latter point owes much to Cohen's work on Hausa merchants of Ibadan (1969).
12. The difference between Weber and Marx, as I see it, is that class is for Weber a purely economic dimension, whereas Marx ponders extensively the question of class consciousness.
13. See Tambs-Lyche, 1995.
14. It will be clear from the following that I regard this term as an over-simplification.

15. See also my discussion of this theme in Tambs-Lyche, 2004, particularly pp. 304-29.
16. In this they share the traditions described by Saraswati (1977).
17. Note, however, that the Bunts are very eager to include the Billavas, their former tenants and labourers, while strong counter-currents among the latter oppose such inclusion.
18. On this point, see Marriott, 1991.
19. Which makes them superior to the Shivallis.
20. This is not the place to discuss theories of memory. By collective memory, here, I imply a socially observable discourse on the past, whose links to memory as a cognitive phenomenon may not be obvious.
21. There are, of course, attempts to date Koti and Chennaya historically. Such attempts generally date them at the sixteenth or seventeenth century. The point here, however, is that such dating does not structure their myth.

Bibliography

Alsdorf, L. (1962), *Beiträge zur Geschichte von Vegetarismus und Rinderverährung in Indien*, Wiesbaden: F. Steiner.

Ammann, J.J., n.d., *Ein Missionsleben unter den Tulu's. Lebensskizze des Basler Missionärs Johann Jakob Ammann*, Basel: Verlag der Basler Missionsbuchhandlung.

Anderson, B. (1983), *Imagined Communities: Reflections on the Origins and Spread of Nationalism*, London: Verso.

Appadurai, A. (1991), 'Global Ethnoscapes: Notes and Queries for a Transnational Anthropology', in R.G. Fox (ed.), *Recapturing Anthropology*, Santa Fe: School of American Research Press.

Arasaratnam, S. (1987), 'India and the Indian Ocean in the Seventeenth Century', in Das Gupta and Pearson, 1987: 94-130.

Babb, L.A. (1975), *The Divine Hierarchy: Popular Hinduism in Central India*, New York: Columbia University Press.

Bailey, F.G. (1957), *Caste and the Economic Frontier*, Manchester: Manchester University Press.

———(1959), 'For a Sociology of India?', *Contributions to Indian Sociology*, III, pp. 88-101.

Baily, C.A. (1989), *Rulers, Townsmen and Bazaars: North Indian Society in the Age of British Expansion*, Cambridge: Cambridge University Press.

Baily, S. (1997), 'Caste and "Race" in the Colonial Ethnography of India', in P. Robb (ed.), *The Concept of Race in South Asia*, Delhi: Oxford University Press, pp. 165-218.

———(1999), *Caste, Society and Politics in India from the Eighteenth Century to the Modern Age: The New Cambridge History of India, IV-3*, Cambridge: Cambridge University Press.

Barth, F. (1963), 'Introduction' in *The Role of the Entrepreneur in Social Change in Northern Norway*, Oslo: Universitetsforlaget.

———(1966), *Models of Social Organization*, London: Royal Anthropological Institute.

———(1967), 'Economic Spheres in Darfur', in R. Firth (ed.), *Themes in Economic Anthropology*, London: Tavistock.

———(1969), 'Introduction', in F. Barth (ed.), *Ethnic Groups and Boundaries*, Oslo: Universitetsforlaget.

———(1975), *Ritual and Knowledge among the Baktaman of New Guinea*, New Haven: Yale University Press.

Bateson, G. (1972), *Steps to an Ecology of Mind*, New York: Random House.

Berreman, G.D. (1961), 'Caste in India and in the United States', *American Journal of Sociology*, 66, pp. 120-7.

Béteille, A. (1990), 'Race, Caste and Gender', *Man*, 25, 3, pp. 489-504.

Bhatt, G. (1975), *Studies in Tuluva History and Culture*, Manipal: published by the author.

Blunt, E.A.H. (1931), *The Caste System of Northern India with Special Reference to the United Provinces of Agra and Oudh*, London: Oxford University Press.

Bouchon, G. (1987), 'Sixteenth Century Malabar and the Indian Ocean', in Das Gupta and Pearson, 1987: 162-84.

Bourdieu, P. (1972), *Esquisse d'une théorie de la pratique*, Génève: Droz.

———(1980), *Le sens pratique*, Paris: Editions de Minuit.

Brouwer, Jan (1995), *The Makers of the World*, Delhi: Oxford University Press.

Brückner, H. (1995), *Fürstliche Feste. Texte und Rituale der Tulu-Volksreligion an der Westküste Südindiends*, Wiesbaden: Harassowitz.

Buchanan, Francis (Hamilton) (1807/1999), *A Journey from Madras through the Countries of Mysore, Canara, and Malabar*, 3 vols. Originally published in London, 1807. Reprint Delhi/Madras, Asian Educational Services, 1999.

Carreira, E. (1990), 'Les Kamat et le commerce français en Inde, 1778-1819', *Moyen Orient et Océan Indien*, 7, pp. 157-77.

Carrin, M. (1998), 'Le spectacle des *bhuta.* Observations sur les rapports du théatre et du rituel', in L. Bansat-Boudon (ed.), *Théatres Indiens. Purusartha* 20, Paris: EHESS, pp. 247-67.

———(1999), 'Les multiples bouches de la verité: la possession des médiums au Karnataka', in J. Assayag and G. Tarabout (eds.), *La Possession en Asie du Sud. Purusartha* 21, Paris, EHESS, pp. 383-419.

———(2002a), 'La forêt desenchanté: relations de pouvoir et cultes de *bhuta* au pays Kanara', in J. Pouchepadass (ed.), *L'homme et la forêt en Inde du Sud*, Pondichéry and Paris, IFP and Karthala, pp. 293-339.

———(2002b), 'Retour au bousquet sacré: réinvention d'une culture *adivasi*', in M. Carrin and C. Jaffrelot (eds.), *Tribus et basses castes. Résistance et autonomie Dans la société indienne. Purusartha* 23, Paris: EHESS, pp. 233-64.

———(2008), 'Le service religieux de guérison: savoir et biographie des guérisseurs tulu', in I.G. Zupanov and C. Guenzi (eds), *Divins Remèdes. Médicine et Religion en Asie du Sud. Purusartha* 27, Paris: EHESS, pp. 99-131.

Carrin, M. and H. Tambs-Lyche (2008), *A Peripheral Encounter: Santals and their Missionnaries, 1867-1900*, Delhi: Manohar.

———(2010), 'À quelle Nation se vouer? Les représentations diversifiées de l'Etat au Sud Kanara, Inde'. *Journal des Anthropologues*, nos. 118-19: 305-35.

Carrithers, M. (2000), 'On Polytropy: Or the Natural Condition of Spiritual Cosmopolitanism in India: The Digambar Jain Case', *Modern Asian Studies*, 34 (4): 831-61.

Carrithers, M. and C. Humphrey (eds.) (1991), *The Assembly of Listeners: Jains in Society*, Cambridge: Cambridge University Press.

Chandrasekhara, H.L. (1990), *Sri Annamacharya: A Philosophical Study*, Mysore: Vidyashankara Prakashana.

Chinnappa Gowda, K. (1983), *Bhutaradhane: Kelavu Adhyayanagalu*, Mangalore: Tuluva Prakashana.

Chitrapur Saraswat 1971: Census Report and Directory (1972), Mumbai: Kanara Saraswat Association.

Claus, P. (1970), 'Kinship Organization of the Bant-Nadava Caste-Complex', unpublished Ph.D. thesis, Duke University.

———(1978), 'Terminological Aspects of Tulu Kinship: Kin Terms, Kin Sets and Kin Groups in the Matrilineal Castes', in S. Vatuk (ed.), *American Studies in the Anthropology of India*, Delhi: Manohar, pp. 211-41.

Cohen, A. (1969), *Custom and Politics in Urban Africa*, Berkeley: University of California Press.

Cole, A.H. (1959), *Business Enterprise in its Social Setting*, Cambridge, Mass.: Harvard University Press.

Conlon, Frank F. (1974), 'Caste by Association: The Gauda Sarasvata Brahmana Unification Movement', *Journal of Asian Studies*, 33, pp. 351-66.

———(1977), *A Caste in a Changing World: The Chitrapur Saraswat Brahmins, 1700-1935*, Berkeley: University of Calfornia Press.

Das Gupta, A. and M.N. Pearson (eds.) (1987), *India and the Indian Ocean 1500-1800*, Kolkata: Oxford University Press.

Dave, H.T. (1967/1974), *Life and Philosophy of Shree Swaminarayana*, 2nd rev. edn., Bochasan: Akshar Purushottam Sansthan.

Davis, K. and W.E. Moore (1945), 'Some Principles of Stratification', *American Sociological Review*, April, pp. 242-9.

Davis, R.H. (1997), *Lives of Indian Images*, Delhi: Motilal Banarsidass.

Dirks, N.B. (1987/89), *The Hollow Crown: Ethnohistory of an Indian Kingdom*, Cambridge and Mumbai: Cambridge University Press and Orient Longman.

Douglas, M. and Baron Isherwood (1979/1996), *The World of Goods*, London: Routledge.

Dubashi, Vamana M. (1918), 'Gauda Saraswata Brahmana Jnatichi Kamgiri', *Maharashtra Saraswata*, 2, pp. 36-61.

Dumont, L. (1957), 'For a Sociology of India', *Contributions to Indian Sociology*, no. 1, pp. 7-22.

———(1965), 'The Functional Equivalent of the Individual in Caste Society', *Contributions to Indian Sociology*, VII, pp. 13-61.

———(1966), *Homo Hierarchicus*, Paris: Gallimard.

Dutt, C.C. (1960), *The Culture of India as Envisaged by Sri Aurobindo*, Mumbai: Bharatiya Vidya Bhavan.

Eidheim, H. (1971), 'Entrepreneurship in Politics', in H. Eidheim, *Aspects of the Lappish Minority Situation*, Oslo, Universitetsforlaget, pp. 10-24 (originally published in F. Barth (ed.), 1963 (op. cit.).

Ellsworth, E.W. (1991), *Science and Social Science Research in British India, 1780-1880*, New York: Greenwood Press.

Esnoul, A.M. (n.d.), *Ramanuja et la mystique vishnouite*, Paris: Seuil.

Fischer, G. (1906), *Erquickung auf dem Wege. Missionsarbeit auf der Station Karkala von 1898-1904*, Basel: Verlag der Basler Missionshuchhandlung.

Fonseca, J.N. Da (1878/1986), *An Historical and Archaeological Sketch of the City of Goa.* Originally published by Thatcher & Co., Bombay, Reprint 1986, Delhi: Asian Educational Services.

Frykenberg, Robert E. (1989), 'The Emergence of Modern "Hinduism" as a Concept and as an Institution , in G.D. Sontheimer and H. Kulke (eds.), *Hinduism Reconsidered*, Delhi: Manohar.

Furnival, J.S. (1939), *Netherlands and India: A Study of Plural Economy*, Cambridge: Cambridge University Press.

Gangopadhyay, B. (1964), *Marriage Regulations among Certain Castes of Bengal*, Poona: Deccan College.

Ghurye, G.S. (1932/1969), *Caste and Race in India* (5th edn.), Bombay: Popular Prakashan.

———(1962), *Gods and Men*, Bombay: Popular Book Depot.

Hagen, E.E. (1962), *On the Theory of Social Change*, Homewood, Illinois: Dorsey Press.

Haley, A. 1976, *Roots*, New York: Doubleday.

Hannerz, U. (1996), *Transnational Connections*, London and New York: Routledge.

Hardiman, D. (1996), *Feeding the Bania: Peasants and Usurers in Western India*, Delhi: Oxford.

Hartenstein, K. (ed.) (1935), *Das Werden einer Jungen Kirche im Osten*, published by the author.

Hegde, P. Suvasini (1999), *Whispering Memories (Travelogue)*, Mangalore: Hemamshu Prakashana.

History of Higher Education in South India, 2 vols. (1957), Madras: University of Madras.

Hobsbawm, E. (1975), *The Age of Capital 1848-1875*, London: Weidenfeld and Nicholson.

Hocart, A.M. (1927), *Kingship*, London: Oxford University Press.

———(1950/1938), *Caste: A Comparative Study*, London: Methuen.

———(1970/1936), *Kings and Councillors*, Chicago: University of Chicago Press.

Honko, L. (1986), 'The Birth of the Finnish National Epic', in U.P. Upadhyaya (ed.), *Folk Epics of Tulunad*, Udupi: The Regional Resources Centre for Folk Performing Arts.

Honko, L., C. Gowda, A. Honko and V. Rai (1998), *Textualizing the Siri Epic and the Siri Epic: As Performed by Gopala Naika*, 2 vols., Helsinki: Academia Scientiarum Fennica.

Inden, R.B. (1976), *Marriage and Rank in Bengali Culture*, Delhi: Vikas.

———(1978), 'Ritual, Authority and Cyclic Time in Hindu Kingship', in J.F. Richards (ed.), *Kingship and Authority in South Asia*, Madison: University of Wisconsin.

Jackson, W.J. (2007), *Vijayanagara Visions: Religious Experience and Cultural Creativity in a South Indian Empire*, Delhi: Oxford University Press.

Jacobsen, K. (2003), *Hinduismen*, Oslo: Pax forlag.

Jacobson, D. (1977), 'Flexibility in Central Indian Kinship and Residence', in K. David (ed.), *The New Wind: Changing Identities in South Asia*, The Hague: Mouton, pp. 263-83.

Jaffrelot, C. (1993), *Les nationalistes hindous*, Paris: Presses de la fondation nationale des sciences politiques.

Jain, R.K. (2002), *Between History and Legend: Status and Power in Bundelkhand*, Hyderabad: Orient Longman.

Jayashankar, S. (1999), *Temples of Kerala, Census of India 1991*, Delhi: Controller of Publications.

Jha, D.N. (1974), 'Temples as Landed Magnates in Early Medieval South India (*c.* AD 700-1300)', in R.S. Sharma and V. Jha (eds.), *Indian Society: Historical Probings*, Delhi: People's Publishing House, pp. 202-16.

Kamath, M.V. (1983), *The Innovative Banker: T.A. Pai, His Life and Times*, Manipal: T.A. Pai Memorial Committee.

Kamath, M.V. (1991), *A Banking Odyssey: The Canara Bank Story*, Delhi: Vikas.

Kamath, S.U. (2001), *A Concise History of Karnataka*, Bengaluru: Jupiter Books.

———(ed.). (1982), *Karnataka State Gazetteer*, Part 1, Bangalore: Government of Karnataka.

Karve, Irawati (1953), *Kinship Organization in India*, Poona: Deccan College.

Kini, U.J. (n.d.), *The Tonse Kini Family Tree*, Udupi: the author.

Klostermaier, K.K. (1994), *A Survey of Hinduism*, Albany: State University of New York Press.

Kothari, R. (2002), *Memoirs*, Delhi: Rupa.

Krishna, N. (2000), *Balaji-Venkateshwara: Lord of Tirumala-Tirupati*, Mumbai: Vakil, Feffer and Simons Ltd.

Kuduva, P.R.(1996), 'Aryavartadar prachatinam vaishnava patha: Shri Kashimata Samsthana' *and* 'Shri Parthagalu matha' in Shri Venkata Prasada, *Centenary Souvenir of the Shri Laxmivenkatarama Temple, Udupi*, Udupi: The Shri Laxmivenkatarama Temple.

Kuduva, V.N. (1972), *History of the Dakshinatya Saraswats*, Madras: Samyukta Gowda Saraswat Sabha.

Lachaier, P. (1999), *Firmes et entreprises en Inde. La firme lignagère dans ses réseaux*. Paris: IFP–Karthala–EFEO.

Lévi-Strauss, C. (1952), 'La notion de structure en ethnologie', in *Social Structure*, Wenner-Gren Foundation International Symposium on Anthropology, New York: Wenner-Gren Foundation.

Lobo, M. (2000), *Distinguished Mangalorean Catholics (1800-2000)*, Mangalore: Camelot.

———(2002), *The Mangalorean Catholic Community: A Professional History/ Directory*, Mangalore: Camelot.

Longva, A.W. (1997), 'Walls Built on Sand', Doctorate thesis, University of Oslo.

Machado, Prabhu (1999), *Sarasvati's Children*, Bangalore: I.J.A. Publications.

Madan, T.N. (1965), *Family and Kinship: A Study of the Pandits of Rural Kashmir*, Bombay: Asia Publishing House.

———(1982), 'The Identity of the Householder among the Kashmiri Pandits', in T.N. Madan (ed.), *Way of Life: King, Householder, Renouncer: Essays in Honour of Louis Dumont*, Delhi: Vikas, pp. 223-49.

———(1987), *Non-renunciation: Themes and Interpretations of Hindu Culture*, Delhi: Oxford University Press.

Madsen, S. Toft (1992), *Udupi Hotels: A Case of Ethnicity Based Non-virulent Development*, Lund: Research Report No. 25, Department of Sociology, Lund University.

Malamoud, C. (1989), *Cuire le monde. Rite et pensée dans l'Inde ancienne*, Paris: La Découverte.

Männer, J.F.A. (1886), *Tulu-English Dictionary*, Mangalore: Basel Mission Press.

Marriott, McKim (1976), 'Hindu Transactions: Diversity without Dualism', in B. Kapferer (ed.), *Transaction and Meaning*, Philadelphia: ISHI.

———(1989), 'Constructing an Indian Ethnosociology', *Contributions to Indian Sociology*, n.s., 23, pp. 1-39.

———(1991), 'Multiple Reference in Indian Caste Systems', in D. Gupta (ed.), *Social Stratification*, Delhi: Oxford University Press, pp. 49-59. (Originally published in 1968 in J. Silverberg (ed.), *Social Mobility and the Caste System in India*, The Hague: Mouton.

Mauss, M. (1966), *The Gift: Forms and Functions of Exchange in Archaic Societies*, London: Cohen and West.

Mayer, A.C. (1958), 'The Dominant Caste in a Region of Central India', *Southwestern Journal of Anthropology*, 14, pp. 407-27.

———(1960), *Caste and Kinship in Central India*, London: Routledge and Kegan Paul.

———(1981), 'Perceptions of Princely Rule: Perspectives from a Biography', *Contributions to Indian Sociology*, n.s., 15, pp. 127-54.

McClelland, D.C. (1965), 'Achievement Motivation can be Developed', *Harvard Business Review*, no. 6 (November/December).

McClelland, D.C. and D.G. Winter (1969), *Motivating Economic Achievement*, New York: Free Press.

Menefee, S. (1969/1984), *The Pais of Manipal*, 2nd rev. edn., Manipal: The Academy of General Education.

Meter, Karl van (1994), *Textes essentiels: La Sociologie*, Paris: Larousse.

Moraes, G.M. (1927), *Mangalore: A Historical Sketch*, Bombay: Indian Historical Research Institute.

Narayanan, M.G.N. and K. Veluthat (2002/2000), 'Bhakti Movement in South India', in D.N. Jha (ed.), *The Feudal Order: State, Society and Ideology in Early Medieval India* (paperback edition), Delhi: Manohar, pp. 385-410.

Njammasch, M. (1992a), 'Die Dorfgemeinde im Maitrakareich', *Beiträge des Sudasien Instituts*, Humboldt-Universität zu Berlin, 1, pp. 1-49.

———(1992b), 'Die Flur-und Besitzverhältnisse im Dorf Madasara auf kathiawar im Jahre 675 n.Chr.', *Beiträge des Sudasien-Instituts*, Humboldt-Universität zu Berlin, 2, pp. 27-68.

———(1993), 'Freie Bauern und Pächtern im grühmittelalderlichen Indien', *Beiträge des Sudasien-Instituts*, Humboldt-Universität zu Berlin, 5, pp. 1-61.

Pai, M. Govinda (1997), 'Flashes from the Past', in M.G. Pai, *Indiana: Studies in Indian Culture, History and Civilisations*, Udupi: Rashtrakavi Govinda Pai Samshodana Kendra, pp. 765-858.

Pareto, V. (1966), *Sociological Writings*, selected and introduced by S.E. Finer, London: Pall Mall Press.

Parry, J.P. (1980), 'Ghosts, Greed and Sin: The Occupational Identity of the Benares Funeral Priests', *Man*, n.s., 21, pp. 453-73.

Patel, H.G. (1966a), 'Anawari: The System of Social Status Among the Lewa Patidars', *Journal of the Gujarat Research Society*, XXVII, pp. 1-4.

———(1966b), 'The Change in Structural Unit and Attitudes Towards Marriage by Exchange', *Sociological Bulletin*, no. 2.

Pearson, M.N. (1973), 'Wealth and Power: Indian Groups in the Portuguese Indian Economy', *South Asia*, 3, pp. 36-44.

———(1976), *Merchants and Rulers in Gujarat: The Response to the Portuguese in the Sixteenth Century*, Berkeley: University of California Press.

———(1981), 'The Port City of Goa: Policy and Practice in the Sixteenth Century', in *Coastal Western India: Studies from the Portuguese Records*, New Delhi: Concept.

Peterson, I. Viswanathan (2003), 'Tanjore, Tranquebar and Halle: European Science and German Missionary Education in the Lives of Two Indian Intellectuals in the Early Nineteenth Century', in R. Frykenberg (ed.), *Christians and Missionaries in India: Cross-Cultural Communication since 1500*, London and Grand Rapids: Routledge and William B. Eerdmans, pp. 93-126.

Pfeffer, G. (1976), 'Puris Sasandörfer. Basis einer regionalen Elite', Doctoral thesis, Freie Universität Berlin.

Pocock, D.F. (1972), *Kanbi and Patidar*, Oxford: Clarendon.

———(1973), *Mind, Body and Wealth*, Oxford: Blackwell.

Priolkar, A.K. (1961), *The Goa Inquisition*, Bombay: the author.

Quigley, D. (1993), *The Interpretation of Caste*, Oxford: Clarendon.

Ramesh, K.V. (1970), *A History of South Kanara*, Dharwar: Karnataka University.

Rao, V. (2002), *Living Traditions in Contemporary Contexts*, Hyderabad: Orient Longman.

Rex, J. (1970), *Race Relations in Sociological Theory*, London: Weidenfeld and Nicholson.

Robertson, R. (1992), *Globalization*, London and Newbury Park: Sage.

Rothermund, D. (1993), *An Economic History of India from Pre-colonial Times to 1991*, 2nd edn., London: Routledge.

Rudolph, L.I. and S.H. Rudolph (1955), 'The Political Role of India's Caste Associations', *Pacific Affairs*, 28, pp. 235-53.

———(1978), 'To the Brink and Back: Representation and the State in India', *Asian Survey*, 18, 4.

Saki (1998), *Making History: Karnataka's People and Their Past*, vol. 1: *Stone Age to Mercantilism*, Bangalore: Vimukthi Prakashana.

Saletore, B.A. (1936), *Ancient Karnataka*, vol. 1: *History of Tuluva*, Poona: Oriental Book Agency.

Index